AMERICAN VISTAS
1607–1877

American Vistas
1607–1877

Seventh Edition

Edited by

LEONARD DINNERSTEIN

and

KENNETH T. JACKSON

New York   Oxford
OXFORD UNIVERSITY PRESS
1995

Oxford University Press

Oxford   New York   Toronto
Delhi   Bombay   Calcutta   Madras   Karachi
Kuala Lumpur   Singapore   Hong Kong   Tokyo
Nairobi   Dar es Salaam   Cape Town
Melbourne   Auckland

and associated companies in
Berlin   Ibadan

Published by Oxford University Press, Inc.,
200 Madison Avenue, New York, New York 10016

Oxford is a registered trademark of Oxford University Press

Library of Congress Cataloging-in-Publication Data
American vistas / edited by Leonard Dinnerstein
and Kenneth T. Jackson.—7th ed.
p. cm.   Includes bibliographical references
Contents: [v. 1.] 1607–1877—[v. 2.] 1877 to present.
ISBN 0-19-508783-6 (v. 1)—ISBN 0-19-508784-4 (v. 2)
1. United States—History.   I. Dinnerstein, Leonard.
II. Jackson, Kenneth T.
E178.6.A426   1995
973-dc20   94-7567

9 8 7 6 5 4 3 2 1

Printed in the United States of America
on acid-free paper

For
Myra Dinnerstein

PREFACE

It is now more than two decades since we first embarked on our project of bringing together a series of historical essays that combined interest with readability and which could be used in conjunction with a survey text or a wide variety of other books. We have been gratified by the initial reader response as well as the enthusiasm with which our subsequent editions were received. The comments that we have read indicate that there are a large number of instructors who find the combination of traditional and off-beat essays on the American past suitable to their own teaching styles. We are particularly pleased that *American Vistas* has been used by a wide diversity of people in every region of the country as well as in Canada and overseas. It reaffirms our belief that the American past can be both enlightening and instructive to people who are fascinated with the development of societies.

For this revision we have made a searching reexamination of the contents and have kept only those essays we believe have been particularly successful in the past. Letters from users and comments from other colleagues and scholars clearly indicated which pieces were most suitable for college classes. We have tried to follow this advice whenever possible. Many of our selections fit so well into the teaching patterns of a large number of introductory courses that it seemed an injustice to students and teachers alike to eliminate them. On the other hand, more recent scholarship and the changing emphasis of societal and classroom interests have resulted in new selections on women, witchcraft, adolescents, Catholics and First Amendment freedoms, the African-American experience, and military activities during the Civil War.

Several former teaching assistants at the University of Arizona made suggestions about inclusions and incisions. For their valuable insights we would like to thank Allen Broussard, Susan Hill, John Krueckeberg, Renee Obrecht Como, and Phyllis Smith.

Tucson   L. D.
New York   K. T. J.
November, 1993

CONTENTS

AMERICAN VISTAS
1607–1877

The Puritans and Sex

EDMUND S. MORGAN

● *In 1630, after an arduous Atlantic crossing aboard the Arabella, John Winthrop and a small band of followers established the Massachusetts Bay Colony. In their "Holy Commonwealth" the Puritans emphasized hard work, severe discipline, and rigid self-examination and self-denial. Ministers had great political influence in the theocratic government, and profanation of the Sabbath day, blasphemy, fornication, drunkenness, and participation in games of chance or theatrical performances were among their many penal offenses. Even today the term "puritanical" suggests narrow-mindedness and excessive strictness in matters of morals and religion. Yet, as Daniel Boorstin and others have observed, the Puritans were not simply an ascetic group of fanatics who prohibited all earthly pleasures. Actually the severity of their code of behavior has frequently been exaggerated. The Puritans were subject to normal human desires and weaknesses, and they recognized that "the use of the marriage bed" is "founded in Man's nature." Moreover, numerous cases of fornication and adultery in the law courts of New England belie the notion that all Puritans lived up to their rigid moral ideology. In the following essay, Professor Edmund S. Morgan cites numerous examples of men and women, youths and maids, whose natural urges recognized no legal limits. In viewing their enforcement of laws and their judgments of human frailty, we may find that the Puritans do not always conform to their conventional stereotype as over-precise moralists.*

Henry Adams once observed that Americans have "ostentatiously ignored" sex. He could think of only two American writers who touched upon the subject with any degree of boldness—Walt Whitman and Bret

From *New England Quarterly*, XV (1942), 591–607. Reprinted by permission of the author and the publisher.

Harte. Since the time when Adams made this penetrating observation, American writers have been making up for lost time in a way that would make Bret Harte, if not Whitman, blush. And yet there is still more truth than falsehood in Adams's statement. Americans, by comparison with Europeans or Asiatics, are squeamish when confronted with the facts of life. My purpose is not to account for this squeamishness, but simply to point out that the Puritans, those bogeymen of the modern intellectual, are not responsible for it.

At the outset, consider the Puritans' attitude toward marriage and the role of sex in marriage. The popular assumption might be that the Puritans frowned on marriage and tried to hush up the physical aspect of it as much as possible, but listen to what they themselves had to say. Samuel Willard, minister of the Old South Church in the latter part of the seventeenth century and author of the most complete textbook of Puritan divinity, more than once expressed his horror at "that Popish conceit of the Excellency of Virginity." Another minister, John Cotton, wrote that

> Women are Creatures without which there is no comfortable Living for man: it is true of them what is wont to be said of Governments, *That bad ones are better than none*: They are a sort of Blasphemers then who dispise and decry them, and call them *a necessary Evil*, for they are *a necessary Good*.

These sentiments did not arise from an interpretation of marriage as a spiritual partnership, in which sexual intercourse was a minor or incidental matter. Cotton gave his opinion of "Platonic love" when he recalled the case of

> one who immediately upon marriage, without ever approaching the *Nuptial Bed*, indented with the *Bride,* that by mutual consent they might both live such a life, and according did sequestring themselves according to the custom of those times, from the rest of mankind, and afterwards from one another too, in their retired Cells, giving themselves up to a Contemplative life; and this is recorded as an instance of no little or ordinary Vertue; but I must be pardoned in it, if I can account it no other than an effort of blind zeal, for they are the dictates of a blind mind they follow therein, and not of that Holy Spirit, which saith *It is not good that man should be alone.*

Here is as healthy an attitude as one could hope to find anywhere. Cotton certainly cannot be accused of ignoring human nature. Nor was he an isolated example among the Puritans. Another minister stated plainly that "the Use of the Marriage Bed" is "founded in mans Nature," and that consequently any withdrawal from sexual intercourse upon the part of husband or wife "Denies all reliefe in Wedlock vnto Human necessity: and sends it for supply vnto Beastiality when God gives not the gift of Continency." In other words, sexual intercourse was a human necessity and marriage the only proper supply for it. These were the views of the New England clergy, the acknowledged leaders of the community, the most Puritanical of the Puritans. As proof that their congregations concurred with them, one may cite the case in which the members of the First Church of Boston expelled James Mattock because, among other offenses, "he denyed Coniugall fellowship vnto his wife for the space of 2 years together vpon pretense of taking Revenge upon himself for his abusing of her before marryage." So strongly did the Puritans insist upon the sexual character of marriage that one New Englander considered himself slandered when it was reported, "that he Brock his deceased wife's hart with Greife, that he would be absent from her 3 weeks together when he was at home, and wold never come nere her, and such Like."

There was just one limitation which the Puritans placed upon sexual relations in marriage: sex must not interfere with religion. Man's chief end was to glorify God, and all earthly delights must promote that end, not hinder it. Love for a wife was carried too far when it led a man to neglect his God:

> ... sometimes a man hath a good affection to Religion, but the love of his wife carries him away, a man may bee so transported to his wife, that hee dare not bee forward in Religion, lest hee displease his wife, and so the wife, lest shee displease her husband, and this is an inordinate love, when it exceeds measure.

Sexual pleasures, in this respect, were treated like other kinds of pleasure. On a day of fast, when all comforts were supposed to be foregone in behalf of religious contemplation, not only were tasty food and drink to be abandoned but sexual intercourse, too. On other occasions, when food, drink, and recreation were allowable, sexual intercourse was allowable too, though of course only between persons who were married to each other. The Puritans were not ascetics; they never wished to prevent the enjoyment of earthly delights. They merely demanded that the pleasures of the flesh be subordinated to the greater glory of God: husband and wife must not become "so transported with affection, that they look at no higher end than marriage it self." "Let such as have wives," said the ministers, "look at them not for their own ends, but to be fitted for Gods service, and bring them nearer to God."

Toward sexual intercourse outside marriage the Puritans were as frankly hostile as they were favorable to it in marriage. They passed laws to punish adultery with death, and fornication with whipping. Yet they had no misconceptions as to the capacity of human beings to obey such laws. Although the laws were commands of God, it was only natural—since the fall of Adam—for human beings to break them. Breaches must be punished lest the community suffer the wrath of God, but no offense, sexual or otherwise, could be occasion for surprise or for hushed tones of voice. How calmly the inhabitants of seventeenth-century New England could contemplate rape or attempted rape is evident in the following testimony offered before the Middlesex County Court of Massachusetts:

> The examination of Edward Wire taken the 7th of october and alsoe Zachery Johnson. who sayeth that Edward Wires mayd being sent into the towne about busenes meeting with a man that dogd hir from about Joseph Kettles house to goody marshes. She came into William Johnsones and desired Zachery Johnson to goe home with her for that the man dogd hir. accordingly he went with her and being then as far as Samuell Phips his house the man over tooke them. which man caled himselfe by the name of peter grant would have led the mayd but she oposed itt three times: and coming to Edward Wires house the said grant would have kist hir but she refused itt: wire being at prayer grant dragd the mayd between the said wiers and Nathanill frothinghams house. hee then flung the mayd downe in the streete and got atop hir; Johnson seeing it hee caled vppon the fellow to be sivill and not abuse the mayd then Edward wire came forth and ran to the said grant and took hold of him asking him what he did to his mayd, the said grant asked whether she was his wife for he did nothing to his wife: the said grant swearing he would be the death of the said wire. when he came of the mayd; he swore he would bring ten men to pul down his house and soe ran away and they

followed him as far as good[y] phipses house where they mett with John Terry and George Chin with clubs in there hands and soe they went away together. Zachy Johnson going to Constable Heamans, and wire going home. there came John Terry to his house to ask for beer and grant was in the streete but afterward departed into the towne, both Johnson and Wire both aferme that when grant was vppon the mayd she cryed out severall times.

Deborah hadlocke being examined sayth that she mett with the man that cals himself peter grant about good prichards that he dogd hir and followed hir to hir masters and there threw hir downe and lay vppon hir but had not the use of hir body but swore several othes that he would ly with hir and gett hir with child before she got home.

Grant being present denys all saying he was drunk and did not know what he did.

The Puritans became inured to sexual offenses, because there were so many. The impression which one gets from reading the records of seventeenth-century New England courts is that illicit sexual intercourse was fairly common. The testimony given in cases of fornication and adultery—by far the most numerous class of criminal cases in the records—suggests that many of the early New Englanders possessed a high degree of virility and very few inhibitions. Besides the case of Peter Grant, take the testimony of Elizabeth Knight about the manner of Richard Nevars's advances toward her:

The last publique day of Thanksgiving (in the year 1674) in the evening as I was milking Richard Nevars came to me, and offered me abuse in putting his hand, under my coates, but I turning aside with much adoe, saved my self, and when I was settled to milking he agen took me by the shoulder and pulled me backward almost but I clapped one hand on the Ground and held fast the Cows teatt with the other hand, and cryed out, and then came to mee Jonathan Abbot one of my Masters Servants, whome the said Never asked wherefore he came, the said Abbot said to look after you, what you doe unto the Maid, but the said Never bid Abbot goe about his businesse but I bade the lad to stay.

One reason for the abundance of sexual offenses was the number of men in the colonies who were unable to gratify their sexual desires in marriage. Many of the first settlers had wives in England. They had come to the new world to make a fortune, expecting either to bring their families after them or to return to England with some of the riches of America. Although these men left their wives behind, they brought their sexual appetites with them; and in spite of laws which required them to return to their families, they continued to stay, and more continued to arrive, as indictments against them throughout the seventeenth century clearly indicate.

Servants formed another group of men, and of women too, who could not ordinarily find supply for human necessity within the bounds of marriage. Most servants lived in the homes of their masters and could not marry without their consent, a consent which was not likely to be given unless the prospective husband or wife also belonged to the master's household. This situation will be better understood if it is recalled that most servants at this time were engaged by contract for a stated period. They were, in the language of the time, "covenant servants," who had agreed to stay with their masters for a number of years in return for a specified recompense, such as transportation to New England or education in some trade (the latter, of course, were known more specifically as apprentices). Even hired servants who worked for wages were usually single, for as soon as a man had enough money to buy or build a house of his own and to get married, he would set up in farming or trade for himself. It must be emphasized, however, that anyone who was not in business for himself was necessarily a servant. The economic organization of seventeenth-century New England had no place for the independent proletarian workman with a family of his own. All production was carried on in the household by the master of the family and his servants, so that most men were either servants or masters of servants; and the former, of course, were more numerous than the latter. Probably most of the inhabitants of Puritan New England could remember a time when they had been servants.

Theoretically no servant had a right to a private life. His time, day or night, belonged to his master, and both religion and law required that he obey his master scrupulously. But neither religion nor law could restrain the sexual impulses of youth, and if those impulses could not be expressed in marriage, they had to be given vent outside marriage. Servants had little difficulty in finding the occasions. Though they might be kept at work all day, it was easy enough to slip away at night. Once out of the house, there were several ways of meeting with a maid. The simplest way was to go to her bedchamber, if she was so fortunate as to have a private one of her own. Thus Jock, Mr. Solomon Phipps's Negro man, confessed in court

> that on the sixteenth day of May 1682, in the morning, betweene 12 and one of the clock, he did force open the back doores of the House of Laurence Hammond in Charlestowne, and came in to the House, and went up into the garret to Marie the Negro.
>
> He doth likewise acknowledge that one night the last week he forced into the House the same way, and went up to the Negro Woman Marie and that the like he hath done at severall other times before.

Joshua Fletcher took a more romantic way of visiting his lady:

> Joshua Fletcher ... doth confesse and acknowledge that three severall nights, after bedtime, he went into Mr Fiskes Dwelling house at Chelmsford, at an open window by a ladder that he brought with him the said windo opening into a chamber, whose was the lodging place of Gresill Juell servant to mr. Fiske. and there he kept company with the said mayd. she sometimes having her cloathes on, and one time he found her in her bed.

Sometimes a maidservant might entertain callers in the parlor while the family were sleeping upstairs. John Knight described what was perhaps a common experience for masters. The crying of his child awakened him in the middle of the night, and he called to his maid, one Sarah Crouch, who was supposed to be sleeping with the child. Receiving no answer, he arose and

> went downe the stayres, and at the stair foot, the latch of doore was pulled in. I called severall times and at the last said if shee would not open the dore, I would breake it open, and when she opened the doore shee was all undressed and Sarah Largin with her undressed, also the said Sarah went out of doores and Dropped some of her clothes as shee went out. I enquired of Sarah Crouch what men they were, which was with them. Shee made mee no answer for some space of time, but at last shee told me Peeter Brigs was with them, I asked her whether Thomas Jones was not there, but shee would give mee no answer.

In the temperate climate of New England it was not always necessary to seek out a maid at her home. Rachel Smith was seduced in an open field "about nine of the clock at night, being darke, neither moone nor starrs shineing." She was walking through the field when she met a man who

> asked her where shee lived, and what her name was and shee told him. and then shee asked his name, and he told her Saijing that he was old Good-man Shepards man. Also shee saith he gave her strong liquors, and told her that it was not the first time he had been with maydes after his master was in bed.

Sometimes, of course, it was not necessary for a servant to go outside his master's house in order to satisfy his sexual urges. Many cases of fornication are on record between servants living in the same house. Even where servants had no private bedroom, even where the whole family slept in a single room, it was not impossible to make love. In fact many love affairs must have had their consummation upon a bed in which other people were sleeping. Take for example the case of Sarah Lepingwell. When Sarah was brought into court for having an illegitimate child, she related that one night when her master's brother, Thomas Hawes, was visiting the family, she went to bed early. Later, after Hawes had gone to bed, he called to her to get him a pipe of tobacco. After refusing for some time,

> at the last I arose and did lite his pipe and cam and lay doune one my one bead and smoaked about half the pip and siting vp in my bead to giue him his pip my bead being a trundell bead at the sid of his bead he reached beyond the pip and Cauth me by the wrist and pulled me on the side of his bead but I biding him let me goe he bid me hold my peas the folks wold here me and if it be replyed come why did you not call out I Ansar I was posesed with fear of my mastar least my mastar shold think I did it only to bring a scandall on his brothar and thinking thay wold all beare witnes agaynst me but the thing is true that he did then begete me with child at that tim and the Child is Thomas Hauses and noe mans but his.

In his defense Hawes offered the testimony of another man who was sleeping "on the same side of the bed," but the jury nevertheless accepted Sarah's story.

The fact that Sarah was intimidated by her master's brother suggests that maidservants may have been subject to sexual abuse by their masters. The records show that sometimes masters did take advantage of their position to force unwanted attentions upon their female servants. The case of Elizabeth Dickerman is a good example. She complained to the Middlesex County Court,

> against her master John Harris senior for profiring abus to her by way of forsing her to be naught with him: . . . he has tould her that if she tould her dame: what cariag he did show to her shee had as good be hanged and shee replyed then shee would run away and he sayd run the way is befor you: . . . she says if she should liwe ther shee shall be in fear of her lif.

The court accepted Elizabeth's complaint and ordered her master to be whipped twenty stripes.

So numerous did cases of fornication and adultery become in seventeenth-century New England that the problem of caring for the children of extra-marital unions was a serious one. The Puritans solved it, but in such a way as to increase rather than decrease the temptation to sin. In 1668 the General Court of Massachusetts ordered:

> that where any man is legally convicted to be the Father of a Bastard childe, he shall be at the care and charge to maintain and bring up the same, by such assistance of the Mother as nature requireth, and as the Court from time to time (according to circumstances) shall see meet to Order: and in case the Father of a Bastard, by confession or other manifest proof, upon trial of the case, do not appear to the Courts satisfaction, then the Man charged by the Woman to be the Father, shee holding constant in it, (especially being put upon the real discovery of the truth of it in the time of her Travail) shall be the reputed Father, and accordingly be liable to the charge of maintenance as aforesaid (though not to other punishment) notwithstanding his denial, unless the circumstances of the case and pleas be such, on the behalf of the man charged, as that the Court that have the cognizance thereon shall see reason to acquit him, and otherwise dispose of the Childe and education thereof.

As a result of this law a girl could give way to temptation without the fear of having to care for an illegitimate child by herself. Furthermore, she could, by a little simple lying, spare her lover the expense of supporting the child. When Elizabeth Wells bore a child, less than a year after this statute was passed, she laid it to James Tufts, her master's son. Goodman Tufts affirmed that Andrew Robinson, servant to Goodman Dexter, was the real father, and he brought the following testimony as evidence:

> Wee Elizabeth Jefts aged 15 ears and Mary tufts aged 14 ears doe testyfie that their being one at our hous sumtime the last winter who sayed that thear was a new law made concerning bastards that If aney man wear aqused with a bastard and the woman which had aqused him did stand vnto it in her labor that he should bee the reputed father of it and should mayntaine it Elizabeth Wells hearing of the sayd law she sayed vnto vs that If shee should bee with Child shee would bee sure to lay it vn to won who was rich enough abell to mayntayne It wheather it wear his or no and shee farder sayed Elizabeth Jefts would not you doe so likewise If it weare your case and I sayed no by no means for right must tacke place: and the sayd Elizabeth wells sayed If it wear my Caus I think I should doe so.

A tragic unsigned letter that somehow found its way into the files of the Middlesex County Court gives more direct evidence of the practice which Elizabeth Wells professed:

> der loue i remember my loue to you hoping your welfar and i hop to imbras the but now i rit to you to let you nowe that i am a child by you and i wil ether kil it or lay it to an other and you shal have no blame at al for I haue had many children and none have none of them.... [i.e., none of their fathers is supporting any of them.]

In face of the wholesale violation of the sexual codes to which all these cases give testimony, the Puritans could not maintain the severe penalties which their laws provided. Although cases of adultery occurred every year, the death penalty is not known to have been applied more than three times. The usual punishment was a whipping or a fine, or both, and perhaps a branding, combined with a symbolical execution in the form of standing on the gallows for an hour with a rope about the neck. Fornication met with a lighter whipping or a lighter fine, while rape was treated in the same way as adultery. Though the Puritans established a code of laws which demanded perfection—which demanded, in other words, strict obedience to the will of God, they nevertheless knew that frail human beings could never live up to the code. When fornication, adultery, rape, or even buggery and sodomy appeared, they were not surprised, nor were they so severe with the offenders as their codes of law would lead one to believe. Sodomy, to be sure, they usually punished with death; but rape, adultery, and fornication they regarded as pardonable human weaknesses, all the more likely to appear in a religious community, where the normal course of sin was stopped by wholesome laws. Governor Bradford, in recounting the details of an epidemic of sexual misdemeanors in Plymouth, wrote resignedly:

> it may be in this case as it is with waters when their streames are stopped or damned up, when they gett passage they flow with more violence, and make more noys and disturbance, then when they are suffered to rune quietly in their owne chanels. So wickednes being here more stopped by strict laws, and the same more nerly looked unto, so as it cannot rune in a comone road of liberty as it would, and is inclined, it searches every wher, and at last breaks out wher it getts vente.

The estimate of human capacities here expressed led the Puritans not only to deal leniently with sexual offenses but also to take every precaution to prevent such offenses, rather than wait for the necessity of punishment. One precaution was to see that children got married as soon as possible. The wrong way to promote virtue, the Puritans thought, was to "ensnare" children in vows of virginity, as the Catholics did. As a result of such vows, children, "not being able to contain," would be guilty of "unnatural pollutions, and other filthy practices in secret: and too oft of horrid Murthers of the fruit of their bodies," said Thomas Cobbett. the way to avoid fornication and perversion was for parents to provide suitable husbands and wives for their children:

> Lot was to blame that looked not out seasonably for some fit matches for his two daughters, which had formerly minded marriage (witness the contract between them and two men in *Sodom*, called therfore for his Sons in Law, which had married his daughters, Gen. 19. 14.) for they seeing no man like to come into them

in a conjugall way ... then they plotted that incestuous course,
whereby their Father was so highly dishonoured. ...

As marriage was the way to prevent fornication, successful marriage
was the way to prevent adultery. The Puritans did not wait for adultery
to appear; instead, they took every means possible to make husbands
and wives live together and respect each other. If a husband deserted
his wife and remained within the jurisdiction of a Puritan government,
he was promptly sent back to her. Where the wife had been left in
England, the offense did not always come to light until the wayward
husband had committed fornication or bigamy, and of course there
must have been many offenses which never came to light. But where
both husband and wife lived in New England, neither had much chance
of leaving the other without being returned by order of the county
court at its next sitting. When John Smith of Medfield left his wife and
went to live with Patience Rawlins, he was sent home poorer by ten
pounds and richer by thirty stripes. Similarly Mary Drury, who deserted
her husband on the pretense that he was impotent, failed to convince
the court that he actually was so, and had to return to him as well as
to pay a fine of five pounds. The wife of Phillip Pointing received lighter
treatment: when the court thought that she had overstayed her leave
in Boston, they simply ordered her "to depart the Towne and goe to
Tanton to her husband." The courts, moreover, were not satisfied with
mere cohabitation; they insisted that it be peaceful cohabitation. Husbands and wives were forbidden by law to strike one another, and the
law was enforced on numerous occasions. But the courts did not stop
there. Henry Flood was required to give bond for good behavior because he had abused his wife simply by "ill words calling her whore
and cursing of her." The wife of Christopher Collins was presented
for railing at her husband and calling him "Gurley gutted divill." Apparently in this case the court thought that Mistress Collins was right,
for although the fact was proved by two witnesses, she was discharged.
On another occasion the court favored the husband: Jacob Pudeator,
fined for striking and kicking his wife, had the sentence moderated
when the court was informed that she was a woman "of great
provocation."

Wherever there was strong suspicion that an illicit relation might
arise between two persons, the authorities removed the temptation by

forbidding the two to come together. As early as November, 1630, the Court of Assistants of Massachusetts prohibited a Mr. Clark from "cohabitacion and frequent keepeing company with Mrs. Freeman, vnder paine of such punishment as the Court shall thinke meete to inflict." Mr. Clark and Mr. Freeman were both bound "in XX£ apeece that Mr. Clearke shall make his personall appearance att the nexte Court to be holden in March nexte, and in the meane tyme to carry himselfe in good behaviour towards all people and espetially towards Mrs. Freeman, concerning whome there is stronge suspicion of incontinency." Forty-five years later the Suffolk County Court took the same kind of measure to protect the husbands of Dorchester from the temptations offered by the daughter of Robert Spurr. Spurr was presented by the grand jury

> for entertaining persons at his house at unseasonable times both by day and night to the greife of theire wives and Relations &c The Court having heard what was alleaged and testified against him do Sentence him to bee admonish't and to pay Fees of Court and charge him upon his perill not to entertain any married men to keepe company with his daughter especially James Minott and Joseph Belcher.

In like manner Walter Hickson was forbidden to keep company with Mary Bedwell, "And if at any time hereafter hee bee taken in company of the saide Mary Bedwell without other company to bee forthwith apprehended by the Constable and to be whip't with ten stripes." Elizabeth Wheeler and Joanna Peirce were admonished "for theire disorderly carriage in the house of Thomas Watts being married women and founde sitting in other mens Laps with theire Armes about theire Necks." How little confidence the Puritans had in human nature is even more clearly displayed by another case, in which Edmond Maddock and his wife were brought to court "to answere to all such matters as shalbe objected against them concerning Haarkwoody and Ezekiell Euerells being at their house at unseasonable tyme of the night and her being up with them after her husband was gone to bed." Haarkwoody and Everell had been found "by the Constable Henry Bridghame about tenn of the Clock at night sitting by the fyre at the house of Edmond Maddocks with his wyfe a suspicious weoman her husband being on sleepe [*sic*] on the bedd." A similar distrust of human ability to resist temptation is evident in the following order of the Connecticut Particular Court:

> James Hallett is to returne from the Correction house to his master Barclyt, who is to keepe him to hard labor, and course dyet during the pleasure of the Court provided that Barclet is first to remove his daughter from his family, before the sayd James enter therein.

These precautions, as we have already seen, did not eliminate fornication, adultery, or other sexual offenses, but they doubtless reduced the number from what it would otherwise have been.

In sum, the Puritan attitude toward sex, though directed by a belief in absolute, God-given moral values, never neglected human nature. The rules of conduct which the Puritans regarded as divinely ordained had been formulated for men, not for angels and not for beasts. God had created mankind in two sexes; He had ordained marriage as desirable for all, and sexual intercourse as essential to marriage. On the other hand, He had forbidden sexual intercourse outside of marriage. These were the moral principles which the Puritans sought to enforce in New England. But in their enforcement they took cognizance of human nature. They knew well enough that human beings since the fall of Adam were incapable of obeying perfectly the laws of God. Consequently, in the endeavor to enforce those laws they treated offenders with patience and understanding, and concentrated their efforts on prevention more than on punishment. The result was not a society in which most of us would care to live, for the methods of prevention often caused serious interference with personal liberty. It must nevertheless be admitted that in matters of sex the Puritans showed none of the blind zeal or narrow-minded bigotry which is too often supposed to have been characteristic of them. The more one learns about these people, the less do they appear to have resembled the sad and sour portraits which their modern critics have drawn of them.

2

Anne Hutchinson Reconsidered

WILLIAM G. MCLOUGHLIN

● *By the standards of any century and any society, Anne Hutchinson was a remarkable woman. Born in 1591 in Lincolnshire, England, she emigrated to the Massachusetts Bay Colony to join the Puritans with her husband and family in 1634. There, her personal kindness, her magnetic personality, and her brilliant mind attracted a following. Unfortunately, her espousal of the covenant of grace as opposed to the covenant of works, meaning that she thought that faith alone was necessary for salvation, led John Cotton, John Winthrop, and other Puritan leaders to view her as an "antinomian" heretic. Put on trial for "traducing the ministers," she was found guilty and was banished from the colony in 1637.*

Together with several followers and six of her children, Anne Hutchinson moved first to Rhode Island, then to Long Island, and finally to what is now Pelham Bay Park in the Bronx. There, where the Hutchinson River and the Hutchinson River Parkway, both named for her, meet Long Island Sound, her life came to a tragic end in 1643, when she and all but one of her children were massacred by Indians who had been incited to war by a reckless Dutch governor. The following essay by Professor William G. McLoughlin of Brown University argues that "though long dead, she still speaketh."

So many new and controversial books and articles have appeared about Anne Hutchinson in recent years that it is time to reconsider her place in American religious history. The Antinomian crisis of 1635–37 in Boston, formerly dismissed by most historians as a curious but ephemeral episode of the early history of American Puritanism—a tempest in Boston's teapot—now looms up as a critical turning point in the story

Reprinted with permission from the editor of *Rhode Island History*.

of the Christian churches in our culture. At least six books and numerous scholarly articles were published about Hutchinson in the
1980s. Every history of early Massachusetts now devotes many pages
to her. Although she lived in New England for only eight years, she
left an indelible mark upon its cultural development. It is time to reexamine and reevaluate this remarkable woman.

In its broadest aspects Anne Hutchinson's career iliuminates three
fundamental paradoxes in American civilization: first, our admiration
for vigorous individualism and our respect for duly constituted authority; second, our striving for moral perfection and our commitment
to pragmatic accommodation; and third, our belief in human equality
and our assumption that women are yet somehow not fully equal.
Beyond that, Anne Hutchinson has become a major figure in the history
of American feminism as a forceful symbol of women's role and wom-
en's theology in the churches of America.

In order to understand Anne Hutchinson's place in religious history,
it is necessary to consider her life in the context of the English Reformation. Fifteen years after Martin Luther posted his ninety-five theses
on the church door in Wittenberg, Henry VIII broke with Rome and
established the Church of England, placing himself at its head. But
Henry's theological reforms did not go so far as many wanted, and
Queen Elizabeth did not go much farther when she came to the throne.
By 1603, when Elizabeth died, England was seething with religious
unrest. Radical Christians had now separated from the Church of England in an effort to restore the ideals and practices of the primitive
churches and to move closer to Calvinist theology. These radicals included the Scrooby Pilgrims (called Separatists) who settled in Plymouth
in 1620. Among the more conservative reformers were those called
Puritans, who hoped to reform the Church of England from within.
This was the group that Anne Hutchinson joined.

The Puritan movement opposed the Separatists on the left and the
more conservative Presbyterians of the Church of Scotland on the right.
Those Puritans who came to New England have been described as
Nonseparating Congregationalists because they hoped to abolish the
episcopal structure of the English church and substitute a congregational polity to which only those who underwent a critical religious
experience (salvation by faith through grace) would be admitted as
members. The king and his bishops forced the Separatists out of the

country after 1608, and it looked as though the Nonseparating Puritans would also be suppressed. Yet, although thousands of these Puritans emigrated to New England between 1629 and 1640, the movement continued to grow in Old England until it was able to launch a successful revolution in the 1640s under Oliver Cromwell. By that time Anne Hutchinson had come to New England, and she had already started her own revolution in Boston.

In his book *Wayward Puritans,* the sociologist Kai T. Erikson describes Anne Hutchinson as a woman who lived at the crossroads of early American history. One way to look at this crossroad is to say that the settlers of Massachusetts Bay were facing critical choices about the kind of Christian community they were about to establish in the New World. They wanted it to be a Bible commonwealth, and they wanted it to be "a city set upon a hill," a model for all the world of a perfect Christian state. That vision has cast a long shadow in the nation's history. Today most Americans still believe that the United States is a model for the world, though not quite in Anne Hutchinson's terms or those of the Puritans. In many ways the choices made by the people of Massachusetts in the 1630s shaped our country and brought it to what it is today. We consider ourselves the model of freedom, of idealism, of equal opportunity, and of a stable, orderly, and progressive social system. If the United States is not a Christian nation, it is one clearly formed upon Judeo-Christian principles. In this respect, for better or worse, we owe a major debt to the Puritans. John Winthrop, the leading figure in the Bay Colony, is still cited by presidents and politicians who consider us today a city upon a hill, in special covenant with God, leading the world to the millennium. We like to think of ourselves as a chosen people with a manifest destiny to save the world from error and to make it over in our image.

Yet the New England legacy is ambivalent. We all know that the Puritans were not a very tolerant people and that they had a very rigid view of religious conformity. They expelled Roger Williams and Anne Hutchinson, they whipped and jailed the Baptists, they hanged Quakers, and they put to death people they considered witches. Anne Hutchinson was aware of this double image; she was there when critical decisions were being made, and she spoke in favor of a church-state order different from the one that emerged victorious under Winthrop's leadership.

To Anne Hutchinson, a truly Christian society had to be based upon the ideal of the priesthood of all believers, and the state had to permit the existence of a united church of Christ rooted in a mystical fellowship of those who shared the presence of the Holy Spirit in their hearts. Christian fellowship for her did not distinguish between males and females, rich and poor, and it knew no narrow sectarian or nationalistic covenant with God. Hutchinson also considered John Winthrop and such ministers of the Bay Colony as John Wilson, Zechariah Symmes, and Thomas Welde mistaken in believing that membership in God's church could be discerned by fallible human eyes and measured by the appearances of piety, honesty, and morality, or what were called "good works." Hutchinson was convinced that God worked in many ways not knowable by man or measurable by outward behavior or professions. Furthermore, she believed that in forming churches based upon what she called "the covenant of works" rather than "the covenant of grace," the ministers and lay leaders of the Bay Colony were moving away from the true spirit of the Puritan movement, which had given it strength to stand against persecution in Old England. They were mistaking outward moral behavior for inward grace or salvation. Winthrop's Bible commonwealth seemed to her a retrograde movement that would lead toward a church of hypocrites—people who professed and displayed outward conformity to local norms but who inwardly were not truly one with God. It proved, in fact, to be a movement that foretold the cultural captivity of the churches in America.

Like all Calvinists, Hutchinson believed that men have been so depraved since Adam's fall that they act essentially out of self-interest, and that self-interest leads them to behave according to the standards of the world and not from love of God. Thus most men behave well only out of fear of damnation. In addition, she believed that by insisting that God had made a covenant with the settlers of New England to establish a special community because they were a chosen people, the founders of the colony were creating the same kind of formal, spiritually dead established church that they had fled England to escape. Ultimately this would breed only smugness, complacency, and self-righteousness, with outward forms substituted for inward faith.

Billy Graham preached such Christian nationalism in the 1950s when he said, "If you would be a true patriot, then become a Christian. If you would be a loyal American, then become a loyal Christian." Graham has grown older and wiser and now preaches that God does not make covenants with chosen nations, defining their national enemies as his enemies and their national security as basic to the survival of Christianity.

To many other Americans, however, Billy Graham's earlier view seems perfectly reasonable, and for that we have John Winthrop and John Wilson to thank. For what they established in their city upon a hill, after banishing heretics, was a community in which "grace flowed through the loins of the saints," a New Israel in the New World. It was a community with a hierarchical and patriarchal social structure led by elect males and organized in parish churches. This, they firmly believed, was God's way. It was, in fact, the purified church and state for which England was to undergo a drastic revolution under Cromwell.

When we come to examine closely what was labeled Antinomianism (against law) by Winthrop and the Bay Colony ministers, we recognize today that it is a far more radical definition of church and state than most of us can easily embrace, however much we may admire Anne Hutchinson's courage and audacity. By labeling her an Antinomian, the Puritan leaders branded her as a lawless fanatic who would govern by direct revelation. Her mystical reliance upon the spirit of God within her would undermine all law and order; it would prevent the enforcement of the word of God by civil authorities. Denying that they had any intention of returning to false ecclesiastical or political principles, the leaders of the Bay Colony believed that they were creating a "middle way" between the Anglican Reformation and the radical Separatists, Anabaptists, Familists, and other extremists. Considering themselves practical, realistic, level-headed reformers, they branded Hutchinson as visionary and dangerous. That division between the pragmatist and the perfectionist has been at the basis of American cultural conflict ever since. It poses the binary tension within which the people of this country have oscillated for more than three centuries—a tension between noble idealism and hard-headed expediency. The measure of respect that one accords to Anne Hutchinson or to John Winthrop in evaluating the Antinomian movement in our history is a pretty good index of where one stands within that fundamental polarity.

Anne Hutchinson was a woman who would have left a mark upon any age, but in 1636 she found herself involved in a controversy particularly suited to her talents and temperament. Born in Alford, England, a town north of the old city of Boston, Anne Marbury was one of fifteen children of a crusty, disputatious, strong-willed minister of the Church of England, the Reverend Francis Marbury. Marbury was no Puritan, but like the Puritans he was highly critical of the clergy of the established church. He was imprisoned more than once for publicly denouncing the ignorance, corruption, and incompetence of the Anglican clergy. Anne grew up in Alford, but after her father was reinstated to good standing in the church in 1605, the family moved to London, where Marbury became a pastor. The Marburys may well have rubbed shoulders with William Shakespeare in the streets of that metropolis.

Living in an era of political and religious turmoil, Anne Marbury appears to have mastered all of the fine points of Anglican and Calvinist theology. She read her father's books of theology and sharpened her native intellectual ability through regular discussions with her father and siblings. We know little of her physical appearance, but all accounts agree that she was remarkable for her nimble wit, her strong assertiveness in debate, her bold presentation of her own position, and her genuine compassion in helping other women both by medical care and by psychological and spiritual counseling. Hutchinson was not so mystical that she thought babies dropped from heaven into the cabbage patch. She had good reason to learn all she could about health care, for the body, she believed, was the temple of the soul, and for the reborn it became the dwelling place of the Holy Spirit. Physical birth and spiritual rebirth were logically connected in her thinking.

Her father died in 1611 when she was twenty. A year later she married William Hutchinson, a prosperous cloth merchant. They lived in Alford, her childhood home. It is not clear just when she made the decision to join the Puritan movement, but from her later account her religious conversion appears to have occurred during the 1620s. This was after she and her husband had discovered the Reverend John Cotton preaching in the town of Boston twenty-four miles south of Alford. They traveled there regularly to hear him, and he had a profound effect upon their own religious transition from the Anglican to the Puritan persuasion. That Anne was no radical at this time seems indicated by her refusal to be swept into the Separatist movement.

Tensions within the Anglican Church reached a critical point in the 1630s. John Cotton was expelled from his position by the archbishop for his Puritan leanings, and in 1633 he left for New England to join

John Winthrop and the founders of the Bay Colony. Anne Hutchinson persuaded her husband to follow Cotton, and in 1634 they reached Boston with their children. During her lifetime Anne was to bear fifteen children, like her mother, and this was part of her incentive to become a midwife.

Life in the primitive village of Boston was extremely difficult. Although there were several towns in the colony, the total population in the Massachusetts Bay area at that time was only about four thousand. Boston itself held just one-quarter of these, or roughly two hundred families. Most of them lived at first in small log houses with thatched roofs and one or two rooms. Shortly after the Hutchinsons arrived, they were admitted to the Boston church in which John Cotton and John Wilson were preaching. The colony was already becoming involved in quarrels fomented by Roger Williams. Williams had become a Separatist, and he urged the Bay Colony to follow the example of the Pilgrims at Plymouth and announce its own separation from the unredeemable Anglican Church. He went even farther and denied the right of the civil authorities to enforce religious conformity and church attendance, and for this he was banished in 1635. There is no record that Anne Hutchinson or her husband ever lifted a finger to defend Williams or to oppose his banishment. Separation of church and state was apparently not part of her teaching; she was content to work for reform within the existing church structure.

Anne Hutchinson was teaching theology at this time to some of the women of Boston. They met weekly in her home to discuss the sermons preached by John Cotton and John Wilson. Her exposition of theological fine points and her lively leadership in the discussions later attracted male visitors to her meetings, among them Governor Harry Vane. While her husband rose to important positions in the church and in the state, Anne quickly established herself as a significant religious and social force in that small community. Her role as a religious leader became evident when her brother-in-law, the Reverend John Wheelwright, came to Boston from England in 1636. Hutchinson and those who admired her urged that Wheelwright be appointed as a third minister of the Boston church. And that was when she began to arouse opposition.

She wanted Wheelwright to join with John Cotton because she had come to distrust the preaching of John Wilson. Wilson, she told those at her meetings, was preaching that people could prepare themselves to receive grace and be part of the elect for whom Christ died; by leading prayerful and pious lives, they could provide a pure vessel into which the Holy Spirit would be poured. Wilson was also preaching that it was a pretty good proof that someone was one of the elect and had been regenerated by the Holy Spirit if he or she led a moral, upright, and industrious life. The Puritan ethic was defined in terms of piety, morality, honesty, industry, sobriety, and thrift. But while this was a commendable moral ethic, Anne Hutchinson did not believe that moral behavior entitled anyone to church membership or that it was any proof of election. Such beliefs were a corruption of true Christianity, she felt, for they meant that people who lived moral lives from self-interest and people whose thrift, sobriety, and industry helped them grow wealthy would be assumed to be converted by God, when in fact they may well have been spiritual hypocrites or spiritually deceived into believing they were of the elect. Preaching that people could work their way into the church through their good behavior, or could bind God to save them by preparing themselves for salvation, incorrectly interpreted true doctrine; that is, salvation by faith alone. It also limited God by appearing to make salvation a contractual arrangement between equals: when men or women did their part and lived piously, soberly, and uprightly, then God was obliged to do his part and send them grace.

The Church of England admitted persons on the basis of these beliefs, and this, Hutchinson felt, could only lead backward in New England. As historians can now demonstrate, she was correct, for gradually the spiritual fervor of the early Puritan movement waned. After 1640 Puritanism became institutionalized and routinized. As the New England churches lost their original pietistic spirit, they lapsed into institutions whose members were admitted in adulthood almost as a matter of course; a kind of birthright membership developed. But the leaders of the Bay Colony did not foresee this change. They believed Anne Hutchinson was insulting them and their cause, and they said so.

New England Puritanism contained a number of basic paradoxes and inconsistencies, and Hutchinson adroitly put her finger on these incompatible elements. At the time, however, she seemed to be seeing heresy where there was none. In fact, the logic of her beliefs seemed to undermine all church organization and ritual. Since God's grace was,

for her, unconditional (or arbitrary), it mattered little how people behaved in their outward lives. In addition, she insisted that even salvation
could not wholly save mere humans from sin. Ultimately she claimed
that only the truly elect could discern other truly elect persons, and
that the elect recognized each other through the mystical operation of
the Holy Spirit dwelling within them. Worst of all, however, her teachings led to the denigration of the Bay Colony's civil and ecclesiastical
leaders, whom she called false leaders and false preachers.

John Wheelwright was not selected to become a pastor in the Boston
church, although Governor Harry Vane supported the Hutchinsonians
in their effort to have him appointed. John Winthrop's opposition
proved decisive in this controversy. It now became clear that a major
dissension was brewing. Matters were made worse when Wheelwright,
in a fast-day sermon soon after his failure to attain office, boldly asserted that the true followers of God would and should do everything
in their power to assert control over the colony to save it from corruption. "We must all prepare for a spiritual combat," Wheelwright
said. "Behold the bed that is Solomon's; there is three-score valiant
men about it, valiant men of Israel, every one hath his sword girt on
his thigh.... They must fight, and fight with spiritual weapons ... we
must all of us prepare for battle and come out against the enemies of
the Lord. And if we do not strive, those under a covenant of works
will prevail."

In this sermon the colony's leaders found a clear threat of insurrection. While Wheelwright specifically said that he spoke only of spiritual
and persuasive means of asserting control, his opponents took him to
mean otherwise. They put him on trial for fomenting sedition against
duly constituted authority. In March 1637 they convicted him. Soon
after, the authorities passed a law prohibiting anyone with Hutchinsonian leanings from entering the colony. Six months later John Wheelwright was banished, and all who had supported him were forced to
give up their guns. Many were then disfranchised, and other Hutchinsonians were banished also. In most history books this is considered
a victory for law and order by practical leaders who rightly saw that
only anarchy could result from the presence of two such opposing
factions in the colony.

The final act in this drama came when a synod of ministers from
Massachusetts and Connecticut made a list of all the erroneous views

of the Hutchinsonians. They discovered eighty-two heretical positions dangerous to the stability of the commonwealth and the truth of Calvinism. Several ministers were then delegated to confront Anne with these errors and to persuade her to recant them. Most of the errors were so farfetched—such outrageous perversions of her teaching—that she disclaimed them readily and was indignant that they were ever imputed to her. But there were several presumed errors that she could not deny, especially those that condemned the doctrine of preparation for grace, denied that good works were evidence of election, and affirmed that God's grace was unconditional. John Cotton at first seemed to defend her position, but he later turned against her. In November 1637 she was convicted of libeling (or "traducing") the ministers of the colony and sentenced to banishment.

Because she was pregnant, her banishment was delayed, and she spent the winter under arrest. In March 1638 her church placed her on trial for heresy, and she was excommunicated. Later that month she and about half of her followers left Massachusetts for Rhode Island. The leader of this group, which included several of the most influential men of the colony, was William Coddington (another group of her followers went to Exeter, New Hampshire, with John Wheelwright). Coddington and the Hutchinsons received timely assistance from Roger Williams in Providence, who helped them to purchase Aquidneck Island from the Narragansett Indians.

All that we know of Anne Hutchinson's beliefs we learn from the stenographic report of her trial and from other reports by her enemies. She left no theological writings of her own. Most historians have agreed that the trial was not fairly conducted, that Anne was denied ordinary rights, and that she defended herself so ably that she almost succeeded in thwarting her accusers. But when she said that God revealed various things to her directly, and that one of these was his promise that Massachusetts Bay would be destroyed if its leaders continued to persecute her, she provided a convenient handle for her own conviction. People who believed that God spoke to them directly, and who therefore placed God's voice above the voices of the learned ministers and the duly elected magistrates, were clearly unfit to remain in the kind of Bible commonwealth that the majority favored in 1637.

Hutchinson meant to say that the elect were not bound to obey the law of the Mosaic or Abrahamic covenant, the law that said "Obey my laws and you will be my people." But in her excitement she seemed to be saying that the covenant of grace enabled the elect to know God's will even in future events of a secular nature. To her, the covenant of works, and her opponents' belief that only a learned ministry and God-ordained magistracy knew the truth, were such departures from true religion that they would bring down destruction upon the colony. But she put this badly. It was one of the few times her keen intelligence failed her.

Historians have noted that her banishment was meant to indicate to conservative Puritans in Old England that the New England Puritans were able to use their middle way of church-state relations to control fanaticism without bishops, church courts, and a king who was head of the church. In addition, banishing Anne Hutchinson made her a cautionary or monitory figure to other females who might assume the right to venture out of their proper sphere.

While a careful reading of her trial record and other statements can show us what the Hutchinsonians stood for in the debate over Calvinist doctrines, we have much less evidence to describe how they felt about organizing a social order. Here we must rely upon what little is known about their own colony at Pocasset (now Portsmouth) in Rhode Island. The records of this community are very scanty, but from what little survives, it does not appear that Anne Hutchinson and her friends were particularly radical. Although they said that they would not persecute anyone for conscience, we know that the Puritans said the same thing; to the Hutchinsonians, as to the Puritans, it was not persecution to whip, jail, or hang a heretic, for one could only "persecute" a truly good and orthodox person. We know how the Hutchinsonians dealt with Samuel Gorton, an eccentric mystic who believed that women as well as men should be allowed to preach: when Gorton appeared in Pocasset, after being banished from Boston and Plymouth, he was whipped and banished from the town in 1639. We know too that Pocasset, like Boston, was organized in accordance with wealth, education, and social position. The well-to-do were given more land and high office, while the poor were relegated to inferior status. We also know that the Pocasset settlement was not a very stable one. In 1638 Coddington and some of the other leaders were deposed from office and left in a huff for the southern end of the island, where they founded a town called Newport.

It was reported to those in Boston that Anne Hutchinson continued to expound the word of God in Pocasset, but it seems doubtful that she did so outside her own home. There is no record of her leading a church or of any meetinghouse being built in the town. In fact, while it is known that John Clarke preached in Pocasset, there is no record that he founded a church there (though he later did so in Newport). Under the Hutchinsonian theology it is difficult to see how a visible church could have been founded unless everyone was willing to accept the right of those who believed they were of the elect to choose the church's members on the basis of their own mystical knowledge of each other's sainthood.

Antinomianism did not produce religious stability in Pocasset. When John Clarke moved to Newport, he became a Baptist. Anne Hutchinson's sister, Katherine Marbury Scott, went to Providence and convinced Roger Williams to become a Baptist also (he left the denomination after a few months). Some Hutchinsonians questioned the practice of infant baptism, though there is no evidence that Anne Hutchinson ever did. The members of Clarke's church later split over whether to worship on the Lord's Day (Sunday) or on the Jewish Sabbath (Saturday), and this led to the formation of the Seventh-Day Baptist denomination. After 1656 many of Hutchinson's followers joined the new sect called the Society of Friends, or "Quakers."

From this history it can be argued that the Puritans were right to see a kind of anarchy inherent in the Hutchinsonian position and a certain confusion arising from reliance upon the teaching of the Holy Spirit dwelling within the heart of each believer. But all of this misses the point. Anne never said she was a system builder. She opposed the idea of institutionalizing the doctrine of salvation by faith alone. And, as we know, Roger Williams did no better when he separated church and state. The proliferation of various ways of being Christian was one of the legacies of both these early Rhode Islanders.

In 1642 William Hutchinson died. He had been Anne's anchor through the years of controversy—always supportive, always loyal. It was reported that Anne had forced him to renounce his position as a magistrate in Pocasset because she had ceased to believe that God had ordained the institution of magistracy. How could saints be governed by secular authority? Why should they be, when the Holy Spirit dwelt in them? It was not, of course, that she believed the elect were perfect and could never sin. On the contrary, she said that they could sin as much as reprobates and still retain their election; she never doubted the Puritan doctrine of the perseverance of the saints. This left her open to the charge of believing that sin must originate with God and that sinners are not responsible for their own behavior because the Holy Spirit is living within them and guiding them. Her strict interpretation of unconditional election led to what some considered a fatalistic reliance upon God. But for her, fatalism was perfectly consistent with man's fallen state, God's omnipotence, and the necessity of total reliance upon God's will.

The last act in Anne Hutchinson's history began with her decision, after her husband's death, to move with her unmarried children to the Dutch colony of New Amsterdam. There she lived at Pelham Bay (southeast of present-day Eastchester) until the Dutch inadvertently stirred up an Indian rebellion. Among the first settlers to be killed by the Indians were Anne and four of her children. And so her life ended, in August 1643, with Anne a victim of the white man's theft of the Indian's land—a sin that Roger Williams had denounced in Boston a decade earlier, but that Anne Hutchinson had never mentioned.

This, then, was the historical context of the Antinomian movement. It remains to summarize some of the different ways in which historians have been interpreting that movement since then. Here I will be recapitulating some of the important work done by Professor Amy Lang in her fine study *Prophetic Woman: Anne Hutchinson and the Problem of Dissent in the Literature of New England*. Professor Lang shows very clearly that from Cotton Mather to Nathaniel Hawthorne, the prevailing image of the Antinomian was pervaded by the fact that Anne Hutchinson was a "public woman" and therefore a woman out of her sphere. As Lang demonstrates, early historians of Antinomianism started by connecting her unwomanly conduct with the work of Satan, thus justifying not only her banishment but her final miscarriage after her banishment and her cruel death at the hands of savages.

Later, when the Revolutionary ideology made religious liberty an ideal of the new nation, the Puritans were criticized for failing to tolerate Anne. Nonetheless she was seen as a very eccentric and unstable person, both as a woman and as a theologian. Those who studied her during the nineteenth century tended to find her beliefs of negligible significance and her controversy irrelevant to history; that controversy, it was claimed, was about abstruse points held by Calvinists of an earlier day—points no longer central to Christian thought. But while Anne Hutchinson gradually received more sympathy from historians as a persecuted Christian, she was not exonerated from her unwomanly conduct in leaving the sphere of hearth and home to enter into public debate. In fact, the American Protestants of the nineteenth century (the Victorian era) were convinced that she was more sinful for being unwomanly than for believing in the covenant of grace. Professor Lang makes a good case that Emerson did not really consider her a true forerunner of Transcendentalism (though some Transcendentalists thought she was) and that Hawthorne probably had her in mind when he branded the eccentric (and adulterous) Hester Prynne with a scarlet letter in his novel of that name.

Until the twentieth century the best Hutchinson could obtain from historical study was a concession that she was a pious and godly woman, that her trial was a grave miscarriage of justice, and that her theology was so recondite as to have not been worthy of any trial. Still she remained a cautionary figure in a male world; her real sin was forgetting that she was only a woman and that God had not ordained women to engage in the difficult and learned practice of Biblical exegesis or in the rough-and-tumble of worldly politics. In fact, until the middle of the twentieth century, most historians, being male authority figures, felt that Anne Hutchinson was a rather brazen, arrogant hussy; that however bright she was, she was really guilty of improper behavior, a scandal to the norm of female domesticity. As Professor Lang puts it, "The gender-specific problem of the public woman figures [in] the dilemma of maintaining the law in a culture that simultaneously celebrates and fears the authority of the individual." Privately we admire Anne Hutchinson as a strong-minded individual, but for male authority figures she was always a threat and her womanhood was therefore held against her.

Beginning with the works of Perry Miller in the 1940s, however, a new set of perspectives began to appear. Miller and his pupils reexamined Puritanism and redefined the importance of the Antinomian movement. Through his emphasis on theology as a major feature of the Puritan community, Miller gave the Hutchinsonians a new significance in the history of the Bay Colony. Recognizing and pinpointing the redefinition and institutionalization of Puritanism in the New World, he was the first to depict the Hutchinsonian movement as the turning point in Puritanism's decline. Miller clearly delineated, at last, the significance of the Puritan belief in preparation for grace and in church membership based upon the evidence of good works. He showed that Anne Hutchinson was upholding an older pietistic approach to the Puritan movement, while Winthrop and her other opponents were more interested in order and stability than in theology.

In this line of argument Miller was followed by his pupil Edmund S. Morgan, whose 1958 volume *The Puritan Dilemma* is still the most widely used textbook on Puritanism. Morgan claimed that Anne Hutchinson was Winthrop's intellectual superior in every respect except political common sense. He argued that Winthrop railroaded Anne Hutchinson out of the colony because it was not big enough for both of them, but he concluded his analysis of the movement by claiming that no other choice was possible if the colony was to survive. Writing as a hard-headed neoliberal in the 1950s—in an era when liberals spoke of "the end of ideology" and favored pragmatic solutions to political problems—Morgan had even less sympathy with Hutchinson's theological position than his mentor did. For him, "the Puritan dilemma" was how to live in this world and still be a good Calvinist; in these terms Anne Hutchinson was unrealistic, for she was more concerned with following the logic of her views, regardless of practical consequences, than with accommodating to the world.

Following Morgan's book sociologists and psychologists began to study the Antinomian crisis from other viewpoints, those inspired by Erik Erikson's famous studies of Martin Luther and Mahatma Gandhi. One sociologist, Kai Erikson, concluded in 1966 that Hutchinson and her "odd opinions" deviated too far from the acceptable norms of Massachusetts society. Following Emile Durkheim, Erikson maintained that persecution of social deviants marks the health of society, for it gathers the community into a solid phalanx against those who threaten its accepted beliefs and values. Although few Bostonians understood the theological quibbling that led to Anne's banishment, Erikson believed, they were agreed that her behavior was out of line with what was expected of respectable, decent, orderly, and normal Puritans. He was willing to concede that her being a woman was one of the marks of her deviance, but he also followed Miller and Morgan in arguing

that pragmatically speaking, Winthrop stood for common sense and
Anne Hutchinson for fanaticism. No one was to blame in such a sce-
nario, however, for society sets its own standards and defines its own
deviants. The sociologist simply charts the middle of the road in terms
of those who are driven off into the gutter.

A few years earlier Emery Battis had utilized both sociology and
psychology to analyze the Antinomian movement in the most intense
detail yet provided by a historian. In *Saints and Sectaries* Battis concluded that Anne Hutchinson's behavior was psychologically abnor-
mal. She had too intense a relationship with her father; too emotional
a bond with her father-figure, John Cotton; too little concern for her
spineless husband, William. Her psychological instability led her to
challenge other male authority figures, said Battis. Anne battled for her
own psychological needs rather than for theological and ecclesiastical
concerns, and the latent psychological meaning of this struggle is more
important that the overt civil or theological meaning.

Why, then, did so many other, more psychologically stable people
in Boston side with Anne Hutchinson? Here Battis pointed out another
latent meaning in the controversy; drawing on Max Weber, he analyzed
the wealth and social standing of those who supported her. Battis's
statistical analysis led him to conclude that most of the staunch An-
tinomians were merchant entrepreneurs, men of rising wealth, while
most of their opponents were landed gentry with more traditional views
of social order. The rising merchant class differed from the old landed
class in desiring less restraint upon business enterprise. These entrepreneurs chafed under the efforts of the Puritan gentry who dominated
the legislature (and who clung to an older, medieval social ethic) to
pass laws regulating wages and profits. The entrepreneurs also disliked
the clerical denunciations of "filthy lucre" and the clerical insistence
that people remain in the social rank to which they were born. Hutchinson's views appealed to these "new" men because these views were
closer to a new individualistic, laissez-faire social ethic, one that would
limit the regulatory power of the state and exalt the free enterprise of
the rising middle class. Anne Hutchinson, it seemed, was not the Tho-
reau of Massachusetts Bay but the Ayn Rand.

Finally, in the 1970s, a group of feminist historians entered the field
and produced important new reevaluations of the Antinomian crisis.
For these writers, Antinomianism is one of the earliest examples in our

culture of the way in which gender issues govern social power and behavior. Anne Hutchinson's theological contributions to Puritanism, these historians said, were ignored and denigrated primarily because Hutchinson dared to challenge male hegemony. The leaders of Massachusetts Bay decided to make an example of her as a symbol of the danger posed to society when a woman leaves her God-appointed sphere. This feminist viewpoint totally reversed the interpretation of the early nineteenth-century historians. It exalted Hutchinson for daring to be a woman and daring to assert woman's equal role; it eulogized her as a compelling symbol of the new movement for equal rights for women.

Anne Hutchinson has also become a contemporary symbol of a major gender revolt within our churches, where women theologians like Mary Daly, Rosemary Ruether, and Elizabeth Fiorenza are critical of the patriarchal basis of the Christian church and demand that the Bible itself be reexamined to expose its bias against women. Instead of disparaging Hutchinson's theology as abstruse or mere "quibbling" over Calvinist exegesis, feminists argue that her willingness to stand up as a woman and seek theological change marks Hutchinson as a martyr to both women's history and church history. She is now cited as an example of what is necessary today if the Christian churches are to become relevant again in modern society. Hutchinson preached the priesthood of all believers, and from this ideal derives the equality of women in Christianity and their right to do everything a man can do in church and civil affairs.

I am not personally convinced that Anne Hutchinson was consciously trying to empower women—that is, to give them a special or equal role in the church as women. In fact, at her trial she made a point of stressing that she never taught theology at the meetings in her home when men attended. Nevertheless her behavior demonstrated her belief that God's message could and should be defended by women as well as by men when it was being perverted, and that women could minister to fundamental human concerns in spiritual affairs as effectively as men could. Just as she was a medical and psychological minister to women in her daily life, so, as a Christian, she asserted a sphere of influence that she believed was not only perfectly legitimate in the Christian order but also obligatory. God spoke through all of his saints regardless of gender, and they were all bound to uphold his truth.

In what I have been saying about historical reinterpretations, I am not simply reciting the truism that every age makes past symbols into relevant examples of contemporary concerns. In seeking a "usable" past, too often we distort it. The study of African-American history, for instance, is not just a search for tools for the present civil rights movement; more importantly, it is an effort to understand how and why black slavery and white racism obtained such a strong hold on our culture. Similarly, studying the Puritans' quarrel with Anne Hutchinson can give us a better understanding of the founding of American civilization and how that quarrel gave it shape. While each new interpretation of the Antinomian crisis may reflect the particular concerns of its age, it can also help us to see more clearly who Anne Hutchinson was and what she and John Winthrop represented both for their times and for ours. Different historians may emphasize different aspects of that affair, but taken together they are all helping us to deal with the living past. As William Faulkner once said, "The past isn't dead; hell, it isn't even past." Anne Hutchinson has thus become, like Christianity itself, a many-splendored thing. She lives because she was with us at a vital crossroads in our past, and because her actions help us to comprehend more clearly the vital religious, social, and feminist crossroads in the present. It is the best possible tribute to her that, though long dead, she still speaketh.

3

Indians and Colonists in Virginia and New England: A Contest for Power

ROGER L. NICHOLS

● *Racial thought is as old as civilized man. It has been a part of European and Oriental culture since antiquity, and its elements have existed in India, China, Egypt, Palestine, and Greece. It is hardly surprising that the United States has always been a racist society; the earliest colonists simply brought with them to the North American continent the attitudes and prejudices that prevailed in Europe in their day. The English, for example, considered themselves to be God's chosen people and thought of those of different skin color as being inferior.*

The Indians along the East Coast were obviously of a different skin color, and in addition they were unlettered, unwashed, unclothed, and "uncivilized." Initially, however, many colonists believed that the natives were descendants of the lost tribes of Israel, and they made honest, if somewhat misguided, efforts to Christianize them. Moreover, the Europeans also discovered that the Indians were "of a tractable, free, and loving nature, without guile or treachery"—to quote a seventeenth-century eyewitness. These native people were especially open with their knowledge and experience. For example, after the first desperate winter at Plymouth, during which time half the Pilgrims died, the Indians gave the survivors food and taught them to grow corn under primitive conditions. The following November, after a bountiful harvest, the two groups jointly celebrated America's first Thanksgiving.

But, as Professor Roger L. Nichols indicates in the following essay, red-white relations deteriorated rapidly during the seventeenth century. Pressed by increasing numbers and eager to provide more space for their expanding society, the white settlers pushed farther and farther inland, thus forcing the Indians to battle for their very existence. As the struggle took on more violent dimensions, myths of the worthlessness and brutality of the Indians had to be fabricated to justify the slaughter that ensued. Past experiences contradicting the image of the Indian as a savage had to be forgotten.

As you read the Nichols essay, you might consider that Adolf Hitler often pointed to the American Indian experience as a justification for his expansionist policies in Europe. After all, he suggested, the Nazis simply wanted to do what the white man had done in the United States—subjugate the native peoples and appropriate the land for use by a more civilized, powerful, and advanced culture.

When the English reached North America during the 1580s they sought wealth, fame, and adventure, but to their disappointment they found an environment suited only for farming. More important, in the long run, the regions they claimed and tried to settle were not vacant, but included substantial numbers of Algonkian villagers. To these resident Indians the English appeared as violent, unpredictable, and thoroughly dangerous invaders so they tried to discourage the newcomers through diplomacy, economics, and warfare. Repeated clashes between the two led to eventual English victory and their domination of the coastal regions in Virginia and New England. The frequent warfare and resulting hatred and suspicion between the invading Europeans and the resident tribes shaped attitudes on both sides and laid the foundations for poor relations between whites and Indians that continued through much of American history.

The two sides viewed their situation from vastly different perspectives. The Indians looked upon the colonists as possible allies against their local enemies, and as the source of valuable goods. At the same time the villagers assumed their superiority over the invaders who proved unable to feed themselves much of the time. In the long run, however, the Algonkians resented and feared the Europeans as greedy invaders who took land and food with little payment to the rightful owners. Certainly, given the dozens of tribes living near the coast, specific ideas and reactions varied widely, but these attitudes describe their general responses to the English. At the same time the intruding colonists considered their culture and technology far superior to those of the Indians. As bearers of civilization and Christianity they expected to be welcomed and acknowledged as superior beings. Indian reluctance to accept European preeminence puzzled and then angered the colonists. This, in turn, led to repeated clashes and eventual English victory and domination in both Virginia and New England. Despite this general pattern real differences existed in the relations between the native peoples and the invaders in the two regions and those need careful attention.

In general, friction and violence between the tribes and the colonists resulted from a tangle of basic causes and misunderstandings by people on both sides, and there is plenty of blame to be shared. The English added to the difficulties quickly. In fact, even before their permanent settlements in North America took root, they and other Europeans introduced epidemic diseases like smallpox and measles that swept away thousands of the coastal villagers. Whether the Indians recognized the source of these disastrous plagues or not, they came to fear English violence and treachery from the earliest meetings of the two groups. At Roanoke Island off the coast of North Carolina during the 1580s the English blamed nearby villagers for the loss of a silver cup. When the Indians did not produce the lost item, the English burned their crops and villages. In other instances English ship captains kidnapped whatever Indians they could induce to board their ships and took them to be sold as slaves in the West Indies or brought them back to England as curiosities. In either case, having experienced kidnapping, arson, and murder at the hands of the whites, it is no wonder that the coastal tribes viewed the invaders with a wary mixture of suspicion and hostility.

In Virginia hostilities between the English and the Indians began even before the Europeans reached Jamestown, and they continued sporadically for nearly seventy years. Landing about sixty miles up the James River brought the English into immediate contact with the so-called Powhatan Confederacy which had developed in the decade before the Europeans arrived. Through this group of thirty Algonkian tribes Powhatan dominated the region. Apparently he saw the Europeans as serving his needs and he sought to get an alliance with them against his Indian enemies and competitors. A highly intelligent leader, Powhatan quickly realized that the English represented both an opportunity to strengthen his confederacy and a potential threat to his leadership. Hoping to get more than he gave to the invaders, he tried to persuade the English to give or trade him two of their cannons, but without success. Yet despite stringent controls on trading or selling arms to the tribes, a small stream of muskets, powder, and shot came into the Indians' possession. Whenever possible the English strove to reduce the number of guns available to the tribes, and at times they demanded that the chiefs return all runaways and firearms to the colonial officials.

While the Indians strove to equip themselves with European weapons, the English struggled to survive. Either unable or unwilling to raise enough crops to meet their needs, the colonists began an aggressive campaign to extort food from the nearby villagers. Led by the Captain John Smith, the English sought to end the sporadic Indian attacks, and during the winter of 1608–09 Smith launched a belligerent effort against the Indians. He demanded the submission of entire villages, publicly humiliated local leaders, seized hostages, and extracted foodstuffs from one village after another. In one instance Smith dragged a village chieftain into the nearby stream threatening to drown or decapitate him if the villagers refused to provide corn. Having gotten what he wanted from the Indians, Smith put the luckless chief in chains and brought him to Jamestown as a hostage. The Captain blundered badly when he mistreated and humiliated Chief Opechancanough, the brother of Powhatan and his eventual successor. While at his village, Smith took Opechancanough by the hair while pointing his musket at the enraged Indian's chest and demanding that the villagers fill the colonist's boat with corn. The chief had already proven himself strongly anti-English, and this affront only made matters worse. In fact, little more than a decade later it was Opechancanough who organized and led the all-out attack on the Jamestown colony.

Indian headmen soon realized the extent of the English threat, and they did everything they could to thwart European expansion. Some of the warriors got and learned how to use firearms effectively. While the colonists strove to split Indian ranks, the villagers stressed their cultural solidarity by refusing to sell food to the invaders, by fleeing when the whites approached their towns, and by actual hostilities. These tactics nearly destroyed the fledgling colony and by the winter of 1609–10 the settlement faced collapse. At this point the Indians had won. As the English prepared to abandon Jamestown and return to

England, however, Lord de la Warr arrived with more colonists and supplies, as well as a renewed determination to smash Indian resistance to the English invasion of Virginia. This led to continuing aggression by both sides for another four years as English numbers grew and their wilderness skills improved. Columns of heavily armored colonists marched back and forth across the tidewater regions of Virginia, and by 1614 they had cleared much of the James River Valley of Indian resistance, forcing Powhatan to seek peace.

The defeat so weakened Powhatan that he surrendered leadership of the Indian confederacy, and soon his militant brother Opechancanough became the dominant figure. Although the coastal tribes had ceased hostilities, they did not accept the English as allies or friends. Rather they nursed their deep resentments and waited for better times. Powhatan's willingness to accept peace in 1614 had convinced the English to try other steps to gain control of Indian-white relations in Virginia. By 1616 officials there received orders to try peaceful means to gain tribal cooperation, and for the next several years the colonists worked to spread English culture, religion, and language among their neighbors. For a time the whites proved so eager to attract Indian adherents that they included muskets, powder, and ammunition in their trade and gifts with the nearby tribes. The colonists urged the Indians to send some of their children to Jamestown to learn European ways, something the villagers had little interest in doing. Tribal customs included exchanging children, but the colonists had no intention of having their children raised as Indians. Clearly neither group wanted to surrender its own culture.

The colonial authorities tried several other approaches in their efforts to incorporate Indians into the long-range development of Virginia. When the villagers refused to send their children into the English community to live, Governor Thomas Yeardley decided to recruit entire families. Any Indians who would move into town or to live among the English would receive a house, land for crops, and even some livestock. He hoped that while the adults learned the workings of the colonial economy and society, the children would be in school or working as apprentices and that both parents and children could be converted to Christianity. Backing for this approach came from England too. By 1619 the Church of England began sending funds for missionary and educational activities among the tribes. A year earlier the Virginia Company officers had designated the use of ten thousand acres of land to pay for an Indian college. Clearly the English hoped that education and possible conversion of young Indians would solve colonial problems with the tribes.

While England hoped for peace between the races, few individual settlers wholeheartedly shared that goal. Some leaders realized this. For example, George Thorpe, one of the strongest proponents of dealing kindly and fairly with the Indians, never considered that the villagers would reject English measures of good will. Rather he complained that the colonists themselves seemed to hate and fear their neighbors, and noted that most of the English denounced the Indians, with "nothinge but madedictions and bitter execrations." Even the missionaries and teachers destined to work among the native people lost patience with their lack of progress in "civilizing" the Indians. In 1621 one of the ministers complained that there was no hope of converting the tribes "till their Priests and Ancients have their throats cut."

There is little evidence to suggest that the Indians wanted to join any English-dominated biracial society. While the ethnocentric English congratulated themselves on their efforts to "civilize the savages," leaders of the Powhatan Confederacy learned white military skills, acquired weapons and ammunition, and fostered a growing resistance to the invaders. While ethnocentrism on both sides caused some friction, land ownership and use created the major point of dispute between the colonists and their tribal neighbors. Nevertheless, until John Rolfe, one of the leading planters, developed a marketable strain of tobacco, the Europeans were too few and occupied too little land to pose much threat. His success launched a veritable "tobacco craze" that swept the colony sending colonists streaming into the woods and onto lands cleared by the villagers.

Once the English realized tobacco was to provide an economic base for their colony they took Indian lands at every opportunity. For example, some whites seized cropland while the Indians were away on their annual migrations to gather seafood or to hunt, claiming that the fields had been abandoned. As early as 1615 several chiefs of minor tribes agreed to mortgage all their land in exchange for grain because of poor crops that year, and it is unlikely that colonial officials explained the legal implications of the agreement to the Indians. Within three years Governor Samuel Argall noted that the local tribes could no longer pay their debts and tribute, and if those being described were the same people whose lands had been pledged as security for the food loan several years earlier, the English would have taken the crop land for tobacco production. In fact, English landgrabbing became so widespread that one observer commented that the Virginia tribes lived in "dayly feare" that the colonists would take all of their lands and force them to move west into the territory of their long-time enemies.

While this occurred, Powhatan surrendered leadership of the Indian confederacy and his younger brother Opechancanough assumed effective command. Having distrusted the colonists since their arrival, and with a deep resentment for his mistreatment at the hands of John Smith some years earlier, the new chief strove to shape the confederacy into an effective force to block further English domination. Opechancanough exercised his skills with care. He expressed peaceful intentions to the colonists repeatedly and even swore that the sky would fall before he would break the tentative peace between the races. Still, the Indian leader saw the magnitude of the English threat and did everything within his power to prepare for eventual warfare. He encouraged the warriors to get firearms and to learn how to defend themselves against European military tactics. In fact, he was so successful at calming colonial fears and getting weapons and training for his men that in 1616 several Indians participated in a public parade of musketeers held at Jamestown.

Other Indian leaders helped Opechancanough focus anti-English feelings among the tribes. While some cooperated in urging a growing military preparedness, others tried different tactics. A prominent war chief named Namattanew proved especially able at fanning the flames of hatred among the tribes. Known as "Jack of the Feathers" by the English, this veteran of the pre–1614 fighting had proven ability as a leader and also as a marksman. The English feared this charismatic leader because of his skill in focusing tribal discontent against the colony through native religious practices. Jack encouraged a growing warrior cult based on strong cultural pride, a belief in the spiritual powers of the tribal deities, and the existing anti-English bitterness then present in the tidewater villages. He persuaded the warriors that his spiritual powers made his cloak of feathers impervious to English guns and that the Indian men would enjoy the same protection in battle if they used the ceremonies he prescribed. What influence "Jack of the

Feathers" had remains unclear, but certainly confederacy leaders, in particular Opechancanough, welcomed his nativist message and used the major Indian cultural regeneration movement then taking place as another way to strengthen their resistance to the colonists.

By 1619 the potential battle lines between the races had been drawn. Between that year and 1622 another 3,500 colonists seeking Indian land arrived in Virginia. Obviously, the tribes faced the unhappy alternatives of being driven from their homes, of becoming part of a despised underclass in the colony, or of attacking the invading whites. Indian leaders appear to have considered only one of the options—that of warfare—seriously. Opechancanough led a confederacy well united by cultural pride, a deep sense of continuing mistreatment and injustice at the hands of the English, and a zealous religious assurance of religious superiority and protection from the colonists' weapons. When the English killed Namattanew—Jack of the Feathers—they gave the Indians a cultural martyr and an incident around which Opechancanough could mobilize the continuing anti-English sentiment within the confederacy.

Rallying his forces secretly on March 22, 1622, the Indian leader launched a coordinated series of raids that devastated the colonial settlements. At least 345 colonists died the first day, one-fourth of the settlers, and this so-called Massacre of 1622 set off an intermittent and vicious war. Indian warriors destroyed the scattered farms while ably defending their villages and ambushing and repulsing or destroying attacking columns of colonial militiamen. The warriors became so bold that they used a fleet of sixty canoes to attack the ship *Tiger* as it lay at anchor on the Potomac River. Unable to win any open battle and terrified of further Indian victories, the English turned to treachery. They proposed peace negotiations, and when Opechancanough and two hundred of his followers met them for talks, the colonists poisoned the Indian's drinks. The chief and a few of his men escaped unharmed, but many died. The English decapitated and mutilated their victims, bringing "parte of their heades" as grisly trophies back to Jamestown. Despite this cowardly act and the initial advantages the tribes had enjoyed at the start of the conflict, in the long run the English brought their superior economic resources and larger population to bear to gain a one-sided victory.

The 1622 "Massacre" and the ensuing war ended the modest early efforts to merge colonial and tribal societies. Trade, education, religion, and military threats had all failed. The tribal people wanted little to do with the invading Europeans, and ten years of intermittent warfare made that clear to both sides. After 1622 the English moved quickly to occupy all of the cleared village land vacated by the scattered tribes, and the Indians never regained any of their former fields. In fact, colonial authorities made ever-increasing demands on the Indians as the growing white population continued to spread across the countryside. Disputes over cattle rustling, and over English land-grabbing from the tribes continued to disrupt relations between the two groups.

These grievances and news that the English were fighting a civil war at home persuaded the aged Opechancanough to try another all-out war against the colonial settlements. In 1644, although he was so feeble that he had to be carried to battle on a litter, the chief still commanded enough respect that his men attacked the colonists again. As they had two decades earlier, the Indian forces caught the English by surprise and inflicted major defeats and many casualties. Once again, however, the war proved a disaster for the Powhatan Confederacy, and by 1646 the English had won and forced another one-sided peace agreement on their defeated enemies. Opechancanough was captured, taken to Jamestown as a prisoner, and there was shot by one of his guards. His successor accepted a position clearly subordinate to the English. The tribes living nearest to the colonists thereafter remained in a permanently subservient status, surrendered much of their land, and agreed to remain out of specified regions reserved for the whites. After this defeat the tribes of coastal Virginia never again regained the level of cooperation and organization they had enjoyed earlier in the century. They remained, defeated, divided, and scattered, and under the watchful and suspicious eye of the conquerors. As such they ceased being a major independent force in colonial affairs or even a major danger to the expanding settlements.

By the 1670s when the last major Indian war of the seventeenth century took place in Virginia, the tribal population had plummeted sharply. A 1669 colonial census only mentions eleven of the twenty-eight tribes listed in 1608 by John Smith. While the number of tribes had dwindled, total Indian population declined even more rapidly if the 1669 figures are at all accurate. The estimated 30,000 Indians reported as present in 1608 had melted down to a mere 2,000 by 1669. Even if the earlier figure was inflated, this drop demonstrates the catastrophic impact of the European invasion and settlement of the Virginia coastal region.

With so few Indians remaining in colonial Virginia, the result of the last white-Indian conflict was never in doubt. By the 1670s squabbles among contending groups of colonists brought war to the tribes along the frontier. Disputes over the fur trade caused an incident between the Doeg Tribe and a trader named Thomas Mathews. In retaliation, Virginia militia units crossed the border into Maryland where they attacked the nearby Susquehannock Tribe by mistake. After the whites treacherously murdered five of the chiefs who had asked to parley, enraged warriors swept south into Virginia attacking exposed frontier settlements. Hopelessly mixed with a bitter quarrel among contending groups of Virginians over who was to control the fur trade, the colonial government, and the direction of future Indian policy, the fighting along the frontier escalated into what became known as Bacon's Rebellion. When that conflict ended, the local tribes signed another agreement with the English. This treaty placed the defeated Indians in a position of total subordination to the English. They agreed to pay annual rent for their land, and accepted the idea that they held their territory at the pleasure of the King. This 1677 treaty signalled the end of fighting between Indians and colonists in coastal Virginia, and demonstrates the continuing decline of Indian strength and independence as they contended with the invading Europeans.

In New England, relations between the races followed a similar pattern, although the details varied and the major conflict came a half century later than in Virginia. English sailors visited the New England coast before colonial settlers did, and while there they set the scene for later disputes with the local tribal people. In 1605 an expedition on the *Archangel* kidnapped five Abenakis and took them back to England. The English hoped that once the captives learned the language and returned to their home villages they would mediate relations between the invaders and the New England tribes. This did not happen. A few years later, in 1611, Edward Barlow seized three villagers from the mainland and three more at Martha's Vineyard before returning to Europe. In 1614 Thomas Hunt and his companions captured twenty-four more Indians, taking them south to be sold into slavery among the Spanish. All of these incidents occurred prior to any concerted effort to establish permanent settlements along the New England coast, but they gave the resident Indians there an indication of the treatment they might expect from the Europeans.

As they had done in the south, these actions brought suspicion and violence between the Indians and the English, but the initial situation in New England differed substantially from that in Virginia for several reasons. When the first colonists arrived, they did not encounter any grouping of tribes similar to the Powhatan Confederacy of Virginia. Rather, in 1616–18 a series of plagues had swept through the coastal tribes with a virulence hard to imagine. Whether a single catastrophic disease or a combination of several, the result was a demographic disaster. During the early 1620s while traveling through the region Thomas Morton reported seeing brush-filled corn fields, abandoned villages, and piles of "the bones and skulls" of the dead. Scholars who have examined the sources for this human destruction estimate that as many as 75 to 90 percent of all the people living in some coastal villages may have died from diseases within those few years.

The regions most heavily hit lay directly in the path of the first Pilgrim and Puritan settlements, and to the English the destruction of the local villages appeared as a sign that "divine providence made way for" their colonial settlement activities. For the Indians the impact of the disease and deaths proved an unmatched disaster. The epidemics shattered existing diplomatic alliances, strained or broke village economies, weakened the influence of tribal religious ideas and leaders, and endangered the mere existence of what had been well-established villages and tribes. Still reeling from the impact of these losses, the villagers were too busy trying to rebuild their lives and societies to expend any major efforts to destroy the first English settlements. Although they opposed European expansion when they could, in New England the local people had neither the inter-tribal organization nor the centralized, coordinated leadership enjoyed by the Virginia Indians.

Another basic difference between the New England Pilgrims and their Virginia counterparts was that from the start the northern colonists feared that the Indians might destroy them. Even before they landed at Plymouth in 1620, William Bradford, the Governor of the colony, noted their fears and wrote that the villagers reputed savagery made "the very bowels of men to grate within them and make the weak to quake and tremble" when they thought of Indians. This view of the local population certainly colored Pilgrim actions toward them, and despite Bradford's urging that the Plymouth colonists deal peaceably with their Indian neighbors, this did not occur. Miles Standish, a sort of New England version of John Smith, took the lead in applying intimidation and force to white-Indian relations. Apparently he assumed that once the villagers came to "respect" the English they would decide to cooperate and would help the intruders with food, protection, and cooperation. His aggressive policy did not always achieve the goal of peaceful coexistence that the English desired. Yet no major conflict between the invading English and the local Algonkians occurred during the early years of Pilgrim settlement.

Peaceful relations came for a variety of reasons. Despite a few early skirmishes the coastal peoples were still too badly shaken by the plagues of a few years earlier to present any major obstacle. More important was the reluctance of the powerful Wampanoag Tribe to meet the English until they determined that the invaders were too few and too weak to present any immediate threat. They watched the colonists struggle to survive during the winter of 1620–21, and then in March, 1621, Wampanoag chief Massasoit, his brother, and sixty armed warriors arrived at Plymouth. As the Pilgrim leaders wondered how they could meet the chief without inviting his entire party into the settlement, Squanto, an English-speaking captive living among the Wampanoags, arrived to serve as translator. Described as "a spetiall instrument sent of God for their good," his presence lessened Pilgrim fears and they welcomed the visitors into the settlement. Their talks produced an alliance between the tribe and the settlers in which the two groups agreed to a mutual defense pact against other peoples in the region.

In this instance the situation in New England differed sharply from that in Virginia as the Indians nearest the English became their allies rather than their competitors and eventual enemies. At the same time, the Wampanoags hoped to use their alliance with the colonists to strengthen their own relations with the Narragansetts, their dangerous competitors to the west. Obviously the Indians looked at the invading colonial settlers in much the same way that Powhatan had done in Virginia a decade earlier as they strove to incorporate the English into the existing web of inter-tribal relations. Yet there was a major difference in the two situations. In Virginia Powhatan operated from a position of local dominance, while in New England, Massasoit needed

Pilgrim help against his neighbors just to retain his influence. There was little question of his dominating the region.

Relations between the colonists and the New England Indians remained peaceful most of the time, although rumors of conspiracies and several minor incidents of English aggression did mar the picture. Still, by the mid–1620s the patterns of Pilgrim-Indian relations appeared clear. The two peoples had come to tolerate each other and avoided major violence for the rest of that decade. By 1630, however, the advance parties of the vast Puritan migration from England surged into eastern Massachusetts, changing the situation drastically. Benefitting from earlier Pilgrim peace with the local tribes, from the demographic havoc the plagues of 1616–18 had wrought among the Indians and from their own large population, the new colonists felt little threat of major war. At the same time, because the Massachusetts tribe and several other related small villages remained weak and considered the Abnaki to the north a worse threat than the English, they had little reason to attack the colonists. Rather they welcomed the Puritans as allies and protectors.

From the start, in New England, divisions and competition weakened the native peoples' ability to resist white encroachment. Nevertheless, continuing rivalry and friction resulted from the ongoing English efforts to expand their control over the economy, political-legal structure, diplomacy, and even culture of the Indian communities. Although determined to avoid major war if possible, the Puritans moved quickly to extend their influence over every phase of tribal life. To accomplish this they tried to manipulate people and events to ensure their rapid local dominance. At a glance Puritan efforts to control the local situation appear similar to actions by the Jamestown colonists in Virginia, but the relationships between whites and their Indian neighbors differed in the two regions. Therefore, what brought long and bitter war in Virginia caused only the modest-sized Pequot War of 1636–37 during the early decades of English settlement in the region.

That conflict provides a graphic example of English ethnocentrism and their determination to use divided Indian loyalties and inter-tribal rivalries for their own advantage. The Pequot War led to clear-cut English supremacy over the people of coastal New England. Competing Dutch traders, overlapping land claims among competing English

groups, divisions among the Pequots and competition with the Narragansetts all played a role in this struggle. As the whites extended
their settlements and trading activities, the Pequots began to lose their
prized role as middlemen in the growing trade, so the Indians began a
series of raids in the Connecticut Valley to reassert their dominance.
A major smallpox epidemic in 1633–34 further complicated the situation as it spread death among other coastal groups. At that point a
semi-piratical trader named John Stone sailed his small vessel up the
Connecticut River, hoping to kidnap Pequots for ransom. The Indians
turned the tables on Stone, however, when they stormed his craft and
killed him and his eight companions. Regardless of the circumstances,
the colonists decided that they could not ignore that the Indians had
killed nine Englishmen, so they demanded that the Pequots pay reparations and submit themselves to colonial authorities. Finding themselves isolated by white diplomacy, in November 1634 the Pequots
signed a treaty with the Massachusetts officials. Through this agreement
they accepted English settlement in Connecticut and the colonists' control of the interracial situation there.

During the next several years depredations and violent incidents
continued, so the English demanded that the Pequots pay reparations
and turn over the accused individuals for punishment. Usually the
Indians refused to do this. In the summer of 1636 the murder of another
English trader brought things to a head. First the colonists secured
Narragansett neutrality. Then they accepted Chief Uncas and a seceding
band of Pequots now calling itself the Mohegans as allies. Having
isolated the Pequots diplomatically, the English in 1636 launched a
series of attacks against the tribe. The war proved swift, brutal, and
decisive, and when the fighting ended many Pequots had been killed.
The victorious English treated the survivors harshly too. Some they
sold into slavery, but the rest they placed under the watchful eye of
Uncas of the Mohegans or of Miantonomo of the Narragansetts. The
colonial authorities convinced these tribal leaders to sign the Treaty of
Hartford in 1638 which made them responsible for keeping the region
at peace, or at least making certain that the remaining Pequots would
cause no further trouble. The destruction of the Pequots did not end
all friction between the colonials and the Indians in New England, but
it halted major fighting there for nearly four decades.

During that time Puritan leader worried about the presence and influence of Indians in their New World Garden of Eden. Torn between a desire to convert the tribes to Christianity on the one hand, and to maintain their social and doctrinal purity on the other, the colonists struggled with the issue of how best to deal with their neighbors. By the 1640s the authorities decided to bring both Christianity and English-style education to the villagers, and they began this effort by ordering county courts to provide funds for both missionary and educational activities. Despite these stated goals there was little money and no immediate action. In order to help Indians who might want to adopt some aspects of white culture, the colonists needed to learn at least some of the local Algonquian languages, but few bothered doing that. The Thomas Mayhews, father and son on the island called Martha's Vineyard, and John Eliot, who worked in Massachusetts, were the clear exceptions. In Rhode Island and Plymouth the colonists supported modest missionary efforts, too, but with less success than in either Massachusetts or on the coastal island. The difficulties of expressing complex theological concepts inhibited missionary activities, but ingrained English ethnocentrism and Indian determination to retain their cultural beliefs slowed the acculturation program as well. Nevertheless, remnants of the Massachusetts and a few other small coastal tribes accepted English teaching and practices. Gradually John Eliot organized a dozen so-called Praying Towns where the inhabitants were segregated from both the English and the other Indians. By the 1670s colonial authorities listed an Indian population of some 2,500 converts living in these villages, perhaps a fifth of the native people left in Massachusetts.

The Puritans tried to disrupt local culture in other ways, too. Teachers and schools in theory accepted Indians as well as whites for class, and some native children attended the schools. By the 1660s colonial authorities paid "a score or more" of Indian boys to attend schools in Cambridge and Roxbury, hoping that they could be prepared for entrance into Harvard. On Martha's Vineyard Thomas Mayhew conducted a school for about thirty Indian children there. Some adult Indians managed to learn to read English and by 1651 Eliot employed several Indian teachers to expand the work among other villages. In 1654 Harvard organized an Indian college within the school, and two years later the authorities there even built a separate building to hold twenty Indian students. Only a handful of young Indians ever got to

Harvard during the seventeenth century, however, and for most of them the experience was a disaster. Several died while at college, while others contracted diseases which killed them later. One was murdered, and at least one dropped out of the school. Discouraged by the lack of response, college authorities assigned some of the space in the Indian College to the Cambridge Press. Like the Virginia effort to establish Henrico College for tribal young people some decades earlier, the Massachusetts effort to incorporate the Indians bore little fruit.

In addition to using religion and education to acculturate their tribal neighbors the Puritan colonists sought to apply English government and laws whenever possible. As the number of whites increased through the decades, so did the pervasiveness of their legal system in dealing with the Indians. In the long run, English insistence on imposing their legal practices and control over the tribes caused as much difficulty for the native people as any element in the whites' program. For the Puritan settlers, their religious beliefs and cultural experience led them to insist that through the government man strove to attain God's desires for society. For the Algonquian peoples of New England, however, nothing could have been farther from their conceptions. They recognized no formal relationship between individuals and any government. Rather the village, clan, and family provided the framework for their lives. Justice revolved around personal relationships and family obligations rather than a set of laws, and they settled disputes either by paying compensation for damage or injury to others, or through physical retribution when compensation proved inadequate or unsatisfactory.

Each treaty signed by a tribe and a colonial government proved a vehicle for the expansion of English influence. White officials used treaty agreements and the legal system to extend their authority over the tribes gradually. At first, they worked through village leaders, making them responsible for the return of stolen property and the surrender of villagers accused of breaking English laws. The colonial authorities regulated which, if any, Indians could buy land, alcohol, or firearms. Gradually they admitted the villagers to the jury system, but Indian jurors were rare unless both parties in a suit were Indians too. The whites assumed that their courts treated the Indians fairly and equally, but that was not the case. When tribal members were convicted for a particular crime, they usually received harsher or more physical punishments than did whites convicted of the same offense. For example, while a colonist might pay a fine, an Indian would be whipped, pay a larger fine, or both. As the two races had more experience with each other, more Indians participated in the court system, with Plymouth even making a provision that Indian witnesses need not take an oath before their testimony. Despite these changes, English power gave them control with a corresponding weakening of Indian independence, culture, and values throughout New England.

Having expanded their authority in economics, religion, education, and law, the New Englanders came to dominate their neighbors. Yet continuing rumors of tribal conspiracies and English paranoia about the Indians drew both groups into the last major conflict in that area, King Philip's War. This struggle was much more than a simple Indian-white fight. It resulted from long-term trends of English expansion and aggression, inter-colonial competition over land and influence between Plymouth, Connecticut, and Massachusetts, ongoing rivalries among the Narragansetts, Wampanoags, and Mohegans, stresses between Christian Indians and the traditional villagers, and the ambitions and personal influence of individual chiefs. Whatever the specific causes, this conflict pitted colonist against Indian in the most bitterly contested war between the two in the history of New England, and the colonial victory marked the complete domination of the region by the intruding Europeans.

The inter-racial difficulties grew out of the increasing white dominance of the region through trade, law enforcement, education, and religion. While these trends accelerated, tribal leadership underwent significant change. Massasoit, the long-time Wampanoag sachem who had been a friend and ally of the English, died during the 1660s and his eldest son Wamsutta took over leadership of the tribe. The new chief died suddenly in 1662 leaving Metacom to assume command. King Philip, as the English called the new leader, reaffirmed his father's earlier treaty of peace and friendship with the colonial authorities, yet at the same time he took a more openly independent stance toward the colony than had his father or brother. An astute leader, he recognized the threat for the tribes the expanding settlements posed, and he sought to strengthen Indian abilities to resist English domination. While trying to do this, he also strove to discredit the Narragansetts and the Mohegans by telling the whites of Indian plots by those peoples against them. Clearly Philip hoped to gain favor with the English and then use his good standing with them to deflect white activities that might reduce his influence or damage Wampanoag interests.

For nearly a decade, from the mid-1660s to the mid-1670s, Metacom worked to achieve his goal of continued Indian independence. During that time English officials in Plymouth sought to publicly humiliate the chief while they tried to disarm and dominate his tribe. In 1667 Metacom complained that jealous chiefs in other tribes had falsely accused him of plotting with the French against the nearby English. Two years later he reported that the Niantic and Mohegan leaders had met to plot war against the colonists. The meeting took place, but apparently was just an ordinary multi-tribal ceremony with no particularly anti-English overtones. These actions did little to give Metacom credibility with the Plymouth authorities. By early 1671, he and his advisors appeared before the Plymouth officials to explain their acquisitions of weapons. When their answers to the whites' questions seemed evasive, the English demanded that he sign a new treaty of submission, surrender the guns, and return home. The chief had little choice but to submit, and left Plymouth humiliated and nursing strongly anti-English feelings.

By 1675 Indian resentment over real and imagined slights, anger over English land-grabbing, and colonial fears of an Indian conspiracy set the stage for the violence to follow. In January that year John Sassamon, a Christian Indian who had reported continuing anti-English actions among the Wampanoags, was found dead. The circumstances of his death convinced the English that Sassamon had been murdered in retaliation for reporting news of tribal activities to the whites. Eventually a single Indian testified that three Wampanoags had killed the victim, and in June 1675 the accused stood trial in Plymouth. The jury found them guilty and the last of the three to be executed admitted the crime before his death. Because one of the convicted men was an advisor to King Philip, the Plymouth officials assumed that the sachem had ordered the killing. From there it was only a matter of weeks until violence erupted, and that led quickly to all-out war.

Hysteria swept through the English settlements as rumors of Indian alliances, raids, and atrocities circulated freely, and by mid-June roving bands of warriors began to strip and burn abandoned farms and other buildings. As soon as the nearby colonies learned of the hostilities, they sent troops to help force the local tribes to either join or avoid the growing conflict. The Narragansett leaders assured the English of their peaceful intentions, but several bands of that tribe later participated in the fighting. Some of the Nipmucks joined Philip's forces, too, but the other tribes either stayed neutral or supported the colonial armies against the Wampanoags. Even the Christian Indians from the Praying Towns volunteered to help the whites, but English bigotry and suspicion of those people limited their use. Once fighting began, war parties swept through the outlying settlements destroying many of them and sending terrified refugees fleeing to the larger towns. By August, 1676 most of the fighting had ended as Philip and his followers went down to defeat. Indian auxiliaries killed the Wampanoag sachem, and the English sold his wife and son into slavery in the West Indies.

The war brought immense destruction and population loss to both colonists and the New England tribes as entire towns and villages were abandoned, and the population of both combatants dropped sharply. Nevertheless, the conflict proved more critical to Indian survival than to that of the colonists. The whites had crushed the Wampanoag, Nipmuck, Pocumtuck, and Narragansett tribes, while they already dominated the much-reduced Pequots and the Mohegans. Most of the individual survivors of the defeated tribes surrendered to the colonial victors, but some fled out of the region seeking homes among related people in New York and even in Eastern Canada. Those villages and individuals who remained found themselves at the mercy and under the clear domination of the New England colonial governments. While the whites, too, lost heavily, they had the population base and economic base to rebuild their societies. For the New England tribes, King Philip's war proved as disastrous a defeat as the 1622 and 1644 conflicts in Virginia had for the tribes there. Indian defeat in 1676 came to be understood as not just an immediate disaster for the Indian, but rather the last major step in the process of inter-racial relations. As the English grew stronger the tribes fell continually farther under the colonists' domination and control.

By the end of the 1670s it was clear in both North and South that the English dominated all of the areas where they had settled. Their laws, economy, social organization, military actions, and religion had triumphed. For the Indians this meant that they faced the future as defeated people, living in a country controlled by their enemies, the conquering English. Unfortunately, the precedents of warfare and cultural domination set in the seventeenth-century colonial settlements continued to shape American attitudes toward the tribes for most of the next three centuries, and only since 1960 have responsible national leaders begun to redress the earlier dismal relations between the United States and the Indians.

4

Witchcraft, Sexuality, and the Cunning Woman in Salem

LOUIS J. KERN

● *Although the practice of black magic predates Christianity, the period between about 1450 and 1750 witnessed an explosion of fear, hysteria, and chaos with regard to the imagined spread of witch lore. Seeking to convert all the peoples of Europe to the true faith, the Catholic Church in particular banned pagan religion and practices and began to prosecute supposed witches. Trials, convictions, and executions became commonplace on the continent and reached a crescendo during the Spanish Inquisition, when as many as one hundred persons were burned as witches in a single day. Mass executions sometimes took on the qualities of a carnival, where spectators could buy food, souvenirs, and rosaries.*

Late in the seventeenth century, this fanaticism spread to the American colonies and especially to Salem, Massachusetts, where in 1692 many persons were condemned as witches. Not surprisingly, most of the victims were women because, as Professor Louis J. Kern of Hofstra University reminds us in the following essay, female sexuality was itself mysterious and threatening. And witches were thought to be especially aggressive and innovative in their desire for physical intimacy.

The belief in the power of magic is as old as civilization itself. Magic constituted a transcendent, sacred order of knowledge that commanded principalities of the air and infernal forces of immense scope and power. The apparent ability of its adepts to control the lives and destinies of their fellows and to sustain or destroy society as a whole gave rise to a profound aura of fear and awe that surrounds the realm of magic in

Courtesy of the *Essex Institute Historical Collections,* published by the Peabody and Essex Museum, Salem, Massachusetts. This essay appeared in issue number one of volume 129, pages 3–38.

the popular mind. From the earliest times, therefore, a close association arose between the rituals of magic and those of religion. Indeed, as Jules Cambarieu has observed, the magical incantation may well have been "the oldest fact in the history of civilization."

In pre-Christian times, a distinction between two forms of magic—white (licit) and black (illicit)—was widely recognized. Illicit magic operated through the invocation of demons to hinder or injure its victims. Licit magic sought to forfend the disastrous consequences of demonic intervention in human affairs. The early Church Fathers blurred this distinction between theurgy and diabolical magic. Saint Augustine charged all practitioners of the magical arts with "criminal tampering with the unseen world," and maintained that "both classes are the slaves of deceitful rites of the demons whom they invoke under the names of the angels."

In the popular mind, however, the distinction between harmful magic, grounded in devil worship, and beneficial, propitiatory spells and incantations, endured. Despite severe ecclesiastical and secular penalties for trafficking in the magic arts, the common people persisted in believing in their efficacy, and continued to consult practitioners of occult rites. The force of custom, then, sustained the practice of magic as an alternative form of spiritual power and a body of powerful, arcane lore that coexisted (albeit not very peacefully) alongside Christian beliefs and ecclesiastical rites. Such an uneasy tenure on the popular mind was not acceptable to the Church, and gradually Christian apologists were able to subsume much of traditional magical practice under the rubric of the diabolical by employing the term "witchcraft," which had theretofore constituted but one branch of the magical tree, to signify the dire spiritual threat of a far from moribund occultism.

Witchcraft, derived from the Anglo-Saxon term, *wiccian* (which meant to practice sorcery), came to include *veneficium* (compounding and/or administering drugs, potions, or philters), and *incantatio* (to recite magical words, to work charms, or to bewitch). Since these two practices, at least in their more beneficent forms, were also attributes of white (good) magic, what was taken as the essence of the detested and execrable practice of witchcraft, as defined by Christian authorities, was the implied intent of the practitioner, expressed as *maleficium*—the noxious or pernicious infliction of injury or harm upon another. The Church built upon and co-opted the popular traditions and images of sorcery and magic in defining the rites and practices of witches, and effectively forged links between the vulgar persistence of ancient pre-Christian beliefs, which continued to enjoy wide popularity, and the explicit inversion of Christian doctrine through the self-consciously heretical worship of Satan. Such characteristic acts of witchcraft as compacts with the Devil, the suckling of familiars, sexual relations with demon lovers or Satan himself, and the witches' Sabbat also allowed the Church to annex to the practice of the ancient religion the full corpus of mortal sins.

Witchcraft was constructed as the mirror image of orthodoxy; it constituted a deviant organization of religious and social life that gave precedence to physical over spiritual experience. It became the duty of all true believers to root out and extirpate the full panoply of its execrable practices wherever they might be found. The full weight of the ecclesiastical establishment was brought to bear against *maleficium* in an extensive, European crusade against witchcraft that spanned three centuries (1450–1750) and resulted in over 100,000 formal prosecutions. The witch-hunts and persecutions, whose primary victims were women, were greatly facilitated by Innocent VIII's bull *Summis Desiderantes* (1484), which linked the prosecution of witches to the apparatus of the Inquisition, specifically directing inquisitors and other ecclesiastical and secular authorities to execute all practitioners of witchcraft and other diabolical arts.

An extensive literature of witchcraft was produced that detailed the horrors and crimes perpetrated by the adepts of this ancient art and came to comprise a set of guidebooks to the examination and trial of suspected witches. While there is a substantial variety of interpretation among these works, there is a notable orthodoxy on fundamentals. A central dogma, from which there is scant deviation, and which is sustained by an objective study of the statistical record of prosecutions and executions, is that witchcraft is a predominantly female crime. So inveterate was this belief that it became the basis for juridical expectation and popular suspicion. In places where the witch-hunts provoked mass hysteria—Geneva in 1546, Labourd in 1609, Lorraine between 1580 and 1595, and Salem in 1692, for instance—it became a virtually self-fulfilling prophecy that led to the condemnation of thousands of women.

Nicholas Remy asserted that "it is not unreasonable that this scum of humanity should be drawn chiefly from the feminine sex," for "women excel in their knowledge of witchcraft." In the late fifteenth century, two Dominican inquisitors, writing under the imprimatur of the papal see, penned a popular manual for the persecution and extirpation of witches. This comprehensive volume, the *Malleus Maleficarum* (1486), inextricably linked evil, the erotic, and the feminine, and brilliantly wove together official doctrine and popular prejudice. It defined "wicked women" as those consumed by "infidelity, ambition, and lusts," and argued that

> since of these three vices the last chiefly predominates, women being insatiable, etc., it follows that those among ambitious women are more deeply infected who are more hot to satisfy their filthy lusts; and such are adulteresses, fornicatresses, and the Concubines of the Great.

There were two important corollaries to the basic assumption that "far more women are witches than men." Both related to the irreducibly erotic nature of witchcraft beliefs and practices. The first held that, if women were the agents of diabolical forces in their character of witches, men were their object, their victims. Therefore, "men are more often bewitched than women." The second corollary sought to explain the seeming incongruity of the ideologically prescribed superior sex being victimized by the subordinate and weaker sex. "The reason for this," we are told,

> lies in the fact that God allows the devil more power over the venereal act, by which the original sin is handed down, than over other human actions. . . . And the venereal act can be more readily and easily bewitched in a man than in a woman.

The ability of the Devil, operating through his unquestioning human followers, to "cast spells upon the venereal act," demonstrates that diabolical power preeminently "lies in the privy parts of men."

The literature on witchcraft makes clear that witches' sorcery and sexual magic were considered essentially identical. But while traditional magical intervention in the amatory affairs of the common people may be found in this literature—use of occult powers and potions to secure affection, to enhance the libido, and to curse the faithless paramour—

the overwhelming intent of sexual spells was to induce male impotence. In general, it was maintained that witches afflicted men by means of their seductive wiles, through "their dances, their obscene kisses," they "contrive[d] to send demons and evil spirits into a man's body."

Those evil spirits erected potent impediments to the male's genital functions. They affected both the mental and the physical aspects of sexual behavior. In the first instance, they might "so disturb a man's perception and imagination as to make the woman appear loathsome to him." Even more devastatingly, they might destroy the basis of male sexual capacity through spermatoschesis, spermatemphraxis, or the incapacity of the erectile power. But the sexual power of witches that cast a cold horror of brute, visceral fear over the male imagination was the threat of the utter and complete disappearance of the sexual organs. For, "there is no doubt," the *Malleus Maleficarum* insists, "that certain witches can do marvellous things with regard to male organs." Although they cannot actually remove the organs, they can make their victim effectually incapable of perceiving them. When this apparent removal of the sexual organs is

> performed by witches, it is only a matter of glamour; although it is no illusion in the opinion of the sufferer. For his imagination can really and actually believe that something is not present, since by none of his exteriour senses, such as sight or touch, can he perceive that it is present.... so that it seems to him that he can see and feel nothing but a smooth body with its surface interrupted by no genital organ.

Passages like these are indicative of the efforts of orthodoxy to palliate male fears of female sexual power and to undermine the vestigial beliefs in the old religion of magic that were all but inseparable from popular ideas and folk custom. Indeed, the assurances of the superiority of Christianity over diabolical magic are commingled with reiterations of traditional folk belief that are but indifferently glossed and ineffectively subsumed under the orthodox construction of the powers of witchcraft. A story recounted in the *Malleus*, for example, has all the qualities of a bawdy folk tale. It arises in the context of a widespread and persistent belief that some witches

> collect male organs in great numbers, as many as twenty or thirty members together, and put them up in a box, where they move

themselves like living members, and eat oats and corn, as has been seen by many and is a matter of common report.

Once, so the story goes,

> a certain man ... when he had lost his member ... approached a known witch to ask her to restore it to him. She told the afflicted man to climb a certain tree, and that he might take which he liked out of a nest in which there were several members. And when he tried to take a big one, the witch said: You must not take that one; adding, because it belonged to the parish priest.

Beneath the comedy of this story, the unreasoning fear of female power exercised through the dark arts is apparent. In the first instance, it is evident that witches have coldly and calculatedly assembled their organ collections through manipulation of what is considered the hyper-sexuality of the female. They have worked their will on the male community "through their [men's] carnal desires and the pleasures of the flesh." Secondly, it indicates a fear of male sexual loss of control—the penis has an independent life of its own; it is not subject to the control of the (male) will. And it is precisely the male's inability to control his penis that has made it possible for the female as witch to seduce and unman him. Fear of male sexual inferiority is also implied in the subject's attempt to appropriate the largest penis in the collection. Finally, the story underscores the superiority of the old faith over the new in two ways. First, the witch has seduced and deprived of his virile member the local surrogate of the church universal; and then, the only recourse to having been "collected" is to propitiate the evil forces in the person of the witch. Even in cases where a male victim had been deluded by a "glamour" that merely prevented his perception of organs still attached, their restoration often required the magical contrectation of the witch herself. As a young man described the process,

> the witch touched him with her hand between the thighs, saying: "Now you have what you desire." And the young man ... plainly felt, before he had verified it by looking or touching, that his member had been restored to him by the mere touch of the witch.

As self-conscious representatives of anarchic, unbounded, and ungovernable female sexuality, witches were also believed to be a threat to male potency and self-control through their ability to seduce men into satyriasis or *philocaption* ("inordinate love"), whereby "a man is so bound in the meshes of carnal lust and desire that he can be made to desist from it by no shame, words, blows or action; and when a man often puts away his beautiful wife to cleave to the most hideous of women." Women, even when promised the handsomest of lovers, are frequently depicted in this literature as virtuously resisting temptation. Females were of two types—the dangerously lascivious and diabolically cunning witches, and the upright matrons and irreproachable virgins. It was free indulgence of feminine sexuality—promiscuous and nonreproductive in nature—that separated the conventional from the deviant woman. Typically, witches were initiated into their craft through an act of sexual intercourse. For example, a woman, tutored by one of the relatively rare males executed for witchcraft, "as the price of her learning ... had been defiled by him and made pregnant."

But what most characterized the hypersexuality of the female, as represented by the conventional depiction of the witch in the literature of inquisition, was copulation with the Devil. So essential was diabolical intercourse to the ideal type of the witch, that one writer could unqualifiedly maintain that

> it has been revealed in the examinations of witches that they all have this connection with Satan. The Devil uses them so because he knows that women love carnal pleasures, and he means to bind them to his allegiance by such agreeable provocations. Moreover, there is nothing which makes a woman more subject to a man than that he should abuse her body.

The usual pattern in these matters was for the witch to seal her/his covenant with the Devil by a sexual union, and for carnal connections to play a major role in the rites of the Sabbat. Orthodox authors, however, could only conceive diabolical sexuality as unnatural, and therefore depicted it as unpleasurable in some degree for the women involved. The bulk of witches' testimony reported in these guides to prosecuting witches sustains the sense of acute physical distaste associated with intimate contact with Satan. As one witch confessed,

> she had several times taken in her hand the member of the Demon which lay with her, and that it was as cold as ice and a good

finger's length, but not so thick as that of a man. [Nevertheless], when Satan coupled with her she had as much pain as a woman in travail.

In a literature written exclusively by men, exhibiting a fascination with the intimate details of female sexuality, both psychological and physical, male sexual fears and fantasies ran rampant. Male sensitiveness about penis size and a vindictive insistence on the castigation of female sexual desire characterize the assessment of the putative unrestrained eroticism of the sex life of the typical witch. "All female witches," we are told, "maintain that the so-called genital organs of their Demons are so huge and so excessively rigid that they cannot be admitted without the greatest pain." Individual witches testified that the Devil's organ, "even when only half in erection, was as long as some kitchen utensils," that it felt "like a spindle swollen to an immense size so that it could not be contained by even the most capacious woman without great pain," and that it was "long environ la moitié d'une aulne, de mediocre grosseur, rouge, obscur, et tortu, fort rude et comme piquant." One witch asserted that "although she had many years' experience of men, she was always so stretched by the huge, swollen member of her Demon that the sheets were drenched with blood."

Some male authorities were reluctantly forced to conclude, given the weight of testamentary evidence, that for most witches, "it is wholly against their will that they are embraced by Demons, but . . . it is useless for them to resist." Such a conclusion, that diabolical intercourse was ravishment, soothed the bruised male ego and minimized the threat of feminine sexuality. But not all authors were willing to accept the logic of the witch-hunters and remained obdurately defiant. A Scottish woman, for instance, stoutly maintained of her demonic paramour that "he is abler for us that way than any man can be, onlie he ves heavie lyk a malt-sek; a hudg nature, verie cold, as yce."

Apparently Satan, in his infinite incarnations, was not alone "abler" for witches but for their more orthodox and conventional sisters as well, for the other great strain of eroticism in the witchcraft literature was that of the demon lover or incubi and succubi. On the question of the nature and issue of the intercourse of a human being and an incubus (literally, "lying above," male) or a succubus (literally, "lying beneath," female) there was heated controversy in the literature. Some maintained that such hypostatized apparitions were fallen angels or *eudemons,* while others contended that they were the incarnation of the spirit of evil or *cacodemons.* The most heated controversy, however, emerged over whether such demonic-human unions could produce progeny, and if so, what the effectual means of generation was. Though there were some dissenters, the consensus of opinion seems to have held that such unions could be fruitful; but some disagreement remained over precisely how it might be possible for supernatural intervention to operate through natural means.

A Spanish medical authority of the sixteenth century claimed that the whole process was a kind of eugenics in reverse that would eventually produce the Antichrist by means of natural biological evolution. "What Incubi introduce into the womb," he asserted,

> is not any ordinary human semen in normal quantity, but abundant, very thick, very warm, rich in spirits and free from serosity. This moreover is an easy thing for them, since they merely have to choose ardent, robust men, whose semen is naturally very copious and with whom the Succubus has connexion, and then women of like constitution, with whome the Incubus copulates, taking care that both shall enjoy a more than normal orgasm, for the more abundant the semen the greater the venereal excitement.

Most writers were reluctant to accept the concept of demon lovers as super progenitors since both popular culture and conventional wisdom (grounded in Aristotelian ideas about the physical world) emphasized the coldness of the Devil and his associates. But the notion of the succubus/incubus pair as a supernatural force that magically united the male and female germs of two human parents, who remained mutually unconscious of the other's role in the reproductive process, proved at once more enduring and more popular. The supernatural part of the process, predicated upon the demon's ability to change sex at will, is quite straightforward: "the devil is Succubus to a man, and becomes Incubus to a woman."

The crucial distinction between witches' sexual relations with the Devil and the connection of women and incubi is consciousness of the true identity of the lover. Witches are fully aware that their lover is the Devil, having engaged themselves by ritualized covenant to him.

As a consequence, the demon may be visible to the witch's eyes alone, remaining totally imperceptible to any bystanders. In the case of incubi, who essentially delude their mistresses into believing them human, they are quite visible to all human eyes. This distinction was believed to provide one basis for eyewitness identification of a witch, for

> manie times witches are seene in the fields, and woods, prosti-
> tuting themselves uncovered and naked up to the navill, wagging
> and moving their members in everie part, according to the dis-
> position of one being about that act of concupiscence, and yet
> nothing seene of the beholders upon hir; saving that after such
> a convenient time as is required about such a peece of worke, a
> blacke vapor of the length and bigness of a man, hath beene seene
> as it were to depart from hir, and to ascend from that place.

Another example of witchery in sexual congress was the visible use of unnatural means in performing the act. It was discovered, according to a French jurist, that a woman, who had been imprisoned under suspicion of witchcraft,

> had a hole beneath her navel, quite contrary to nature.... the
> witch confessed that her Devil ... had sexual connection with her
> through this hole, and her husband through the natural hole.

What drove women, either witches or more conformist women, to welcome diabolical sex was their very feminity. The physiology of the female body, the delicate balance of their humors, it was believed, made them acutely susceptible to lubricity. For

> they have such an unbridled force of furie and concupiscence
> naturallie, that by no means is it possible for them to temper or
> moderate the same.... Women are also ... monethlie filled full
> of superfluous humors, and with them the melancholike bloud
> boileth.

In the end, the dogmatic belief in the irreducibly lascivious nature of the feminine made it logically necessary to abandon the idea of widespread insemination by incubi. Experience in examinations of witches made it clear that it was only rarely that the Demons act as Succubi: either because it is not the custom of women, whose modesty in this matter they evilly imitate, to take the initiative in inducing men to commit fornication with them; or because the rabble of witches is chiefly composed of that sex which, owing to its feebleness of understanding, is least able to resist and withstand the wiles of the Devil. And certainly, in all the trials of witches that I have had to do with, this has been the one and only example of a Succubus.

Given this uniformly low opinion of feminine morals and women's capacity for self-control in venereal matters, the rational mind is bound to question the existence of such palpable spirits as incubi and to wonder if they are self-conscious inventions "evolved for the sole purpose of hiding the shame of the mothers." But popular belief in the early modern era adhered tenaciously to their existence and, it was maintained, "even to this day nearly all men show by their speech and their thoughts that they truly and firmly believe in the procreation of men by Demons." It might perhaps have been more comforting to the male ego for a husband to believe himself cuckolded by a supernatural rather than a mortal rival, but he would have been nonplussed and disquieted by his wife's response to her dalliance with her "Bawdy Incubus" had he realized, as an English author (speaking of "honest women" in general) pointed out, that "she hath more pleasure and delight (they say) with *Incubus* that waie, than with anie mortall man." This was an indication of how far the popular culture of sexuality and the supernatural diverged in the minds of the two sexes in the late sixteenth century.

The magisterial *Malleus Maleficarum* argues that not simply witches but the entire female gender is deviant, and that when its natural tendencies are enhanced by diabolical power, it threatens the subversion of society and the extermination of the true faith. Deviance and perversion are read as innate female characteristics, for in the biblical account the female arises from one of the precedent male's ribs, but one "which is bent as it were in the contrary direction to a man. And since through this defect she is an imperfect animal, she always deceives." Witches, as the most ambitious, cunning, deceitful, and lewd of women, were accused of every variety of what orthodoxy defined as sexual perversion. Their perversion and deviance threatened the integrity of the Christian community, and their aberrant behavior challenged the righteous order of society. The literature of witchcraft is so rife with descriptions of the diabolical deviance of witches that it virtually comprises a catalogue of contemporary sexual perversions and antisocial behavior. For contemporaries, these two aspects of witchery were integral parts of a monolithic system of demonality at work in the world.

Witches were darkly linked to incest, animal aberrations, necrophilia, anal and oral intercourse, pederasty, homoeroticism, and cross-dressing. These deviations from the sexual norm were usually considered corollaries of the primary sexual activities in which witches were believed to play a central role—sex with the Devil and the incubus/succubus pairings—or part of their general malevolent campaign to seduce the innocent and to subvert an ordered society. Charges of bestiality are a case in point. A typical case of bewitchment involved a young man who fell so "farre in love with his cow" that "for his life he could not come in where she was, but he must needes take up her tayle and kisse under it." Sex with the Devil was often depicted as interspecific and unnatural. The Devil frequently assumed the form of a great goat and "a tousiours un membre de mulet, ayant choisy en imitation celuy de cet animal comme le mieux pourueu." One author, though, turned the argument on its head, asserting that incubi and succubi were

> more noble than man, by reason of the greater subtilty [immateriality] of their bodies, and ... when having intercourse with humankind, male or female, fall into the same sin as man when copulating with a beast, which is inferior to him.

The psychological functions of these explanations for the popular mind are immediately apparent. In the first case, an outré sexual practice, which seems virtually incomprehensible in terms of conventional human erotic motivation, becomes immediately comprehensible and can be used to reinforce conformity to orthodox norms. Much in the same way that our contemporary popular understanding of serial killers as human "monsters" reinforces our fundamental belief in the order of our society and in fundamental human decency, the diabolical explanation of animal aberrations was comforting, and encouraged identification with conventional values. Indeed, this psychological projection mechanism constituted the basis for the popular frenzy that sustained the intellectual structures we have been discussing, that is, the literature and folklore of witchcraft. This was nowhere more evident than in the belief that humans were analogous to lower animals in their relations with demon lovers. Given the much greater frequency of incubi among the preternatural lovers that appear in this literature, the implication of the vicious logic of this argument is certainly the bestialization of the female. Women emerge as potentially a separate, intermediate species, a meretricious, bastardized link in the Great Chain of Being, above the lower animals but below man (in both the gendered and the generic sense), and below the demons of the air.

The inveterate belief that sexual aberrations, while not unique to women, were, when practiced by women, typically more antisocial and represented a more serious threat to orthodoxy and social order, reinforced the vision of female moral inferiority and the need for social control of women. Women of power, women of knowledge—cunning women—were a threat to the established male hierarchies of power, and were frequently subsumed under the broad categories of witchcraft and demonality. Instances of cross-dressing (often in an effort to gain arcane male knowledge or to usurp male power) and the ability to change one's sex, are representative of this set of beliefs. A woman who sought to test the taboo on female presence in a monastery, and who put on male attire to secure entry, provides an example to all rash, presumptuous females. She was resoundingly repulsed by a demon, who forcibly thrust

> her head between her thighs, so that she who had tried to imprint a false kiss upon the holy threshold was forced to kiss the filthy parts of her own body; and she had to exhibit openly to all who wished to see it that sex which she had tried to conceal beneath a man's clothing. The result of this was that no woman thereafter dared to approach the monastery.

Of the limited number of cases of change of sex (which often seems to have resulted naturally from the evolution of congenital hermaphroditism) that appear in this literature, all are from female to male, and it is dogmatically assumed that such changes can be effected by diabolical influences. The few cases of witches "laying on" people in their beds suggest a homoerotic variation on the incubus/succubus theme. These cases exclusively involve child victims, and the intent of the practice, apart from whatever erotic overtones are present, seems to have been to gain nefarious influence over the young. The overt threat to household order and parental authority is also clear. The sole male example involved a pupil and his schoolmaster, who "was in the habit of stretching himself upon his body, placing his mouth on the boy's mouth, which he made him open, and muttering into it."

More real and more dangerously antisocial than these largely symbolic (when not merely potential or imaginary) forms of predominantly female revolt were those activities associated with the cunning women who professed and practiced witchcraft as an ancient form of knowledge and belief. These were the practice of abortion (and sometimes infanticide), "tying the points," and the evil eye. Witches, it was believed, had peculiar power over the health and life of children, and an association between "those midwives and wise women who are witches" and the diabolical rituals of infanticide and abortion is presupposed. These women, it is maintained, kill children "before they have been baptized, by thrusting a large pin into their brains," and "they do even worse; for they kill them while they are yet in their mothers' wombs."

"Tying the points" need not detain us long other than to remark that it comprised, in the popular mind, the most prominent and most feared form of sexual magic. Since we have discussed this aspect of witchcraft at some length above, it should suffice here simply to cite the definition of this practice in ecclesiastical law, which essentially constructed its juridical code in these matters on the foundation of ancient popular belief. The practice undermined the basic social unit of Christian society—the family—by rendering.

> men impotent and bewitched, and therefore by this impediment brought about by witchcraft they are unable to copulate, and so the contract of marriage is rendered void and matrimony in their cases has become impossible.

While this is clearly a predominantly female crime of aggression against males, the Church recognized that it might be as effectively accomplished indirectly by undermining female capacity. "It is to be noted also that impotence of the member to perform the act is not the only bewitchment; but sometimes the woman is caused to be unable to conceive, or else she miscarries." The Church followed popular belief in emphasizing the threat to male potency. The popular term for marital infertility was "tying the points," a colorful idiomatic expression that referred to magically knotting the strings ("points") that attached the codpiece to the hose so that they could not be undone by natural means and thereby preventing male sexual activity.

The evil eye (*mal d'ochio*) tradition represented the survival of an ancient tradition of innate malevolent occult power. Its deleterious effect on the health of those who fell victim to a stare from someone who had the power of the eye was potentially devastating. The operative principle of the evil eye and its power of fascination was believed to be vapors, "conveied out as it were by beames and streames of a certeine fierie force." It was typically associated with certain women. For example, "if anybody's spirit be inflamed with malice or rage, as is often the case with old women, then their disturbed spirit looks through their eyes, for their countenances are most evil and harmful." In fact, such is the highly contagious power of infection of certain categories of women that a person might contact an optical affliction simply by looking upon her, "and although the vision be perfectly clear, yet the sight of some impurity, such as, for example, a woman during her monthly periods, the eyes will as it were contract a certain impurity."

Some authorities opposed the weight of accumulated superstition as it related to occult ocular power, but insisted that a witch could seduce, fascinate, or bewitch by a mere touch of her hand (or, wielding a phallic symbol, her wand). One writer, a jurist, revealed his personal paranoia at the prospect of the male's loss of control in his remark that "if a judge lets himself be touched on the bare arm and hand by the witch, he thereby becomes her advocate."

Such fears were rooted in the belief that witches had literally and completely been defiled and corrupted through their association with the powers of evil, and that the very physical essence of their bodies was imbued with highly communicable, pestilential essences. This may explain the fascination in this literature with the scatological aspects of witchcraft. Since the Devil revels in "external filth and uncleanness," he imparts to his acolytes a taste for "impurity and uncleanness." The physical touch of his body and attendance at his rituals corrupt the taste and sensibilities, for when he occupies a human body he frequently selects that of a corpse, and "often dwells in those parts of the body

which ... harbour the excremental waste of the body.... The gifts of
the Demon also are fashioned from ordure and dung, and his banquets
from the flesh of beasts that have died." The holy water of the witches'
Sabbat was the Devil's urine, and during that ritual as well on diverse
other occasions, witches were instructed "that they should kisse his
Buttockes, in signe of dutye to him." Satan is also able, on occasion,
to "speak through the shameful parts of a woman."

Since the average person might never see and hear this ventriloquist's
feat of the Devil, more certain and publicly verifiable methods of iden-
tifying witches were required. This was the function of the examination
and trial of suspected witches. In the European tradition, the examination was conducted to locate the Devil's mark, with which he had
stigmatized his followers. Diligence and care were necessary in the
search because

> the mark is not always of the same description.... on men it is
> generally found on the eye-lids, or the armpit, or lips or shoulder
> or posterior; whereas on women it is found on the breasts or
> privy parts.

Satan's method of branding witches was detailed by James I of England:

> the Deuill dooth lick them with his tung in some privy part of
> their bodie, before he dooth receiue them to be his seruants, which
> marke commonly is given them vnder the haire in some part of
> their bodye, whereby it may not easily be found out or seene,
> although they be searched: and generally so long as the marke
> is not seene to those which search them, so long the parties that
> hath the marke will neuer confesse any thing.

As a result of the difficulty in locating such a mark, the examination
of a suspected witch required an extremely minute and probing scrutiny
of her/his flesh. If the suspect did not confess, it had been common
practice since ancient times to see to it that "their apparell ... be
changed, and everie haire in their body must be shaven off with a
sharpe razor." The purpose of this procedure was twofold: to facilitate
the location of the Devil's mark, and even more importantly to forfend
the concealment of spells, charms, or drugs that would render the witch
immune to torture or able to maintain silence in the face of vigorous
inquisition.

The location of the Devil's mark is critical to the examination, and was believed to have unique properties. As the mark of Satan's talon, some claimed, it was scarified, and was characterized by "a slight hardening of the skin," and

> the place is entirely bloodless and insensitive, so that even if a needle be deeply thrust in, no pain is felt and not a drop of blood is shed. This fact is held to be so certain a proof of capital guilt that it is often made the base of examination and torture.

Certain aspects of a woman's appearance and antecedents also figured against her in the proceedings of witchcraft tribunals. "Devils attach themselves chiefly to women who have beautiful hair," one authority maintained; while "maides having yellow haire are most combred with Incubus." Intense, quarrelsome women were also suspect, as were "of all other women, leane, hollow eied, old, beetlebrowed women." Of even more importance than physical appearance was family descent, for "it is taken as a great presumption of guilt against the accused if his father and mother, or one of them, are witches. [Indeed], some have maintained that this is an infallible rule; and there seems much to be said for such a view."

European procedure in witchcraft cases, based on ancient tradition and medieval precedent, routinely relied on torture as a means to ascertain the truth of accusations and more particularly to elicit confessions—definitive proof of guilt and sufficient basis for condemnation and execution. On the question of trial by ordeal, there was less agreement. Trial by red-hot iron and trial by boiling water were adamantly condemned by the most authoritative Continental, fifteenth-century witch-hunters' manual, while an English Protestant guidebook of a century later sustained both practices. This suggests some variation in procedure in witchcraft cases by region, by doctrinal belief, and over time. As we turn our attention to the witchcraft trials in Salem, Massachusetts, in 1692, and consider in what ways and to what extent they were influenced by European tradition and practice, it will be useful to keep this divergence of belief and practice in the matter of trial by ordeal clearly in mind.

English legal tradition, from the time of Elizabeth, tended to divide the occult arts into "magicke, southsaying wizards, diuination, iuggling,

inchanting and charming, and witcherie." "Witcherie" was conceived
of as a uniquely feminine offense, the term "witch" signifying a "hagg"
who has been "eluded by a league made with the deuil." The burden
of a witch's offenses was attendance at the Sabbat or Black Mass,
where she would "spend all night after with her sweete hart [the Devil],
in playing, sporting, bankqueting, dauncing, and diuerse other deuelish
lustes and lewd desports, and to shew a thousand such monsterous
mockeries."

New England practice blurred the distinction between one kind of
supernatural activity and another, and subsumed them all under the
comprehensive category of witchcraft. This made for a pragmatic sim-
plification of the legal code, and was quite logical in light of the fact
that contemporary British statutory law ("An Acte againste Conjura-
tions Inchantmente and Witchcrafte," 1 James I, chapter 12), mandated
the death penalty for all three magical categories when their exercise
led to the loss of life or property or materially affected the health, or
welfare of others. Second, convictions of intent without the fact of such
threats to society also merited capital punishment. New England practice also greatly diminished the erotic concerns in witchcraft prosecutions, but could not wholly eliminate them.

Traditional folk concerns rooted in sexual magic played a role in
several of the Salem cases. Bridget Bishop was said to have bewitched
her first husband to death, perhaps an instance of the use of magical
means to achieve revenge on a lover. Her troubled domestic relations
are attested to by the fact that her husband at the time of the Salem
outbreak, Edward Bishop, had brought charges of witchcraft against
her. In the trial of Susannah Martin, William Brown deposed that his
wife had been bewitched by the accused and implied that their marital
relations had been supernaturally impeded. He testified that, about
thirty years before the trial, upon his return from a journey to England,
his

> wife would not owne him but sd they were devorst and Asked
> him wither he did not mett with one M. Benty Abey in England
> by whom he was divorst And from that time to this very day
> have been under a strange kind of distemper frenzy vncapibil of
> any resional action though strong and helthy of body.

Martin's interference in the domestic life of the Browns suggests the persistence of superstitious belief in "tying the points."

Another area of witchcraft that touched on popular erotic fantasy and folklore was fortune-telling and divination. Tituba, Carib Indian slave of the Reverend Samuel Parris, and catalyst for the witchcraft hysteria in Salem, had undertaken to conjure forth the images of the future husbands of her enthralled adolescent audience in the minister's kitchen. Dorcas Hoar had been dabbling in palmistry since the 1670s, and had run into difficulties when she successfully predicted the death of her husband, William Hoar. The suspicions of the village had been aroused because she had declared at the very time she predicted his demise

> yt shee should live poorely so long as her husband willm Hoar did live but ye said will should dye before her and after yt shee should live better.

She had also successfully predicted the order of deaths in other village couples, which made her suspect as one who bewitched others to death and thus feared as a threat to marital unions.

Though not so dramatic and prominent as in the European tradition, there were cases of bewitchment of the genitourinary functions and organs in the Salem records. Bray Williams testified in the proceedings against John Willard that subsequent to his refusal to support Willard, who had been charged with witchcraft, he suffered acute urinary distress. "I cannot express the misery I was in," he told the court, "for my water was suddenly stopd & I had no benefit of nature but was like a man in a Rock." About five days later, after Willard had been arrested and imprisoned, Williams experienced relief, but "in the room of a stoppage I was vexed with a flow of water so that it was hard to keep myself dry," and finally, "I was taken in the sorest distress & misery my water being turned into real blood, or of a bloody colour and the old pain returned excessively as much as before which continued for about 24 hours together."

Another suspect, Wilmott Reed (like Willard, later convicted and hanged), was accused of bewitching essential bodily functions. Charity Pitman testified that Reed, subsequent to a dispute with a Mrs. Syms over missing linen, had cursed the latter for accusing Reed's servant of theft. Reed's imprecation took the form of a wish that "she might never mingere, nor cacare," and as a consequence, "Mrs. Syms was taken with the distemper of the dry Belly-ake and so continued many months" until she removed from Salem.

Benjamin Abbott was tormented, he claimed, by Martha Carrier, who inflicted upon him, amongst other ills, a "sore [that] did breede in my grine." The most telling example, however, was recounted in Cotton Mather's *Memorable Providences* (1689), and provides a glimpse into the paranoid context out of which the Salem episode arose. Mather reported, unequivocally and rather sensationalistically, that in the winter of 1684 one Philip Smith had been "murdered with an hideous Witchcraft." The jury of inquest that examined his corpse "found a Swelling on one Breast, which rendered it like a Womans. His Privities were wounded or burned." This episode suggests an aggressive attack on male sexuality and a conscious effort to achieve emasculation and the transformation of sex not unlike episodes recorded in the European witchcraft literature.

There seems to have been much less overtly diabolical erotic activity in Salem than had been the case in Europe. There is not a single unequivocal reference to sexual relations between a witch and the Devil at Salem. The only supposed case was reported by Edward Bishop, who said of his wife, Bridget, "that the Devill did come bodily unto her and that she was familiar with the Deuil and that she sate up all ye night long with ye Deuill."

Incubus/succubus sex was also less common than in the European tradition, but was certainly not unheard of in Salem. Mercy Short, for example, was visited by demons who would "come and sitt upon her Breast, and pull open her Jaw, and keep her without fetching a Sensible Breath, sometimes for Half-an-hour, and sometimes for several whole Hours together." The specifically erotic content of this case was revealed in Short's response to the incubi: "You pretend a precious deal of Love to mee indeed!... Fine Promises! You'l bestow an Husband upon mee, if I'll be your Servant. An Husband! What? A Divel!"

Richard Coman claimed that Bridget Bishop "in her Red paragon Bodyce," did "lay upon my Brest or body and soe oppressed him yt he could not speake nor stur noe not soe much as to awake his wife althow he Endeavured soe to do itt." He was oppressed by similar visitations on two succeeding nights. Susannah Martin was also accused of acting the part of a succubus. Bernard Peach testified that when he was in bed on a Sunday night he

> saw Susanna Martin come in [at the window], and jump down upon the Floor She took hold of this Deponent's Feet, and drawing his Body up into an Heap, she lay upon him near Two Hours; in all which time he could neither speak nor stirr.

Reports of apparitions in bedchambers with less disturbing consequences and less graphic descriptions were also not uncommon at the height of the witchcraft craze in Salem. These apparitions provide clues to the kinds of aggressively sexual or provocative behavior that led to accusations of witches tormenting men as succubi. William Stacy recalled that during an illness Bridget Bishop "did give him a visitt and withall proferred a great Love for this Deponant in his affliction more than ordinary, at which this deponant admired." At the time of these events, Stacy was twenty-two and Bishop was twenty-seven years of age. The forward older woman, then, visited Stacy while he slept and he awakened to find her at the foot of his bed, whereupon she "hopt vpon the bed and aboute the Roome and then went out." Samuel Gray also testified that he had experienced a nocturnal visit from Bishop, and corroborated Stacy's statements about awakening with something piercingly cold "betweene his lips Pressing hard agt his teeth." Both Stacy and Gray believed Bishop was responsible for the deaths of their daughters.

Contrary to European experience, those accused of witchcraft in Salem do not seem to have confessed to relations with incubi, and I have found only a single example of a male (who was ultimately hanged as a witch) accused of an implicitly sexual offense. John Willard used witchcraft and sorcery upon a single woman, Susannah Sheldon, to the extent that she was "hurt tortured afflicted." His conduct may have constituted what we would today describe as sexual harassment.

The erotic element in the Salem trials seems to have been immediately linked to social disapprobation of what contemporary community standards considered deviant and socially destructive sexual behavior. Bridget Bishop had apparently scandalized her neighbors. John Hale said her home was all but "a house of great profainness and iniquity,"

for she "did entertaine certain people in her house at unseasonable
hours in ye nite to keep drinking and playing at shovel board whereby
discord did arise in other families and young people were in danger of
being corrupted."

One Joseph Ring deposed that he had been inveigled by an acquaintance to an abandoned house near a forest where he encountered Susannah Martin and another woman. The group "had a good fire and
drink it seemed to be sidr this continued most part of the night sd.
Martin then being in her naturall shape." His brother, Jarvis, had
suffered several visits from Martin in her succubus form. The association of the wilderness with unrestrained sexuality is clear here, as it
was in the case of Abigail Hobbs, who routinely slept out in the woods
alone. She told an acquaintance, it was later learned in court, that "she
was not afraid of any thing for . . . she had sold herselfe boddy & soule
to ye old boy." Whether we are to understand this to mean that Hobbs
had had intercourse with the Devil is not clear; in any case, her deviance
by contemporary standards is quite evident.

Males, too, were accused of witchcraft because of social deviance
related to sexuality. George Burroughs, former pastor of Salem Village
and considered by Cotton Mather to be the ringleader of a vast diabolical plot, was charged with murdering (in collusion with his soon-
to-be third wife) his second wife, "because they would have one another." He was also charged with "keeping his two Successive Wives
in a strange kind of Slavery."

It is a striking fact that every case of demon love, and most of the
cases of natural desire resulting in sexually aggressive behavior in the
Salem episode, involved the victimization of the male. This stands in
stark contrast to the European tradition. Quite probably this resulted
from juridical expectations of higher rates of female sexual deviance.
As Carol F. Karlsen has shown, there was an increasing incidence of
sexual offenses committed by females recorded in Essex County as the
seventeenth century wore on. Since prosecutions for sexual offenses
after 1650 increasingly focused on premarital pregnancies and illegitimate births, women came under intense scrutiny; by 1680, sixty percent of prosecutions were of women. The double standard of sexual
justice was reflected in the legal practice of the colony as a whole, for
sixty-three percent of those punished for fornication in Massachusetts
between 1620 and 1689 were women.

Deviance was also inferred in New England, as it had been in the European tradition, from familial association. The taint of witchcraft was not genetically transmitted but was absorbed by contiguity and inculcated by parental example. The most moving case in the records of the Salem trials is that of Sarah Good's daughter, aged four or five years, who was believed to afflict adolescent girls through her evil eye.

The goal of the examination and trial of suspected witches was to establish definitively their deviance and to secure a confession. As John Hale, minister of Beverly, remarked retrospectively, "this matter was carried on ... chiefly by the complaints and accusations of the Afflicted, Bewitched ones, as it was supposed, and then by the Confessions of the Accused, condemning themselves, and others." Cotton Mather, in a letter written to Judge John Richards at the outset of the Salem trials, maintained that the best evidence for conviction was a "credible confession" as opposed to one that "may be the result of only a delirious brain or a discontented heart."

But in the heat and light of the public spectacle, Mather's injunctions about caution were swamped by a flood of popular superstition and prejudice. In no area of the proceedings was superstition, firmly rooted in the centuries-long European tradition, more evident than in the examination of witches and the search for the Devil's mark. Unlike that tradition, however, which saw the mark as outward and visible evidence of the soul contracted to Satan and the body dedicated to spreading diabolism abroad, the Salem witch-hunters tended to emphasize a minor element of the European trials and to combine the idea of the Devil's mark with the notion of the witch's teat, upon which her diabolical familiars were suckled.

Suckling familiars was a preternatural act and therefore became a central point in the physical identification of witches. In the Salem episode as well as in the European tradition, it was never an act exclusive to females. Usually the point of attachment for the familiar's mouth was secret, and no doubt this explains why only those who were supposedly witnessed in the act were credibly taken to nurse through their natural mammary glands. Giles Corey, for example, was described by Susannah Sheldon as appearing with "two turcles hang to his coat and he opened his bosom and put his turcles to his brest and gave them suck."

Just as in the European tradition for the Devil's mark, the location of the more covert teats was gender specific. On the male body, they were found in Salem examinations on the inside of the mouth in the flesh of the cheek, on the shoulder blade, or on the hip. One female witch was said to have had a teat on the lower right shoulder, and Tituba supposedly suckled her familiar between her fingers, but for the most part, these fleshy excrescences were found in the genital area of women.

Bridget Bishop, Rebecca Nurse, and Elizabeth Proctor, upon examination by a committee of nine women and a male surgeon, were found to have "a preternatural Escrescence of flesh between ye pudendum and Anus [the perineum] much like to tetts and not usuall in women . . . and yt they were in all ye three women neer ye same place." The location of these witches' teats on women's bodies in Salem presents a direct line of descent from the European witchcraft tradition, and suggests the persistence of certain bodies of ideas, particularly those linking conceptions of sexuality, sin, and evil to inveterate bodily taboos in the popular mind.

Custom and folk superstitions pertaining to the supernatural seem to have been transmitted somewhat erratically over time and distance. While the basic elements of the drama of the individual soul in its struggle with evil were expressed in a set of symbolic conventions and formulaic rituals associated with witchcraft, the function of particular allegorical and anagogical elements in the system was not immutable. Some associations of ideas were remarkably persistent in the social construction of diabolical magic in the popular mind, while others were more fluid as their meanings shifted to accord with the demands social ideology placed on the systems of cultural belief that sustained it.

A good example of this was the way the incubus/succubus tradition was adapted to the socially determined realities of sexual deviance at Salem. The emphasis on female sexual aggression reflected in the preponderance of malevolent succubi that appear in the trial records represents an adaptation of a traditional cultural system of folk belief to the social construction of gender as expressed in legislation and jurisprudence governing fornication. As we have seen, the fact of sexual deviance had come to be primarily a female responsibility from 1650 on, and Puritan law after 1668 required the questioning of unmarried pregnant women during childbirth to pressure them into naming the fathers of their children. Thus, deviant women became responsible for incriminating their lovers and for reestablishing the socioeconomic balance of the community, since the child would now be supported by its father rather than becoming a burden on the common resources of the village.

The inquisitorial function in cases of unwed mothers fell to the lot of midwives, who thus played an essential role in maintaining community moral standards and protecting its citizens from undue demands on their purses and charitable sensibilities. This may provide some insight into another unique aspect of witchcraft tradition at Salem. There is virtually no concern about the practice of abortion and infanticide among Salem witches and no consistent attempt to link them with midwives. Witches at Salem certainly were accused of afflicting children and, in several important instances, of bringing about their deaths, but the children are typically older (many are adolescents), and there is little interference with pregnancy or childbirth evident in the record.

Essentially, midwives were on the same side as the male magistracy in its attempts to deal effectively with sexual deviance; it would not have done to use them as symbols of witchcraft as the European tradition had done. Since witchcraft trials were part of the broader effort to control social (and especially sexual) deviance, midwives were enlisted to assist in examinations of suspects, a task analogous to their inquisition of unwed mothers. Since such examinations, given expectations about the location of the witch's teat, required close inspection of the genital region, it is not surprising that women often requested the presence of midwives.

Rebecca Nurse, who petitioned the court for a reexamination on 28 June 1692, is a case in point. She noted that physical phenomena discovered on her body were the results of hard travail and difficult births and requested that a new team of women be appointed to examine her. Two of the four women she suggested for the team were specifically identified as midwives. It is notable, too, that the role of midwives in eliciting the name of the father of an illegitimate child partook of the spirit of persecution and the use of physical pain to secure a confession, for it was their practice to refuse assistance in easement of pain during childbirth until the mother had confessed the name of the child's father. The links to the moral and juridical use of torture in witchcraft cases underscore the role of midwives in supporting the established social order in its crusade to control deviance.

As a colonial outpost of the British empire, the immediate legal tradition that would have influenced Salem was that of England. The Act of Parliament of 1604 governed witchcraft cases in England until its repeal in 1735, and is much more specific in its provisions than any colonial statute. Massachusetts statutes of 1641 and 1648 simply provided, as an operative definition of the crime, that the witch "hath or consulteth with a familiar spirit." The colonial laws are skeletal and clearly give little guidance to examiners and prosecutors. The traditions of the English law, much fuller in their elaboration, were selectively applied to the colonial situation. Much more important than statutory provisions for both British and colonial witchcraft proceedings were popular attitudes and beliefs about precisely what behavior constituted witchery. The letter of the law does, however, provide a clear rationale for the most sensational aspect of the Salem prosecutions—the singular importance of the witch's teat as opposed to the Devil's mark, so central a part of European folk belief. The location of the teat provided definitive physical evidence that an individual had entertained and nourished a familiar. The witch's teat was a central element in the juridical literature that arose in England to assist judges to distinguish the natural from the supernatural. Since this was the only characteristic of a witch cited in the law for a capital offense, it became the primary physical condition for execution in the colonial tradition.

The Puritans believed themselves to be modern and scientific in their approach to the natural and supernatural worlds, and therefore the New England tradition tended to reject some of the more colorfully fanciful and credulous beliefs associated with European witchcraft literature. European authors were closer in time and more temperamentally sympathetic to the pagan tales of animal aberrations in which the animal was an incarnation of a god or a spirit. In their compendia, these authors reflected powerful currents of folk superstition and popular magical lore flowing from the lusty sensibilities of pagan eroticism. Puritan emphasis on rationality precluded their following the lead of an author like Henri Boguet, who declared: "I thoroughly believe all that has been written of Fauns, Satyrs and woodland gods, which were no more than demons"; and who could dispute a witch's confession of having copulated with a fowl, saying

> I am of opinion that she meant to say gander instead of fowl, for that is a form which Satan often takes, and therefore we have the proverb that Satan has feet like a goose.

The whole controversy so central to the European literature—whether demons could reproduce through intercourse with human beings or whether they merely provided an alternative mode of human reproduction—found no place in Puritan texts on witchcraft. The Devil was more a threat to the soul than to the body in New England, which helps to explain why there are virtually no straightforward references to intercourse between witches and the Devil in the Salem records. The succubus tradition, however, proved more useful at Salem, and though equally irrational, played a prominent role in accusations of witches. But, then, victimization of males by females, as we have seen, constituted a prominent social and legal fact in Puritan society as related to fornication statutes, and fear of female sexual aggression seemed to be validated by the rising incidence of female offenders. In this context, it becomes easier to understand why there is a preponderance of succubi in the Salem experience, while in the European tradition, incubi were the primary offenders.

The rational position on the incubus/succubus issue was set forth by a late sixteenth-century English author, who argued that "of the evil Spirits *Incubus* and *Succubus* there can be no firme reason or proofe brought out of scriptures," and that "in truth, this *Incubus* is a bodilie disease . . . although it extend unto the trouble of the mind." His cynical rationalism about what he considered the rankest superstitious ignorance is reflected in his assumption that "lecheries [are] covered with the cloke of *Incubus* and witchcraft . . . speciallie to excuse and maintaine knaveries and lecheries of idle priests and bawdie monks; and to cover the shame of their lovers and concubines." Both of the traditions implied here—use of witchcraft to explain sexual deviance and anti-Catholicism—figured prominently in the Salem episode, but that did not prevent the persistence of the succubus belief in the popular mind and, as a consequence, in personal accusations.

Despite a move toward rationality, English cases, too, from the 1580s to the end of the seventeenth century, continued to emphasize certain magical elements. From about 1645, in the English legal tradition, accusations for "entertaining" Satan, in the form of beastly familiars, became increasingly common. While Salem cases revealed little interest in the notion of sex with the Devil, they enthusiastically embraced incrimination for "entertaining."

The tradition of witches cherishing and nourishing their diabolical imps was very strong in English cases, and James I had given the imprimatur of the highest secular authority to the expectation that the teats, which were the outward physical sign of their presence, would be found in the genital region. The resulting dehumanization of the suspected witch was clear in the record of one seventeenth-century English case where, after a diligent and minute search, examiners had found "in her secret parts 2 white pieces of flesh like paps and some swore they were like the teats of an ewe, & some like the paps of a cat." I have found no evidence that English practice in physical examination of witches followed European precedent in shaving the entire body of the suspects, but the remarks of James I on the location and cunning concealment of these teats or marks strongly suggest the wisdom of thorough depilation. At Salem, the strip search of witches was a standard feature of examinations in cases of witchcraft, but like English practice, there is no evidence to support the continuation of the earlier European practice of systematic removal of all body hair. The tradition of associating diabolical contact with the genital region of the female body, however, remained central to Salem belief and practice.

An idiosyncrasy of the seventeenth-century English tradition arose from its emphasis on the physicality of the relationship between the witch and Satan. Since the Devil typically appeared to women in the shape of a man, he was believed to seduce them through the lusts of the body, to seal a diabolical covenant. But whereas the European tradition had pondered the question of whether such sexual contacts resulted in diabolical progeny, the English stressed the literal indwelling presence of evil in the witch. Butterflies, bees, and mice were described as apparently emerging from the private parts of various witches, and one Margaret Mixter cried out "that Satan was within her," and onlookers "saw a thinge come from under her coats in likeness and shape of a beaver brush [tail]." It is clear that these physical entities that had taken up residence within women's bodies were often considered to be their familiars, but they also seem to have been, from another point of view, the monstrous spawn of diabolical intercourse. There is no evidence of this explicit belief in the Salem records despite the prominence of familiars in accusations, yet the supposition of the location of the witches' teats in the genital area suggests at least a subliminal persistence of this tradition.

The Salem emphasis on familiars and the witch's teat represented a direct line of descent from the biblical texts and Stuart practice as determined by the king. In the early Salem cases, especially the confessions of Tituba and William Barker, detailed descriptions of the inverted rites of the unholy Sabbat, and sealings of diabolical covenants by signing the Devil's book, figured prominently. As the number of cases grew and a body of victims (the afflicted) came forward, accusations and confessions came to focus on proof of the fact of apparitional affliction; spectral evidence took precedence over customary belief. The personality of the Devil and his direct role in matters of witchcraft was downplayed, and the presence of evil became more spiritual than physical. In these ways, procedural practice at Salem diverged from the Stuart example.

In Salem, the broad Protestant tradition (as opposed to a narrowly sectarian Puritan one) played an important role in the social construction of witchcraft. Cotton Mather, for instance, linked early witches with the Catholic and specifically Irish traditions as well as with French influence and the pagan savagery of the Indian population. English reticence about detailed discussions of sexual aspects of witchcraft seems to have prevailed at Salem as well, but that does not mean that sexuality did not play a significant role in the Salem trials: it was simply expressed in less direct ways. There is certainly no evidence to suggest that prudery or sexual delicacy played any role at Salem. Nevertheless, when we compare the testimony in seventeenth-century fornication cases with the witchcraft trials at Salem, the deviation of the latter from contemporary standards of popular public parlance becomes clear. Fornication trials were replete with detailed, eyewitness accounts (as the law required) of sexual acts, and not infrequently earthy Anglo-Saxon terms for sexual organs and acts were uttered openly in court.

Rejection of the central Continental concept of sexual intercourse between witches and the Devil and the focus on spectral evidence, which moved witchcraft activity to a primarily supernatural plane, seems to have been grounded in the rejection of Catholic superstition and ecclesiastical precedent, for the tradition of witchcraft's power over the venereal act arose directly out of the 1484 papal bull of Innocent VIII. No doubt a desire to distinguish the crimes of witchcraft from those less threatening and more typical, frequent forms of sexual deviance, like fornication and adultery, was also involved in the de-emphasis on witchcraft as sexual magic.

Judicial practice and standards of evidence also played important roles in establishing the nature of witchcraft proceedings at Salem. In the European tradition, inquisitorial procedure came to dominate witchcraft trials by the late fifteenth century. These trials, conducted after 1550 in secular courts, allowed the initiation of proceedings by accusers (who sustained no criminal liability in bringing such charges), and permitted judges wide discretion (including use of torture) in accumulating evidence necessary for conviction. The standards of proof in such cases were based on the Roman law of treason, and mandated either the testimony of two eyewitnesses or the confession of the accused.

The English tradition was the only one in Europe that did not follow inquisitorial procedures in witchcraft trials but instead relied on the jury system. The effect of this divergence of English legal practice from that of the Continent in these matters was to allow rumor, hearsay, circumstantial evidence, and the establishment of fact by a single uncorroborated witness.

Salem practice in the witchcraft trials adopted a syncretic approach. As in the inquisitorial framework, accusers played a prominent role and judges conducted the proceedings so as to confirm accusations, to elicit confessions, or to build up an overwhelming body of evidence. Two witnesses to the fact of witchcraft were required, but "one single witness to one Act of witchcraft, and another single witness to another such fact, made two witnesses against the Crime and the party suspected." This standard, much closer to the English single-witness criterion than to European legal tradition, made the rule for sufficient testamentary evidence in a capital felony less rigorous than for sexual violations, much less serious criminal offenses. Two eyewitnesses of the deed were required for conviction in these cases.

Though this was common Massachusetts practice in witchcraft cases, there was precedent for establishing a stricter standard of evidence in the issue of the case of Goody Glover in 1679. Governor Simon Bradstreet and a panel of magistrates dissented from the jury verdict and reprieved Glover on the grounds that "they did not esteem one single witness to one fact, and another single witness to another fact, for two witnesses, against the person in a matter Capital."

Contrary to the long tradition of European witchcraft, but in accord with contemporary English practice, torture was generally discountenanced at Salem, and trial by ordeal, especially the popular trial by water, widely employed in England, was rejected. The New England legal code expressly rejected the use of torture, but a letter of John Proctor, one of the accused, from Salem prison in July 1692, suggests that some physical duress was used to extract confessions.

Proctor claimed two of Martha Carrier's sons were induced to confess when "they tied them neck to heels till the blood was ready to come out of their noses." And, of course, there was the case of Giles Corey, pressed to death because he refused to plead when charged with witchcraft. But these were exceptions to the rule in the Salem proceedings. In general, they seemed to follow Cotton Mather's advice that "far from urging the un-English method of torture," intense questioning and other methods that "hath a tendency to put the witches into confusion" should be employed to elicit confessions. In fact, the role of torture in the Salem trials was reversed. The victims of physical abuse who occupied center stage were the afflicted, whose "tortures increased continually," and were endlessly described in minute detail in court testimony. Indeed, the tortures of those afflicted by spectral agents became a central body of evidence for the conviction of those accused of witchcraft at Salem.

Puritan ecclesiastical and secular authorities sincerely believed that they were conducting the Salem trials on the basis of enlightened, rational, scientific principles of jurisprudence and human behavior. Certainly, in comparison to seventeenth-century English standards—especially in regard torture—the Salem cases were conducted in a physically more humane way. But the Puritans, despite their efforts to downplay the personal, sensual presence of the Devil (perhaps they had overused his metaphorical presence in the literature produced to rationalize the Indian wars of 1636–37 and 1675–76, in which the dusky complexion of savagery was equated with that of the Black Man), had been unable finally to subdue the persistent folk beliefs about the active presence of evil in everyday life that were rooted in the popular lore and superstition of both England and Europe. Despite the inveterate Protestant bias against the irrationalities and superstition of Catholicism, the bulk of the evidence brought forward in the trials by accusers sustained important traditions associating witchcraft with sexual magic, and the examination of witches to locate the Devil's mark or witch's teat, long part of the European and English traditions of witchcraft, and carrying powerful implications (though never openly stated at Salem) of sexual congress with the Devil, fed into and reinforced (though in diminished form) popular beliefs about witchcraft and the practice of sexual magic. As the definitive European witchhunters' manual, the *Malleus Maleficarum* (1486) had observed, "witchcraft is not taught in books, nor is it practiced by the learned, but by the altogether uneducated. What the Puritan elite discovered was that the beliefs as well as the practice were sustained by the common people, and once the chords of superstition had been touched in the popular mind, folk traditions, vulgar rhythms, and ancient hermetic harmonies would call the tune.

5

The Double Bonds of Race and Sex: Black and White Women in a Colonial Virginia Parish

JOAN REZNER GUNDERSON

• *The institution of slavery started on the North American continent as an attempt to cope with severe labor shortages. The first boatload of Africans arrived in 1619, and for the next forty years blacks were sometimes treated as indentured servants—workers who toiled for a fixed period of time and who were then free to pursue their own lives—and sometimes kept forever in bondage. Not until the 1660s did the custom develop to keep all African-Americans in permanent servitude. Thereafter, the African slaves provided the bulk of the laboring force in the southern colonies. Slavery existed in the North also during this period, but the institution was generally curbed, and the bondsmen released, well before the Civil War. In the South, by contrast, the invention of the cotton gin in 1793 created an enormous need for slaves to support an essentially agricultural economy, and it took a terrible conflict and many hundreds of thousands of battle deaths before the "peculiar institution" was finally abolished.*

As Joan Rezner Gunderson points out in the following essay, black, female slaves were doubly damned in colonial America. As women, they knew the pain of childbirth and frequent death, and they suffered the common discrimination against members of the second sex. As slaves, they knew the horror of forced separation from children and loved ones, and the futility of being unable to control their own destiny.

Phillis, a Black Slave, and Elizabeth Chastain LeSueur, her mistress, worked and raised families together for over thirty-two years in King

Joan Rezner Gunderson, "The Double Bonds of Race and Sex: Black and White Women in a Colonial Virginia Parish," *Journal of Southern History*, LII (August 1986), 351–72. Copyright © 1986 by the Southern Historical Association. Reprinted, without footnotes, by permission of the Managing Editor.

William Parish, Virginia. In their small world, about thirty miles west of Richmond, shared ties of gender created a community of women but not a community of equals. The bonds of race and slavery provided constraints that divided the experience of Phillis from that of Elizabeth. Like most women of their day, they left but a faint trail through the records. Elizabeth Chastain LeSueur was probably the older, born about 1707, while all that is certain about Phillis is that she was born before 1728. Both women died sometime after David LeSueur's estate went through probate in early 1773. Both bore and raised children, worked at the many domestic tasks assigned to women in the colonies, and experienced the growth of slavery in their region. The similarities and differences between their lives (and the lives of the other women of the parish) reveal much about the ways gender and race interacted in the lives of colonial women.

The lives of black women such as Phillis have yet to be explored in depth by the new social historians. We have, however, learned something about the lives of women like her mistress, Elizabeth Chastain LeSueur. In recent years historians have examined the life expectancy of seventeenth-century blacks, the effects of demographics and demand upon the introduction of slavery in the Chesapeake, the impact of a black majority upon South Carolina development, the patterns of slave resistance in eighteenth-century Virginia, and the structure of eighteenth-century slave families. In all of this the black woman appears as a cipher, notable in the seventeenth century and first part of the eighteenth by her absence and by her lack of overt resistance to slavery; she seems essential only to the study of fertility. But just as the experience of white women such as Elizabeth Chastain LeSueur differed from that of white males in the colonies, the black female's experience in slavery differed from the male's, and to ignore that difference would be to misunderstand the nature of slavery. Gender not only separated female slaves from males, it also forged bonds with white women. After all, black women lived among whites, and in order fully to understand their lives, it is necessary to compare their experiences with those of white women. Only then can we begin to understand what it meant to be black and female in colonial Virginia.

This essay looks at slavery from a comparative female perspective in King William Parish during the eighteenth century. The findings suggest that the bonds of a female slave were twofold, linking her both to an interracial community of women and setting her apart as a slave in ways that make evident the special burden of being black and female in a white, patriarchal society. The local parish records, including tithe records for nearly every year between 1710 and 1744, provide a unique opportunity to illuminate the role of the black woman in a small plantation setting and to document the development of slavery within a new community just as it became the major labor source for the colony.

The slave women who arrived at King William Parish in the early eighteenth century did not make a simple transfer from an African past to an English colonial present (even with intermediary stops). Rather, they came to a community itself in transformation from a French Protestant refugee culture to an English colonial one. The Virginia House of Burgesses created King William Parish for Huguenot refugees who settled at Manakin Town in 1700. Changing county boundaries placed the settlement at various times in Henrico, Goochland, Cumberland, and Chesterfield counties before 1777. The tiny handful of slaves present before 1720 belonged to a community in which French was the dominant language. The decade of the 1720s, during which the first expansion of the slave population occurred, is also the period in which the Huguenot community leadership and property passed into the hands of those who, like Elizabeth Chastain LeSueur, either had arrived in Virginia as infants or had been born there. An epidemic in 1717–18 greatly disrupted the community and its institutions, speeding the transfer of leadership to a new generation.

The economy of King William Parish, based on wheat and other grains, was also in transition, and the adoption of slavery was a reflection of this change. The first black women thus had to adapt to both a culture and an economy in transition. In the 1720s some land passed into English hands, and tobacco became a secondary crop. Slavery and tobacco together grew in importance in the parish over time. English interlopers did not introduce either slavery or tobacco, but they did provide a bridge to the agricultural patterns of the rest of the colony. The first slaveholding families in the community, including Elizabeth LeSueur's family, were French, and the purchase of slaves signified their claim to be members of the gentry.

When Abraham and Magdalene Salle purchased Agar, an adult black female, in 1714, she joined a handful of other blacks at Manakin. The only other black woman, Bety, had arrived in the parish the year before.

Agar began and ended her three decades of service in Manakin as part of a black female population outnumbered by black men, but for a decade in the middle (1720–30), she was among the majority or was part of an evenly divided black population. Since black and white women in the Chesapeake were also outnumbered by men, Agar was part of a double minority. In King William Parish the circumstances of immigration had created nearly even sex ratios for both races. By 1714, for example, the white community had only slightly more adult men than women. Recent studies throughout the Chesapeake have documented the shortage of black women in slave communities, and while the sex ratio at King William Parish favored men, it was seldom as severe as that reported for other areas. Thus the sense of being part of a female minority was less obvious than elsewhere in the colony.

The King William Parish slave population grew slowly. The originally unbalanced black population achieved a better balance between the sexes, then became more one-sided, and finally returned to a nearly balanced state (see Table 1). By 1720 Agar was one of four black women out of a total of seven slaves in the community. Throughout the 1730s the adult sex ratio became more skewed, leaving women outnumbered 2:1, but well before the Revolution it had balanced. Overall, from 1710 to 1776, the parish's adult sex ratio for blacks was 6:5, or nearly even. This is very close to the ratio that the whites of the parish had achieved by 1714. Thus only early in the settlement's history did the majority-minority experience of black and white women diverge.

Interplay between patterns of importation and natural increase explain the shifting sex ratios. The more balanced sex ratios of the early years were an unintentional outgrowth of purchase patterns for imported slaves. Upriver slave purchasers received the leftovers from importation. Since adult males were the most desirable, and also available in greater numbers, the Tidewater planters purchased nearly all males in the early part of the eighteenth century. Conversely, the slaves who reached the Piedmont in these earlier years included proportionately more women and children. By mid-century the majority of imports went to the Piedmont, providing an expansion of male field labor and unbalancing the sex ratios. As a nativeborn slave population came of age beginning in the 1750s, the ratio was once more evenly balanced.

Throughout Agar's life at Manakin (1714–c. 1748) she was con-

TABLE I

Number and Sex Ratio of Adult Blacks in Manakin
1711–1744

Year	Males	Females	Unknown	Sex Ratio
1711	2	0	0	2:0
1712	5	0	0	5:0
1713	3	1	0	3:1
1714	4	2	0	2:1
1715	4	3	0	4:3
1717	6	3	0	2:1
1719	6	3	0	2:1
1720	3	4	0	3:4
1723	11	11	0	1:1
1724	11	11	0	1:1
1725	8	9	0	8:9
1726	8	7	0	8:7
1730	31	21	6	3:2
1731	28	19	10	7:5
1732	30	21	0	11:9
1733	33	24	3	4:3
1735	45	22	0	2:1
1744	66	51	0	11:8.5

SOURCE: Tithe lists, King William Parish Vestry Book: 1744 Tithe List in Brock, ed., *Documents*. 112–16.

stantly part of a racial minority, for whites outnumbered blacks until after 1750. By the late 1730s black men and women comprised half of the tithables of King William Parish. Since white women were excluded from the count of tithables, and since there were many more white children than black, Agar and other blacks were still part of a minority in the community, but among a majority of those who worked the fields. Agar probably died in the late 1740s, a few years after the LeSueurs purchased Phillis. Phillis lived in a community almost evenly divided between whites and blacks and between men and women, but belonging to a numerical majority did not loosen either the bonds of slavery or gender.

Ironically, black women had an opportunity for a more normal family life than did black men because they were less desirable purchases. Because black women were outnumbered by men in King William

Parish, it was easier for women to form families. Even so, the evidence suggests that black women took their time. Several factors complicated a black woman's search for a partner. The dispersed patterns of ownership meant few black women lived in a slave quarter or with other blacks. Initially blacks, and especially black women, were scattered singly or in small groups among those families who owned slaves. Over one-third of the families owned some slaves or rented them. No family before 1744 paid taxes on more than six blacks over age sixteen. Before 1744 only two or three families owned enough slaves to have both adult males and females. Thus black women had to search for mates on nearby farms. Furthermore, many black women lived relatively short times in Manakin, disappearing from the tithe records after only a few years. Bety, the first female slave in the parish, for example, appears on only four tithe returns. Such transience delayed the process of forming a family. In the early years this experience did not necessarily set black women apart from whites; immigrants of whatever race tended to marry later. As the community aged, however, the black woman's delay in starting a family did set her apart, for native-born white women began families earlier than their immigrant sisters, black or white.

There is only fragmentary evidence to suggest whether the slaves of Manakin were imported directly from Africa, or the West Indies, or if they were purchased from other colonial owners. Almost all slaves bore Anglicized names. The names of the slaves do suggest that the same kinds of compromises between African and English cultures that Peter H. Wood found in South Carolina also existed in colonial Virginia. The process of having the county courts decide the age of young immigrant slaves has identified a small percentage of the black population in King William Parish as imports. Importers usually registered newly arrived Africans at a county in the Tidewater and then brought them upriver for sale. Thus the records in the King William Parish area do not normally distinguish between slaves imported from abroad and those born elsewhere in Virginia.

Whatever these names may reveal about the origins of Manakin's black residents, black and white women were subjected to the same gender-imposed cultural restraints in naming. Of course, only white males had the security of a stable surname, but putting that issue aside, naming patterns reveal a subtle power structure in which gender played as important a role as did race. It is fitting that the first black woman resident in King William Parish was called Bety, because Bett (Beti, Bety, Betty) would prove to be one of the most common names for slave women in the parish. Of the 737 blacks studied, the 336 women bore only 71 names. Nine of these names were used seventeen times or more and account for over half of all the women. Conversely, the 401 men bore 117 names, only 5 of which were used seventeen times or more, representing only one-quarter of all male names. Thus the men bore more individualistic names. The men's names included those with more recognizable African roots such as Ebo, Manoc, and Morocco. The women's names were more Anglicized. The most common female names among slaves were western names that closely resembled African ones, such as Betty and Jude. Hence the names represent a compromise of cultures. It is possible that the lack of recognizable African roots reflected the insistence by owners that black women fit the cultural norms for women while accepting the idea that black men might be "outlandish."

Slave naming patterns may have been affected by the French community. Manakin whites bear frustratingly few names, especially among women. Nine women's names account for over 90 percent of the more than 600 white women associated with the Manakin community before 1776. While both black and white women drew their names from a much smaller pool than did men, the pool of black names had a diversity to begin with only eventually matched by white families who added new names through intermarriage. That black women shared the same names more frequently than black men parallels the pattern of the white community. But there was a further commonality among women's names that cut across racial lines. Slave names were often the diminutives of white names, for example, Betty for Elizabeth and Will for William. White women also were known by diminutives such as Sally, Patsy, and Nancy. They appear this way even in formal documents such as wills. Nicknames and diminutives are not used for adult white males. Hence diminutives were shared by women, both black and white, but not by all groups of men. White women shared in unaltered form several common names with black women, including Sarah, Hannah, and Janne. Male slaves did not bear the same names as white males, although a white youth might be called by a nickname such as Tom, which was also a common slave name. On legal documents and at adulthood, however, white men claimed the distinction granted by the formal versions of their names. Slaveowners apparently found it more necessary to distinguish between white and black males than to distinguish between white and black females by changing the form of their names or choosing names for slaves not used by whites. Such distinctions in naming patterns helped to reinforce the status and power of white men.

The records unfortunately do not reveal who did the naming of black women, whether immigrant blacks influenced the choice of names assigned them or whether owners or mothers chose the names of black children. Control over the power of naming was an important indicator of the power relationship that existed between owner and slave, but general cultural constraints also shaped the choices made by whoever exercised that power. Tradition greatly limited the naming patterns of whites. The oldest children bore grandparents' names, the next oldest were their parents' namesakes, and younger children were named for siblings of their parents. Occasionally a family would use the mother's family name as a first name for a younger child. However, the important point is that general cultural constraints determined naming patterns, not individuals, and the gender constraints of Virginia meant that women of both races shared a naming experience that offered them fewer choices, accorded them less individuality, and reinforced a dependent status.

Childbirth is an experience shared by women of all races, but in King William Parish the patterns of childbearing reveal another way in which black women lived within a community of women and yet encountered a separate experience. Next to the ordinary rhythms of work, childbirth may have been the most common experience for women. Pregnancy, childbirth, and nursing provided a steady background beat to the lives of women in the colonies. Recent research has shown that colonial white women made childbirth a community event, infused with rituals of support by other women, and that these rituals of lying-in were shared with black women. The evidence from Manakin, however, suggests that the risks of childbirth were greater for black women than for white. Although they may have participated in the rituals surrounding childbirth, black women were the center of attention less frequently because they had fewer children; moreover, participation in this women's culture required them to abandon some of their African traditions. Truly, childbirth was a bittersweet experience for black women.

The fragmentary King William Parish Register includes the records of births of slaves among forty-eight owners for the years from 1724 to 1744. The parish register reveals only the owner's name, not the mother's, but since most white families claimed only one or two black women it is possible to trace the childbearing history of individual women. The average birth interval was about 28 months, but was often less than two years. The experience of Marie, a slave of Jean Levillain, illustrates the point. Marie's first two children were born 19 months apart, followed by intervals of 24, 25, 11, 14, and 30 months. In general, for the black women of Manakin, the most frequent interval was 20 months. Fifty-six percent of the birth intervals were between 15 and 34 months. However, another quarter of the intervals fell into a block running 36 to 47 months. The interval between births, however, was much more ragged than these figures suggest. Many women had long gaps in their childbearing histories. Other women had few or no children. For example, Pegg, the slave of Barbara Dutoy, had only one child in twelve years.

While the average and median for childbirth intervals were similar for black and white women in the parish, there were also major differences. The black woman was much more likely to have an intermittent history of childbirth with long gaps, ending much sooner than it did for the whites of Manakin. Birth intervals for whites were more tightly clustered around 24 months than black births. Seventy-four percent of the white births fell in the interval between 15 and 34 months (see Table 2). Elizabeth Chastain LeSueur, for example, bore children every two to three years with almost clockwork regularity from 1728 to 1753, while her slave Phillis had two children 30 months apart and then had no more children for at least seven years.

The child-spacing patterns for black and white women of King William Parish provide important clues to the adaptation of black women to American slavery and their participation in a community culture surrounding childbirth. African customs of nursing were different from those of Europeans. In Africa women often nursed children for more than three years, abstaining from sexual relations during that period. Black women continued these patterns in the Caribbean slave com-

TABLE 2

Birth Intervals for Women Associated with Manakin

Interval in months	Black Births 1724–1744		White Births 1701–1783	
	number	percent	number	percent
0–8	0	0	2	1
9–14	6	9	5	3
15–19	10	14	23	11
20–24	12	17	58	29
25–29	15	21	44	22
30–34	3	4	25	12
35–39	8	12	22	10
40–44	7	10	4	2
45–49	3	4	5	3
50–54	1	2	6	3
55–59	0	0	2	1
60+	5	7	6	3
Total	70	100	202	100

SOURCES: King William Parish Register in Brock, ed., *Documents*; William Macfarlane Jones, ed., *The Douglas Register* (Richmond, Va., 1928).

munities, as did seventeenth-century blacks in the Chesapeake. The secondary cluster of birth intervals of three to four years suggests that a number of immigrant black women, including Phillis, continued that tradition in the Manakin area. European women, however, nursed for a shorter time and had resultingly closer birth intervals of about two years. Marie and a number of other black women in the parish adopted the shorter European traditions of nursing. Whether this adoption of European custom came at the urging of owners or as part of a cultural accommodation by black women, the result was that Marie and others like her had one more bond with white women.

In another way, however, the birth intervals explain how childbirth set black and white women apart, for black women had many fewer children per mother than the white women did. Childbearing histories for twenty-eight black women and fifty-five white women appear in Table 2. Twice as many white women provided almost three times the number of birth intervals as did black women. The difference may be a result of fewer black births, owners more frequently forgetting to register black births, or a combination of the two. All of the possibilities suggest a different experience for black women. Other evidence, such as estate inventories, suggests that fewer births account for most of the difference. Because many black women lived in King William Parish for fewer than their total childbearing years, it was necessary to transform the raw figures into data for a stable community in order to make comparisons with the experience of whites. A stable population would have been represented by just under nineteen black women living in the parish continuously throughout the twenty-year period. They would have averaged 6.01 children to produce the births actually registered. While this compares favorably with figures for the total children born to the French immigrant generation at King William Parish, it is considerably lower than the average number of children born by the later generations of white settlers at Manakin. Some white women also ended their childbearing after only a few children, or had long gaps due to the death of a spouse or physical problems, but most produced a steady stream of children spaced two years apart. If black women had borne children spaced at the average interval without interruption, it would have taken only 14.2 years to reach the family size indicated by the stable population calculations.

That most black women were immigrants and most whites were native-born accounts for some of the difference in numbers of children, for immigrant women often delayed starting families while searching for mates or found their marriages disrupted. Others reached menopause before they had been in the Manakin area twenty years. The gaps in the middle of black women's childbearing years, however, are at least as significant as any shortening of the years at risk by late starts. Those mid-life gaps in childbearing were due in part to black life expectancy. Africans and other immigrants to the South had high death rates, even in the more healthful eighteenth century. Disruptions caused by the death of a partner could inhibit the total number of children a woman bore, especially while the black community was small, for finding a new partner might take years. Although white women also lost partners, by 1730 the population of King William Parish was colonial-born and more resistant to the endemic fevers. Thus their marriages were more stable. The slave population, however, continued to be heavily immigrant and thus continued to have a higher rate of

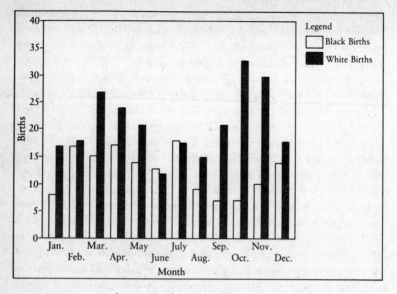

FIGURE I Birth months for Manakin children, 1724–1750.

marriage disruption. Transfers of ownership and removal to other areas increased the possibility of separation from partners and hence lowered the number of children born.

Childbearing was a part of the rhythm of a woman's life, but that rhythm had a different beat for black women. All twelve of Elizabeth LeSueur's children were born in October, November, or December. Phillis's known childbirths, however, were in April and October. Two-thirds of King William Parish's black births, however, occurred between February and July. The months of August through January saw relatively few black births. Black women, then, usually conceived during the months of May through October. The white women of Manakin show a much different pattern of births. Births were heavy in the fall and early spring and lowest in June, July, and August (see Figure I). White conceptions were lowest in the fall; blacks were lowest in the deep winter. Black women thus were in the later stages of pregnancy during the heavy labor season of spring planting. Surely this affected their health.

The puzzling question of why black women had their children on a different cycle from white women has no ready solution. Black women were certainly not planning their pregnancies in order to receive reduced work loads during the spring, because there is evidence that the loads were not reduced. It is possible that black men and women had more contact with each other during the summer and fall while they were tending and harvesting crops. In the cold months black women may have been kept close to the plantation house working on domestic projects such as spinning, and thus were not free to meet with their partners. White women had no such constraints. Opportunity for conception increased when the cold months brought white men closer to the hearth fires.

The white women of Manakin expected their children to survive to adulthood. A black woman could not. King William Parish death records are fragmentary, so slave deaths appear only in a few cases where the record of birth includes a note of the infant's death. Circumstantial evidence, however, suggests high infant and child mortality. Only 44 out of 151 of the slave children whose births were recorded in the parish register appear in any other legal and church record, and for some that second appearance was as a child. Death explains many of the disappearances. For example, Beti, slave of Gideon Chambon, bore children Jean (John) in 1727 and Marye in 1733. When Chambon's estate inventory was filed in 1739 neither child appeared on the list. Given Chambon's age and economic condition, the most likely explanation is that the children died, not that he sold or gave them away. Similarly, Magdalene, born in 1744, does not appear in any records after the filing of John Harris's will when she was seven. Owners registered two and three children by the same name over the years. John Chastain, for example, registered the births of black newborns named Fillis on March 24, 1745/6 and June 12, 1753. Only one slave of that name appears on his estate inventory. Likewise, Bartholomew Dupuy's slave Sara bore sons named Jack in both 1727 and 1730. Apparently they were doing what many families also did following the death of a white child, that is, replacing it by another of the same name.

The work patterns of black women fostered the high death rate among their children by exhausting mothers and making infant care difficult. The experiences of Aggy, a slave of the Levillain family, provide some clues to the relationship between work, childbearing, and infant mortality. Aggy (Agar) had been born in Manakin on August

7, 1733, as the slave of Jean Levillain; she passed by will to Jean's son Anthony Lavillain in 1746. Four years later, when Aggy was seventeen, Anthony died intestate, leaving Aggy the property of Anthony's new-born daughter Mary and the subject of an administered estate for the next fifteen years. Aggy's first child was born when she was eighteen. Two years later she had another. Throughout those years she worked in the fields, while the administratrix of the estate, Elizabeth Lavillain Young Starkey, recorded expenses for "nursing" both small children. The youngest, a girl, died by age three. In 1763 Aggy, by then thirty, again became pregnant. The pregnancy was not easy, however, for the records show payments to Mrs. Chastain for treating Aggy "when sick" and attending Aggy's lying-in.

Aggy's life illustrates the black pattern of work and childbearing in King William Parish. Beginning in her teens Aggy had two children spaced two years apart, but then there was a ten-year gap before she had another child. From 1754 to 1756 Aggy was hired out. Then she returned to work with the other slaves growing tobacco, wheat, and corn for the estate. John Levillain, Anthony's brother and, after 1754, Mary's guardian, did see that Aggy got medical treatment during her difficult later pregnancy, but the records Levillain filed with the court for income to the estate credit her with the same share of work on the crops as other slaves, so he had not reduced her work. Such practices would increase the risk of infant mortality.

The records for the Manakin area do not reveal much about the birth customs for black women, but Charlotte Chastain's appearance during Aggy's lying-in was not the only time a white midwife was paid for the delivery of a black woman's baby in the Manakin area. Thus while the Manakin families might not have been rich enough to provide the elaborate lying-ins for black women that Mary Beth Norton has described, the birth experience was not left entirely to the black community. Since we also know that black women helped at the births of white children, the physical act of giving birth may have been one of the most significant ways in which black and white women served each other in a single community.

As with the other aspects of their lives, work both separated and brought black women together with whites. Virginia's tithe laws made clear the distinctions. White women such as Elizabeth Chastain LeSueur were not counted in figuring the tithe. In fact, they only appeared on the tithe lists when widowed with slaves or male children sixteen years or over. On the other hand, black women like Phillis were counted. Ironically, it is easier to trace black women from year to year in the community since they are listed on the tithes than it is to trace white women. Eventually, in 1769, free black women received the same exemption as white women, but slave women remained a part of the tithe. In other words, black women were considered a basic part of the agricultural labor force in a way that white women were not. Undoubtedly, Phillis had spent part of her time working in the LeSueur fields. When the LeSueurs purchased her they had no children old enough to help with farm work, and David and Elizabeth LeSueur were planting without any regular help. Phillis's arrival assured Elizabeth that she could withdraw from occasional help in the fields to her many household duties and garden.

While white women seldom worked away from home, black women sometimes did. Slave rentals kept the labor supply flexible, cut costs for care by owners, and provided an income for widows and orphans. Two major sources for rental slaves were estates managed to provide an income for widows and orphans, and wealthy farmers who hired out their surplus women and children slaves. Women slaves were hired out more frequently than men. Thus black women might be separated from family and friends in order to secure the income that allowed a white woman to remain on the family farm. Agar, who had arrived at Manakin in 1714, spent the 1730s hired out by the widow Magdalene Salle, while the family's other adult slave, Bob, stayed on the plantation. Only when Magdalene's son came of age and assumed management of the plantation did Agar return to the plantation. Widow Barbara Dutoy also rented her slaves to other residents of Manakin from 1726 to 1733. In both cases rental gave the widow an income without the worry of planting. It allowed minimum disruption to the widow's life, but at the expense of disrupting the slave woman's life.

Surviving orphans court records and wills document other hiring out of slaves in the Manakin area. Jean Levillain hired out Aggy from 1754 to 1756 for a charge of about £4 each year. Some hiring was short-term. James Holman hired out a black woman for two weeks time while managing Peter Martin's estate. In addition, nine children's births appear in the parish register without their owners paying tithes on an adult woman. The mothers were probably rented out and appeared under the renter's name on the tithe list. A hired slave could move frequently; for example, Lucy seems to have been hired by Abraham Salle in 1724, Jack Griffin in 1732 and 1733, and Pierre Louis Soblet in 1734 and 1735. The rental of female slaves thus seems to have been an integral part of the Manakin labor system, allowing aspiring farmers to add to their small labor forces while providing income for widows and orphans. Once again the community's perception of black women primarily as field hands set black and white women apart.

Phillis might have spent much of her time in the fields, but she also worked with Elizabeth LeSueur on the many tasks associated with women's work. Domestic work was not a single occupation but a variety of highly skilled tasks shared by women on the plantation. For example, clothmaking occupied both white and black women in the Manakin area. When David LeSueur died in 1772, the family owned working farms in both Buckingham and Cumberland counties. Only the home plantation in Cumberland, however, had cotton, wool and cotton cards, a wool wheel, two spindles, four flax wheels, and parts for two looms. Elizabeth obviously oversaw and worked with Phillis and Phillis's two grown daughters in the making of a variety of cloth. The LeSueurs were not unusual, for inventories throughout the Manakin region mention several crops including flax, the tools necessary to produce linen thread, and, somewhat less frequently, looms for weaving. The Lavillain estate, for example, purchased two spinning wheels. These wheels were for the use of Aggy and Nan, slaves of the estate who continued to be credited with a share of the crops of tobacco and grains. John Levillain simply added cloth production to the women's field duties. The usefulness of women in the tasks of cloth production may have encouraged owners to purchase women slaves. From its beginning the colony at Manakin provided Virginia cloth, used to clothe slaves and the poor. Black women worked with white women in this production on the small farm, thus providing another way in which a community of women cut across racial lines.

The smallness of slaveholdings and the relatively short life expectancies of owners created major instabilities in the lives of black women that exceeded the uncertainties of life for their white mistresses. Although owners recognized that black families existed, and while there is convincing evidence that kinship ties were strong among blacks, the value of slaves as property meant that black family stability was tied to the life cycle of their owners. Short life expectancies and parental willingness to establish adult children on farms of their own as soon as possible accelerated the cycle in the Manakin area. Life patterns in the late seventeenth and early eighteenth centuries were such that most Chesapeake parents expected to die before all their children came of age. One result of this expectation was the willingness of parents to give adult children their shares of the estate when they came of age or married. For example, Elizabeth Chastain's brother John and sister Judith were already living on their shares of land when their father Peter wrote his will. Thus even a long-lived owner was no guarantee of stability in a slave family.

Most blacks in the Manakin area changed hands upon the death of an owner or the coming of age of a child of the owner. Because slaves were valuable legacies to children, they were often divided among several heirs. Daughters, especially, received slaves as their share of the estate, either as dowries or legacies. With slaveholdings small, black families were divided at each period of change within the white family. Most bequests in the Manakin area (except for life interests to widows) were of one or two slaves. David LeSueur, for example, granted each of his eight surviving children one slave. Phillis, her two oldest children, and another male (probably husband to her daughter) stayed with their mistress, Elizabeth Chastain LeSueur, but all of Phillis's younger children and grandchildren were scattered. Owners when possible left very small children with slave mothers or bequeathed the slave mother to a married son or daughter and the slave's children to the children of the son or daughter. Thus black women received some recognition of bonds with children not accorded to men. In fact, the estate appraisers often perceived infants and mothers as one, giving a single value to a mother and her small child. Frequently they did not even bother to list the infant's name.

Black women might wait for years before the pain of such divisions became real. While the marriage of older children of the owners caused some separation among black families, the major estate divisions came when the owner died. Many estates remained intact for years awaiting the coming of age of minor children or the remarriage or death of a widow. Thus the fate of black women (and men) depended on the fate of their white mistresses. For example, Kate was a slave of Anthony Rapine when he died in 1737. Rapine gave his wife, Margaret, a life interest in half the estate with all eventually to go to his daughter. Maryanne Martin. Since Maryanne and her husband lived with the Rapines, Kate's life went on unchanged. In 1740 she bore a daughter. Hannah. Three years later Maryanne Martin was widowed and soon after she remarried. She deeded Kate and Hannah to her year-old son, Peter Martin, shortly before remarrying. In 1747, ten years after Anthony Rapine died, the estate was finally divided between Margaret Rapine and Thomas Smith, who had married the now-deceased Maryanne. Kate and Hannah (by then age seven) were listed together on the inventory and passed into Smith's possession. He then turned Kate and Hannah over to Peter's new guardian in 1749. At last, after twelve years, Kate and Hannah were forced to move. The black woman on a larger estate had a better chance of remaining with kin following the death of an owner. The few large estates included in the study divided slaves on the basis of where they lived, often giving a particular farm and its slaves to an heir.

The slave woman lived and worked in a very small community at Manakin. Since each family owned only a few slaves, a black community could not exist on a single plantation. The farms at Manakin were small enough (the original allotments were 133 acres each) that visiting between farms would be possible, and thus a wider community might have existed. The birth patterns, however, suggest that such visiting was limited. Although the dispersed black population might have hindered the formation of a black community, the tasks of the black woman put her in constant contact with whites. Family members on a small farm labored in the fields alongside the slaves, and women's chores such as spinning might be done with the wife and daughters of the owner. Historians have speculated that slaves who lived on small plantations or in areas isolated from a black community probably adopted white values and customs more readily than those who could fashion a creole life-style with other blacks. For the black woman this meant partial acceptance into the special world of women's society. Such acceptance made more poignant the contrast in birth rates, child morality, and family stability between blacks and whites.

Life for black women in the Manakin area was filled with insecurity. Some risks, such as childbirth, were shared with white women, but others were not. As part of a double minority black women enjoyed a favorable marriage market, but dispersion of holdings threatened the families formed by black women with separation. Some slaves on large plantations could begin to develop distinct creole societies near Manakin, but that was possible only after 1750 and only for a small proportion of slaves. Slave rentals, which affected women more than men, added another dimension of instability to that ensured by the short life spans of spouses and owners. The decisions made by widows to remarry, farm, or hire out slaves for income not only determined whether white families would remain intact, but whether black ones would too. Most black women in the Manakin area lived on small farms or quarters where their field work was supplemented by sharing in the household tasks of the white women on the farm. The "bonds of womanhood" surrounded her life as much as the bonds of slavery, beginning with the very choice of a name. Childbearing was especially frustrating for the black woman, filled with the pain of frequent infant death, heavy workloads when pregnant, and separation from children. But childbirth also meant sharing in a woman's network that stretched across racial lines. The life of a black woman was thus constantly subjected to the cross-pressures of belonging to a woman's subculture without full membership.

6

Land of the Unfree: Legal Limitations on Liberty in Pre-Revolutionary America

LINDA GRANT DEPAUW

● *In 1776, representatives of thirteen British colonies in North America boldly affixed their signatures to the Declaration of Independence. Arguing that all men were endowed by their creator with certain "inalienable" rights, they gave liberty as the purpose of the new United States. Based on the theory of natural rights, which had been espoused earlier by John Locke and Jean Jacques Rousseau, the Declaration of Independence is the most important of all American historical documents.*

Actually, the notion of freedom was rather new in 1776. Until the twentieth century, in many parts of the world serfs were bound to the land, meaning that they lacked the freedom to come and go as they pleased without undue restraint. Freedom of religion, the right to worship with groups of one's own choosing, was unknown before the Protestant Reformation. The right to vote and to hold office was practically nonexistent before the nineteenth century, as was freedom of speech and of the press. Prior to the Habeas Corpus Act (1679) in England and for centuries thereafter in most countries, a person could be seized or kept in prison indefinitely without trial or hearing.

Even in the United States, long known as "the Land of the Free," the concept of liberty has expanded only gradually. The idea of equality, for example, has come only slowly to be associated with the idea of freedom. And for specific minorities, women and blacks being notable examples, many liberties are seen only as operative for white men. But whatever its shortcomings, the United States has usually come

"Land of the Unfree: Legal Limitations on Liberty in Pre-Revolutionary America." *Maryland Historical Magazine*, volume 68, number 4, 1973. Article is reprinted courtesy of the Maryland Historical Society.

> *closer to the ideals and spirit of the universal symbol of free-*
> *dom, the Statue of Liberty, than have other nations of the*
> *world.*

The fortune that Thomas Jefferson pledged with his life and sacred honor in support of the declaration that all men are created equal and endowed with inalienable rights to life, liberty, and the pursuit of happiness included, in the summer of 1776, almost two hundred slaves. The incongruity of a slave-owning people basing their Revolution on such exalted doctrines did not escape remark by contemporaries any more than it has escaped notice by historians. "How is it" sneered Samuel Johnson, "that we hear the loudest *yelps* for liberty among the drivers of negroes?" The Loyalist Thomas Hutchinson dryly observed that there seemed to be some discrepancy between the declaration that all men were equal and a practice that deprived "more than a hundred thousand Africans of their rights to liberty."

Even those Englishmen who sympathized with the American cause were repelled by the paradox. "If there be an object truly ridiculous in nature," Thomas Day commented, "it is an American patriot signing resolutions of independence with the one hand, and with the other brandishing a whip over his affrighted slaves." And the patriots themselves were not insensitive to it. "I have sometimes been ready to think," Abigail Adams wrote to her husband, "that the passion for liberty cannot be equally strong in the breasts of those who have been accustomed to deprive their fellow creatures of theirs." Patrick Henry confessed amazement that men as sincerely "fond of liberty" and genuinely religious as himself tolerated slavery. "Would anyone believe," he asked, "I am the master of slaves of my own purchase!"

Historians writing about the age of the American Revolution have tended to ignore the paradox more frequently than they have attempted to resolve it, but in recent years serious attention has been given to the enslaved blacks, and such New Left historians as Jesse Lemish and Staughton Lynd have pointed out the limitations on the rights of such groups as merchant seamen and urban workers. Yet the full magnitude of the paradox is still unmeasured, for it appears that the contradiction between Lockean ideals and social practice in the year 1776 was not only more pronounced than contemporaries and traditional historians described but even exceeds the dimensions suggested by recent historians of the New Left. Had Lockean dicta been applied to all the human beings in British North America on the eve of the Revolution, and had all been permitted to enjoy the natural and legal rights of freemen, it would have been necessary to alter the status of more than 85 percent of the population. In law and in fact no more than 15 percent of the Revolutionary generation was free to enjoy life, liberty, and the pursuit of happiness unhampered by any restraints except those to which they had given their consent.

The unfree of Revolutionary America may be conveniently considered in five categories: Negroes, white servants, women, minors, and propertyless adult white males. These categories overlap and the proportion of the total population falling into each of the categories differed from one part of the country to another. Thus there were proportionately more women in New England than in backcountry North Carolina, many more blacks, proportionally, in Virginia than in New Jersey, and a larger proportion of disfranchised adult white males in South Carolina than in Massachusetts.

It is also true that legal limitations on liberty do not necessarily coincide either with a psychological sense of freedom or with social practices. The unfree were rarely, in face, exploited to the full limit allowed by law. Nor has there been any attempt in this brief essay to present a precise description of legal status based on the myriad of local traditions, statutes, and common law interpretation. The following summaries claim to be correct in outline, not to have exhausted the complexities of the subject, which are vast and largely unstudied. It is clear, however, that for each of the unfree groups the law placed definite theoretical limits on the rights Locke viewed as inalienable.

The black slaves, the most visible of the colonial unfree, comprised approximately 20 percent of the colonial population, a proportion twice as great as that formed by the black population of the United States today. These slaves were legally chattel property. The law saw no self-evident right to liberty attached to the person of the dark-skinned laborer from Africa, and, indeed, the law had little concern for his right to life. The deliberate murder of a slave was not necessarily a felony in Virginia before the Revolution, for the law assumed that no one would intentionally destroy his own estate. Slaves had no right to hold property of their own and enjoyed the use of no more than the master allowed. As for the third right in Jefferson's trinity, pursuing happiness, if that took the form of taking time off from the master's work, it was a punishable offense.

There were a small number of free blacks in Revolutionary America, most of them in the North. Their status was superior to that of the slave, but they were still limited politically, socially, and economically in all of the colonies. For most legal purposes there was no distinction made between free and enslaved Negroes. They might have some time they could call their own for pursuing happiness, but they were forbidden to pursue it in a tavern. In Rhode Island a free black man could not even purchase a quart of cider.

White servants in colonial America comprised a class perhaps half as large as the slave force but unbalanced in age and sex distribution in favor of young adult males. Their status was superior to that of Negroes but still substantially below that of freemen. In many ways the servant was merely a slave with prospects of eventual freedom and whose entry into his lowly station had been more or less voluntary. When, in November 1775, Lord Dunmore attempted to lure blacks into the British army by offering them freedom as a bounty, the same offer was extended to white servants.

The servant's labor belonged to his master twenty-four hours a day, seven days a week. Like the black slave, he was a chattel. He had no property himself but what his master allowed. He could not marry without his master's permission and, like a black man, he could not drink liquor in a tavern. Running away and disobedience were severely punished, and stories of inhuman cruelty to white servants are common. Like a slave, a white servant could be sold against his will away from his wife and family or seized to satisfy his master's debts. There seems little to recommend the legislation governing servants over that governing blacks—with one exception. White servants, unlike slaves, had personal rights to life and contract rights to a minimum standard of living. They could bring suit to enforce these rights and courts would enforce them even to the extent of freeing the servant outright.

The legal status of colonial women was determined by the tradition of the British common law with certain modifications forced by pioneer American conditions, most of which were made before the end of the seventeenth century. Blackstone's *Commentaries*, which began to circulate as an admired authority among colonial lawyers in the decade before the Revolution, described a theoretical position for English females that varied substantially from that held by free English men. Under common law, Blackstone taught, a woman ceased to exist if she married, for she and her spouse became one flesh and the flesh was his. She was no longer responsible for her debts or even for all of her personal actions. She had no legal control over any property either inherited or earned. And if her husband judged her disobedient or saucy he could chastise her as he did his children and servants. This was considered proper as he might be held responsible for her misbehavior in cases short of murder and high treason. Although divorce laws were relatively liberal for a time in the seventeenth century, a reaction in the Revolutionary era made divorce, regardless of cause, practically impossible for a woman to obtain.

The status of unmarried women, both widows and spinsters, was considerably better. By a law of 1419 known as "couverte de Baron" an unattached woman, the "Feme Sole," was entitled to engage in business enterprises on her own account. A widow was entitled to one-third of the family estate and might be willed even more. So long as she did not remarry she could invest or dispose of this property as she wished. There was, however, great social pressure on women to marry. Although women made up almost half of the total population when all age groups are included, the sex ratio of men to women in the marriageable age group (i.e., between sixteen and sixty) was extremely high—160.8 men to every 100 women. Consequently spinsters were few and they were generally propertyless dependents in the home of a male relative. Widows commonly remarried before their husbands had been buried a year—unless they were remarkably unattractive, elderly, or poor. Those in the last category, who could not support themselves on one-third of their deceased husband's estate, would be subject to the poor laws unless a male relative could be found to take them in. The poor law prescribed compulsory labor for the poor so that impoverished widows might be bound out to serve as domestics. In Wareham, Massachusetts (admittedly an exceptional case) there was an annual auction of indigent widows.

Americans under the age of twenty-one, a clear majority of the population in 1776, were legal infants, and the right to liberty of such persons was far from self-evident to the founding fathers, although they were aware that it seemed to follow, at least for older children, from the Lockean premises. It would be a mistake to confuse the class of legal minors in Revolutionary America with modern adolescents. Blackstone declared a boy of twelve fit to take an oath of allegiance and a girl of seven ready to be given in marriage. The age of discretion for most purposes fell between seven and fourteen and all children above this age group were subject to capital punishment for felonies and bore most of the responsibilities if not the privileges of adults. Children entered the labor force well before they entered their teens, and they developed a degree of maturity and experience in the world that would be considered unhealthily precocious today. The large number of men in their early twenties who served competently as field officers in the Revolutionary armies and sat in the Continental Congresses could only have appeared in a society that considered teenage boys adults even though it deprived them of full legal rights. Male children of the age of sixteen were taxable and liable for militia duty. And since the population of colonial America was generally young, sixteen being the median age, unfree males between sixteen and twenty-one comprised one quarter of the total taxable male population. In an age when the mortality rates among infants and children were high and when a youth of sixteen had less than an even chance of surviving to the age of thirty, the loss of even a few years of liberty was a significant grievance.

Furthermore, theories of child nurture in colonial days were distinctly grim, based on the still formidable patriarchical traditions that had prescribed death for a "rebellious and incorrigible son." Obedience to parents was a duty imposed by divine as well as human law to be enforced by corporal punishment if necessary. Minors were expected to work for their parents as soon as they could walk, but they had no personal property rights before they came of legal age. Authority over children above ten or fourteen was frequently transferred from the natural parents to a master. The institution of apprenticeship was still viable at the time of the Revolution and was the usual path for a young man who did not intend to become a farmer but wished to learn a trade. Girls might also become apprenticed. Apprenticeship articles were drawn to standards set by colonial legislatures and generally required the consent of the child as well as of his parents. But children of poor or otherwise incompetent parents might be sold against their will to masters who promised, sometimes deceitfully, to provide for them adequately and teach them a trade before they came of age.

Once apprenticed, a child's labor belonged to the master as fully as did that of any servant. Even visits to his own parents could be forbidden and the free-time conduct of apprentices was subject to the same sort of restrictions that applied to adult servants or slaves. Disobedience to a master as to a father could be punished with the whip. If a child came to detest the trade his father apprenticed him to, or if the master failed to make him proficient in the craft, his entire future would be warped, for once of age and free it would be too late to begin again to acquire the skills needed to make a living.

These four groups—Negroes, servants, women, and minors—together comprised approximately 80 percent of the two and a half million Americans in the year 1776. The legal doctrine applied to these classes excluded them from the category of persons who should enjoy the "inalienable rights" of which the Declaration speaks. But perhaps the most significant mark of their unfreedom was their usual lack of a right to vote, for the privilege of consenting to the laws was the essential right of a free man in Lockean theory. Indeed, the very word "enfranchise" was defined in the eighteenth century as the equivalent of the word "emancipate"; it meant "to make free."

Interestingly enough, the prohibition on the suffrage does not appear to have been absolute either in law or in fact for any of the unfree groups. Colonial suffrage legislation tended to be vague. Only Virginia, South Carolina, and Georgia specifically confined the franchise to white voters and there are recorded cases of Negroes, mulattoes, and Indians actually casting ballots. When in 1778 a provision excluding blacks from the suffrage was inserted in the proposed Massachusetts constitution, a citizen observed in the *Independent Chronicle* that "a black, tawny or reddish skin is not so unfavorable in hue to the genuine son of liberty, as a tory complection." Rare instances of bond servants casting votes are known and enough servants presumed to exercise the franchise in Albany, New York, to necessitate their specific exclusion from participation in city elections in 1773.

Only Pennsylvania, Delaware, South Carolina, and Georgia specifically disfranchised females who otherwise qualified as property holders. When Hannah Lee Corbin protested to her brother Richard Henry Lee in 1778 that Virginia women ought not to be taxed if they had not the right to vote, he replied that "women were already possessed of that right," and, apparently, some women did vote for a time in Virginia as well as in New England and the middle colonies. But these cases were rare and it is significant that Mrs. Corbin did not know she had the franchise until her brother so informed her.

Only six states explicitly stated that voters must be twenty-one years of age (Pennsylvania, South Carolina, Virginia, Connecticut, New York, and North Carolina), and there are recorded cases of young men under legal age occasionally registering their votes.

In all likelihood, however, the liberality of colonial suffrage legislation was due to careless draftsmanship rather than to any desire to permit members of the unfree classes to vote. The intention was to limit the franchise to free, adult, white males and others who voted slipped through by accident as a result of laxity among election inspectors. Indeed, we know of such cases chiefly because they served as grounds for complaint in disputed elections.

A fifth group of colonial Americans, adult white males with little or no property, was deprived of the vote in colonial elections and so fell short of full liberty in the Lockean sense. But they were privileged above the other unfree groups since they were legally entitled to acquire property and were protected from physical abuse except such as was administered by public authority after trial as punishment for offenses against the state. Some of these disfranchised males were idiots, invalids, or residents of workhouses. Others were simply too poor to qualify under the arbitrary property requirements of the various electoral laws. Statistically they are the least significant of the unfree, although they have had more than their share of attention from critics of consensus history. They made up between 5 and 10 percent of the total population. If they are added to the 80 percent of the population in the other unfree categories, which were limited not merely in their political rights but in their rights to personal liberty and property as well, then only 10 to 15 percent of the American population remain to qualify as "freemen" in the fullest sense.

It is curious that this startling statistic has somehow escaped comment by historians. While the enslavement of Negroes and disfranchisement of some adult white males may be noted in passing as undemocratic elements in pre-Revolutionary America, the disfranchisement and worse of the other unfree classes is accepted without remark even in our enlightened age. Thus, Elisha P. Douglass defines democracy in his *Rebels and Democrats* as "a political system in which all adult males enjoyed equal political rights." Robert Brown writes in *Middle-*

Class Democracy and the Revolution in Massachusetts, "The only valid approach...is to find out how many adult men could vote out of the total adult male population," and he concludes that "if anything with the appearance of a man could vote there was little problem of a restricted electorate." And finally, the author of this paper casually observed in *The Eleventh Pillar,* "The important ratio is that of qualified voters to adult white males."

Today almost 65 percent of the total population is enfranchised and in law, at least, virtually all of the people are secured in property rights and protected from physical abuse by private parties. Yet even our age finds it self-evident that women and young people should have been excluded from colonial political life. Since this is the case, we should not find it difficult to understand how the men of two centuries ago could accept the contradiction between their Lockean principles and their discriminatory practice without too much discomfort.

It would be both uncharitable and simplistic to dismiss the founding fathers as hypocrites because they tolerated this inconsistency. Some conflict between ideal principles and social practice is inevitable if the ideals are at all noble and the society composed of human beings rather than angels. Nor is such contradiction undesirable. Quite the opposite, since it induces men, who will always fall short of perfection in their experience, to consider the possibility of alternative social arrangements superior to their own. Thus John Adams was vastly amused when his Abigail presumed to apply the Revolutionary slogans to the condition of married ladies. But after puzzling over her remarks for a month he realized that, indeed, he could discover no moral foundation for government that would justify the exclusion of any class of people from full participation. Of course it was "impossible," he wrote to James Sullivan, that the principle of consent should ever be carried so far. But the logic was undeniable and if it were followed to its conclusion "women will demand a vote; lads from twelve to twenty-one will think their rights not enough attended to; and every man who has not a farthing, will demand an equal voice with any other, in all acts of state." Adams seems to have predicted the long range impact of the Revolutionary doctrine accurately enough.

Again, Patrick Henry, facing up to the contrast between his words and his practice of keeping slaves, wrote, "I will not, I cannot justify it. However culpable my conduct, I will so far pay my devoir to virtue, as to own the excellence and rectitude of her precepts, and lament my want of conformity to them."

In the final analysis, however, the contradiction was tolerable to Americans because they compared the extent of liberty in their society not with the Lockean ideal but with the extent of liberty in other contemporary or historically known societies. From this perspective there was no doubt that the Americans of 1776 were remarkably free. Even the slaves, servants, women, and children of America enjoyed positions superior to those held by similar classes in other lands and other times. And surely a land in which more than 10 percent of the population owned property and had a voice in the government was a wonder in an age when the civilized world was ruled by hereditary monarchs and property ownership was a prerogative of aristocrats. Even in England, where the political liberty of the early eighteenth century had made her people the envy of Europe, no more than 25 percent of "the active male population" had voted in even the freest parts of the kingdom—and after the first third of the century even this electorate had dwindled. Yet, to quote J. H. Plumb, "This was England's vast singularity, a unique situation amongst the major powers of the world."

Surely the gap that separated American society from the Lockean ideal was no more impressive than that which separated colonial American society from the societies of Europe. If freedom had a home anywhere in the world in the year 1776 it was in the new Untied States of America. But if "democracy" implies government by consent of the governed or at least by consent of a majority of those governed and not merely of an adult white male elite, then those historians from Bancroft to Brown who have described American society of the mid-eighteenth century as "democratic" are simply wrong. The opinion of Carl Becker and many others that colonial governments "did in a rough and ready way, conform to the kind of government for which Locke furnished a reasoned foundation" is vastly overstated. And the attempts of the New Left history to view the American Revolution "from the bottom up" will be superficial so long as "the bottom" is conceived in a way that still excludes the majority of the population.

7

The Generation Conflict Reconsidered:
Raising Adolescents in Vermont

RANDOLPH ROTH

● *There is no more awkward period in life than that between the onset of puberty and the attainment of full adulthood. Falling approximately between the ages of twelve and twenty-one, adolescence is a time when young people seek gradual emancipation from family rules and try to find an independent place in the community. The transition is rarely easy and is complicated by sexual changes and by powerful social pressures.*

Conflicts with demanding parents did not begin in the 1990s or even in the twentieth century, however. As Randolph Roth reminds us in an essay about adolescence two hundred years ago, few parents have ever known what to make of their teenage children, and few children have ever known what to make of their parents. Contemporary readers will probably be surprised to learn that religious young persons were criticized if their theological views and practices were not in accord with those of their mothers and fathers. But they will not be surprised to discover that the harder the parents pushed, the more the youngsters resisted.

Vermonters take great pride in their eighteenth-century revolutions against Yorker tyranny and the British Empire, and well they should. The society they created was more democratic than any other society formed during the Age of Revolution. Vermonters dedicated themselves wholeheartedly to the principles of freedom, equality, and opportunity. They adopted suffrage for men of all races, no matter how rich or how poor. They embraced religious toleration. They abolished slavery, eschewed discriminatory racial laws, and granted both men and women

Adapted from *The Democratic Dilemma: Religion, Reform, and the Social Order in the Connecticut River Valley of Vermont, 1791–1850*, pp. 46–54.

unprecedented rights to dissolve abusive marriages. They fostered private enterprise and promoted literacy. Nowhere did more families own their own shops and farms. Nowhere did more men and women know how to read and write. And nowhere were citizens better informed about political and social issues.

Today, however, Vermonters have largely forgotten the troubles that democracy caused their forebears. Most people (including many historians) think of Vermonters postrevolutionary era as a period of relative calm, when Vermonters prospered amid the freedom and opportunity of New England's revolutionary frontier. Few people realize that Vermont's struggle for independence and statehood marked only the beginning of Vermont's revolution and that the state would remain in turmoil for another half-century. Democracy, it seems, created as many problems as it solved.

One of those problems was the difficulty pious, churchgoing parents (who comprised the majority of parents in early Vermont) had controlling and disciplining adolescents in postrevolutionary Vermont. Of course, devout New England parents had always had their share of difficulties with young adults. But as Vermont's revolution unfolded, young people became more contrary and assertive. They got into serious mischief, experimenting with alcohol, tobacco, gambling, and sex. Young people also had difficulties transforming youthful religious zeal into mature piety. Vermont parents tried to deal with these problems straightforwardly, doubling their efforts to supervise, discipline, and convert the young, Despite exhortations to righteousness, however, they could not always bring even penitent youths to give up their irreverent attitudes toward certain sins. Nor could they moderate the intense outbursts of moral fervor and religious conviction that occurred at intervals throughout the period among young people. This was especially true if these outbursts got out of hand, and the young converted before reaching moral maturity or—what was worse—turned their perfervid enthusiasm against adult church members, condemning them for inconsistent doctrines and lack of piety.

Henry Stevens, a young Presbyterian farmer and innkeeper from Barnet, demonstrated how reputable, churchgoing young people frustrated churchgoing adults by at once repenting and delighting in their misbehavior. Stevens began a diary in 1811 at age twenty. He expressed regret about not going to meeting more often and lamented that he

lived in a place "inhabited by many young people and Devilish proud."
As he began to confess his misdeeds, however, Stevens often forgot to
be remorseful. His accounts of "boyish courtships" turned into "some
fine stories about some Lyman [New Hampshire] ladies" with whom
Henry and his friends used to dally. Later in the diary a regretful
account of youthful "scrapes" was interrupted by the entry of July 4,
1812. On that day Stevens and several young friends drank grog all
morning, offering seventeen patriotic toasts to their country "in less
than an hour," and marched to the town's Liberty Pole to offer seventeen more "in presence of a Large company. Done well."

How could a youth like Stevens, who in later years would preside
over the Caledonia County Temperance Society, simultaneously lament
and delight in his misdeeds? That question confounded churchgoing
adults throughout Vermont. They knew that human nature allowed
contrary impulses to reside together in weak souls, but they were reluctant to acknowledge that young people lived by two standards and
felt the continual pull of two lives and two sets of values.

Like all but the most otherworldly of their friends and relatives,
young Vermonters dwelt in at least two overlapping but distinct spheres
of social life, one within their churches and one outside in the community at large. Both spheres offered young people opportunities to
meet with neighbors, to flirt with and court the opposite sex, and to
honor their neighborhoods, communities, and country. Whereas one
centered on the church, however, on displaying moral and spiritual
maturity, on striving for unity, on observing Christian rituals and Christian holidays—in other words, on realizing New England's traditional
communal ideals—the other sphere centered on the tavern, on displaying physical strength and physical attractions, on working with
neighbors at raisings and bees, and on militia training and the Fourth
of July.

For men in particular, social life outside the churches revolved around
Vermont's many taverns. There people could congregate casually, gos-
sip, exchange business information, play cards or quoits, while away
inclement weather, celebrate personal triumphs, and mull over failures.
Of course, churches offered some of these attractions, and churches
were the only places where most women could congregate outside their
own homes. But churches were not as numerous as taverns. Nor could
churches keep the hours, offer the comforts, gather the range of neigh-

bors, or provide the atmosphere of easy camaraderie that taverns could. Most devout church members, not to speak of those who were not regular churchgoers, probably spent more time in taverns than in churches.

The sphere of social life outside the churches attracted more inhabitants, including women, to festive gatherings near the taverns. Sporting events were especially popular, even though they sanctioned ostensibly immoral behavior. A wild title match for the wrestling championship of St. Johnsbury, held by lantern light on a Saturday night, went on so late that the referee set back his watch as midnight approached, so that no one who stayed to see who won would "violate" the Sabbath. Horse racing on St. Johnsbury's main street was also popular; especially memorable to residents of that town was "the superior equestrienneship of Sally Tute ... who leaping on a barebacked horse called for a glass of stimulant and challenged any man of the crowd to overtake her." These contests drew admiring throngs who wanted to cheer for their neighborhood champions and celebrate the physical strength, horsemanship, courage, and tenacity so admired on the farming frontier.

Most frequent of all social events in Vermont were the various raisings and bees held to make light work of arduous physical tasks. At raisings, neighbors would come together to construct the frame for a building. The builder would purchase the building materials, send out the invitations, and supply reinforcing beverages. Under the influence of those beverages, workers often held contests to see who could perform the most daring acrobatic feat. In 1804, Ziba Tute (Sally's brother) assured himself a place in history when he stood on his head on the ridge pole of the new St. Johnsbury meetinghouse.

Bees gave Vermonters another chance to socialize. Quilting bees, spinning bees, chopping bees, and goose-plucking bees brought neighbors together, but apple-paring bees and corn-husking bees were the truly popular events of the season, particularly among young people. Both sexes were present at these gatherings, hard cider was plentiful, and "sparking" was encouraged. At husking bees the young men were allowed to kiss the young women whenever anyone came up with a red ear of corn.

The major events of the year in Vermont, however, were the patriotic holidays, the militia training days, and the Fourth of July. The militia would turn out in full force on these occasions, and liquor flowed freely. It was the custom for militia captains to "treat" their men from early morning on to sustain their strength and enthusiasm. As a result, unfortunately, accidental shootings were all too common. But intoxication allowed the men to level all distinctions among themselves and to celebrate their freedom as Americans. Getting drunk was a way for men to assert that as Americans they were free to do as they pleased and did not have to answer to anyone. According to historian William Rorabaugh, the urge to level distinctions and celebrate being as American was one of the reasons alcohol consumption rose to twice today's per capita rate in Vermont and in the nation at large in the years after the Revolution. Like patriotic songs and martial fervor, alcohol drew neighbors together and reinforced their sense of themselves as a defiant, liberated people.

Patriotic holidays served other purposes as well, particularly for the younger participants. Young men took the opportunity to show they could outdrink, outdrill, and outsloganize any patriot in Vermont. They took pride in having "done well" before friends, neighbors, and, most especially, the young women in the crowd.

This sphere of Vermont life, and that which centered on the church, were inhabited by much the same people. Most church members participated in the social life outside their churches, and most people were included to some degree in the circle of a church. The spheres were not necessarily inimical to each other. Christians young and old felt it possible to be pious and at the same time patriotic, good-natured, and neighborly to those outside their churches. Still, the spheres were distinct, and potential for antagonism was great, particularly as hard drinking and patriotic celebrations became more prevalent after the Revolution. In the church's circle, patriotism and good fellowship were not to be sought (and were indeed censured) as ends in themselves. Conversely, in the community sphere, where patriotism and good fellowship were valued as ends in themselves, rectitude and piety were admirable, but there was a point beyond which quibbling over the morality of a national policy or a neighbor's actions became bad manners.

These spheres posed a perpetual problem for pious adults, whose mission "to be in but not of the world" required them to participate in the social life outside their churches without becoming creatures of that life. The burden of that problem rested most heavily, however, on young Vermonters who were of an age to be attracted by the worldly sphere and who were all too ready to place camaraderie ahead of their duty to God. The young also had to face temptation without having mastered the subtle code that told adult church members when they had partaken enough of revelry, when they had shown enough charity toward human frailty, when they should chastise, when they should let matters pass.

Thus it was not strange that young people like Henry Stevens were doomed to repeat what in more sober moods they knew to be sins. Reconciling the demands of two worlds was a problem most young people were not equipped to deal with. As both a tavern owner and a promising Presbyterian, Stevens was forced to confront this problem head on, for he lived in two worlds, amidst piety and promiscuity, and knew the attractions of both.

Drinking and carousing among young people were not the only problems that confronted Christians. Fervent evangelicals also faced problems that had their source solely in the religious sphere—in particular, premature conversions. It was natural for evangelical parents to tell their children at an early age how Christ had died for their sins and how only conversion—the evangelical experience of being "born again" in which God fills the sinner's soul with saving grace—could bring peace and salvation. They meant to make children think seriously about God and to encourage them to consider and pray over their own souls. Such conversations produced the desired effect with surprising frequency. Children would try to improve their behavior and would sit down with their friends and play preacher to them—a common enough pastime before the games of cowboys and Indians or cops and robbers came into being. But at times young children were terrified. They hid during thunder and lightning storms for fear of dying before receiving God's grace. Some even made mild attempts at mortification of the flesh. Joel Winch, a young Hartland boy, recalled in his memoirs (written at the age of twenty-one) that he thought "much about dying" after such a conversation with his father, and would "git alone and cry."

Few parents knew what to make of children who were so desperately concerned about their souls. Joel Winch's parents, who were dedicated evangelical Congregationalists, had no wish to discourage their twelve-year-old son from seeking God, but they had hoped he would be a little older before he found Him. Joel did not yet know, they thought, what real sin or real religion was about. His mother tried to reclaim her son and, as Joel wrote later, "being a quick woman twitted me of my pretending to be good." She was none too gentle in her teasing, however, and Joel was crushed. "O how it sunk me down," he wrote. For three years he lived with the knowledge of his own sinfulness. When at last the Lord "broke into" Joel's soul at age fifteen, "the Congregationalist professors would take no notis of that which the Lord had don for me." It was not at that time customary for the church to accept young people as full members.

Joel did gain admittance to the church while still a teenager, as did a number of other young people, even though "it made some talk" among church members. Their elders feared that no matter how fervent the religious commitment the young professed, it was at bottom unreliable. At the age of fourteen, fifteen, or sixteen, young people, particularly those from farm, artisan, and laboring families, were entering the most difficult years of their lives. It was then that they would begin working, often for long periods away from home—the girls as domestics, the boys as farmhands or apprentices. Their wages would go toward augmenting the family income, building dowries, or, in the case of males, toward saving for a farm or a shop. Once they reached the age of twenty-one, young people were responsible for themselves and could "journey" wherever they wished to find suitable employment. Until then, however, their parents controlled their destinies.

It was the prevailing notion among Christian parents that responsible relatives, neighbors, and fellow‹church members handled young people better than did parents, because they did not face rebellion against specifically parental authority and because they were not reluctant to administer strict discipline out of the "false" love that sometimes prevented parents from correcting their children. Putting children out was not always a solution to disciplinary problems, however. There is little evidence that masters and mistresses actually had any less trouble than parents in governing young people. Then, too, even when parents were careful in their selection of an employer, the moral and spiritual lives of their children were sometimes neglected. Masters and mistresses might prove less warm toward the church than parents expected and allow their wards to stay home on the Sabbath or to strike up friendships with freethinkers. That was certainly true for Joel Winch, who flirted briefly with deism while working a season for an easy-going, free-thinking farm family. Under these circumstances young converts could quickly become backsliders.

The greatest problem for those who converted at a young age, however, was the temptation to cast off religion for a while and return to carefree, reckless ways. A few truly rebelled, indulging in drunkenness or fornication; others sought release in flirtation, pranks, or vandalism. Upon his return from journeying in the fall of 1800, Joel Winch fought with his parents and fell headlong into sin. He stayed out nights, leaving his parents to fear that he had compromised several young women in the neighborhood. In fact he and his friends were trying to start a witchcraft scare. They opened people's doors, made "all manner of noises," threw carts down wells, and put hogs in cow pens and cows in hog pens. Joel grew "more hardened in sin, more bald in Deviltry, more subtle in my plans, more engaged to presew what I undertook. I was afraid of nothing but Jestis." The seriousness of what he was doing did not strike him until he tried to seduce a young Baptist girl at a party and was repulsed. Her righteous rejection of him made him realize that he had become an ally of the Devil. In his own defense, he protested that he was not as bad as some of his friends. He did not dance, swear, or play cards, for he knew he "could not have the name of being religious" if he did so.

Joel's behavior was typical of many young converts who backslid. They behaved frivolously or wickedly, but were careful not to do anything that would injure their churches. Their sins were committed in secret and were usually minor, having to do with wasting time, gossiping, daydreaming about parties and courting, or fishing when there was work to be done (one young man confessed to catching 1,117 fish in two years). They suffered remorse periodically and rededicated themselves to Christ for weeks or even months, only to lapse again. Unable to live in two worlds at once, they traversed the cycles of sin and salvation.

Even when young people turned to Christ for good, they often confounded their friends, relatives, and congregations with rigorous searches for doctrinal truth and purity. They could do so privately, or they could do so openly and aggressively. Unwilling to confront the leaders of her church, or perhaps merely loath to make trouble, Lois Leverett of Windsor decided secretly that predestination and infant damnation were unscriptural foolishness. She also covertly rejected the evangelism of her Congregationalist forbears. In religion, as in love, she would not allow herself to be "smitten," and she opined that Windsorites caught up in the frenzy of a revival in 1810 were "almost crazy," adding that the revivalists "work too much upon the passions of the people." A voracious reader, she thought deeply about religious issues and had a clear sense of her own sinfulness, but shrank from discussing religion with the pious Mrs. Niles, whose submissive acceptance of the contradictions implicit in faith made her uneasy. She relied strongly on intellect to resolve religious questions; after all, she wrote, "the design of religion was not to bewilder, but enlighten our understandings and the plea of ignorance will not avail us." Not to exercise the intellect on any matter would result, she felt, in a "relapse into feminine style."

There were a great many young people in Vermont who not only rejected their parents' faith but went so far as to leave their parents' churches—particularly Congregationalist, Baptist, and Presbyterian churches, which adhered to New England's traditional ideals—over some difference in scriptural interpretation or social style. Lois Leverett, finding Windsor's Old South Congregational church insufficiently enlightened and genteel, joined the Episcopalians as an adult. Twenty-year-old Elias Smith of South Woodstock, distressed at not finding the Baptist doctrines he learned as a child supported by the Bible, demanded that open discussion of complex theological questions be allowed in his church. When his request was denied, he quit to found an egalitarian denomination, later known as the Christian Church, that would allow honest disagreements among sincere Christians.

Joel Winch likewise left his parents' church, when he decided it lacked the dignified, quiet, holy manner of Methodist prayer meetings. When its council ordered him to "come out from among" the Methodists "and be separate and tutch not the unclean thing," Joel determined "to stand fast in the liberty whare in Christ had made me free." He asked embarrassing doctrinal questions in church meetings and rallied support for a policy of granting letters to members wishing to join competing evangelical churches. The minister pressed for Joel's excommunication. He was hurt by Joel's charges that he was "prejudiced" and felt betrayed by the righteous, unyielding insurgency of a youth he had sheltered and supported even in his darkest times. But the majority voted to give Joel his letter. The outraged minister and his supporters withdrew to form a more orthodox Congregational church. Joel later heard that the minister had "told som of his friends about a Dream that he had one night (viz) that he had a Snake that he had brought up in his bosom and it bit him but his wife was friendly to it &c. This he called J. W." The minister learned what an intense, zealous youth could do to a ministry and a church.

Backsliding and overzealousness presented enduring problems for Christians and their communal ideals. In part, of course, the problem was that young people were just that—young and immature. They had few of the attachments of adulthood that provided a firm basis for social, moral, and spiritual maturity: a spouse, a household, a shop or farm, respectable friends, and a commitment to the community and its values. It took time to acquire such connections and commitments. Young Vermonters remained half in and half out of the adult world at least until their mid-twenties or early thirties.

After the Revolution, adult church members in Vermont deliberately chose to let the young mature in their own good time. In a radical departure from the ways of their fathers, they decided not to subject the young to anything more than gentle moral suasion. Moderate Calvinists abandoned efforts to use church councils to discipline the young by the 1790s, the Woodstock Congregationalists in 1783 being the last to exclude baptized nonmembers from the watch and care of the church. In addition, evangelical churches no longer required that applicants for admission confess past sins, except when the sins had been committed so recently as to place the sincerity of the person's change of heart in doubt. Only the Scottish Presbyterians in Barnet and Ryegate continued the practice of confessing sins beyond 1810, because they had brought it with them from Scotland in the 1790s, and all but one of their churches would soon stop.

Most important, evangelicals decided after the Revolution not to encourage or press for youthful conversions. The data on ages at conversion for males show that even during revivals, the typical convert was well into maturity in this period and far older than typical converts during southern New England's Great Awakening of the eighteenth century. Eighty percent of new female members of Congregationalist and Baptist churches were married by the time they entered the church. (The Scottish Presbyterians in Barnet differed; among them the mean age at conversion remained below thirty prior to 1815.) Church members did not censure or disregard all youthful conversions, for they believed that God elected souls when He pleased; still, they were wary of them. Several churches had to vote down, as scripturally unsound, efforts to deny admission to converts solely on the basis of their youth.

The retreat spread as pious adults began grudgingly to tolerate a greater range of excesses, particularly by young people, on public occasions. They issued no audible protests against the continuation of the St. Johnsbury wrestling match into the Sabbath. They refrained from condemning the rowdiness among young people that accompanied the raising of that town's meetinghouse. Members of one church actually sided against their minister in favor of several young converts who had "returned to their sports, carousing, and dancing," maintaining "that abstinence from mirthful recreation could not be expected of those who were in the heat and vigor of youth." A new balance of power had been struck between adult church members and their young and potential members.

There were now religious and political movements in Vermont that were hostile to the traditional Calvinist faiths and communal ideals that most adults embraced, and pious parents recognized that they could drive the young into those movements if they pressed them too hard or if, on the other hand, they failed to take them seriously. That was precisely what happened to Lois Leverett, Elias Smith, and Joel Winch. Alternately pressured and chaffed by their elders, they were driven further away from their parents' traditional faiths. Parents' problems were only compounded, according to historian William Gilmore, by the dramatic increase in literacy and reading in postrevolutionary Vermont. Young people now had ready access to unorthodox books and periodicals of every stripe.

In addition to there being new alternatives available, the attitudes of young people seemed to have undergone a change. Relative to southern New England, workers were in great demand in Vermont and opportunities for marriage and for independent proprietorship were plentiful. The young considered their futures secure. Therefore they may have been truly less careful of their reputations than before. It is also possible that the Revolution compounded the problems of adult Christians by leading young people to confuse their right to hold their own religious and political opinions with their ability to arrive at opinions that were as valid as those of their elders. Young people had on occasion challenged the beliefs of authorities in southern New England before the Revolution, but on a less widespread basis.

The revolution and migration to New England's northern frontier had thus destabilized relationships between parents and adolescents in Vermont in ways adult Christians had not foreseen. Pious adults, particularly those who were members of New England's traditional Calvinist churches, believed it would be easier to preserve traditional values on New England's revolutionary frontier. However, in Vermont they found themselves confronting the inescapable dilemma of democratic life: how to preserve order, morality, deference, and hierarchy in a society formally committed to freedom, equality, tolerance, and opportunity. It was not until after 1815 that adult church members began to address this dilemma successfully, at least where young people were concerned, and even then their success was due more to changing economic circumstances than to any imaginative new measure they tried. An economic decline reduced opportunities for marriage and self-employment, thereby altering the balance of power between generations. Since success in an increasingly competitive economy depended on a reputation for reliability and restraint, young people were forced to abide by stricter standards. Finding their children more tractable, parents intensified their efforts to control and discipline them.

The generational conflicts of the first postrevolutionary years still bear witness, however, to the dramatic effects of democracy on a democratic people. Vermont's revolution not only created an independent state; it transformed a society.

8

Society and Republicanism: America in 1787

JAMES A. HENRETTA

● *Unlike the situation in Nazi Germany, where each military officer swore a personal oath of allegiance to Adolf Hitler, newly commissioned officers in the armed forces of the United States do not swear allegiance to the President, or to Congress, or even to the nation itself. Rather, they promise loyalty to a piece of paper, to a document drawn up at the Federal Constitutional Convention at Philadelphia in 1787, to the Constitution of the United States. The concise document consists only of a preamble, seven articles, and twenty-three amendments; its very brevity gives it power. Indeed, the constitution is remarkable in that it is revered by persons on both the extreme right and the extreme left of the political spectrum.*

As Professor James A. Henretta of the University of Maryland notes in the following essay, Americans were as divided by gender, race, and class in 1787 as they would be two centuries and more later. And then, as now, they were united by their constitution and their republican ideology even as they debated the meaning of liberty and equality.

"In all times," John Winthrop told the first Puritan migrants to the Massachusetts Bay colony in 1630, "some must be rich, some poor, some high and eminent in power and dignity, others mean and in subjection." A century and a half later his descendant James Winthrop likewise pointed to the power of the rich and well-born. "Every society naturally divides itself into classes," he wrote in 1788, and men who compose "the *natural aristocracy* ... will command a superior degree of respect.'" John Winthrop praised rule by the privileged few, but his descendant condemned it. In 1788 James Winthrop emerged as a

Reprinted from *This Constitution*, No. 15, Summer, 1987.

leading Massachusetts Anti-Federalist. He opposed ratification of the Philadelphia Convention because its system of "government is so constituted as to admit but few to exercise to the powers of it." In his eyes, it did not provide "for a genuine and fair representation of the people."

This dialogue between the Winthrops underlines the radical nature of the American Revolution. The repudiation of British rule ended the traditional colonial social and political order. The Declaration of Independence spoke of human equality, of the right of all people to enjoy "life, liberty, and the pursuit of happiness." Ordinary Americans quickly used their new-found freedom. In 1778 voters in James Winthrop's Massachusetts rejected a state constitution proposed by the Assembly. "Said Constitution and Form of Government," the residents of the small western town of Greenwich explained,

> Entirely Divests the good People of this State of Many of the Privileges which God and Nature has Given them . . . and [gives] away that Power to a few Individuals, which ought forever to remain with the People. . . .

The republican doctrine of popular sovereignty placed ultimate authority in the hands of "the People." But who were "the People"? Did "the People" include women as well as men? Black slaves as well as free whites? Did the republican doctrines of political liberty and legal equality imply social equality as well?

Between 1776 and 1789 Americans passionately debated these questions. The fate of the revolution—and the republican experiment—seemed to hang in the balance. This extraordinary intellectual and political ferment stemmed in part from the contradictions within republican ideology. Some Americans gave an "aristocratic" definition to republicanism; they championed rule by the "natural aristocracy." Other citizens argued for a "democratic" republic characterized by greater legal and political equality. The harsh economic conditions of the 1780s increased social tensions and raised the stakes of this debate. The resulting political factionalism led to the writing of Philadelphia Constitution. These ideological and economic conflicts likewise shaped the debates over ratification. In particular, they explain Madison's astute analysis of social and political factions in *Federalist* No. 10.

REPUBLICANISM

Europeans were especially conscious of the relationship between the social order and republicanism. In his famous *Letters from an American Farmer* (1782), the French essayist Hector St. John de Crevecoeur explained that Europe was ruled by "great lords who possess everything, and a herd of people who have nothing." In America, historical development had eroded the foundations of traditional hierarchical society; here, there "are no aristocratical families, no courts, no kings, no bishops...." Europeans also pointed out that the American Revolution had instituted legal equality, further undermining social privilege and hierarchical authority. "The law is the same for everyone both as it protects and as it punishes," one visitor noted. "In the course of daily life everyone is on the most perfect footing of equality."

Like James Winthrop, Europeans were well aware that legal equality had not prevented the formation of social classes in the United States. "Wealth, power and higher education rule over need and ignorance," one visitor declared bluntly. Yet class divisions in America differed from those in Europe. The colonies had lacked—and the republican state constitutions prohibited—a legally privileged class of nobles. The absence of an aristocracy of birth encouraged many Americans to seek upward mobility and to create class divisions based on achievement. "In Europe to say of someone that he rose from nothing is a disgrace and a reproach," an aristocratic Polish visitor explained in 1798. "It is the opposite here. To be the architect of your own fortune is honorable. It is the highest recommendation."

Some Americans disagreed. Many Patriot leaders held "aristocratic-republican" values. These men and women preferred a society based on inherited wealth and family status. They questioned the wisdom of a social order based on equality of opportunity and financial competition. During the War many small-scale traders had reaped windfall profits from military supply contracts and sharp dealing in scarce commodities. "Fellows who would have cleaned my shoes five years ago, have amassed fortunes, and are riding in chariots," complained Boston's James Warren in 1779. Such envious sentiments were echoed by established families who wished to preserve their social and political dominance. Many American political leaders likewise lamented the demands for political equality generated by the Revolution. "Depend upon it, Sir," the aristocratic-republican John Adams declared in a private letter, "it is dangerous... to alter the qualifications of voters." If property qualifications for voting were lowered, he warned,

> there will be no end to it. New claims will arise; women will demand a vote; lads from twelve to twenty-one will think their rights not enough attended to; and every man who has not a farthing, will demand an equal voice with any other, in all the acts of state.

The result would be "to confound and destroy all distinctions and prostrate all ranks to one common level." Like John Winthrop, John Adams still believed that some men were high and eminent, while others were lowly and should be in subjection.

WOMEN AND THE FAMILY

Nonetheless, republican ideology challenged all social privilege, even the patriarchal relations of power within the family. Previously, religious writers had accorded preeminent authority to the male head. "The Husband is to rule his Family and Wife...," Boston minister Benjamin Wadsworth had declared in *The Well-Ordered Family* (1712). "Wives submit your selves to your own Husbands, be in subjection to them." In 1776, Abigail Adams questioned this system of patriarchal authority. She urged her husband John and the other men in the Continental Congress to "Remember the Ladies, and be more generous to them than your ancestors [were]." "We know better than to repeal our Masculine system," the future president replied with jocular condescension, "in Practice you know we are the subjects. We have only the name of Masters."

In fact, legal rules ensured male dominance in the new republican family. Statutes enacted by state legislatures perpetuated traditional English common law restrictions on married women. William Blackstone, the famous English jurist, had pointed out that under common law, "the very being or legal existence of the woman... during marriage is incorporated and consolidated into that of the husband." This legal condition of "coverture" limited the rights of married women to own property, to sue, or to make contracts and wills. These common law rules deprived American women of most legal rights until the 1840s, when many state legislatures passed Married Women's Property Acts. Even then, less severe forms of legal inferiority restricted women's lives through most of the twentieth century.

Yet "democratic-republican" ideology encouraged demands for the legal emancipation of women even as republican practice denied them. In 1779, Judith Sargent Murray of Gloucester, Massachusetts, composed an essay "On the Equality of the Sexes" and published it in 1790. Murray stressed the importance of mutuality in marriage: "Mutual esteem, mutual friendship, mutual confidence, *begirt about by mutual forbearance*." Similar sentiments were widespread among young, well-educated, upper-class women. They tried to reconcile the republican doctrine of equality with the cultural reality of female subordination. "I was never of opinion that the pursuits of the sexes ought to be the same," seventeen-year old Eliza Southgate of Maine wrote to a male cousin, "each [sex] ought to have a separate sphere of action." "Yet to cultivate the qualities with which we are endowed [she continued] can never be called infringing the prerogatives of man." "The men say we have no business" with politics, Eliza Wilkinson of South Carolina complained, "but I won't have it thought that because we are the weaker sex as to bodily strength we are capable of nothing more than domestic concerns. They won't even allow us liberty of thought, and that is all I want."

A few American public leaders responded positively to female demands for greater equality, but usually with male needs in mind. In his *Thoughts on Female Education* (1787), the Philadelphia physician Benjamin Rush advocated the intellectual training of women, so they would "be an agreeable companion for a sensible man." Rush and other men of affairs likewise praised "republican mothers" who instructed "their sons in the principles of liberty and government."

Ultimately, the concept of "republican motherhood" altered the character of the family and of American society. The main impetus came from religion. Beginning in the 1790s, Christian ministers celebrated women's role as moral educators. "Preserving virtue and instructing the young are not the fancied, but the real 'Rights of Women'," the Reverend Thomas Bernard told the Female Charitable Society of Salem,

Massachusetts. "Give me a host of educated pious mothers and sisters," echoed Thomas Grimké, a South Carolina minister,

> and I will do more to revolutionize a country, in moral and religious taste, in manners and in intellectual cultivation than I can possibly do in double or triple the time, with a similar host of men.

Grimké did not exaggerate. Women played a central role in the Second Great Awakening (1790–1830), the evangelical revivals that made Christianity an important part of the emerging American national character. Many married women now used their moral position as "guardians of virtue" to achieve a position of near-equality within the home. Women trained in religious academies entered the paid work force as teachers, while other women actively campaigned for social reform and for women's rights. Republican ideology and religious idealism had transformed the traditional cultural rules governing the status of women in American society.

SLAVERY AND PROPERTY

Democratic-republicanism and Christian idealism also threatened the institution of slavery, a prime feature of the American legal order. In 1787, no fewer than 750,000 blacks (20 percent of the entire population of the United States) were held in hereditary bondage. But now their servile status was the subject of political debate. In 1784, Virginia Methodists condemned slavery, using both religious and republican arguments. They declared that slavery was "contrary to the Golden Law of God on which hang all the Law and Prophets, and the unalienable Rights of Mankind, as well as every Principle of Revolution."

These arguments laid the intellectual basis for black emancipation in the northern states, where there were relatively few slaves. By 1784, Massachusetts, Pennsylvania, Connecticut, and Rhode Island had either abolished slavery or provided for its gradual end. Two decades later, all states north of Delaware had adopted similar legislation.

The abolition of slavery in the North exposed additional contradictions within republican ideology. American patriots had fought the

British not only for their lives and liberty, but also for the rights of private property. Indeed, the three values were closely linked in republican theory. The Massachusetts Constitution of 1780 protected every citizen "in the enjoyment of his life, liberty, and property, according to the standing laws." The Virginia Bill of Rights went further; it asserted that the "means of acquiring and possessing property" was an inherent right. Like John Adams, the authors of most state constitutions believed that only property owners could act independently and restricted voting rights to those with freehold estates. For them, republicanism was synonymous with property rights.

There was the rub. For slaves were property. The abolition of slavery in Massachusetts in 1784, James Winthrop pointed out, meant that "a number of citizens have been deprived of property formerly acquired under the protection of law." To protect white property rights, the Pennsylvania Emancipation Act of 1780 did not free slaves already in bondage. The Act awarded freedom only to slaves born after 1780—and then only after they had served their mothers' masters for twenty-eight years. In fact, American republican ideology was ultimately derived from ancient Greece and Rome and was fully compatible with slavery. "As free men," the poet Euripedes had written of his fellow citizens in the ancient Greek republics, "we live off slaves."

This aristocratic-republican combined with economic self-interest to prevent the emancipation of slaves in the South. Slaves accounted for 30 to 60 percent of the southern population and represented a huge financial investment. Most southern political leaders were slaveowners, and they actively resisted emancipation. In 1776, the North Carolina legislature condemned the actions of Quakers who freed their slaves as "highly criminal and reprehensible."

Understandably, southern blacks sought freedom on their own. Two white neighbors of Richard Henry Lee, a signer of the Declaration of Independence, lost "every slave they had in the world," as did nearly "all of those who were near the enemy." More than five thousand blacks left Charleston, South Carolina, with the departing British army. Other American slaves bargained wartime loyalty to their patriot masters for a promise of liberty. Using a Manumission Act passed in 1782, Virginia planters granted freedom to more than ten thousand slaves.

Yet black emancipation in the South was doomed even before the expansion of cotton production gave slavery a new economic rationale.

The rice planters of Georgia and South Carolina strongly opposed emancipation throughout the revolutionary era. Their demands at the Philadelphia Convention resulted in a clause (Article I, Section 9) that prevented Congress from prohibiting the transatlantic slave trade until 1808. By that time, southern whites had imported an additional 250,000 Africans—as many slaves as had been brought into all the mainland colonies between 1619 and 1776.

Nonetheless, republican ideology and evangelical Christianity profoundly affected the lives of many black Americans. By 1787, thousands of blacks in the Chesapeake states had joined Baptist and Methodist churches. The Christian message promoted spiritual endurance among some blacks and prompted others to resist slavery by force. In 1800, Martin and Gabriel Prosser plotted a slave uprising in Richmond, Virginia. They hoped to capture the governor and to seize the arms stored in the state capital. Their "cause was similar to the Israelites'," Martin Prosser told his followers.

> I have read in my Bible where God says, if we worship him, we should have peace in all our land and five of you shall conquer a hundred, and a hundred of you a hundred-thousand of our enemies.

White Virginians nipped the insurrection in the bud, but it renewed their fears about the democratic implications of republicanism. During the War, slaves had "fought [for] freedom merely as a good," St. George Tucker suggested, but now they "claim it as a right." "Liberty and equality have brought this evil upon us," a letter to Virginia *Herald* argued following Gabriel's Rebellion, for such doctrines are "dangerous and extremely wicked in this country, where every white man is a master, and every black man is a slave."

ARTISANS AND FARMERS

Democratic-republicanism appealed not only to women and blacks but also to artisans and yeomen farmers. These men formed the vast majority of the voting population. Prior to Independence, they usually elected leading landowners or merchants to political office and deferred to their superior social status. Religious conflicts during the First Great

Awakening (1740 to 1765) partially undermined these deferential attitudes. As Baptist leader Isaac Backus explained in 1768, "the common people [now] claim as good a right to judge and act for themselves in matter of religion as civil rulers or the learned clergy."

Political revolution translated these anti-elitist sentiments into ringing affirmations of popular power. In 1776, the voters of Mecklenberg County told their delegates to the North Carolina Constitutional Convention to "oppose everything that leans to aristocracy, of power in the hands of the rich and chief men exercised to the oppression of the poor." The new state constitutions dramatically increased the political influence of ordinary citizens. Lower property qualifications for voting gave urban artisans greater power; and reappointment of the state legislatures on the basis of population gave greater representation to ordinary western farmers.

The results were dramatic. Before 1776, only 17 percent of northern assemblymen were "middling" farmers and artisans, those with tax assessments of less than £2,000; by the 1780s these social groups constituted no less than 62 percent of the representatives. The democratic-republican thrust of the American revolution had undermined the hierarchical social order of John Winthrop and had created state governments in which, as James Winthrop put it, there could be "a genuine and fair representation of the people."

Democratic-republican demands for greater equality contributed to the intense political and constitutional struggles of the 1780s, as did an overcrowded agricultural economy. Thousands of white tenant farmers yearned to escape the hierarchical rural society of the Chesapeake states, while landlords sought to keep them at home. "Boundless settlements," a letter in the Maryland *Gazette* warned in 1785, will open "a door for our citizens to run off and leave us, depreciating all our landed property and disabling us from paying taxes."

A rapidly growing population pressed on landed resources in New England as well. In the typical town of Kent, Connecticut, one hundred fathers and 109 adult sons lived on the town's 103 farmsteads. Previous generations of Kent parents had subdivided their lands to provide for their many offspring; now their small farms would support only a single heir. Yeomen families faced declining prospects and even the loss of their land. "The *mortgage of our farms*, we cannot think of," the farmers of Conway, Massachusetts protested,

to be *tenants* to *landlords*, we know not who, and pay rent for
lands *purchased with our money*, and converted from howling
wilderness, into the fruitful fields, by the *sweat of our brow*,
seems . . . truly shocking.

To provide for their families in these hard times, many rural residents
turned to household manufactures. In the small village of Hallowell,
Maine, the daughters of Martha Ballard learned to weave, as did most
of the town's young women. The resulting surge in household cloth
production dramatically reduced American dependence on British manufactures. During the Revolution, artisans in the town of Lynn, Massachusetts, had likewise raised their output of shoes. By 1789, the town
turned out 175,000 pairs of shoes each year, and by 1800, no fewer
than 400,000 pairs. The efforts of these women and men laid the
foundation for American self-sufficiency and prosperity. As Alexander
Hamilton noted proudly in 1792, the countryside was "a vast scene of
household manufacturing . . . in many cases to an extent not only sufficient for the supply of the families in which they are made, but for
sale, and even, in some cases, for exportation."

Merchant entrepreneurs such as Ebenezer Breed of Lynn, Massachusetts, directed many of these rural enterprises. They employed farm
women and children to sew the soft uppers of shoes or to spin yarn,
and rural males to weave cloth for market sale. Their entrepreneurial
activities helped many Americans to maintain their standard of living
during the commercial and agricultural recession of the 1780s.

This new capitalist system of production for market also increased
economic conflicts. Rural workers and merchant entrepreneurs were
indispensable to each other, but their interests—like those of merchants
and farmers—were not always identical. Many backcountry farmers
went into debt to expand household production or provide farmsteads
for their children. As debts increased, so too did defaults and law suits.
The courts directed sheriffs to sell the property of bankrupt farmers
and artisans to pay merchant creditors and court costs.

Commercial debt had been a feature of American life since the 1760s.
"Mark any Clerk, Lawyer, or Scotch merchant," warned North Carolina farmer Herman Husband. "We must make these men subject to
the laws or they will enslave the whole community." Actually, merchants usually had the law on their side so, during the 1760s, Husband

and his followers intimidated judges, closed courts by force, and broke into jails to free their arrested leaders. Anti-merchant sentiment during the 1770s pushed forward the independence movement in Virginia, where Scottish traders had extended credit to more than 32,000 tobacco planters. And it appeared yet again in western Massachusetts in the 1780s. Between 1784 and 1786, the Hampshire County Court heard 2,977 debt cases. Angry Massachusetts farmers defended their property from seizure by closing the courts.

Farmers—like women and slaves—now used the democratic-republican heritage of the American revolution to justify their actions. They met in extra-legal conventions and spoke of the "Suppressing of tyrannical government." Led by Revolutionary War veteran Captain Daniel Shays, these farmers eventually rose in outright rebellion. As the Massachusetts aristocratic-republican Fisher Ames lamented, "The people have turned against their teachers the doctrines which were inculcated in the late revolution."

The republican ideology of liberty and equality had raised the expectations of a majority of "the People" while leaving them in an inferior social position. In 1787, American women were still legally subordinate to males, and most blacks were still legally enslaved. Legally-mandated taxes and court proceedings threatened the livelihoods of thousands of yeomen farmers and artisans. Yet "the People" also included lawyers like Ames and James Winthrop, established merchants like Bostonian James Warren, slaveowning planters like Thomas Jefferson, and shoe-industry entrepreneur Ebenezer Breed. As James Madison astutely argued in *Federalist* No. 10,

> A landed interest, a manufacturing interest, a mercantile interest, a moneyed interest, with many lesser interests, grow up of necessity in civilized nations, and divide them into different classes, actuated by different sentiments.

Madison's goal at the Philadelphia Convention had been to create a public arena in which this "variety of parties and interests" could pursue their own goals without invading "the rights of other citizens."

PARTICIPANTS AND SPECTATORS

Like James Winthrop, many Americans doubted that the Philadelphia Constitution represented the correct constitutional formula. The Constitution was ratified only by narrow majorities in the major states of Virginia (89 to 79), Massachusetts (187 to 168), and New York (30 to 27). Yet by July 4, 1788, the Constitution had become the supreme law of the land, and thousands of Philadelphians turned out for a celebratory parade. A band played "The Federal March," and a float carried a oversized framed reproduction of the Constitution itself.

The parade also demonstrated social and political divisions outlined in Madison's *Federalist* No. 10. Most of the five thousand participants marched not as individual republicans, but as members of distinct occupational or social groups. Farmers cast seed before them. Weavers operated a loom on their horse-drawn float, while printers ran a press. Behind the floats marched groups of artisans and professionals—barbers, hatters, lawyers, clergymen, and political leaders. Most blacks, women, and white laborers watched from the sidewalks.

All of these Americans joined together to cheer their republican revolution and their new national constitution. But many remained as spectators, both of the parade and of the political process. And those citizens who participated did so with a heightened sense of their respective social identities and economic interests. The United States began its history with a society legally divided by gender and race, and with a polity divided by class position and economic interest.

Two hundred years later, Americans remain sharply divided by race and by economic and social inequalities, although united by their Constitution and their republican ideology. Now, as then, the meaning of liberty and equality remains the subject of intense debate and of political struggle.

9

American Catholics and the First Amendment, 1776–1840

PATRICK W. CAREY

• *Until John F. Kennedy served as president of the United States without turning the government over to the Vatican, many American Protestants viewed Catholicism as incompatible with constitutional liberties. Indeed, as late as the 1920s, Catholics were regarded not simply as communicants of an idolatrous church, but as citizens who placed their love and devotion to Rome above their allegiance to the United States. It was widely held that the pope was a political autocrat with a ravenous desire to extend his temporal as well as spiritual influence across the Atlantic Ocean. Wild rumors told of Protestant girls being held captive in convents, of Catholics gaining control of the strategic heights surrounding Washington, and of Knights of Columbus drilling at night and storing arms in the churches. Nor were those the only reasons that Catholic patriotism was suspect. According to some militants, Catholics were responsible for all three presidential assassinations up to that time and for 90 percent of the desertions in World War I. Skeptics were warned that Catholics could be manipulated by priests and reminded of traditional papal interference in the political affairs of Europe. Thus was the Catholic Church often painted as the deadly enemy of free institutions, to be opposed not so much for her religious beliefs as for her dark and deadly political machinations.*

In actuality, as Professor Patrick W. Carey of Marquette University reminds us in the following essay, nineteenth-century Catholics endorsed the first amendment separation of church and state, asking only that it apply to Protestants as well. They felt that the public schools were in fact Protestant

Reprinted from *The Pennsylvania Magazine of History and Biography*, 63 (July, 1989), 323–346, with permission of the editor.

> *schools, and that Catholic children should not be subjected to heretical propaganda. And they regarded their communion with the pope to be purely spiritual and have nothing to do with politics.*

The celebration of the bicentennial of the Constitution, and more specifically in 1989, of the Bill of Rights, demands that Americans reexamine the fundamental values they acknowledge in that document, even if they do not always practice them. Liberty is at the heart of the American value system and has become one of the principal sources of American identity. The First Amendment begins by protecting liberties relating to religion: "Congress shall make no law respecting an establishment of religion, or prohibiting the free exercise thereof." The primacy of religious liberty in the Bill of Rights was more than a literary convention. The bill's framers understood that in a religiously plural society both American identity and republican stability hinged on the free expression of religious beliefs. Religious minorities also appreciated that the liberties secured in the Constitution meant that they would enjoy safeguards against interference from the state, but that they also would have to compete in a voluntaristic religious environment for adherents. Such an arrangement promised a freedom, though, that might loosen religious ties. Perhaps more than any other group in the early republic, Catholics recognized, and wrestled with, the tensions between religious liberty at large and the need to preserve dogma and discipline within a church.

Catholics, like other religious groups in this country, have benefited from, contributed to, and supported in principle as well as in practice the American tradition of religious liberty and separation of church and state. "Nowhere," Elwyn A. Smith argued in 1972, "has the Roman Catholic Church created a more distinctive national policy of church-state relations than in the United States, yet without any breach with the fundamental Catholic tradition." By analyzing what some native mid-Atlantic and recent Irish immigrant American Catholics did between 1776 and 1840 to advance American liberties, what they said about their meaning, and how they reconciled what they did and said with Catholic beliefs, it becomes possible to chart with some precision the early rise and development of the distinctive American Catholic tradition regarding the first American liberties. Some politically active Catholic laity during those years participated in defining America's first liberties and later contributed to the expansion of civil liberties in some state constitutions. Articulate laity and clergy accepted both the non-establishment and free exercise clauses of the First Amendment on the grounds of experience, a republican philosophy of the state, and religious principles—not mere expediency. American Catholics periodically asserted, furthermore, that their support for American liberties was consistent with and not opposed to the authentic Catholic tradition, even though their positions conflicted with clearly articulated early nineteenth-century papal statements.

During the constitution-making period (1776–1791), Catholics were significantly conscious of the tentativeness of America's legislative movements toward general toleration and religious liberty. The Maryland priest John Carroll, although enthusiastic about the gradual extension of religious liberty in the country, was apprehensive about the full extension of those rights to American Catholics. As early as 1784, he acknowledged in a published defense of Catholic teachings that the country was "blessed with civil and religious liberty" and predicted that if Americans had the wisdom to preserve this liberty, the country "may come to exhibit a proof to the world, that general and equal toleration, by giving free circulation to fair argument, is the most effectual method to bring all denominations of christians to an unity of faith."

Carroll, however, also expressed to European correspondents his anxiety about the survival of the American experiments with religious liberty. In 1785 he told a Roman correspondent that he was not sure how long the most recent state acknowledgments of equal toleration would last for Catholics. Religious liberty was a new and revolutionary experiment, and it was on provisional ground as far as Catholics like Carroll were concerned. After 1791 the American Catholic minority grew uneasy about the fragile nature of religious liberty as they faced legal restrictions against Catholics in some state constitutions and the social and cultural intolerance of the "Protestant Crusade."

These circumstances alone make it easy to understand why American Catholics during these years accepted and worked for religious liberty and separation. They were a tiny minority of primarily English-speaking Catholics who were located along the eastern seaboard and who had their own memories of past religious oppression and even current reminders that constitutional religious liberty did not always mean cultural or social religious toleration. For these Catholics, past experience clearly demonstrated that unions of church and state had been detrimental to their own political, civil, and religious interests. John Carroll informed an English correspondent in 1785 that Catholics "have all smarted heretofore under the lash of an established church and shall therefore to [sic] on our guard against every approach towards it." Charles Carroll, Mathew Carey, and numerous others kept alive Catholic memories of the evil effects of established churches and what Carey called the horrors of bloody intolerance.

For Carey, "religious persecution is the real and genuine Antichrist." In the past, persecution had obtained a "glorious triumph over the spirit of Jesus" in Catholic Madrid, Anglican London, and Puritan Boston. It had been almost universal wherever any Christian sect was in the majority. The Quakers, according to Carey, "are almost the only body of Christians, who ever possessed power without persecuting their fellow Christians."

Enlightened Catholic laymen, like Charles Carroll and Carey, freely admitted and deplored the fact that Catholics in Europe had been and were guilty of the crime of religious persecution, even though they had no monopoly on it. In 1774 Carroll wrote: "I execrate ye intolerating spirit of ye Church of Rome, and of other Churches, for she is not singular in that." Whether in the hands of Protestants or Catholics, religious intolerance could produce "only martyrs or hypocrites." Carey, like many others, wanted to bury these past crimes "in eternal oblivion" and engage in mutual forgiveness. Religious persecution was a disorder of the past, and he did not want his own generation of American Catholics to be vilified and held responsible for the "cruelty of their ancestors." For Carey, persecution was a devastating historical practice, not a religious principle. Catholics as well as Protestants and Jews suffered under those practices which were inconsistent with natural rights and the gospel.

If experience had demonstrated the evil effects of established churches, it also had demonstrated the beneficial effects of religious toleration. American Catholic leaders like Bishops John Carroll, John England, and a host of lay and clerical elites periodically appealed with pride to the early Maryland Catholic tradition on religious toleration.

Until the Glorious Revolution, the argument went, Catholics and Protestants enjoyed religious liberty and lived together in social peace. After the American Revolution, the earlier tradition of general toleration was revived.

In 1783, eight years before the ratification of the First Amendment, John Carroll pointed out to a Roman correspondent the benefits of the American Revolution for American Catholics in particular. "You are not ignorant, that in these United States our Religious system has undergone a revolution, if possible, more extrordinary [sic], than our political one." Free toleration, if not full religious liberty, was allowed for all Christians in all states of the union, and in Pennsylvania, Delaware, Maryland, and Virginia Catholics were able to enjoy all civil rights. Such freedom, Carroll explained, was "a blessing and advantage" that Catholics had the duty to preserve and to improve.

Catholics tried to do just that. Prominent American Catholic laymen, motivated by a zeal for the public good as well as their own self-interests, helped initiate and extend legislation on religious liberty and separation at both the state and federal levels. Even moreso than Pennsylvania's, the eighteenth-century Maryland Catholic experience is particularly instructive in this regard. Charles Carroll was the most significant Catholic proponent of general toleration and religious liberty. In 1774 he defended the rights of Catholics to speak out on political matters in Maryland and protested the irrational system that made religious affiliation a civil disability. In 1776 he helped write the Maryland state constitution which provided for general religious liberty, but only for Christians.

Charles Carroll also signed the Declaration of Independence, an act which he later interpreted as the first step in a movement toward universal religious liberty. He told a friend in 1829 that, when he signed that document, he had in view "not only our independence of England but the toleration of all sects, professing the Christian Religion, and communicating to them all great rights." Carroll's 1829 recollection may not have been historically accurate, but it was consistent with his general perspectives.

Daniel Carroll of Maryland and his fellow Catholic Thomas Fitzsimons of Philadelphia were elected to the United States House of Representatives and took part in and approved the formation of the United States Constitution and the Bill of Rights. Although their contributions were not singularly significant, they did participate, more as American citizens than as Catholic laymen, in the establishment of religious liberty and separation of church and state. In 1789 Carroll was appointed to a congressional committee assigned to frame the First Amendment. He supported an amendment that would secure the equal rights of conscience and explicitly forbid any establishment of religion at the national level. Such an amendment, he asserted, would be the most helpful measure the Congress could enact to attach the American people to the federal government. He was not particularly concerned about the precise wording of the amendment as long as it secured the rights of conscience.

After the ratification of the Bill of Rights, a few American Catholic politicians expanded the meaning and application of religious liberty when they helped remove from some state constitutions clauses that had severely restricted civil rights for Catholics. The Catholic layman Francis Cooper (1764–1850), a Jeffersonian Republican, was elected to the New York State Assembly in 1806, but he refused to take the constitutional oath of office because, he claimed, it violated his religious freedom, requiring as it did a renunciation of foreign allegiance "in all matters ecclesiastical as well as civil."

Cooper's fellow parishioners at St. Peter's in New York City petitioned the legislature to remove the odious clause against Catholics, because it violated the liberal principle of the First Amendment and New York State's constitutional acknowledgment of equal religious liberty. The prescribed oath, they argued, subjected Catholics "to a religious test, to which their consciences are opposed" and which "operates upon them as an absolute disqualification" for office. Catholic allegiance to the bishop of Rome was purely spiritual and had nothing to do with American civil liberties. The petition succeeded. Once the odious clause was removed, Cooper took the revised oath and assumed his seat in the Assembly.

A North Carolina Catholic layman, Judge William Gaston (1778–1844), also helped remove legislative disabilities against Catholics. In 1835 he argued before the North Carolina Constitutional Convention for a "total abrogation of Religious Tests" from the state's constitution. The state's constitution declared that "no man who shall deny the being of God, or the truth of the Protestant religion, or the divine authority of either the old or New Testaments, or who shall hold religious principles incompatible with the freedom and safety of the State, shall be capable of holding any office or place of trust or profit, in the civil department within this State." Gaston asserted in opposition to this religious test that "anyone who is prohibited from certain civil rights because of the exercise of his religious opinions suffers a grievous wrong." Even if the clauses never had previously affected anyone, still they were tyrannical: "All unnecessary restraint on freedom of thought or action, is tyranny, and all unmeaning and inoperative restraint, folly." A majority of the state legislature considered Gaston's arguments for a "total abrogation" of the religious clauses and his support for religious freedom dangerously "latitudinarian." The legislature, however, voted to replace "Protestant" with "Christian" to provide room for Gaston and his fellow Catholics in public offices. It was not the "total abrogation" that Gaston had in mind, but, given the circumstances, it was the most he could obtain.

A few Catholics, although active in promoting their own rights to full religious liberty in this country, also lobbied publicly for the eradication of civil disabilities for all religious groups, not just for Catholics. Mathew Carey of Philadelphia and Bishop John England of Charleston, South Carolina, in particular, argued periodically that the principle of religious liberty was universal and should be universal in application. Both condemned the abominable persecution of the Jews throughout Christendom, abhorred Maryland's exclusion of Jews from office-holding, and called for a repeal of Maryland's legal restrictions against the Jews. Bishop England also supported the emancipation of Jews in England, Bavaria, Damascus, and Rhodes, and initiated or joined numerous committees in Charleston to promote these causes.

Catholics accepted neither the Protestant evangelical nor the exclusively rationalist arguments for religious liberty; nonetheless, they shared much with both traditions in the United States. Although Catholics accepted the individual's natural rights to liberty, their particular constellation of arguments for religious liberty was not exclusively based upon individualism nor autonomy in regard to religion. Revelation and reason combined to provide arguments for religious liberty in society and for a communal tradition in religion that respected the individual's rights within the context of a magisterial churchly tradition.

John Carroll was well aware, as he admitted in his private correspondence of 1784, that few in the Catholic communion outside of the United States had spoken out vigorously to support religious liberty. He wanted Catholic theologians in Europe to argue the case for universal toleration—as had Joseph Berington in England and Arthur O'Leary in Ireland. He supported the principle and practice of religious liberty and occasionally indicated the reasons for his support, but he never developed any systematic arguments. Bishop England gave the clearest American Catholic definition and defense of religious liberty. For him, it was "the right of every man to follow the dictates of his conscience in the belief of doctrines purely religious *without being subject, on that account,* to civil pains and disabilities." Catholic arguments for religious liberty were based upon experience, revelation, and reason.

The experience of religious liberty provided a powerful and perhaps widely shared Catholic argument for religious liberty. It operated like a self-evident principle upon most Catholics. Principles must be tested by their effects, the pragmatist would say, and American Catholics were pragmatists when it came to religious liberty. Experience demonstrated that religious liberty was beneficial not only for Catholics but for all in society. It achieved, in other words, *salus populi* (i.e., public peace and prosperity), the ultimate purpose of the state.

American Catholics also periodically invoked three traditional Christian principles to support American religious liberties. First, they had recourse to the traditional distinction between the spiritual and the temporal realms. The spiritual realm generally referred to the church's powers to provide means for eternal salvation. The temporal referred to the state's powers to provide for public peace, justice, and material prosperity. Catholics, like other Christians, found support for this traditional distinction in the Bible: "Give to Caesar the things that are Caesar's, and to God the things that are God's" (Matt. 22:21), and "My kingdom is not of this world" (John 18:36). Of the two realms, the spiritual was superior to the temporal. Christianity had refused to recognize the state's powers as ultimate. It placed God beyond and indeed over the power of the state, repeatedly asserting that it was better to obey God than man in cases of conflict between the two realms.

American Catholics also frequently appropriated the traditional Catholic principle of the freedom of the church (i.e., *libertas ecclesiae*) to justify their support for religious liberty and separation. The church, constituted by divine design, so the Catholic argument went, had been given its independence from the state, and, therefore, no state had the power to arrest from the church what God had given it.

The three traditional principles provided the general theoretical context for American Catholic arguments. The principles themselves and the biblical passages that supported them had been variously interpreted and applied in the long history of the Christian West. They were repeatedly used, for example, to defend the various unions of church and state throughout history. In the United States, however, these traditional principles began to be interpreted in new ways as the American experience itself became a testing ground where the principles were reinterpreted and reapplied. The ancient distinction between the spiritual and the temporal was applied to the American separation of church and state. The superiority of the spiritual reinforced the American constitutional view of the state. This superiority did not mean, as it had in some previous periods of Christianity, that the church was superior to the state in all things, but only in reference to the ultimate salvific end of humankind. The state had its own autonomy in reference to the temporal ends of human existence.

American Catholic constitutional views of the state, although reinforced by the three traditional principles, had their most immediate source in Enlightenment ideas. American Catholics, like other Americans, had been significantly influenced by Enlightenment ideas of natural rights and a compact view of the state. While still in Europe as a young priest, John Carroll, using natural rights language, spoke of the "idea of an original equality, or of the common rights of mankind" when criticizing the slavish dependence of the citizens he observed in some states in Europe. Whether Federalists or Jeffersonian Republicans, American Catholics accepted a constitutional view of the state, and that meant in particular that the state had no divinely established powers to determine heresy or to defend orthodoxy.

The state's powers were limited by the divinely constituted natural rights of conscience, by the spiritual constitution of the church, and by the people as the only source of political power. The U.S. Constitution, John England argued, explicitly acknowledged the government's incompetence "to legislate upon religion or morals, directly or indirectly." It simply had no power over opinion and religious persuasions. It protected the rights of individuals and minority religious groups—no matter what religious denomination was in a majority in the country. "If ninety-nine hundredths of the present population," England argued, "were to become Catholics to-morrow, they would be morally criminal did they exclude the remaining hundredth portion from any civil, or political, or religious right; and under our constitution the attempt would be usurpation, and therefore invalid."

Catholic apologists like England argued repeatedly that their acceptance of a constitutional view of the state was not inconsistent with their religious beliefs, as some Protestants had charged. In the past Catholics had lived under a variety of forms of government and had entertained various philosophies of the state. There was no such thing as an authentic Catholic doctrine of the state because there was no divine revelation on the subject. Catholics were free to live under and construct whatever philosophy of the state that the mind could devise. A constitutional view of the state, however, was consistent with Catholic principles and a Catholic understanding of revelation, even though it did not have its source in revelation.

A natural rights philosophy also informed the American Catholic view of religious liberty. The right to worship, John Hughes noted, was grounded in "a spiritual concern between man and his God" and that right, because it was inherent in nature, was indefeasible, inviolable, inalienable, and common to all men. "The rights of *conscience,* in their personal relation, are as inalienable as the rights of *memory;* and it is just as absurd to talk of 'surrendering' the one as the other." The prerogative of believing, *"as an act of the mind,* bids defiance of all *external power."* Demetrius Augustine Gallitzin, a Pennsylvanian like Hughes and a pastor of Loretto, argued in *A Defence of Catholic Principles* (1815) that Catholics as well as Protestants were agreed "in believing that no authority merely human possesses any right in controlling the consciences of men." The U.S. Constitution, unlike civil constitutions in many Protestant as well as Catholic countries, had simply acknowledged, not granted, that right.

Christian revelation, too, supplied Catholics with explicit arguments in support of religious liberty. Christian faith and church membership was of its very nature voluntary. In Catholic theology faith was indeed a gift of God's grace, but it was also a free act of human response. No temporal force should be used to change, promote, or sustain religious opinions. Christians, John England maintained, should follow the Jesus who "taught truth, and gained converts by persuasion." He used no temporal pains, penalties, or promises to communicate his truth to his followers. He used only spiritual means. And if the church itself should find anyone in error, it should follow Christ's example and "endeavor to reclaim him by argument and persuasion," not by force.

The Christian principle of universal charity was another reason for accepting religious liberty. In civil life, John England wrote, we should respect and love all persons, "forget the distinctions of Religion, and look upon every child of Adam as a brother." The unity of all humanity in one blood and the evangelical admonition to love one's neighbors imposed upon all citizens a duty to respect each person's God-given right to believe and to express what was considered true. Civil respect was not just a matter of putting up with one another, it was a positive Christian principle of love.

England also periodically appealed to an argument from Christian eschatology to demonstrate his acceptance of religious liberty. A society in which there was a mixture of religions was very much like the gospel parable of the wheat and the tares. Only God could distinguish between the two. In the time before His final judgment, therefore, Christians should live together in peace and love, and "leave the final judgment [about errors in matters of religion] always to God."

American Catholic support for religious liberty can sound very much like religious "indifferentism"—that is, the view that all religions were equal and that all religious doctrines were indeed relative. This was not the case. John Carroll and John England distinguished between religious liberty as a principle that should guide persons in civil life and a religious indifferentism that had no regard for doctrinal truth in religious life. The constitutional state had a duty to be perfectly neutral and indifferent to religious truth. The Christian, however, could never be neutral with regard to religious truth. The same creator who gave all humans the gift of liberty also gave them the duty to search for the truth and to preserve it when they found it. Although all Christians had the freedom to search for the grounds of their Christian beliefs, no Christian had the liberty to depart from what God had revealed. The Christian understanding of freedom, unlike the rationalist, was not based upon neutrality in the search for truth. John Carroll approvingly quoted the Baptist John Leland to argue that the Christian must be open to rational conviction in his or her search for the truth of doctrines and facts, but this did not mean that he or she had to be "absolutely indifferent to them, before he begins that inquiry." For the Christian, faith seeks understanding. Freedom of inquiry starts with a basic commitment to the truth that is in Christ. It is that truth, in turn, that makes the Christian free.

Liberty within religious life was not a license to believe whatever suited one's fancy or whatever was most useful. It was the means that led toward truth. Truth had to be based upon either the authority and testimony of God or the evidence of reason. Any religious person who maintained opinions for which he could show neither the evidence of revelation or reason was not acting responsibly. Catholics, like many other Christians of the era, had a supreme confidence in reason's ability to discover evidence for particular religious beliefs.

Enlightened Catholic apologists like Carroll and England argued that a reasonable search for the truth would lead individuals to accept the Catholic church as the true Christian church. Investigation of all the evidence, moreover, would demonstrate that the Catholic church alone had the divinely constituted means to judge infallibly between true and false Christian doctrines. This did not mean that Catholicism should have exclusive rights in the political and civil order. It meant that the determination of what constituted Christian doctrine was the prerogative of the spiritual not the civil realm.

American Catholics could accept religious liberty and American religious pluralism, work with believers and non-believers toward the general welfare of society, believe that persuasion was the only means of propagating religious truth, and still maintain that Catholicism was the true religion. Religious indifference, therefore, was not the basis of their acceptance of religious liberty. They accepted it as a natural right and a constitutional principle that had foundations in reason, revelation, and experience.

Most articulate Catholics agreed on the meaning of religious liberty and saw the separation of church and state as an instrumental means to achieve that liberty. Thadeus O'Meally, a priest of St. Mary's in Philadelphia, reflected the views of many Catholics when he wrote in 1852 that the "peculiar situation" of the American separation of church and state was the "only natural order of things." Richard Meade, a lay trustee at St. Mary's, agreed. For him, Christ repeatedly told his disciples that "His Kingdom is not of this world" and Saint Paul reaffirmed this when he argued that priests were ordained for things "pertaining to God." O'Meally and Meade employed these arguments ideologically to foster the trustees' causes in Philadelphia, but the arguments they and numerous other lay Catholic trustees throughout the country used illustrated their commitment to the American proposition.

American Catholics, however, did not understand the non-establishment clause of the First Amendment in the same way. Some, like the Maryland Carrolls, saw in the non-establishment clause a restriction upon the government's preferential support for one religion. Others, like John England, saw in it an almost total restriction upon the government's support for any religion.

The Maryland Carrolls opposed the establishment of a specific national or state religion. Although they accepted Maryland's constitutional preference for Christianity, they did not consider this an attempt to establish religion. It did not seem to bother them that the constitution restricted the civil rights of Jews.

John Carroll rejected church establishments like those in England and France because he believed that they always involved a surrender or forfeiture of a divinely endowed ecclesiastical independence. Establishments destroyed *libertas ecclesiae*. Carroll's views of non-establishment, like those of many Maryland Christians, were not absolutist. Catholics like Carroll approved, for example, the 1776 Maryland constitutional provision that granted the state legislature a discretionary power to oblige all citizens to contribute to the support of the religion and minister of their choice or to designate the funds for the poor. In 1785, however, Carroll indicated that Catholic citizens joined together with Presbyterians, Methodists, Quakers, and Baptists to oppose a minister's salary bill that would have activated the legislature's discretionary power. They were unwilling in this case even to accept a non-preferential approach to state aid to religion because they believed the bill would in fact give the Protestant Episcopal church a "predominant and irresistible influence." In principle, if not always in practice, however, they could and did accept a non-preferential approach to governmental aid.

Daniel and John Carroll in particular reflected this Maryland Catholic tradition. They simultaneously rejected a state establishment and supported non-preferential state aid to the churches. As a Maryland state senator in 1788, Daniel Carroll introduced legislation that would protect without partiality or preference the rights of all Christian churches to incorporate and govern their own temporalities. Like many of his contemporaries, he believed that state aid could legitimately be given to all Christian sects as long as it was given without discrimination.

After his consecration as the first bishop of Baltimore and after the ratification of the First Amendment, John Carroll twice (once in 1796 and once in 1800) supported a Catholic Indian missionary's appeal to the federal government for financial support for the missionary's work among the Indians on the Wabash. The missionary had been granted an annuity by the federal government to serve in the Indian community there, but the government had failed to provide the annuity for at least two years. Carroll wrote to the United States Secretaries of War on both occasions and simply requested that the government comply with its contract with the priest. President George Washington had recommended to the Congress that the federal government enact a beneficent policy toward the Indians that would tend to their "civilization" and teach them the advantages of the Christian religion. Some clergymen, Catholics among them, offered to take part in this work and were granted a yearly allowance by the government. The missionaries' functions were twofold: to render important services to the United States by "humanizing & *moralizing*" the Indians and by fostering in them friendly dispositions to the United States. Like many in the United States, John Carroll saw no contradiction between the First Amendment and governmental financial support for works that combined religious and public benefits.

John England articulated a very different understanding of non-establishment, particularly at the federal level of government. He printed the First Amendment on the masthead of his diocesan newspaper, the *United States Catholic Miscellany*, and generally understood it to put severe restrictions upon governmental aid to any and all religions. He held that

> there never was a union of church and state which did not bring serious evils to religion.... But I do know that the Founder of our faith did not unite the church and state; ... Without writing harshly of thousands of good and better men who differ from me in opinion, I am convinced that a total separation from the temporal government, is the most natural and safest state for the

church in any place where it is not, as in the papal territory, a complete government of churchmen.

What did a "total separation" mean? For England, government had no competence to legislate for religious purposes, either to prohibit meat on Fridays, the drinking of whiskey, or the distribution of mails on Sundays. It had no powers to regulate religion, nor morals; its only power was to manage civil and political concerns. Government was not to be, as some would have it, a nursing father to the church. A Roman Catholic legislator, like all legislators, was to be regulated by the political powers that were conferred upon him. His duty "is to legislate only for the temporal welfare of the state, not upon the religious concerns of the people." It would be "criminal" for him to "use his power openly or covertly for the checking of heresy, or the elevation of his own Church."

Nor did the government have the power to use taxes to support, directly or indirectly, any religious purposes.

> Now I deny at once, that Congress has any power whatever to interfere directly or indirectly with the temperance societies or education, or missionary societies, or with the conduct of individuals in respect to either. Any legislative action of Congress upon either of those subjects would be direct usurpation, palpably invalid, and dangerous to the liberties of the republic: and as such, it would, and it ought to be resisted.... Congress has no power to nurse the Evangelist, nor to frown upon the Papist; it cannot prefer the Christian to the Jew; nor bestow one cent either to plant the Gospel in Monrovia, to build a synagogue at Grand Island, or a mosque in New York.

As a young priest in Ireland and as a bishop in the United States, England had vehemently opposed all state financial aid to religion because he believed the church would, by accepting such aid, lose its freedom. It was a violation of political justice, too, he believed, for Great Britain to "give to an hierarchy with which one third of the nation is not in communion a revenue drawn from the whole people." For Bishop England, religious liberty could be fully and adequately protected only by a "total separation" of religion from government.

As a young priest in Philadelphia, John Hughes also rejected the idea of government aid for religious purposes. In an 1833 polemical debate,

Hughes chided John Breckinridge and the Presbyterians whose religious schools and colleges "feed at the public treasury of the State." He claimed that "the Catholic colleges, and houses of education never beg at the doors of government for any such aid. They hold that the institution which, in this country, is not able to support itself by its own intrinsic merit, ought not to exist."

In the early antebellum period, when they had few developed institutions, Catholics like England and Hughes had a more radical view of the non-establishment clause and of the voluntary nature of the church than they would later hold as the pressures of building multiple institutions tested their pocketbooks. The more radical interpretation, however, faded fast after 1840.

In 1840 Hughes experienced a severe case of amnesia regarding his earlier interpretation of non-establishment when, as bishop of New York City, he appealed to city government for non-preferential financial aid for his Catholic schools. His application reflected the exigencies of building a host of Catholic institutions that were deemed necessary to preserve Catholic separateness in a turbulent sea of anti-Catholicism. After the 1840s, American Catholic petitions for state funds increased as their school systems developed; their understanding of separation of church and state also tended to be uniformly in favor of non-preferential state aid. The tradition of England and the younger Hughes disappeared from Catholic consciousness and was replaced exclusively by the tradition articulated by the Carrolls.

American Catholics' participation in the advancement of religious liberty and separation and their assertions of their acceptance of the principle as well as the legal practice of both had very little influence upon the dominant American view that Catholicism was systematically opposed to both. Catholics could not in principle accept religious liberty and separation of religion and government, so the argument went, because they belonged to a church that not only favored the union of church and state, but in principle supported persecution for the sake of enforcing its own perception of truth and justice in society. It was, after all, the church of the Inquisition. It had used the arm of the state to extricate heresy, believing that error had no rights in society. How could Catholics, except from motives of expediency, accept American religious liberty?

The force of this question came to haunt American Catholics. They were from conviction committed to the American proposition, but they were repeatedly called upon to answer for the weight of history. They could have escaped this task by separating from Rome because their communion with Rome was a continual reminder of the freight of the past, but none wanted to do that.

It was not only the past that Catholics had to answer for in the early nineteenth century. Pope Gregory XVI's 1832 encyclical *Mirari Vos* had opposed in principle and practice religious liberty, freedom of the press, and separation of church and state because he saw religious indifferentism as their source. Such liberties were a threat to civil as well as ecclesiastical unity and stability. The pope condemned religious indifferentism as that "perverse opinion" which held that it is "possible to obtain the eternal salvation of the soul by the profession of any kind of religion, as long as morality is maintained." From this "shameful font" arose "that absurd and erroneous position which claims that *liberty of conscience* must be maintained for everyone. It spreads ruin in sacred and civil affairs, though some repeat over and over again with the greatest impudence that some advantage accrues to religion from it." Liberty of conscience, the pope continued, provided "a pestilence more deadly to the state than any other." Experience had demonstrated the devastating damage to society that this "single evil" brings. Experience also demonstrated that the union of church and state was always "favorable and beneficial for the sacred and the civil order." He warned that the "shameless lovers of liberty" who desired to separate the church from the state want to break that mutual concord between the two. The pope called upon princes and governmental officials to exercise their resources and authority to support his desire to restrict religious liberty, preserve the union of church and state, and defend the Catholic church. "Placed as if they [the princes] were parents and teachers of the people, they will bring them true peace and tranquility, if they take special care that religion and piety remain safe."

Here were principles and a recourse to experience that were opposed to American ideals and indeed to the American experience itself. The pope did not aim his attacks directly at the American experience. The encyclical was meant to quiet liberal Catholics in France, but the sweep of his statements on modern freedoms clearly conflicted with American Catholic ideals and experiences. Protestants found in it proof positive that Catholicism was opposed to American liberties.

Although American Catholic bishops agreed with the pope's condemnation of religious indifferentism and licentious liberty, they did not agree with his views of religious liberty and separation, and, perhaps more importantly, they did not share his historical experiences. The pope had associated the ideas of religious liberty and separation with the French Revolution and with the devastating consequences it had upon the European Catholic church. In 1837, five years after the publication of the encyclical, the American bishops issued a joint pastoral letter and, without any reference to the contrary opinions found in the papal encyclical, they reaffirmed their own understanding and acceptance of America's first liberties. Civil allegiance had nothing to do with spiritual allegiance, they wrote. They accepted the pope's spiritual supremacy and simultaneously denied that he had "any civil or political supremacy, or power over us [as Catholics]."

From the days of John Carroll, American Catholics had understood their communion with the pope to be purely spiritual; it had nothing to do with politics. They repeatedly asserted that they were not responsible for past or present papal pretensions to and exercises of political powers. Although they did not make too much of it, they claimed that they had the right to reject papal teachings on political matters, because the pope had no divinely commissioned competence in the area of politics and there were no grounds in either scripture or tradition for these secular matters.

Antebellum American Catholics did not attribute as much magisterial authority to the encyclical *Mirari Vos* that their successors would attribute to post-Vatican I (1869–1870) papal encyclicals. Before the definition of papal infallibility, most American bishops, unlike their Protestant opponents, did not look solely or primarily to the papal office for the definition of authentic Catholic doctrine. The bishops considered themselves as an authentic part of the teaching church and believed that they could accept and promote America's first liberties without violating the essentials of the Catholic tradition.

The encyclical, Catholics like John Hughes argued, did not articulate authentic Catholic doctrine on modern constitutional freedoms. When Presbyterian John Breckinridge of Philadelphia, for example, charged that the papal rejection of civil and religious liberties was authentic Catholic doctrine, Hughes simply denied that what the pope taught was indeed Catholic doctrine. There was no Catholic "doctrine," for example, on the press because God made no revelation on the subject; consequently, " *'liberty*, or the *restraint* of the *press'* forms no 'principle or doctrine' of the Catholic religion."

For Hughes, no infallible Catholic doctrine on civil and religious liberty existed: "No such doctrine *can even* become a portion of that [Catholic] creed, which would *forfeit* its claims to infallibility, the moment it should teach *as* a 'tenet revealed by Almighty God,' any article that had not been taught and believed from the beginning of Christianity." Past unions of the Catholic church and the state were historically conditioned arrangements that had nothing to do with revelation and Catholic doctrine. Catholic discipline in the past had certainly provided for these unions and had certainly denied religious liberty, but past disciplinary canons and the facts of history were not infallible Catholic doctrine. American Catholics made distinctions where their opponents did not.

Mirari Vos certainly contradicted American Catholic experiences and principles regarding church and state. It would be anachronistic, however, to expect early nineteenth-century American Catholics to see such papal pronouncements as an articulation of the authentic Catholic tradition. The pope's view of a confessional state was simply contradicted by the American Catholic constitutional view of the state. Neither view of the state was grounded in authentic Catholic doctrine. Plenty of room for freedom of opinion on this issue existed within the Catholic tradition. Nonetheless, the problem of Catholic allegiance to the American constitutional view of the state would continue throughout the nineteenth and early twentieth centuries because popes continued to maintain a confessional view of the state and, in American society, the pope continued to be perceived as the authentic and only interpreter of the Catholic tradition. The distinctions that the antebellum Catholics made between spiritual and temporal communion, doctrine and discipline, doctrine and theological opinion, principle and facts of history were simply lost in religious controversy.

The early American Catholic tradition on religious liberty and separation demonstrates how American Catholics reinterpreted their own Christian heritage in the light of their political and civil experiences in American society, how they relativized former Catholic understandings of church-state arrangements, and thus how they were enabled by experience, conviction, and principle to accept the first liberties. That they did not share the same interpretation of the non-establishment clause will come as no surprise to those who are aware of the variety of interpretations that clause has received in American history. What may be of some surprise is that there was a radical American Catholic interpretation of non-establishment that has generally remained buried in dusty tomes. Some would undoubtedly prefer to leave it there.

This early tradition also demonstrates something of the tensions involved in American Catholic identity throughout the nineteenth and early twentieth centuries. Convinced by experience and by principle of the rightness of the American proposition, American Catholics were nonetheless simultaneously in tension with Rome and some of their Protestant and secular opponents in American society over the Catholicity of their convictions. That tension continued until the *Declaration on Religious Liberty* at the Second Vatican Council in 1965.

The Republican Wife: Virtue and Seduction
in the Early Republic

JAN LEWIS

● *The sexual attraction of men and women for each other is as old as the species and is among the most powerful of all human drives. It has existed in all nations, all cultures, and all times. Thus, one would think that romantic passion would have nothing much to do with political ideology. But, as Professor Jan Lewis argues in the following essay, the metaphor of marriage was important in the early years of the United States.*

Male lust was considered so powerful that it needed to be directed toward positive outcomes. Indeed, when a man was in love he was particularly vulnerable to a woman's benevolent influence. According to this theory, a bachelor could be seduced into virtue by the female who was the subject of his desires. Quite simply, the height of a young lady's power was reached during the period of "love and courtship," when the gentleman would be so desperate for the favors of his beloved that he would gladly reconsider his temper, his habits, and even his ideology.

The darker side of male passion was as threatening to the nation as to women themselves. The "base seducer," for example, was a man so anxious to satisfy his sexual appetite that he would take advantage of the innocence of "pure womanhood." Such a person would resort to falsehood and perjury to make a conquest. Without the ideal of a republican wife, without the example of virtuous intimacy, he could also be expected to be a poor prospect for responsible citizenship. Thus does Professor Lewis suggest that even the most intimate relations of life could set the pattern for the nation itself.

William and Mary Quarterly, 3d ser., 44 (October, 1987), 689–721. Jan Lewis is an associate professor of History at Rutgers University

When the American colonists commenced rebellion against the British government and assumed the separate and equal station to which they believed the laws of God and nature both entitled them, they found in marriage—"that SOCIAL UNION, which the beneficent Creator instituted for the happiness of Man"—a metaphor for their ideal of social and political relationships. In the republic envisioned by American writers, citizens were to be bound together not by patriarchy's duty or liberalism's self-interest, but by affection, and it was, they believed, marriage, more than any other institution, that trained citizens in this virtue. Thus "L," writing in the *Royal American Magazine* in 1774, explained why this "social union is so essential to human happiness." The married man, he wrote, "by giving pleasure ... receives it back again with increase. By this endearing intercourse of friendship and communication of pleasure, the tender feelings and soft passions of the soul are awakened with all the ardour of love and benevolence.... In this happy state, man feels a growing attachment to human nature, and love to his country." Marriage was the very pattern from which the cloth of republican society was to be cut.

Revolutionary-era writers held up the loving partnership of man and wife in opposition to patriarchal dominion as the republican model for social and political relationships. The essays, stories, poems, and novels that established this model created in republican marriage an ideal that drew upon recent social trends and infused them with political meaning; in so doing, their authors created for women an important new political role, not so much as a mother, as Linda K. Kerber has suggested, but, rather, as a wife. As an indispensable half of the conjugal union that served as the ideal for political as well as familial relationships, the Republican Wife exemplified the strengths and weaknesses of the Revolutionary era's notion of woman's role and, indeed, of republicanism itself, neither can be understood fully except in the context of the other.

Because historians have begun to question whether American political discourse in the period 1775–1815 can be understood in terms of republicanism alone, it is important to note that the adjective "republican" will be used here much as Americans of the period used it—to signify not only classical republicanism but also that fusion of civic humanism and evangelical ardor achieved by Americans at the eve of the Revolution. The key to republicanism is virtue, the self-sacrificial and disinterested quality that was prized in both sacred and secular traditions. The premium that republican thought placed upon disinterestedness has obscured the revolutionary nature of its views about women. To be sure, republican theorists were unwilling to think of women, or any other group, as having different and perhaps antagonistic interests; hence, they did not address women as a separate group. Republicanism assumed, however, that America's dawning glory would cast its beneficent rays upon the whole of society, a new and different society in which women would be required to play a new and unprecedented role.

If we would understand the role designed for women in the early national era, we must look to that body of Anglo-American literature that addressed political issues indirectly and found a wide and appreciative audience among the rapidly expanding reading public. Jay Fliegelman has shown that when we read those popular literary, pedagogical, and didactic works for their political meaning, we gain a new perspective on both the development of political thought in the eighteenth century and the intimate connections between family and polity in eighteenth-century thought. Much of the commentary about woman's nature and her proper role can be found in novels and in the fiction and essays of the growing number of popular magazines.

Americans drew no clear distinctions between that which was "fiction" and that which was not, between works addressed to men and works addressed to women, or even between British literature and original American creations; nor should we. Moreover, what concerns us here is the meaning that American men and women might derive from popular literature. The moral message in what might seem a diverse body of works was remarkably consistent. Magazine editors, for example, aimed both to instruct and to entertain, devoting their periodicals to "knowledge and entertainment," "entertaining knowledge and instructions," and "amusement and instruction." They and their readers could find knowledge entertaining and a properly written piece of fiction instructive. Indeed, fiction served to illustrate the workings of character. In the moral world of the eighteenth century, character was all, and the study of character was an important aspect of moral philosophy, itself a branch of post-Newtonian natural science. Here art and science might fuse.

Similarly, although some periodicals seem to have been addressed primarily to men and others to women, most welcomed both sexes as readers and authors and printed articles that presumably were of interest to both sexes. In fact, no magazines intended exclusively for women were published in America until early in the nineteenth century. The themes of courtship, marriage, and seduction figured to a greater or lesser extent in a wide range of early national publications, not only the *Boston Women's Magazine* but also, for example, Paine's *Pennsylvania Magazine* and Webster's *American Magazine*. The topic of marriage was not reserved to women or their magazines, for it was an issue of public, indeed political, import.

Finally, we must note that much of what was read in America had been written in Britain. Popular British novels were brought out in American editions, and American editors, unable to fill their periodicals with original works, borrowed freely from each other and from each other and from their British counterparts. Yet what matters is not only the origin and intent of such works but also the lessons Americans might have derived from them. Bernard Bailyn has shown the special meaning British political writings may have had for Americans immersed in an imperial crisis. So also with the literature of marriage.

Indeed, a British work might be edited for the American audience in ways that would make it more applicable to the American situation. In *Clarissa*, the novel of the patriarchal family par excellence, the heroine is, as Fliegelman has put it, "purely a victim caught between two tyrannies," that of the father and that of the seducer. Although Richardson held the disobedient daughter partly responsible for her sad fate, eighteenth-century American editions of the book removed that assessment of the heroine from both the subtitle and the introduction, making Clarissa instead the innocent victim of male arrogance, imperiousness, and design. Yet *Clarissa* was more than a seduction story; it was a political parable with particular lessons for Americans, as a fearful John Adams recognized when he observed that "Democracy is Lovelace and the people are Clarissa."

Americans who aimed for the separate station of a viable republic would have to learn better than Clarissa how to resist the tyrannies and seductions that republican theorists were certain they faced. Because eighteenth-century thought placed the family and the state on one continuum, that of "society," and did not yet—as in the nineteenth century would—erect a barrier between the private sphere of the family and the public one of the world, it could dramatize issues of authority in terms of relationships between members of a family. Accordingly, the young woman's quest for a suitable husband and her attempt to navigate between the eighteenth-century's Scylla of overweening power and its Charybdis of seductive liberty was the nation's plot as well.

Americans, successfully completing a revolution against one sort of tyranny, were bound to conclude that their young men and women also could achieve independence. The anti-patriarchalism of Revolutionary ideology dictated that tyranny presented the most immediate and obvious threat to American happiness, and patriarchal domination the chief obstacle to happy and virtuous marriage. According to the republican view, patriarchs such as "The Inexorable Father" who was "unfeeling as adamant, hard of heart as the nether mill stone," threatened always to block the happiness of their children; in this case, the father refused to let his daughter marry a promising young physician who was too honest to enrich himself by overcharging his patients.

So resonant was this anti-patriarchal theme that well after the Revolution American magazines published articles excoriating "parents" ... who are daily offering up the honour and happiness of their children at the shrine of interest and ambition," much as the British government had sacrificed its American colonies. Instead, "marriages should be contracted from motives of affection, rather than of interest." Fortunately, such unions were possible in "happy America," where partible inheritance—"provided our conduct does not render us unworthy"—formed "the basis of equality and the incitement to industry and caution." If America's sons and daughters were educated to "virtue and good morality," they would choose to marry for love rather than interest. Being capable of exercising sound judgment, children were not obligated to obey the injunctions of narrow-minded or rapacious parents.

The rhetoric of marriage bears the same relationship to the prevailing customs as does republican ideology to the events it sought to shape and define: in each case, the terms of analysis explained long-range trends by turning them into dramas enacted by villains and heroes— or, more commonly, heroines. Historians of the family have shown that parental control of marriage declined over the course of the eighteenth century, while children's autonomy increased. That trend had its roots in the Reformation; Protestantism, with its insistence that "mutual comfort" was one of marriage's primary purposes, had licensed the consensual, affectionate union. Although American Puritan ministers still retained for parents, by virtue of their supposedly superior wisdom, a key role in selecting their children's mates, they nonetheless recognized that "marriage is one of the weightiest actions of a person's life, and as the Yoke fellow is suitable or unsuitable, so that condition is like to be very comfortable or uncomfortable." Nor did wealth establish a potential spouse's suitability. As Cotton Mather rhymed it, "The Wretch that is alone to *Mammon* Wed, / May chance to find a *Satan* in the Bed." Interest alone, whether personal or dynastic, had never been an acceptable basis for marriage in the colonies; what changed were, on the one hand, determinations of who was best qualified, the parents or the children, to recognize merit in a potential spouse and, on the other, perceptions of how likely the affections of marriage were, in and of themselves, to assure lasting happiness. During the eighteenth century, parents grew less willing or able to exert the full range of pressures at their command to shape their children's destinies; the balance tipped in favor of the younger generation's discretion.

Thus rhetoric that implicitly likened late eighteenth-century parents to designing court ministers, bent upon subjecting their dependents, grossly exaggerated the control that parents retained over their children's marriages and, in fact, overstated the power parents had held a century earlier. Nonetheless, the rhetoric of marriage, much like that of politics, served both to expose underlying fears and to legitimate and encourage patterns that had already come to prevail.

Republican theorists endeavored to show how, in a post-patriarchal world, citizens could govern themselves, how they could form a society bound by love rather than fear. Because they deemed marriage the school of affection, authors who wrote about the institution were addressing one of their age's most pressing questions: how to make citizens fit for a republic. For example, if the choice of a mate were, or should be, the individual's, he or she must know how to select wisely. And if the parents no longer did, or should, have control, substitute parents could still give advice, which they did at great length in numerous tracts and essays. Parents did not abdicate; rather, they refashioned themselves into friendly paternalists who exerted influence in their families by more subtle, psychological means and in the wider world by words of friendly counsel. Thus the author of "A Father's

Advice to his Daughters" recommended that his own daughters and those of other men "place confidence in those who have shown affection for you in your early days, when you were incapable of making them any return." Yet even those dethroned patriarchs who posed as kind advisors believed they best served young men and women by enabling them to choose wisely their own partners.

What sort of man made the ideal husband? He was republican virtue incarnate, moderation personified. He was "devout without superstition, and pious without melancholy,... careful without avarice, [manifesting] a kind of unconcernedness without negligence." He should be well educated but not "a pedant." A woman should look for "virtuous conduct, good temper, discretion, regularity and industry," and a "mild and even" disposition. Unlike her European sisters, who supposedly married to raise their status, the American maid aimed at—and hoped to maintain—a happy medium, a domestic version of that steadily improving yet never-changing society that Gordon S. Wood has identified as the ideal society of republican dreams. Thus the happily married woman would find that her husband "would always be the same, and always pleasing."

The good husband was like the good citizen; he wed "not by interest but by choice," and "he treats his wife with delicacy as a woman, with tenderness as a friend." He "ever studied the happiness of the woman he loved more than his own." In fact, the ideal husband resembled more than a little the popular portrait of the Revolutionary War officer, which is precisely the occupation Royall Tyler chose for the hero of his play *The Contrast*. To ensure that the officer/suitor's character could not be mistaken, Tyler dubbed him "Colonel Manly" and gave him such quintessentially republican opinions as that ancient Greece declined because "the common good was lost in the pursuit of private interest" and that "the man who can plant thorns in the bosom of an unsuspecting girl is more detestable than a common robber, in the same proportion as private violence is more despicable than open force, and money of less value than happiness." The qualities that made a man honorable in public life, then, distinguished him as a potential husband as well.

Men, likewise, were supposed to select republicans as their life partners. As the author of "On the Choice of a Wife" put it, "virtue, wisdom, presence of mind, patience, vigour, capacity, and application, are not *sexual* qualities; they belong to all who have duties to perform and evils to endure." Echoing standard Protestant assumptions, Americans and the British writers they chose to republish argued that the most important considerations in the selection of a wife were her "qualifications as a *companion* and a *helper*." The choice was difficult, for women were not equally qualified. Suitors should be wary of frivolity and mere physical beauty or what the author of "The Intrinsic Merits of Women" called "the fashionable follies of the age." It was not that all women were suspect but that only certain types—great beauties, heiresses, and coquettes—were likely to be dangerous. Thus "the husbands of beauties are the most miserable of husbands.... Vexed by the vanity, exhausted by the extravagance, tortured by the inconstancy... life, instead of a blessing, becomes to them a purgatory." The republican gloss is equally evident in the simple reminder that "riches... will never alone afford happiness to their possessors."

Men and women both were thus advised to seek for their mates what we can recognize as embodiments of republican ideology. They were warned at even greater length to avoid certain notorious types, those associated with the despicable aspects of European court life: flatterers, deceivers, flirts, fops, coxcombs, coquettes, and all persons lacking in honor and virtue. Indeed, writers devoted so much effort to delineating the characteristics of the coxcomb and coquette that one cannot help suspecting that the type, rather than presenting a bona fide threat to naive American beaux and belles, served as a distillation, much like the tyrannical ruler or the designing minister, of what the age most feared. Flirts and fops, coxcombs and coquettes romp through the pages of republican literature with abandon. Their names are code words that signify luxury, vice, and deceit; their presence in a story points almost without exception to an unhappy ending. They promise ruin not only for themselves and their victims but also for the infant nation, for they practice habits that were commonly believed to spell the death of republics. So reasoned the author of "The Philosophy of Coquetry": "so long as the sensualities and pride of one sex shall delight in luxurious habits and ostentatious living; so long as the vanities of the other shall be gratified by splendid personal decorations, costly refinements, and glittering equipages—or, more philosophically speaking, so long as we shall be enslaved in a refined state of society, by numerous and factitious wants, we shall look in vain for disinterested alliances, and an union of the sexes resulting from mental attachment."

Reform began with the individual; a republican society required virtuous men and women. That belief permeates the purportedly "True Story" of "Eugenia—or the Coquette." The girl of the title had parents who were "dissipated and luxurious.... [T]hey looked forward to immense wealth.... Pride, pomp, and luxury dazzled their eyes." Indeed, "without a particle of principle, [Eugenia's] father countenanced depredation, at a time when the hirelings of tyranny were not sparing in the arts of devastation." In this republican vision a nation could be no better than the individuals who constitute it. In this story a sad fate for the nation is averted when Eugenia, who has inherited her parents' vices, jilts the decent young man who had courted her, freeing him to marry "a woman, who boasts only those real charms.... which constitute the perfect wife.... [A]s she never experienced the deceit of a fop, so he congratulates himself that he has escaped from the smiles of a coquette." Significantly, Eugenia herself is almost incidental to the story. It is her parents, stand-ins for a corrupt British government, and their ability to thwart a truly affectionate union that are most feared. In such a view, to fall for a coquette is to surrender republican virtue, and to flirt is to commit an act of treason.

When courtship and marriage are infused with political meaning, women inevitably and inescapably become political beings. Make no mistake: these first formulations of a feminine political role were not fundamentally feminist. They were not devised by women in particular, nor was their aim primarily to enhance the position of women. The dynamic, rather, was republican and anti-patriarchal: it juxtaposed the virtuous, independent child and the oppressive, corrupting parent, and it found in the union of two virtuous individuals the true end of society and the fit paradigm for political life. Such a conceptualization of the relationship between family and polity represents more a subtle shift than a clean break from earlier models. When Puritans designated the family "a little commonwealth," they meant it to be "a schoole wherein the first principles and grounds of government and subjection are learned: whereby men are fitted to greater matters in Church or commonwealth." In such a family the relationship between parent and child was most important.

When anti-patriarchalists in the eighteenth century substituted marriage for parenthood as the fundamental familial relationship, they did not, however, question the assumption that the family was but the society in miniature. Society still appeared as the family writ large, with the same sorts of relationships deemed appropriate for both the as-yet-undifferentiated spheres of home and world. Yet in shifting interest from the parent-child nexus to the husband-wife bond, eighteenth-century authors necessarily raised women to a new moral and political stature. When the key relationship in a society is that between father and son or ruler and subject, women may conveniently be ignored; when the most important relationship is between conjugal equals, and when the family is still seen as the correlative of the larger society, then women can no longer be overlooked. If the affectionate union between a man and his wife, freely entered into, without tyrannical interference, is the model for all the relationships in the society and the polity, then the wife, as an indispensable half of the martial union, is a political creature.

To the extent that the success of the republican endeavor rested upon the character of citizens, republicanism demanded virtue of women, not because it numbered them as citizens but because it recognized how intimately women, in consensual unions, were connected to men. A virtuous man required a virtuous mate. Moreover, republicanism called upon every means at its disposal to assure male virtue. That obsession with virtue, deriving its force from the fusion of Protestant and republican notions of character, persisted long after the Revolution had been won and the Constitution ratified. Well into the nineteenth century, Americans linked the fate of their nation to the virtues of its people. Even if, as several historians have suggested, certain thinkers, before the end of the eighteenth century, had embraced liberalism and its premise of the self-interested individual, popular writers and, presumably, their audience had not. One writer put it emphatically: "Private vices are *not* public benefits." That rejection of Bernard Mandeville infused much of the early national literature, and that conceptualization of society—which continued to see the family as the microcosm of the wider world and to insist that "public good must grow out of private virtue"—held out a significant role for women.

"A woman of virtue and prudence is a public good—a public benefactor." She has the power to make "public decency...a fashion—and public virtue the only example." And how is woman to accomplish that great end? By her influence over the manners of men. Indeed, "nothing short of a general reformation of manners would take place, were the ladies to use their power in discouraging our licentious manners." Such a role might seem trivial did Americans not consider "the general reformation of manners" one of the young nation's most important goals, and did they not think women fully capable of contributing to it. Women might begin by reforming themselves, for "there is not a more certain test of national depravity, than that which presents itself in the degeneracy of female manners."

Male manners, however, were of more concern, and in changing them women were to play their most important role. So argued men, such as the essayist who held that women who were the beneficiaries of a "virtuous and refined education" might contribute "no less to public good than to private happiness. A gentleman, who at present must degrade himself into a fop or a coxcomb in order to please the ladies, would soon find that their favor could not be gained but by exerting every manly talent in public and private life." That same view could be expressed by a woman—for example, Miss C. Hutchings, who assured her fellow boarding-school graduates of the influence of "female manners on society in general": "were all women rational, unaffected and virtuous, coxcombs, flatterers and libertines would no longer exist." Such arguments rested on several important new assumptions. First, although the concern with "manners" betokened an upper-class emphasis upon gentility, the insistence that women are— or can be—a moral force transforms manners into mores, into the moral foundation of the society. Thus "it is ... to the virtues of the fair ... the society must be indebted for its moral, as well as its natural preservation." Second, women play their moral role not by denying their sexuality, by becoming "passionless," but by using it to tempt men to be good.

This conceptualization of female influence seems to have intrigued men and women in the decades just after the Revolution. Magazines printed and reprinted numbers of articles with similar titles and sentiments: "Female Influence," "Scheme for Increasing the Power of the Fair Sex," "The Influence of the Female Sex on the Enjoyments of Social Life," "The Power of Beauty, and the Influence the Fair Sex might have in Reforming the Manners of the World." These, with a host of similar articles, argued that the potential for beneficial female influence was almost unlimited.

The height of a woman's influence was reached during the period of "love and courtship," which, "it is universally allowed, invest a lady with more authority than in any other situation that falls to the lot of human beings." A young man who addressed his classmates at Columbia College's commencement elaborated: "She can mold the taste, the manners, and the conduct of her admirers, according to her pleasure." Moreover, "she can, even to a great degree, change their tempers and dispositions, and superinduce habits entirely new." Thus it was not in childhood that a man was most malleable; rather, it was when, grown to maturity, he sought the favors of a young lady that he was most susceptible to influence. "By the judicious management of this noble passion [love], a passion with which the truly accomplished of the fair sex never fail of inspiring men, what almost miraculous reformations may be brought about?"

Once she had seduced him into virtue, the married woman's task was to preserve her husband in the exalted state to which her influence had raised him. "It rests with her, not only to confirm those virtuous habits which he has already acquired, but also to excite his perseverance in the paths of rectitude." The boldness of this formulation is stunning. What earlier Americans perceived as Eve's most dangerous characteristic, her seductiveness, is here transformed into her capacity for virtue. Woman was to lead man into rectitude, to lure him to the exercise of manly virtue. What miraculous reformations became possible when the attraction between the sexes, which for millennia had been considered the cause of the fall of mankind, could be transformed into the bedrock of the nation! Women indeed had great power—nothing less than the ability, as one magazine implored, "to make our young men, not in empty words, but in deed and in truth, republicans."

That was why so much importance was attached to the education of women. Passion could and must be tempered by reason. If Eve's daughters could deserve, as one young woman put it, to be "extolled for the beauties of their minds instead of their persons . . . , then would mankind enjoy that happiness which was first intended for the happy pair in Paradise." Were women properly educated, "then will the halcyon days dawn, and human nature appear in its highest beauty and perfection." Few topics excited more interest in the early national period than education, for it seemed to hold the key to making "our women virtuous and respectable; our men brave, honest, and honorable—and the *American* People in general *an* EXAMPLE *of* HONOUR *and* VIRTUE to the rest of the world." Writers were not always clear or certain about whether the American people were naturally virtuous or whether, instead, they merely had unusual potential to be so; hence the extremes of millennial hope and overwhelming fear, as men and women envisioned both the prospect of paradise on earth and the potential for disastrous failure.

Unless we recognize how grandiose American expectations could be and how terrifying was the possibility that they might not be realized, we cannot fully appreciate how central female education was to the republican agenda. While it is true that some reformers advocated educating women so that they, in turn, could teach their children, the more important consideration, always, was to make women into fit companions for republican men and, especially, reliable guarantors of masculine virtue. Hence, as one man put it, "would the females keep in view the influence they possess over our education, they would not fail to perceive an attention to their own as nearly connected with the welfare of mankind. . . . Do they admire and respect the man of sense, and treat with contempt the coxcomb and the fop, [a young man] will, to recommend himself to their esteem, form himself to usefulness and virtue." No one argued that women were naturally more virtuous or pure than men; rather, they had the capacity to overcome weakness and become good.

Nor, certainly, were all women natural republicans; the books and magazines of the age are populated with as many coquettes and flirts as coxcombs and fops. Human nature was malleable, and if it could be bent toward the good, to make a republican, it might also be warped toward evil, creating a coxcomb or coquette. Obviously, those who believed in the malleability of character rejected Calvinistic assumptions about innate depravity, and nowhere is their departure from the older orthodoxy more clear than in their expectations of feminine virtue. Thus one essayist advised women of the enormous power they had at their disposal: "as *Milton* says, *The world lies all before them*, and it is theirs to mould into what shape they please."

That paraphrase and application of the penultimate lines of *Paradise Lost* are a good deal more sanguine than the original. So optimistic a reading of Milton, with its suggestion that the world was Eve's to make, even into a new paradise, drew upon millennial hopes that had become an integral part of American culture. To be sure, such expectations did not always express a literal believe in the imminence of Christ's thousand-year reign, and they were often dampened by a lurking fear that they might not be realized. Still, the Revolution unloosed a flood of optimism—so much, in fact, that some Americans could begin to think of themselves as "new" men, veritable American Adams, given the opportunity to make the world and themselves anew. As Paine put it, America "has it in her choice to do, and to live as she pleases. The world is in her hands." This persistent strain in American thought is well known to students of American culture. Yet there could be no Adam without an Eve; in the garden, as described in Genesis and by Milton, Adam had a companion who sinned first. Without Eve, Adam presumably would have remained in Paradise; that reminder of woman's unhappy role in effecting human destiny had never been far from the minds of Puritan ministers such as Cotton Mather. To the extent that the Fall was the most compelling of all biblical episodes for Puritans, woman played a central, and unenviable, role in the central drama of mankind. Milton's version of the Fall achieved wide popularity in America at the end of the eighteenth century, and not just among the heirs of the Puritans; his Eve, although more sympathetic than the stock Puritan version, still bore primary responsibility for the great calamity.

Thus, to move to a more helpful view of human potential, it was necessary first to come to terms with the Fall. Several avenues were available. One was to shift the focus of religion from Fall to Redemption; that path was taken, particularly in the nineteenth century, as American Protestantism became more Christocentric. Another option was for Adam, in effect, to go his own way, without Eve, remaking the world as an all-male paradise; classic American literature, written by men, followed that route in the nineteenth century. But Americans of the late eighteenth century, steeped as they were in orthodox readings of the Bible, and reminded of them by Milton, could not remake Adam and give the story of the Fall a happier ending without first remaking the woman who had been first in sin. And that is precisely what they did.

Some revamped Eve clearly and consciously, offering new exegeses of Genesis, as did the author of "The Nobility of Woman Kind," who reasoned that "the man gave us death; not the woman. The woman did amiss ignorantly and from deception: But the man knew, that he did amiss." Judith Sargent Murray, writing in the *Massachusetts Magazine* under the pen name "Constantia," offered an even more positive assessment of Eve's brief residence in Eden. Eve's motive in eating the forbidden fruit, Murray suggested, was admirable; she hungered for knowledge. Even though Adam could see that his mate had grown no wiser, he nonetheless tasted the fruit himself. His motive? "A base pusillanimous attachment to a woman!... Thus it should seem, that all the arts of the grand deceiver ... were requisite to mislead our general mother, while the father of mankind forfeited his own, and relinquished the happiness of posterity, merely in compliance with the blandishments of a female." Thus could common assumptions about feminine moral weakness and masculine intellectual strength be turned cleverly on their heads.

Still, most writers who wished to revise popular evaluations of Eve did not take so assertively a feminist a tack as to reinterpret the story of the Fall. For one reason, they might be refuted by traditional readings that kept a culpable sensuality, both feminine and masculine, at the center of the story. Instead, those who were inclined to paint the first mother in more flattering hues tended to focus not so much upon her unhappy departure from Eden as upon her more pleasing qualities when she was still there. Here Americans took their cue from Milton, and in the years just after the Revolution his Eve "began to emerge as a pattern of womanly perfection." Sometimes an author quoted Milton directly, as did Dr. John Gregory, an Edinburgh physician whose *Legacy* to his daughters was popular in America: "Milton had my idea, when he says of Eve 'Grace was in all her steps. / Heaven in her eye. In every gesture of dignity and love'." Samuel Low, author of the play *The Politician Out-witted*, must have assumed that his audience would recognize his source when he quoted the same lines, without attribution, to describe his heroine.

Often Milton's influence was indirect but unmistakable; his "fair angelic Eve," created "for softness ... and sweet attractive grace," served as model for the ideal woman who would display "softness and delicacy of manners, unaffecting beauty, unassuming worth, modesty happily blended with good humour." The Miltonic influence is also clear in a poem entitled "Female Character," published in 1792:

> Queen of every gentle passion,
> Tender sympathy and love;
> Perfect work of Heav'nly fashion,
> Miniature of charms above.
>
> Love and grace in rich profusion,
> Soft'ning man's ferocious soul;
> All creation's fair conclusion,
> Form'd to beautify the whole.

Woman is the last of God's works, created not, as the pre-Miltonic tradition had it, to bring about man's fall, but rather to remind him, after that event, of the paradise they had once shared and hoped still to regain.

Jay Fliegelman has noted that Milton's description of Eve played an important role in "the secularization and feminization of 'grace'" in the eighteenth century as the word took on an aesthetic meaning. By the same token, woman, "Heav'n's last best gift," promised salvation; she, like Christ, pointed the way toward redemption. Yet it is redemption with a difference, for when sacred history is rewritten in such a way—as American popular writers would have it—that woman is gracious and man has not yet sinned, then we can imagine the time before the Fall when the world was Paradise and our first parents

> In naked majesty seemed lords of all,
> And worthy seemed, for in their looks divine
> The image of their glorious Maker shone...

It was to this image of prelapsarian godliness that Americans, in the era just after the American Revolution, responded.

The Republican Wife, then, was Eve, and republican marriage represented Paradise, a veritable "heaven on earth." Taking their model from Milton's hymn to wedded love in Book IV of *Paradise Lost*, American publications described marriage in unabashedly Edenic terms. "The house of the married man is his paradise.... In the existence of a married man, there is no termination[;] when death overtakes him, he is only translated from one heaven to another." Marriage is "the highest state of human felicity, and resembles that of the beneficent beings above." For this reason the choice of a marriage partner was so important. A correspondent to the *Christian's, Scholar's, and Farmer's Magazine* put it simply: "The Choice of a Wife" was one "on which not only [mankind's] present welfare, but even their everlasting felicity may depend."

The Edenic vision of marriage, then, served to bridge the anti-patriarchalism of the eighteenth century and the domesticity of the nineteenth. If the patriarchal model of familial relationships was suited to a hierarchically organized society, and if, as Nancy F. Cott has suggested, domesticity went hand in hand with mid-nineteenth-century democratic liberalism, the Edenic vision fit just as nicely with the canons of republicanism. Like republicanism itself, Edenic republican marriage presented itself as egalitarian. Republican characterizations of marriage echoed with the words *equal, mutual*, and *reciprocal*, and marriage was described as a friendship between equals. An essay "Addressed to the Ladies," for example, urged "every young married woman to seek the friend of her heart in the husband of her affection. There, and there only, is that true equality, both of rank and fortune, and cemented by mutual interests, and mutual . . . pledges to be found. . . . There and there only will she be sure to meet with reciprocal confidence, unfeigned attachment and tender solicitude to soothe every care." Indeed, no word better summarizes republican notions of marriage than *friendship*. "Marriage is, or should be, the most perfect state of friendship. Mutual interest produces mutual assistance." Another writer defined the good marriage in almost the same words as "the highest instance of human friendship." In fact, "love" was nothing more than "friendship raised to its highest pitch."

Marriage, quite simply, was friendship exalted. Its pleasures derived from "mutual return of *conjugal love*. . . . When two minds are . . . engaged by the ties of reciprocal sincerity, each alternately receives and communicates a transport that is inconceivable to all, but those that are in this situation." Marriage was intended, another writer concluded, "to be the basis and the cement of those numberless tender sympathies, mutual endearments and interchanges of love between the mutual parties themselves, which make up not the morality only, but even the chief happiness of conjugal life." Marriage was moral because it fused "virtuous love and friendship; the one supplying it with a constant rapture, the other regulating it by the rules of reason." True marriage was quite unlike "those unnatural and disproportionate matches that are daily made upon worldly views, where interest or lust are the only motives." True marriage was proportionate; put another way, it was symmetrical. Indeed, the mutuality and reciprocity that republicans so prized were inconceivable in an asymmetrical union—the "slavery" of so-called barbaric cultures, in which women were thoroughly subordinated to men.

That republican marriage was symmetrical does not mean that it was fully egalitarian; rather, men and women were opposite sides of the same coin or, as a popular fable had it, two halves of a being that had once been sundered. Neither could be whole until it found its other half. Nor could the halves be fully moral when separate, for Eve's love and Adam's reason were equally necessary to the prelapsarian vision. As heirs to the Enlightenment, American republicans sought the happy medium between—or, more precisely, a fusion of—passion and intellect, head and heart. Eighteenth-century moral philosophy, as it was popularized in American magazines, taught both that passion must be regulated by reason and that "no real felicity can exist independent of susceptibility and affection, and the heart of him who is cold to the soothing voice of friendship, dead to the melting strains of love, and senseless to the plaintive pleadings of distress, is a mansion only calculated for demoniac spirits, or a cheerless dwelling for disgust and spleen." Adam and Eve, reason and love, are each indispensable, and the symmetrical marriage brings them together.

For this reason—that in checking passion and socializing reason the conjugal union made mankind truly virtuous—marriage was the model for society. The single life, according to John Witherspoon, writing as "Epaminondas" in the *Pennsylvania Magazine* on the eve of the Revolution, "narrows the mind and closes the heart." He asserted unequivocally the "absolute necessity of marriage for the service of the state." The pure love of marriage formed the basis for "social virtue," for "while other passions concentrate man on himself, love makes him live in another, subdues selfishness, and reveals to him the pleasure of ministering to the object of his love.... The lover becomes a husband, a parent, a citizen." The "marriage institution," then, "is the first to produce moral order." For that reason, "marriage has ever been considered by every wise state the sinew of its strength and the foundation of its true greatness." Marriage formed the basis of all other relationships, both in the family, because it led to parenthood, and in the society, because it schooled men in the disinterested benevolence that was supposed by republican ideologues to constitute virtue. In sum, as an essayist in the *Key* put it, "nothing is so honourable as MARRIAGE, nothing so comfortable both to body and mind. . . . It is marriage alone that knits and binds all the sinews of society together and makes the life of man honourable to himself, useful to others, and grateful to the God of nature. . . . Is there anything on earth nearer heaven?" Lest that promise of heaven-on-earth be insufficient to persuade his readers, the writer continued: "That MAN who resolves to live without WOMAN, or that WOMAN who resolves to live without MAN, are [*sic*] ENEMIES TO THE COMMUNITY in which they dwell, INJURIOUS TO THEMSELVES, DE-STRUCTIVE TO THE WORLD, APOSTATES TO NATURE, and REBELS AGAINST HEAVEN AND EARTH." The man or woman who proposed to live alone, then, was heretic and traitor both.

Like republicanism, the doctrine of symmetrical marriage subordinated individual interest to the greater good of the whole. Accordingly, marriages based upon interest were to be loathed; true marriage was the model for disinterested benevolence. Unlike the canon of domesticity, in which "women's self-renunciation was called upon to remedy men's self-alienation," idealized republican marriage required men and women both to display virtue. Male and female were two halves of one whole whose name was concord; the ideal marriage was a scene of prelapsarian harmony. As the author of "On the Necessity of Domestic Concord" noted, "peace" was more important even than "plenty." In order for "harmony" and "concord" to prevail, husband and wife were to be of one mind; they could not disagree. To prevent a conflict-filled marriage, one must choose one's mate wisely; probably no consideration was more important than "a similarity of sentiments and dispositions," for where there is "an union of souls, and a consistent harmony of mental ideas . . . discord will keep at an awful distance, and an universal sympathy, productive of an ineffable bliss, will ever attend them. . . . O happiness divine! source of concordant minds!" An essayist in *New York Magazine* expressed the same idea more matter-of-factly: "There cannot be too near an equality, too exact a harmony, betwixt a married couple." Indeed, "the idea of power on either side should be totally banished."

Conjugal affection, then, was not coercive. Nor did it admit of any "selfish or sensual alloy." Marriage was the republic in miniature; it was chaste, disinterested, and free from the exercise of arbitrary power. And, like republican citizens, husband and wife were most likely to find happiness when, as Witherspoon suggested, they shared the same rank, the same education, and the same habits of life.

It is tempting to suppose that the ideology of the republican marriage was but the rhetorical manifestation of the newly affectionate conjugal union, and that both rhetoric and reality represented positive and progressive change. Yet we must remember that republicanism, like Janus, looked to the past as well as to the future; it focused more upon the welfare of the society than the well-being of the individual. Thus it had an implicitly anti-individualistic dimension, one that was exposed whenever conflict arose. We can see that tendency in the ideal of marital concord, which could be—and was—used to legitimate both coverture and the exclusion of women from direct participation in politics. Indeed, the rhetoric of harmony seems almost a gloss upon the doctrine of marital unity—the English common law fiction that in marriage the husband and wife are one, and the husband is the one. It has puzzled some historians that American Revolutionaries did not jettison coverture along with other pieces of undemocratic British baggage such as primogeniture and entail. Yet republican theorists prized harmony above all else; they created the ideal of the affectionate marriage not so much to liberate the individual as to assure concord in the family, the building-block of society.

Republicanism aimed to avoid conflict. Hence, using the same principle that predicted that small republics would be the most harmonious, those who applied the theory to the family suggested that husband and wife should share similar dispositions, beliefs, and interests, that they should be as one. Even so, conflict might arise, and the recommendations republicans made to restore harmony in such unfortunate cases expose the limitations of the republican model for family and polity alike.

The ideal, of course, was equality; no good republican would have disagreed with the egalitarian sentiments expressed by the woman who styled herself "A Matrimonial Republican." "The obedience between man and wife," she wrote, "is, or ought to be mutual." The catch was in the "ought to be," for here the weaknesses in the republican ideal show through. What, for example, was a wife with an errant husband to do? Although it was certainly true that "man has no more right to sin with impunity than woman," husbands seemed to fall more often, and it became a wife's duty to lure her errant mate back to rectitude with "the charm of good humour and uncomplaining sweetness." In other words, only redoubled feminine virtue could reclaim a husband from masculine vice. "Dispute not with him, be the occasion what it will," advised one writer. Better to let errors go unremarked, warned another, than to "strike too often the unharmonious string." Indeed, "the best way of a married woman to carry her points is to yield sometimes." Harmony, then, took precedence over equality; in the interest of concord a woman would sometimes have to forbear.

But why not the husband? In a truly reciprocal marriage would not the two parties compromise? Almost all essayists who addressed the issue of conflict in marriage argued that it was the wife who had to bend. The responsibility for anchoring marriage fell disproportionately to women because they were, supposedly, more compliant than men, or, at least, they would find it "necessary, for political purposes, to consider man as the superior authority." The symmetrical marriage thus gave way, under very little pressure, to a disproportionate one in which the wife, in order to maintain domestic tranquillity, was expected to defer.

Deference, of course, was the solution republicans offered for the problem of conflict in the polity; persons deficient in judgment or inferior in status, they believed, should simply yield to those of superior wisdom. Yet although, as Wood has shown, Federalists offered the Constitution as a "republican remedy" for the republican vice of disharmony, no similar rearrangement was forthcoming for the family. Indeed, as Americans showed increasing acceptance of conflict in the market and the polity, they became less willing to tolerate it at home.

The insistence upon feminine deference revealed fears about conflict in the society and nation, and not merely concern about unhappy marriages. Indeed, very few of the essays that enjoined women to complaisance mentioned those character flaws we might expect women to have confronted most frequently in their mates: irritability, distasteful habits, slovenliness, insensitivity, an inability to earn an adequate income, or even the arbitrary exercise of power. Rather, the single failing that drew the most censure—and also the most extravagant claims for the power of female influence—was infidelity. Stories with titles like "The Way to Reclaim Him. A Moral Tale" purported to show how supreme feminine virtue could recall an errant husband to the path of rectitude. In that story, as in such another as "Conjugal Prudence," the wronged wife won back her wayward husband by embracing, literally, his mistress and illegitimate offspring, and by insisting upon an education for the children and an annuity (and, implicitly, banishment) for the mistress. Such acts of generosity never failed. The husband in the former story clasped his wife to his breast, "murmured out . . . 'Excellent woman! matchless wife!' " and promised "to remain immutably attached to her alone to the last moment of his existence." Similarly, the husband in the latter exclaimed, "Thou heavenly woman! . . . is it *thus* thou upbraidest me for my infidelity to the most amiable woman that ever existed! O, my love, forgive!—but that's impossible! I am, I will be only yours'."

The authors of such stories seem to be exploring the farthest reaches of self-abasing virtue; they imagine the most extreme instances of domestic cruelty a wife might endure in order to see whether the depths of depravity may be exceeded by the heights of virtue. When the answer is yes, the resolution takes the form of a conversion, with the husband confessing his sins and the wife playing the part, in the words of another contrite fictional husband, of "my guardian angel sent by heaven to prevent my ruin." Stripped of her original culpability, Eve is easily transformed into Christ's surrogate, able to work a sinner's "reformation." "Trust me," the wronged wife says. "I assure you, that search the habitable globe, you will meet with no woman more inclined to serve, love, obey, and oblige you, than your Emilia." Like Christ, the wife has to suffer, and like him, she redeems.

It was, however, equally possible for women to suffer yet not redeem. That was the sad fate of the heroine of Susanna Rowson's *Sarah; or, The Exemplary Wife*, a novel in which "virtue is represented, in all her native simplicity and beauty; and vice . . . is exhibited in her own proper ugliness and deformity." Although "the story is far from being improbable," it is really a parable, with virtue pitted against vice. Virtue is represented by Sarah, a lovely young woman who is forced by mercenary relatives to wed a reprobate, somewhat as if Clarissa had been made, against her will, to marry Lovelace. Although her husband kept a mistress, even bringing her into the home he shared with his wife, and although he despised Sarah for her goodness, she never wavered in her patience, charity, or virtue. When her husband bankrupted himself and even her clothing was claimed by his creditors, she entered into service to support him and herself. And when she discovered his illegitimate child, "said she calmly . . . 'if the child owes its being to you, give orders that it be brought home, and I will see it is properly taken care of; but let me entreat you not to add to the offence already committed against religion and morality, the unpardonable one of leaving your offspring to perish'." Whereupon the errant husband exploded, " 'D—n-t—n. . . . Of all the plagues a man can have, a moralizing, sentimental, canting, hypocritical wife is the worst'." After years of such trials, Sarah died, secure in her conviction that "even in thought she had never dishonoured her husband." Thereupon he married his mistress. Here there is no conversion; virtue will not prevail. Nevertheless, "who of common reflection but would prefer the death of Sarah, resigned as she was, and upheld by faith and hope, to all the splendors, wealth and honors ever heaped upon the heroine in the last pages of a novel" in which a heroine met only an earthly reward? To put it another way, Susanna Rowson expressed doubt about whether feminine virtue *could* prevail in a corrupt world.

The doctrine of the Republican Wife suggested that a good wife could influence a susceptible man; *Sarah* raised the question whether she could reclaim, as well, a man who was confirmed in viciousness. The answer was that she could not. Here was a fundamental dilemma for the new nation: how could virtue be exacted from the vicious? Republican ideology offered a number of plausible ways to encourage the good to be more so; chief among them were education, benevolent reform, and female influence. But it faced an insurmountable obstacle when it confronted men who were beyond all hope of reformation. The problem was infidelity, not merely the faithlessness of a spouse but apostasy itself—the unpardonable sin; for it, republicanism had no cure.

Republican advocacy of virtue was powerless before persons who had no conscience. How bedeviling this problem was can be seen when we examine the conventional seduction story. Tales such as *Charlotte Temple* and *The Coquette* may be considered as not very subtle warnings to young women without dowries that their value lay in their virginity; if they would be sought after on the marriage market, they must keep that commodity intact. The sentimental tale of seduction thus has been seen as an instrument of bourgeois respectability and middle-class conformity. Such a view is not untrue, for surely no early nineteenth-century girl enhanced her marriage prospects by squandering her virginity. Chastity *was* esteemed, but for republican as much as bourgeois reasons. Consider "Reflections on Chastity, or Female Honour," a brief definition printed in at least three magazines before 1800: "What Bravery is in man, Chastity is in woman. This virtue, by making them triumph over every wicked attempt to dishonour them, bestows on them, as the first reward of victory, an universal esteem." Once again we see the symmetrical expectations of men and women; in this case, chastity is the feminine version of the absolute standard of courage expected of Revolutionary War soldiers. For patriots like the Reverend Robert Cooper, cowardice was sin; thus he warned in 1775 that "if . . . you would escape deep guilt before God, and lasting contempt among men, forward you must go. . . . You have, in a word, no alternative, but either to venture your lives bravely, or attempt to save them ignominiously; to run the hazard of dying like heroes, or be certain of living like cowards." Bravery, like chastity, was an absolute; it allowed not the slightest deviation nor tolerated any taint.

Brave men and chaste women were expected to "triumph over every wicked attempt to dishonour them." What Charles Royster has said of this Revolutionary attachment to exacting standards of bravery applies to chastity as well: it reflected an evangelical tendency to establish dichotomies between good and evil, salvation and grace, God and Satan. To waver in one's courage was to fall from grace; similarly, to surrender one's chastity was to sin. Americans of the Revolutionary era held out an impossible standard of purity for women and men both. Yet the Continental army, as Royster has shown, would come to a more workable notion of human capability, as would the political theorists who framed the Constitution. Standards of female virtue, however, fully as unrealistic as the expectation that no soldier would ever feel fear or no citizen advance his own interest, only became more rigid.

In many ways chastity was a fit emblem for republicanism, which, when infused with evangelical ardor, could demand absolute and undeviating virtue from its citizens. Hence we must read the era's popular literature of seduction not merely as cautionary tales addressed to young women but also as political tracts in which men and women explored the possibilities for virtue in a corrupt world. Surely it is significant that the most popular novel of the early national period—indeed, the most popular American novel of all until the publication of *Uncle Tom's Cabin*—was *Charlotte Temple,* Susanna Rowson's classic tale of seduction and abandonment. In this novel it takes not one but two designing men to seduce Charlotte from the path of virtue. The work is begun by Montraville, a Lovelace type who is drawn to the innocent young woman he ensnares but is unwilling to make a disadvantageous match; it is completed by his "friend" Belcour, whose only apparent motivation is to destroy both Charlotte and her faithless lover. Under such an assault, Charlotte's innocence stands not a chance.

Like Charlotte and her forerunner Clarissa Harlowe, the heroines of the sentimental tales of seduction are all sympathetic. Eliza Wharton, *The Coquette,* seemed "to possess both the virtues and the graces"; her weaknesses were "an air of gaiety in her appearance and deportment" and a fatal naïveté. Indeed, the flaws ascribed to the unfortunate heroines were traits that republicans usually valued: "a heart . . . formed of sensibility"; "unsuspecting innocence"; "innocent herself, she expected to find others so"; a mind "pure and unsullied"; "innocence and simplicity"; "amiable, ingenuous and sensible." Pure, innocent, without guile, such young women are nothing less than contemporary versions of Eve; they are endowed with her attributes and given her signs. The unfortunate Amelia, for example, is "one of the fairest blossoms in the garden of society," while Almira is "as beautiful as the daughters of Paradise, as gentle as the breezes of spring; her mind was spotless, and her manners artless." Such innocence fell once from Paradise, and it was destined to fall again and again in countless tales of seduction in the early republic.

We have seen that feminine influence had its limits; no wife could expect to triumph over a thoroughly corrupted man on this side of the grave. Likewise, feminine innocence was at the mercy of masculine vice. No matter how many times the story of the Fall was reenacted, it came out the same way, as a correspondent to the *Gentleman and Lady's Town and Country Magazine* was well aware: "Most angelic and ever-admir'd blossoms of earthly eminence—how few are the instances of thy pure innocence ever reaching the summit of that bliss, uninjured, for which thy Maker intended it." Why? Because of "the wicked designs of artful men, more ravenous than the hungry lions, which go about seeking whom they may devour." Thus he cautioned "the fair daughters of Eve," but could his warning against the "seducers of female excellence" have any more success than God's to Adam and Eve?

How closely the seduction story was modeled upon that of the Fall is even more apparent in a tale entitled "Treachery and Infidelity Punished." Almira, the picture of innocence and "as beautiful as the daughters of Paradise," is seduced by one Lothario: "Oh! the base dissembler—had ingratiated himself too far in her affections: with fondness she listened to his deceitful tales, and with too great avidity devoured his insinuating discourse." Like her mother Eve, Almira fell, for like Eve, she faced the most artful of deceivers, Satan himself, barely disguised.

Without question, most of the fictional seducers are satanic; they are described in terms that leave no doubt about their true nature. Seducers are "those reptiles, those anamacules [sic], who really come under the class of non-descripts in creation." Even when the deceiver is not a snake, he is animal-like, "a lordly brute [who] fixed his cruel fangs" on one who was "gay...lovely...innocent...happy." The seducer "stalks through the polite world like a satiated lion, who wants only the impulse of hunger to sacrifice another victim." The "vile seducer" is indeed subhuman, for he lacks the ability to love. Instead, he perverts affection, preying upon the credulity of the innocent; "falsehood guides [his] tongue, whilst an infamous baseness, under a plausible appearance of love or friendship conceals a heart destitute of every feeling." Indeed, the seducer is the enemy of love, and much like the Devil who envied Adam and Eve their innocent bliss, he plots its destruction.

Hannah Foster modeled Eliza Wharton's seducer at least as much on Satan as on Lovelace. Jealous of the minister Eliza seems to prefer and angered by her virtuous friends, Sanford sets out to trap the lovely girl who has caught his eye. The responsibility is hers, he claims: "If she will play with a lion, let her beware of his paw, I say." *Charlotte Temple*'s Belcour is cut from the same cloth, as are Sidney in "Charles and Amelia, or the Unfortunate Lovers," and Orlando, who contrives Narcissa's fall. In each case, most of the plot is devoted to the stratagems used to "ensnare" the heroine's virtue. Such men, surely, are beyond the compass of normal experience. Each is attracted only to the most singularly virtuous of girls and is not satisfied until he has succeeded in ruining her. Judith Sargent Murray wrote that it was hard to "conceive of turpitude so *enormous*, as that which must excite a being, *deliberately to perpetrate* the *murder of the peace of a fellow creature, without a single apparent motive to stimulate a deed of such atrocity.*" But it should not have been difficult at all; loathsome as the creature was, his prototype could be found in Genesis.

For this reason—that seduction tales essentially reenact the Fall, with the victim cast as Eve and the seducer as Satan himself—we should not read such tales too literally. While they certainly reinforced emerging Victorian standards of sexuality, it is doubtful that this was the primary objective. Rather, they represent another chapter in the early nineteenth century's secularization of religion. In them, the seducer is a secularized—but nonetheless recognizable—version of Satan. The real subject of the seduction stories is not whether young girls should resist sexual temptation, but what hope innocence has in a corrupt world. The answer was grim, and mankind's—not merely Eve's—repeated fall had grave implications not only for women but for all of American society. That was the lesson of "The Seducer: Addressed to the Fair Daughters of America." Its author, typically, was incredulous that a being so depraved as the "base seducer" could exist: "Such a one is a monster in creation. . . . To obtain his desires, he practices every art of dissimulation, and he does not hesitate to violate the most solemn engagements. Falsehood and perjury become familiar to him. . . . Virtue is sacrificed to his lust." Yet it is not only his innocent victim who suffers, for "the peace of individuals, families, and societies is destroyed. . . . Such are more dangerous to meet than bears bereaved of their whelps. They ought like ravenous wolves to be hunted from civilized society." The satanic seducer was an enemy to society, the snake in the grass of the infant republic.

To the list of republicanism's stock villains, to the tyrannical ruler and the designing courtier, we thus must add several other names: those of the coxcomb, the coquette, and—most of all—the vile seducer. All threatened the consensual union that served as the metaphor of what republicans wanted their society to be. Yet if republicanism found ways to vanquish the tyrant and banish the sycophant, it was powerless when confronted by this most insinuating and devilish seducer. He put republicanism, as a system of belief, on trial—and he won. He revealed republicanism's fatal flaw; although it could imagine ways by which reasonably virtuous men and women could make each other more so and might live with each other in harmony, it was utterly baffled by confirmed depravity. In some ways, republicanism represented a quarrel with Genesis. So long as republican-minded men and women could rewrite sacred history in such a way that the Fall never took place and Eve was never tempted, they could imagine themselves inhabiting an earthly paradise, living with their mates in a prelapsarian bliss. But the men and women who were the heirs of the Reformation could never fully forget the Fall; they knew that, when tempted by a deceiver of satanic proportions, humankind would fall and fall again.

The best solution they could devise for the inevitability of sin was the metaphor of republican marriage, in which like-minded and virtuous men and women would guide each other's steps along the paths of rectitude. Yet in their fiction they were drawn irresistibly to the seduction story, and there virtue—and the republic—fell. Most of this discourse, naturally, was expressed in codes; because it was so metaphorical, we cannot read it literally. Clearly, it was not merely sexual lust that republicans found so threatening, but immoderate desires of all kinds, ambition and self-interest chief among them. The vile seducer represented republicanism's inability to come to terms with power, which it tended to equate with evil.

Still, because women figured so prominently in it, we must ask what bearing the literature of republican marriage had for actual republican women. We see embedded in these works many of the themes that historians have already exposed: a growing acceptance of affection as the only proper basis of marriage, increasing respect for feminine virtue, the feminization of religion, the idealization of chastity, and, finally, a growing interest in the possibilities for feminine influence. These themes are all compressed into the person of the Republican Wife: affectionate, virtuous, chaste, and capable of enormous moral authority over her husband. The Republican Wife represented, in the ideology at least, a real and important role. Yet even as an image, she was limited. Indeed, she led to a dead end, for her capability always depended upon masculine susceptibility. She had no more power than man allowed, and even if republican doctrine suggested that men ought to welcome feminine influence, that doctrine held no sway over those who did not subscribe to its credo. That generalization, of course, describes the fundamental weakness in republicanism; it had no power over those who were not or did not want to be virtuous.

In that sense republicanism served women no more poorly than it did men: all were baffled by unalloyed vice. Even though republicanism enhanced woman's status and legitimated improvements in her education as well as her entry into benevolent reform movements, it also placed implicit checks upon her power. And it confronted her with the image of the seduced maid, condemned to fall repeatedly in tale after tale, seemingly incapable of learning from her experience. Women who wanted more status, influence, or power would have to look for another model. Thus the ideal of the wife would give way, by perhaps 1830, to that of the mother. Men might not be malleable, but children were, and they seemed to offer a more promising opportunity for the exercise of influence. Yet before that transition could be effected, the many elements that brought it about would have to fall into place: not merely a sentimental conception of motherhood—already widely shared by the end of the eighteenth century, as Ruth Bloch has shown—but also the removal of the father's place of work from the home, new views on the nature of childhood and child rearing, and, perhaps most important of all, an acceptance of childhood conversion. This shifting of emphasis from woman-as-wife to that of woman-as-mother had important implications for reform, for it rested upon the assumption that women had a special role to play as mothers and that, consequently, they represented a separate interest.

This transition in the conceptualization of woman's nature and her role would have parallels in other aspects of early national life. The 1820s and 1830s may represent a watershed, for not only would the Republican Wife be replaced by the Victorian mother, but in other ways as well the republican synthesis would dissolve, yielding to a more fragmented social vision. In politics, the semblance of an era of good feelings would give way to the second party system. Reform, also, would pass on to a new and more militant phase, beyond benevolence; vague plans for colonization or the eventual abolition of slavery would yield to immediatism, and hopeful schemes to "civilize" the Indian tribes would be replaced by the reality of the reservation. The republic of harmony proved ephemeral; it simply could not work, for it faltered in the face of intransigent slaveholders, Indians who did not want to be white, drunkards who would not give up the bottle, and, most simply, men who would not reform. When confronted by such enormous obstacles, the Republican Wife, like the theory that begot her and like the original woman in whose image she was cast, tasted of the fruit of knowledge and, inevitably, fell.

11

Public Versus Private Education: The Neglected Meaning of the Dartmouth College Case

ELDON L. JOHNSON

• *Almost alone among the great nations of the world, the United States has two distinct systems of higher education— one public and the other private. The reasons for such a dichotomy are many and varied, but if we look for the origins of the American pattern no issue will loom larger than the Dartmouth College case. Indeed, the United States Supreme Court's judgment on this litigation in 1819 is often regarded as the single most important judicial decision in all of American history.*

"It is a small college," noted Daniel Webster (class of 1801) in his eloquent defense, "and yet there are those who love it." He referred to the attempt of New Hampshire to change the college into a state university, to be called Dartmouth University. The charter of the institution, which was established in 1769 under Congregationalist auspices, was the issue in dispute. The state argued that Dartmouth was essentially a public corporation whose powers were exercised for public purposes and were subject to public control. The Dartmouth trustees countered with the claim that the college was a private eleemosynary institution.

Chief Justice John Marshall, in giving the opinion of the high court in 1819, ruled that Dartmouth's charter was a contract within the meaning of the United States Constitution and that as a contract it could not be repealed or altered by legislation. The Dartmouth College decision was a stunning defeat for those in every state who wanted to transform the colonial colleges into state universities under public control. In essence, the Supreme Court ruling meant that Harvard, Yale, Princeton, Columbia, Pennsylvania, and similarly char-

*tered institutions were and could remain independent. Hence-
forth, individual states would have to start from scratch to
create their own institutions of higher learning.*

*Dartmouth, meanwhile, went on to great distinction as a
center of academic excellence and established medical, business, engineering, and graduate schools of high quality. Although the institution became a university in fact, its trustees
have always clung to the name which they fought so hard to
keep in 1819—Dartmouth College.*

The Dartmouth College case, its climactic decision coming amidst intellectual and institutional churnings in the formative years of American
higher education, has been examined and reexamined far more for its
constitutional than its education meaning. The U.S. Supreme Court
decision of 1819 is famous in constitutional law for its statements on
private rights and corporation privileges. It is, perhaps, the most quoted
decision of all, but for reasons that have nothing to do with education.
Two great questions remain. What were the educational ideology and
goals in the attempted reform of the Dartmouth charter? ANd what
was the effect on the development of the supposed alternative of public
higher education? Almost no attention has been given the first question,
fundamental though it would seem; and the little attention given the
second, with one notable exception, has been based on questionable
inference. A return to these educational questions seems overdue since
a college was the centerpiece, the state was trying to change it, the
court said what could not be done and intimated what could, and both
the educational ideas espoused and the educational prohibitions imposed must have reverberated down through history for alert ears to
hear. One's curiosity is also piqued by that little explained sentence in
which one historian suggested that public higher education was thus
held back fifty years—an idea since echoed by others without much
examination. The effect on private higher education, bolstered by the
court's vigorous defense of private philanthropy, is much less in doubt
and will be treated here only indirectly.

All know about Daniel Webster and his pleading for the small college
that some still loved (although actually, in number of graduates produced, it was second only to Harvard). All know too about John Marshall, who, as chief justice, wrote what could not be done to the college.

But who knows about William Plumer, governor of New Hampshire, and what this Yankee Jeffersonian was trying to do? And who knows of the overall significance of the Dartmouth College case in the evolution of public higher education? History is a plaster which is hard to change once applied.

It all began in a church quarrel. The relation of Dartmouth's professor of divinity to the local church triggered a larger controversy about who would run the college. Trustees were soon galvanized into factions in their long festering relations with President John Wheelock. Losing his grip after more than thirty years, he invoked the royal charter which the colonial governor had issued in 1769 to Wheelock's father, Eleazar, and went to the New Hampshire legislature for relief. Thus began, in the words of a Dartmouth historian, "a quarrel which was to end in the Supreme Court of the United States, with all the nation looking on." The president, abetted by the minority trustees, memorialized the legislature for public remedy; the opposing trustees took sufficient umbrage to dismiss Wheelock before the resulting legislative investigating committee could report; and the charter (private or public?) became a burning public issue. Newspapers took sides. Pamphlets appeared for and against. Indignation ran against both Wheelock's dismissal and the "dynasty" he tried to perpetuate through the charter.

In time, the issue was politicized. Federalists tended to support the status quo and Republicans favored change; so the New Hampshire election of 1816 was waged on the issue. Afterwards, the new governor, William Plumer, made charter reform one of the two critical issues on which he called for legislative remedy. Following a bitter, protracted struggle of parliamentary maneuver, attempted delay, investigations, and embarrassing divisions (all along political lines), the legislature narrowly voted to "improve" the royal charter carried over into republican times—to make the governance of the college more public and less self-perpetuating, and to conceive the new embodiment as "Dartmouth University." The state injected itself dramatically into college affairs by increasing the number of trustees; giving veto power to a large new board of overseers to be named by the governor and council, who were obligated to inspect the doings of all officers; requiring president and professors to take an oath to support the United States and New Hampshire constitutions; calling for an annual presidential report to the governor on enrollment and the "state of funds"; and guaranteeing "perfect freedom of religious opinion."

But it was not to be so simple. The opposing trustees who were carried over and their college allies dug in their heels, frustrated a quorum, drove governor and legislature to try again with amendments, took the great majority of students off campus for continued instruction, hired the most distinguished lawyers, and carried the matter to the courts. Eventually, the highest state court upheld the act and an appeal was taken to the Supreme Court solely on the grounds that the college charter was a contract inviolate under the Constitution. With Daniel Webster pleading and with other distinguished lawyers participating, Chief Justice Marshall and fellow justices (with one dissent), held for the college in *Trustees of Dartmouth College* v. *Woodward* in 1819. The state legislative act was void because the college was a charitable institution, not a public corporation; hence the charter was a contract and could not be impaired under the Constitution.

What did this mean, at the time and for the future? In looking back, it is now clear that the case originated in differing conceptions of the college mission and of institutional responsibility. It is also clear that it helped shape American higher education in its formative years. Yet the educational significance of the Dartmouth case has been neglected, particularly in understanding what Governor Plumer and his allies were attempting, in ideas as well as in action.

It may be noted at the outset that William Plumer was a public man in the best tradition of the Enlightenment in early America. He was an independently minded, self-educated lawyer who made significant political and intellectual contributions, both locally and nationally. At twenty-six years of age, he entered the state legislature, where he served eight terms and rose to speaker of the house and president of the senate. The revised state constitution of 1792 was so much of his shaping that opponents called it "Plumer's Constitution." Despite his professed indifference when out of public office, politics kept calling him back from law, farm, and books—once to the United States Senate, 1802–1807, and repeatedly to the governorship of New Hampshire, in 1812, and for three yearly terms from 1816 to 1819. Plumer began as a Federalist but deplored blind party loyalty and, despite his initial dislike and suspicion of Jefferson, eventually shifted to the Republican party.

While not so consistently liberal as Jefferson, Plumer pressed religious liberty wit such fervor that he provoked violent recriminations. He embraced reform and thought well ahead of his time: in treatment of prisoners and debtors, in legal codification, in educational philosophy, and in advocacy of an income tax. Beyond that, he had ideas about virtually everything, as shown in the 186 essays he wrote and published between 1820 and 1829. He was widely read, often quoting Bacon, Montaigne, Locke, Rousseau, Pope, Gibbon, and Adam Smith. His private library was almost half the size of Dartmouth College. From his exposure to the nation's capital in the formative years, he resolved to write the definitive history of North America and was encouraged to do so by Jefferson, John Quincy Adams, and others. What he left, instead, were many useful biographical remnants and significant aid to new regional historical societies. All in all, he was a fiercely independent man of intellectual substance, "a man of conviction, of stubborn courage, and of devotion to principles wider than his own horizons and nobler than his own character." Paying tribute to the local bar which so helped shape the young Daniel Webster in Portsmouth, New Hampshire, biographer Henry Cabot Lodge named Plumer as "the most eminent and "a man of cool and excellent judgment," who "was one of Mr. Webster's early antagonists, and defeated him in their first encounter."

This was the man whose position as governor of New Hampshire brought him into the midst of the Dartmouth College controversy. Given his qualities and values, however, it is quite likely that he would have spoken out on the issues of the case in any event. Partisan politics was indeed present. With plenty of initiative from both sides, it sprang both from current interest and past history. It reflected the intense public controversy engendered and testified that a "public interest" was perceived by many common citizens and their leaders. Moreover, as John S. Whitehead pointed out in *The Separation of College and State*, Dartmouth had long followed the collegiate pattern of the time, sought uneasy alliances with the state, asked state favors, and thus incurred political risks from the fierce battle between Federalists and Republicans for state supremacy. Indeed, one line of legal defense held that "our Legislature has often interfered and had thus gained a kind of prescriptive right of interference." Isaac Hill, partisan Republican editor of the *New Hampshire Patriot and State Gazette*, thought that "the future governance of D. College," if "judiciously managed, will be a means of perpetuating the republican majority in the State." When the Federalists attempted to thwart the two great legislative changes of 1816—both judicial reform and charter reform—the college reformers gladly joined the issues for the fall election, and prepared to deal with the unconvinced Dartmouth trustees in the "common interest of our party." The governor was dragged in further than expected because another "long and unpleasant session" was required for patch-up amendments to produce a workable quorum of trustees, with fines for holdouts. In this political climate, the aggrieved and irascible President Wheelock easily precipitated a nasty battle over his reinstatement, which became hopelessly confused with broader governance considerations. However, as a later president controversy from the side of the College said, "It would be unjust . . . to recall this ancient controversy from the side of the College without making the frank acknowledgement that the College invited the interference of the State."

On the charter and governance issues, Plumer clearly acted with competent legal knowledge and legitimate interest in sound public policy. He knew what other states had tried to do, recognized the unsettled legal implications, and had already taken the position that legislatures were incautiously passing acts of incorporation, often "in the nature of grants," without reserving legislative power of repeal or modification "when they cease to answer the end for which they were made, or prove injurious to the public interest." This plea for charters of public responsibility was expressed in Plumer's first gubernatorial message to the legislature four years before the Dartmouth crisis. On vindicating President Wheelock, Plumer's own letters are singularly free of political motivation, although he received commendation for "defense of our venerable friend" and never flinched from battle with the old Federalists. While he once equated Republican victory with "justice to the injured [President] Wheelock," he later wrote that "it has long been a subject of great regret to me that the name of Dartmouth University has been considered as a political party question." Looking beyond presidential restoration, Plumer asked his partisan allies to join in devising "a system . . . to prevent the college being again exposed to similar evils." His subsequent naming of the board members from both parties gave some credibility to his florid hope "that when the sod shall be green on my grave those who survive me will say I have preferred men of merit to political partisans." His concern was for a certain type of institution, more broadly representative, that would reflect his strong views about education with public relevance and responsibility; hence, he fervently urged a trustee to public duty lest "the University remain unorganized . . . and perhaps the current of public opinion [be] turned against the Institution."

Fortunately, we also have a clear picture of Plumer's educational philosophy in a remarkable series of newspaper essays written under the name of "Cincinnatus" two years after the Supreme Court rebuff. He was critical of existing collegiate education and thought it called for radical reform. Such reform would have three major thrusts. It would come from institutions under public control and support, state oriented rather than church oriented. It would emphasize educational application to daily life—the useful, the scientific, the ordinary vocations. It would be open to the poor as well as the rich.

American institutions had become slightly more liberal than the En- glish, but the same "mistaken policy" prevailed, wherein "*the great object of colleges was to educate young men for priesthood,* rather than to qualify them for the duties of civil life." Harvard and Dartmouth were both church-ridden, too subject to "principles unfavorable to the progress of education in the higher branches of literature and science." Hence the usual inquiry was "not whether the public need other col- leges, but whether *particular sects* want them." Instead, colleges should be "formed and governed" without regard to religion or party. "The commonwealth of letters is free—men of erudition of all countries, sects, and parties are its members—and no scholar can be alien from it." Existing colleges were good for the education of the clergy (they needed it, he said) but they should be more—"of a different character . . . suited to the pursuits and business of *this life*." This conviction that contemporary collegiate education was too "monkish" appeared again and again in Plumer's writings; in fact, he thought the ecclesiastical rather than civil emphasis might be "hostile to our republican system."

What was wrong with the colleges was typified by the retention of, and emphasis on, ancient languages and the mode of their teaching. He objected when his children and grandchildren were subjected to Greek, Latin, or Hebrew and rejoiced when French or German was taken. He did not want the prime of life wasted on useless learning and, worse yet, on the form rather than the substance: on the language of the ancients instead of the opinions, ideas, and knowledge possessed by the ancients.

For remedy, Plumer would first put an end to the private-public ambiguity being played upon, as he learned to his sorrow in the Dartmouth case. "When the government of our colleges apply to the people or to the legislature for aid," he wrote, "they represent the college as a *public institution*."

> But when the legislature of the State enact [*sic*] laws for their better regulation and improvement, then the college is to be considered as a *private corporation* exempt from all legislative acts. . . . Let the legislature establish *a public Academy* in each county in the State, subject to the control . . . of civil government. . . . After such academies are established, and the people experience their salutary effects, the legislature will have an easy task to establish a public college or university upon similar principles. Society owes too much to education to justify legislators who neglect the means for its support.

He did not believe that institutions like Dartmouth, many of which received partial public support, were private in the public-hands-off sense held by the Supreme Court; but, if so, then alternative public institutions should be established. Such institutions, moreover, should and would be responsive to the need for new kind of education—useful education.

The academies Plumer conceived would start with "nothing but what is useful and subservient to the business of human life," and the new college or university would correct the mistake of not adopting "effectual measures for instructing youth in the useful arts [and] in science." As "now constituted and governed," however, no college can give "useful and complete education." Plumer underscored the point: "In what school, academy or college are the principles and sciences of agriculture, of commerce, of manufacturers, or of mechanics taught? These are important subjects in which we have a direct and deep interest: for it is from them we derive all the means of substance." Similar sentiments came from Jonathan Baldwin Turner and Justin Morrill forty years later, at the inception of the national system of land grant colleges. It is fitting that in closing his twenty-fifth article on education in the Cincinnatus series, Plumer wrote, "*utility* has been my sole object."

Nor were these educational constructions mere post-Supreme Court rationalizations. While the then new "Dartmouth University" should have given him encouragement, he wrote his friend Salma Hale: "I have long wished to see a fundamental change in these institutions; to have more of the time of students devoted to the acquisition of *useful* rather than ornamental knowledge—the knowledge of *things* rather than that of *words*—and to make proficiency in the *living* rather than the *dead* languages." Then he added plaintively, "I hope for these changes in our university, but I have no reason to expect them" The thing/words, living/dead, useful/ornamental dichotomies were a constant refrain.

Utility led to another reform objective. Since life is short, time should be best used; but the great time needed for college preparation and for learning the dead languages "necessarily excludes a vast proportion of our youth from those institutions." So long as this condition continued, public tax support was not justified. Let the "rich and idle" enjoy such, "but free the common people from the support of establishments in the enjoyment of which they cannot participate." This man who later thought Andrew Jackson's election and "the mad spirit of Jacksonism" the greatest misfortune to befall the nation, nevertheless wrote about education in the context of the "common people," the "common affairs of life," the dangers of "the privileged orders," and the need for more responsive institutions befitting the new republicanism.

What Plumer wanted is best summarized in the positive portion of an essay that criticized the existing colleges with unusual severity. Yes, "even in their present state," they could be of some good:

> But to render them extensively useful to the public, they require a radical reform. They should no longer be schools of theology but civil institutions—instead of being private they should be public establishments, not governed by sectarian priests but by men of literature and science without regard to their professions—instead of *dead* languages, the *living* languages should be taught—the modern discoveries in philosophy and the useful arts should be promptly adopted; and youth instructed in the arts and sciences that are applicable to the business of human life.

These were the educational ideas of the man who led the attempt to amend the Dartmouth charter. They had the immediate potency of his political influence and, on a more enduring basis, they were representative of something larger than himself. During the three or four decades before the ardent advocacy of the 1850s, sentiment for a more responsive kind of higher education was not lacking. It was muted both inside and outside the colleges by dormant enrollments and the flood tide of denominationalism—yet Thomas Jefferson did not stand alone. There were political leaders and opinion-makers who made possible all the early state universities. There were others who promoted particular educational reforms that produced the ingredients later to be clustered together in institutions controlled and supported by state governments. When these unsung authors and actors are brought from obscurity, William Plumer will be prominent among them. If his word was not wholly original nor his deed wholly enduring, he the better reflected his time and the ferment that would later transform American higher education, with an alternative closely allied with the state. He reflected the transitional period in which, according to one historian, family, church, and community influence over education had waned and the "whole range of education had become an instrument of deliberate social purpose."

The first question can now be answered—what educational change was attempted at Dartmouth? As in most political crises, strange bedfellows thought differently but acted together. Some wanted merely to restore President John Wheelock and some merely to defeat political opponents, but what mattered and endured was more substantive. The central attempt was to make Dartmouth more accountable to public authority and needs, in great harmony with the ideals of a democratic secular state and a society of equals. Significantly, that reform effort was the deliberate expression of a sovereign state (the organized New Hampshire public) through all its branches: the executive recommendation, the legislative enactment, and the judicial approval. As the articulate spokesman for many Jeffersonian values of the time, Plumer spelled out the supporting philosophy and the educational results hoped for, once the form was adopted. He gave the rationale from which immediate action proceeded and the goals toward which growth was to be directed. These new desiderata were then put at the mercy of quite inadequate means: transforming an existing institution through state "control" that relied on the presence of state officers without the presence of state taxes. But however rebuffed and delayed, the central idea would persist and later flower in institutions that Plumber and his allies countrywide would have found congenial.

The second question about the effect on the development of public higher education can best be approached by examining what happened in New Hampshire first and then elsewhere. The effect upon Dartmouth itself is important because the strategy of the 1816 legislation was to reform an *existing* institution by launching something public and something called a "university." Deposed President John Wheelock's nephew strongly lobbied for a university divided into colleges, as the law contemplated; and when the new Dartmouth University trustees met without a quorum in 1816, they received a committee report that proposed both some curricular broadening and institutional reorganization, with Colleges of Theology, Medicine, and Law. The curious fact is that Dartmouth unofficially had called itself a "university" as early as 1782 and through the catalogs of the entire 1801–1814 period. That was rather the academic fashion of the time and was abandoned, ironically at Dartmouth, only when the legislature sought to impose precisely that name. Were Webster and colleagues influenced by the fact that in English law "university" meant a public corporation, whereas "college" meant a private charity? before the Supreme Court, Webster derided "the swelling and empty authority" in the "mock elevation to... a university." Even Governor Plumer once conceded that "University" and "College" conveyed no real difference. The profound difference was the existence, nevertheless, of two institutions, competing both legally and often ludicrously for students, keys, books, possession of buildings, commencement dates, and public favor. The incongruity climaxed when both institutions held commencements and both conferred honorary degrees on President James Monroe when he visited New England in 1817. The new state-originated institution was a disaster by any standard, with its unhappy status never better shown than in the accountability report that the new legislation required to be filed with the governor. "University" President William Allen labored valiantly but could report accurately only on the number of students— sixteen. The state of funds, official board actions, and everything else was unknown, ambiguous, or speculative. With remarkable understatement, the president confessed to the governor after the Supreme Court decision that "some officers were discouraged." The short-run effect on the existing college was disastrous, too; but how it recovered and later rose to its present esteemed position is not central to our present purposes.

It was unclear whether Dartmouth was a single college temporarily ruptured by fuzziness about the public-private balance or two institutions already set on contrasting courses. The situation was confounded by the insufficient solution the state attempted, as best shown by the conclusion of two New Hampshire legislative committees that state "control" was necessary but that reform of the charter of the existing college would yield that desired result. Relying on the sufficiency of this remote and indirect public patronage for "the cause of literature and science" (not uncommonly proposed elsewhere in New England at the time), one committee took the view that "the surest and most effectual means ... are to be found in extending to our highest seminary of learning a *controlling* as well as fostering protection— thereby uniting its interests and destinies more firmly with the government of the State." Events were soon to demonstrate that Dartmouth was not the proper subject and a "fostering protection" was not a sufficient method. Furthermore, there is no evidence that Plumer, either as governor or Dartmouth University board member, was determined to force his personal ideas on the new Dartmouth, or that he could have done so through trustees or overseers sometimes as unreliable as executive-appointed judges. He had already failed to wring from the legislature a governing body as publicly representative and responsive (that is, not self-perpetuating) as he wanted. He more than once lamented that his ideas had little hope of acceptance, either under state reform or after the judicial reprieve. He again wrote: "Those institutions are in the hands of men who appear little inclined to change their present course, and still less to acknowledge a right in the people or the legislature to effect a reformation." Whether because of ennui, disillusionment, or decision not to run for gubernatorial reelection, he in 1818 began to excuse himself from university duties and from commencement, with pleas of ill health and hopes for a more useful successor. He apparently did nothing later to foster a public university or to identify with such feeble university-starting efforts as the literary fund gambit of Governor Samuel Bell. Even in logical openings in correspondence with public figures, Plumer withheld comment on university reform, apparently looking back somewhat bitterly on the Dartmouth case as a lost, if not last, opportunity.

Contrary to common assumption, however, this aborted state plan for Dartmouth did not summarily end agitation for state-controlled higher education in New Hampshire. Two great ironies are worthy of mention. In the heat of battle, none other than Daniel Webster suggested the instigation of a plan to create a state-officered "University of New Hampshire" as a means of finding peace; and a loyal Dartmouth trustee group offered a face-saving compromise which would have assured the essential public oversight Plumer sought but could not then gracefully accept. Neither he nor they then knew that trustee acceptance of the compromise would have, because of trustee consent, removed the hinge on which *Dartmouth* v. *Woodward* was to turn. These ambivalent gestures merely recognized, however grudgingly, the durability of the public dimension of the issue; and it remained for Plumer's political successor, Governor Samuel Bell, to make two other valiant attempts to found a separate new university. First, he worked with the 1819 legislature in setting up a committee to devise complete plans for a "public literary institution in this State." But the astutely chosen chairman, President William Allen of the short-lived university, declined the honor because he thought that one college in New Hampshire was enough and he continued to believe that Dartmouth reform of the attempted kind, but with trustee consent, could and should appropriately monopolize legislative patronage. Second, in 1821 the governor and the legislature set up a "literary fund" from a stamp tax on bank circulation. The annual receipts were to support education in the higher branches of literature and science, provided significantly that support should never go to any institution *not* under the direction and control of the state. The muddling of the public-private dichotomy was never better illustrated than when Dartmouth came forward aggressively to seek the money, with willingness to create a Board of Overseers as the "public" price. As the money accumulated, debate ensued on whether to divert it for general state expenses, "for the establishment of a College in some central place," or for schools in the towns. But the public university forces could never muster enough strength to prevail. Their proposed use of the literary fund for a "New Hampshire University" in 1827 passed in the senate, but lost in the house by a two-to-one majority.

That was the high point of public university advocacy in New Hampshire in the half century following the attempted Dartmouth changes. The following year, the new governor began claiming that enough colleges existed in New England, Dartmouth sufficed with its private support, and therefore the towns should receive the literary fund for common schools. As last, that recommendation prevailed. But the seeds of something distinctive, destined eventually to yield fruit, were planted at the same time; that is, the need for agricultural research and training began to be articulated. In the same message that turned off the public university thrust, Governor John bell lucidly spelled out what he thought, in contrast, was needed—"an experimental farm and agricultural school." It was a remarkable prevision of the later land grant college, with emphasis upon practical as well as scientific education, broader student access, student labor, and even an embryonic extension system. This was all too advanced for the lower house, which resolved neither to purchase an experimental farm nor to "adopt any measures in relation to the same."

This history of muddlement and parsimony detracts from the surmise that if the Dartmouth College case had gone the other way, New Hampshire might have had a flourishing state university at once. other evidence magnifies the doubt. First of all, the legislature was not the slightest disposed to provide financial support. To make the reformed Dartmouth "A well-endowed institution" with "a liberal patronage" might have been William Plumer's intention, as his son later contended; but the legislature showed no concurrence. In fact, Plumer was himself a zealot of governmental economy. The state even treated shabbily the university trustees and officers who, after the Supreme Court foreclosure, had to appeal for help on the grounds that they had acted in good faith with the legislature's desire "to improve what was thought to be a public institution." Such help as had been given already to the new "public university" amounted to a four thousand dollar *loan*; and its eventual cancellation (because of no alternative for a defunct institution) was a measure of the legislature's largess.

Things were no better across the river in Vermont, where the incubus of the Dartmouth case did not exist. The spirit of the times, in other words, was well reflected in the studied ambiguity of Governor Jonas Golusha, who said to the Vermont legislature in 1816: "If any further aid to education should be deemed necessary, I doubt not that it will receive all the encouragement that present circumstances of the state will admit." That translated into no aid in 1816, 1817, and 1818. The evidence is that intellectual, political, and budgetary forces stripped Governor Samuel Bell and his enthusiastic senate committee of their confidence in 1820 that a public institution "will sooner or later go into operation under the high auspices of the people of New Hampshire." It was much later, rather than sooner. The New Hampshire College of Agriculture and Mechanical Arts was established in 1866, and the name changed to University of New Hampshire in 1923.

Therefore, the consequences within the involved state would seem superficially to be precisely what Tewksbury said: a fifty-year retardation of the state university movement. The fact is one thing, the causes another, as outlined above. In one sense, quite ironically, New Hampshire had been judicially prompted to do what it presumably wanted to do, only to do it in a more direct way. Certainly, it could have founded an institution beneficially dedicated to that specific place—New Hampshire—since the reasoning of both Chief Justice Marshall and Justice Story had gone to some lengths to show that Dartmouth had no ties to geography or service-to-place. But when it came to the doing, the need for a public alternative was not clearly established. Education dominated by religion was more rather than less popular, despite Governor Plumer's hostility, and the good thoughts about education were drowned out by the bad thoughts about taxes. How slowly the "public" concept had evolved, even in fifty years, is shown by New Hampshire's attempt to piggyback its new land grant college on Dartmouth College once more in 1866. It was a tribute to Dartmouth, which made generous concessions, and it was a vote for governmental frugality; but, foredoomed as an unhappy marriage, it was also an indication that little heed was given either the lesson learned by Plumer or the government's remedy stated by Marshall.

The Dartmouth case had repercussions outside New Hampshire also, both on and beyond the state versus college issue. The interest was greater and the information more widespread than some historians have implied. Even before the case was resolved, the New-York Historical Society was asking Plumer for all relevant documents. The issue of state intrusion was a half-century old and the *North American Review* promptly and approvingly presented the Supreme Court's state-restraining decision in January 1820, because none other "excited deeper interest in the public mind" and all colleges "stood on no surer foundation than Dartmouth College." Likewise thinking Dartmouth's fate "perhaps of equal importance to every other literary and charitable corporation of our country," Timothy Farrar, Webster's former partner, immediately rushed the decision (with its history and pleadings) into print in 1819 to reach the public in addition to the professional audience of the official Wheaton report. The case itself had attracted the nation's best legal talent on both sides, and Governor Plumer had sent his 1816 charter reform message to Thomas Jefferson, prompting approval and the famous reply that "our lawyers and priests generally inculcate this doctrine...that the earth belongs to the dead, and not to the living." With still closer interest, the colleges of the Northeast were clearly aroused. When a College Congress was held in Boston in 1818 with representatives from Yale, Harvard, Bowdoin, the University of Vermont, Williams, and Andover Theological Seminary present, Dartmouth College President Brown was invited but Dartmouth University President Allen was not. The Dartmouth appellants had already asked other colleges to help defer court costs, but President Kirkland of Harvard declined because the highest court might uphold the state decision, increasing its authority a hundredfold and making its application nationwide. Such were then the dubious odds in the public-private battle, with weighty authority on each side. Out of interest among other colleges, a Yale professor did go to Washington to hear the evidence presented. State and college officials, donors, and their legal counsel could hardly have been uninformed, unimpressed, or unaffected after the exhaustive treatment and rounded reasoning, on both sides, in the state court in 1817 and the federal court in 1818–1819.

It is important to remember, however, that the public overlay on Dartmouth was only the first to be tested, not the first to be attempted. Long ago, Lester W. Bartlett summarized the history of post-Revolution attempts at state control in Massachusetts, Connecticut, Pennsylvania, and New York, showing that New Hampshire's later attempt was by no means the most "oppressive" or "threatening," if judged by the percentage of state officials on the college boards. Dartmouth history differed, however, in the complete polarization of forces, the duality of institutions, the legal deadlock, and the firm resolve to derive a guiding precedent from a local example. As Harvard's history before and after showed, legislative tampering (state officers on boards, vetoing powers, visitations) did not keep the institution from being private, yet did not make it public. Nor was the Dartmouth case to be the last. In 1831, for example, the Maine legislature intruded into Bowdoin College to squeeze out President William Allen. Having come there from the headship of the short-lived "public" version of Dartmouth, Allen paradoxically had to switch roles and resort to the federal courts for the same kind of victory that his opponents had enjoyed in 1819.

It was on the public-private distinction that *Dartmouth* v. *Woodward* had the greatest effect nationwide. While the decision meant that the states could no longer reform private colleges without the consent of the trustees involved, unless such power had been reserved, it also called attention quite specifically to how the public *could* do what William Plumer attempted. Chief Justice Marshall wrote: "That education is ... a proper subject of legislation, and placed entirely under its immediate control, the officers of which would be public officers, amenable exclusively to government, none will deny." Therefore, after 1819, every state legislature with collegiate reform ambitions had new limitations upon it and clarified opportunities before it, even if this dictum merely advertised the obvious. As a result, there was increased potential for affecting the establishment and growth of state universities—either hastening or retarding them.

It would be folly to attribute all that later happened to the Dartmouth case, without awareness of many other factors. Some state universities existed before 1819 and those which came after had other initiatives quite apart from Dartmouth, such as the First Amendment impetus to a secular state university; the public land grants, first for new states and later for all states through the Morrill Act; and the changing conception of what was "public" enough to call for governmental response. But the Dartmouth decision thrust in the opposite direction also and became entwined with the great antebellum proliferation of "Christian" colleges, both denominational and non-denominational. In the church-state confrontation born of revolutionary fervor, religion rose to clear dominance in collegiate education. Francis Wayland wrote in 1842: "Almost every college in this country is either originally, or by sliding from its primitive foundation, under the control of some religious sect." In fact, the dominance was so great that the sliding extended even to established state universities, often submerging the public parts and dominating the self-perpetuating boards, as exhibited in all six of the state universities then existing in the original states. That this was a drag on the evolution of "godless universities" cannot be doubted.

A reexamination of the Dartmouth case is a vivid reminder that institutions of higher education have evolved from myriad forces much too complex and attenuated to be explained by sudden events and decisive single cases. It is also a reminder that we, like Plumer and the Dartmouth trustees, are captives of our time and that we are prone to transfer from present to past that which was never there. When we apply "public" to collegiate institutions, we connote the concept of tax-supported, government-owned, and state-run schools, none of which would have been intelligible in 1816. "Private" higher education—untouchable and untouched by the state—had not yet arrived, if yet conceived. Dictionaries and encyclopedias of that time make clear that "public" meant merely what was "done by many," or for the common good,or open to common use—which obviously could have meant a group of "private" individuals. that explains why Governor Plumer thought Dartmouth was already a public institution, why the New Hampshire court unanimously agreed, and why both sides could accept the "guardian care" and "visitorial power" of the state. Two decades later, in his critique of colleges (then virtually all church-controlled), Francis Wayland carefully described them as "public institutions." This confusion between the object of existence and the finality of control also explains why everyone on the "public" side at that time had unwarranted confidence in the sufficiency of state control by the mere laying on of hands via governing boards. Later experience was to show that state support, not a vacuous state presence or concern, was the real key to public higher education. That meant taxation and annual appropriations—again concepts quite foreign to the public-private blurring of 1816, when all kinds of education still relied on unassured annual combinations in which the public and tax parts, if they existed at all, were merely folded into the endowment and current donations parts.

Making a distinction that was to have a profound effect on the relations between state and college, Chief Justice Marshall's language drove a giant wedge into a small fissure. The twin nuclei of private and public could now be separated. They had been conceptually and, in time, would be operationally. But Marshall did not say the poles he identified were the only options. He did not rule out the continuation of some mix between college and state. Not surprisingly, practical men in both college and public life chose for a long time to strive for a balance or an accommodation, rather than an exclusionary extreme. This point is made with convincing documentation by John S. Whitehead, in *The Separation of College and State*. He challenges the conventional wisdom that the Dartmouth College case immediately severed the college-state alliance and clearly set apart public and private higher education. He shows that the Dartmouth trustees accepted their victory as leaving them in the ascendancy in running the college, but they saw no reason to break off the long-standing (if sometimes uneasy) state-college accommodation of mutual gain. As time went on, both at Dartmouth and at other institutions in other states, it was the state rather than the college that opted out of the alliance. With this foreclosure of public support, which went increasingly to public schools and to the public colleges and universities, and with the rise of private philanthropy in American life, the alliance was severed and the public-private distinction became clearly discernible—with President Charles Eliot of Harvard as the chief articulator. That, however, was after 1870. It had taken fifty years to sort out the public-private interest, to pull state and college fully apart, and to find the will as well as the way to separate and maintain "public" and "private" institutions. Interestingly enough, the case followed roughly the same time pattern in gaining its fame on constitutional grounds in "defense of vested rights" against the state, as Webster himself put it.

These were forces which prolonged the reliance on institutions of the familiar type (with a public-private blurring) and resisted the creation of an alternative (with complete separation). Such forces *included* the Dartmouth controversy and its intellectual options but were much larger and, in the aggregate, more conclusive. Gradualism, over a long continuum of interacting forces, was the key. Therefore, to say that the public-private split did not fully materialize until the 1870s is not to deny that forces generated as far back as 1816 and 1819 played a contributing or even determining role. Surely after the Marshal decision cutting off one approach for the state and pointing out another, and after all the intellectual and philosophical debate, "public" had to imply a more activist, initiating, supporting role—thus challenging and gradually replacing the mere authorizing, exhorting, and supervising posture of the state. Plumer's solution did not work. Something more would be required.

At the other pole, the chartered colleges with self-perpetuating boards were given new impetus and governmental immunity that flowered in the "denominational era," and remain as a rich heritage in that great segment of higher education now called "private." Chancellor Kent wrote in his *Commentaries* that the Dartmouth case did more than any other single governmental act "to give solidity and inviolability to the literary, charitable, religious, and commercial institutions of our country." Noting this growth under the new legitimacy, the *Encyclopedia Americana* of 1830 feared that colleges would proliferate on a faulty analogy to the common schools, where "there can hardly be too many of them," little realizing the full potency of that analogy as burgeoning new public institutions were added to the private profligacy.

Rivalry between emerging types of institutions was inevitable. Indeed, it ran to debilitating extremes before the rediscovery that, with creative accommodation, public and private can be complementary. Fortunately, the "public" part was rarely carried to the extreme contemplated in some of the judicial pleadings and opinions—that is, to operation as a wholly undifferentiated and unbuffered part of civil government. Nevertheless, the Supreme Court's separation of public an private went too far in higher education, as it did also in constitutional law. A federal judge recently said that Marshall made it too easy for himself, by "drawing so bright a line between 'a civil institution to be employed in the administration of the government' and 'a private eleemosynary institution,' " and that the court itself no longer feels bound to follow the formulation of 160 years ago. The line was originally blurred; separation was carried too far; blurring is with us again. Meanwhile, much educational history has rolled by, partly shaped by the Dartmouth case.

For those who want to reduce complex historical questions to simplicity, the Dartmouth experience will be frustrating. In fact, to attempt to keep the strains unsnarled and to unfurl a neat answer is to abuse the evidence. The Dartmouth episode in its entirety, not merely the

court case, helps us identify the contributing ingredients of significant change but does not nicely measure their relative weight in the total balance. Beyond doubt, however, it was an event in the formative years of American higher education which helped shape the future. Intellectually, it elicited rough educational ideas and honed them in debate; it strengthened the philosophy of some kind of a higher education alternative, increasingly called "public"; and it hastened the Darwinian effect among educational modes increasingly at odds. Operationally, it defined the options for both state and college; it clarified the inadequacy of state control without state support; and it assured a richer variety of institutional embodiments for the nation. Negatively, the state would thereafter have to respect existing institutional charters or gain the consent of the trustees. There was a chilling effect on state intrusion into higher education governance anywhere anytime. Positively, the state could achieve its purposes via new charters by reserving the appropriate power for later reform, or it could found wholly public institutions committed to the service of a particular place. Conceptually, this great attention to a public alternative could have been a hastening factor in the rise of state colleges and universities—the reverse of the common Dartmouth attribution. But, pragmatically, other factors, chiefly political readiness, were determining. The state had to perceive a need and overcome both
opposition from existing church-related institutions and from reluctant taxpayers. It was effective political will that was tardy, and far more the cause of delay among state universities than the Dartmouth impact.

No one can read the learned decisions by Chief Justice William M. Richardson of New Hampshire and by Justices Marshall, Washington, and Story of the Supreme Court without being reminded that the options all emerged in the context of education, not of commerce—of the small college, not, as later, the big corporation. In restoring that awareness, we are also reminded that with its clashing ideas (including the neglected ones of William Plumer), its national attention and significance, and its effect on the state in relation to both private and public higher education, the Dartmouth controversy was a significant peak, perhaps still inadequately explored, on an important watershed of American educational history.

12

Indian Policy in the Jacksonian Era

RONALD N. SATZ

• As Frederick Jackson Turner, Bernard De Voto, Richard A. Bartlett, William H. Goetzmann, and dozens of other historians have noted, the expansion of the United States from its narrow base along the Eastern Seaboard to almost continental size has been a central fact of American development. The story of the confrontation and eventual domination of the vast and empty spaces by successive waves of pioneer Americans has become our national epic.

Much less attention has been focused on the fact that the settlement of the West ranks among the many examples of naked aggression offered by history. In simple terms, an entire people was removed, a people whose claims to the land often dated back hundreds of years before it was even seen by the first white man. Those Indians that did not die in battle, or from hunger, or from diseases introduced by the new "Americans" were pressed onto reservations that kept getting smaller and smaller, despite treaties and guarantees from the federal government.

That this history was largely ignored for a century and more is hardly surprising given the treachery and the shameful methods used to separate the Indians from what was once theirs. Scholars who did write on the subject were usually so convinced of their own racial and cultural superiority over the native people that their accounts are properly suspect.

The essay by Ronald N. Satz is part of a reappraisal by younger historians of the assumptions held by nineteenth-century policy makers concerning the removal of Indian tribes. Were the claims of these relatively nomadic Indians greater than those of the pioneers who wanted to cultivate the land and create a cornucopia of plenty in the midst of a wilderness?

Reprinted by permission of the author, who is Dean of Graduate Studies and Research at the University of Wisconsin-Eau Claire.

*Or would you agree with twentieth-century historian Satz
(and nineteenth-century English traveler Frances Trollope)
that, as Satz puts it, "Indian removal epitomized everything
despicable in American character"?*

There has long been a tendency among scholars to view the Indian
removal policy of the Jacksonian era in dualistic terms—the forces of
evil supported removal while the forces of humanity opposed it. Recently, Frances Paul Prusha, George A. Schultz, and Herman J. Viola
have attempted to show that enlightened thought supported Indian
removal as a means of rescuing the eastern Indians from the evil effects
of close contact with the advancing white frontier. Yet even these
historians admit that the actual removal prices entailed numerous hardships for the Indians.

This essay is an attempt to assess the goals, execution, and results
of the Indian removal policy in the 1830s and 1840s by focusing
on the application of that policy in the Old Northwest. The events
surrounding the removal of the Five Civilized Tribes from the South
have long been, to use the words of Grant Foreman, "a chapter unsur-
passed in pathos and absorbing interest in American history." This
dramatic episode has, to some extent, obscured similar events taking
place farther north during the same period of time. The Old Northwest provides an interesting test case for an examination of the differences between the rhetoric and the reality of the removal policy. The
Indians in this region were not the beneficiaries of anything approach-
ing the tremendous outpouring of public sympathy for the Cherokees and their neighbors in the Southeast. If the Cherokees faced
a "Trail of Tears" in spite of the great volume of petitions, letters,
and resolutions presented to Congress in their behalf, what happened
to the Indians in the Old Northwest who lacked such enthusiastic public support?

An essential ingredient to an understanding of the Indian policy in
this period is the recognition that President Jackson and his successors
in the White House, the War Department, the Office of Indian Affairs,
and Indian agents maintained that the removal policy would bring at
least four major benefits to the Indians. These included:

   1. fixed and permanent boundaries outside of the jurisdiction of
      American states or territories;

2. isolation from corrupt white elements such as gamblers, prostitutes, whiskey vendors, and the like;

3. self-government unfettered by state or territorial laws; and

4. opportunities for acquiring the essentials of "civilized" society—Christianity, private property, and knowledge of agriculture and the mechanical arts.

Such were the benefits that government officials claimed the removal policy would bring the Indians. As a test case of the application of this policy, let us focus our attention on events in the old Northwest.

President Jackson asked Congress on December 8, 1829, to provide him with authority to negotiate treaties to transfer Indians living east of the Mississippi River to a western location. Jackson and his congressional supporters, in their great rush to push through such legislation, seemed unconcerned about the technical aspects of any great migration of eastern Indians to the trans-Mississippi West. Opponents of the scheme, however, raised several important questions: Would emigration be purely voluntary? Would treaty commissioners negotiate only with acknowledged tribal leaders or would land be purchased from individuals? How many Indians would go? What kind of preparations and resources would be necessary for them? What would be the specific boundaries between emigrant tribes? How would the indigenous tribes in the West react to the intrusion of new people? During the debates on the Removal bill, Tennessean David Crockett warned that it was a dangerous precedent to appropriate money for the executive branch without specifically knowing how the president intended to use it. Crockett warned that if Congress turned a deaf ear to the rights of the Indians then "misery must be their fate."

Unfortunately for the Indians, Congress passed the Removal Act in May 1830, and, despite the opposition of the nascent Whig party, Indian removal became a generally accepted policy in the ensuing decades. Throughout this period, congressional interest focused on patronage, partisan politics, and retrenchment to the detriment of the administration of Indian affairs. While the Whigs found it expedient to condemn aspects of the removal policy when they were struggling to capture the White House, they found it desirable to continue the policy once in office. Henry R. Schoolcraft, an Indian agent in Michigan Territory, poignantly described a serious defect of American Indian policy when he noted that "the whole Indian race is not, in the political scales, worth one white man's vote." The result of this situation, as David Crockett had warned, was misery for the Indians.

Among those who witnessed the actual dispossession of the eastern tribes in the Jacksonian era were two foreign travelers who, while not being authorities on the American Indians, nevertheless clearly recognized the deceptions involved in the treaty-making process. French traveler Alexis de Tocqueville poignantly observed that American officials, "inspired by the most chaste affection for legal formalities," obtained Indian title "in a regular and, so to say, quite legal manner." Although bribery and threats often accompanied treaty making and the formal purchases of Indian land, the United States had legal confirmation of its acquisitions. Indeed treaty negotiators were able to "cheaply acquire whole provinces which the richest sovereigns in Europe could not afford to buy" by employing such tactics as bribery or intimidation. Another European visitor, English Captain Frederick Marryat, accurately reported that "the Indians...are *compelled* to sell—the purchase money being a mere subterfuge, by which it may *appear* as if the lands were not being wrested from them, although, in fact, it [*sic*]is."

President Jackson had early indicated that his primary interest was the removal of the southeastern tribes. Although congressmen from the Old Northwest advised him following the passage of the Removal Act that the time for securing removal treaties in their region was "auspicious," Old Hickory informed them that his immediate concern was to set into motion a great tide of southern Indian emigration. Events in Illinois in the spring of 1832, however, played into the hands of the supporters of Indian removal in the Old Northwest.

In the spring of 1832, a hungry band of a thousand Sac and Fox Indians and their allies left their new home in Iowa Territory and crossed the Mississippi River en route to their old capital on the Rock River. Under the leadership of the proud warrior Black Hawk, this band, which included women and children, entered Illinois in search of food and as a means of protesting against their treatment by white frontiersmen. Mass hysteria swept the Illinois frontier with the news that the Indians had crossed the river. Governor John Reynolds called up the state militia to repel the "invasion" despite the fact that Black Hawk's band was clearly not a war party. The result was a short, bloody conflict brought on largely as a consequence of the actions of drunken state militia. The ruthless suppression of the so-called "Indian hostilities" in Illinois and neighboring Wisconsin in 1832, and the seizure of a large part of the trans-Mississippi domain of the Sac and Fox Indians as "indemnity" for the war, broke the spirit of other tribes in the Old Northwest. Under pressure from the War Department, the Winnebagos in Wisconsin soon signed a removal treaty ceding their land south of the Wisconsin River. One by one, other tribes succumbed to similar pressure.

As critics of the Removal Act of 1830 had feared, the War Department obtained many of these land cessions by bribery. Agents courted influential tribal leaders by offering them special rewards including money, merchandise, land reserves, and medals, among other things. Sometimes treaty commissioners selected chiefs to represent an entire tribe or group of bands. The Jackson administration, for example, secured the title to the land of the United Nation of Chippewa, Ottawa, and Potawatomi Indians in northeastern Illinois, southeastern Wisconsin, and southern Michigan by "playing Indian politics." Indeed, the very existence of the United Nation was the result of the government's insistence on dealing with these Indians as if they were a single unit. Yet neither the great majority of the Chippewas and Ottawas nor all of the Potawatomi bands recognized the authority of the so-called United Nation. The government's policy of dealing with the entity as the representative of all Chippewas, Ottawas and Potawatomis was a clever maneuver to oust these Indians from their lands. By working closely with mixed-blood leaders and by withholding Indian annuities, the War Department secured the desired land cessions from the United Nation in the early 1830s.

During the Jacksonian era, the War Department frequently used economic coercion as a means of securing Indian title in the Old Northwest. Since the 1790s, the department had invested funds appropriated by Congress for purchasing Indian land in state banks or stocks and had paid the Indians only the annual interest on the amount owed them under treaty stipulations. This annuity or trust fund system gave government bureaucrats virtual control over funds legally belonging to the Indians. Although Thomas Jefferson played an important role in establishing the precedent of withholding Indian annuities as a means of social control, this procedure became a standard policy after 1829.

Treaty commissioners, Indian agents, and other field officers of the War Department found that withholding annuities was a convenient means of inducing recalcitrant Indians to sign treaties and to emigrate. Commissary General of Subsistence George Gibson advised the Jackson administration, "Let the annuities be paid west of the Mississippi [River], and there is no reason to doubt that the scheme of emigration would meet with little future opposition." American officials maintained considerable influence over tribal politics by determining who would receive the annuities.

Another measure used to encourage Indians to make land cessions was the inclusion of provisions in removal treaties for the granting of land reserves to chiefs, mixed-bloods, or other influential members of the tribes. The motivation behind this practice was twofold. First, it allowed government officials to combat Indian and American opposition to the removal policy based on the fact that some Indians had demonstrated a willingness and capability of accepting the white man's "civilization." When Andrew Jackson encountered strong opposition to his efforts to remove the Cherokees and the other so-called Civilized Tribes from their Southern domain, he conceded that Indians willing to accept the concept of private property should be allowed to remain in the East on individual reserves and become citizens of the states in which they resided. Secondly and more importantly for the Old Northwest, the practice of providing reserves of land to certain Indians was an ingenious device for bribing chiefs or influential tribesmen into accepting land cession treaties and for appeasing white traders into whose hands their reserves were certain to fall.

Treaty commissioners in Indiana found it impossible to secure land cessions from the Miami and Potawatomi Indians without the approval of the Wabash Valley traders to whom they were heavily in debt. Land speculators and settlers regarded the Miami and Potawatomi reserved sections adjacent to the Wabash River and the route of the Wabash and Erie Canal as choice lands. Wabash Valley traders, Indian agents, and even United States Senator John Tipton ultimately secured most of these lands from the Indians and rented them to white settlers for high profits after the Panic of 1837. By 1840 treaties with the Miamis and Potawatomis of Indiana had provided for nearly two hundred thousand acres of individual reserves. The largest holders of these reserves were not Indians but Wabash Valley traders W. G. and G. W.

Ewing and Senator Tipton. Thousands of acres of Indian land elsewhere in the Old Northwest also fell into the hands of speculators.

In spite of the fact that speculators and traders often pressured the Indians into relinquishing their reserves before the government even surveyed the ceded tribal land, little was done to protect the Indians from such swindlers. Indian Whig Jonathan McCarty, a bitter political adversary of Senator Tipton, introduced a resolution in Congress in 1835 calling for an investigation of the handing of Indian reserves, but no action resulted. Jackson, and his successors in the White House, were anxious to tone down investigations of alleged frauds in Indian affairs in order to avoid possible political embarrassments. Even some of the staunchest opponents of the removal policy benefited directly from the sale of Indian lands. Daniel Webster, Edward Everett, Caleb Cushing and Ralph Waldo Emerson were among those who speculated in Indian lands in the Old Northwest.

In addition to granting land reserves to Indians, the War Department followed the practice of including provisions in removal treaties for the payment of Indian debts to traders as a means of promoting removal. Since the Indians relied heavily on traders for subsistence and advice in the Old Northwest, the inclusion of traders' debts was often crucial to successful treaty negotiations. Although the recognition of these debts helped to promote the signing of land cession treaties, the practice also meant that the Indians lost huge sums of money to men who frequently inflated the prices of the goods they sold or falsified their ledgers. Transactions at treaty negotiations relative to the sale of Indian land, the adjustment of traders' claims, and the like were a complex business, yet many Indians, especially the full bloods, did not know the difference between one numerical figure and another.

The administration of Indian affairs in the mid–1830s was particularly vulnerable to criticism. The Panic of 1837 led many traders to exert political influence on treaty commissioners to have phoney Indian debts included in removal treaties. Commissioners Simon Cameron and James Murray awarded the politically influential American Fur Company over one hundred thousand dollars in alleged debt claims against the Winnebagos in Wisconsin in 1838 in return, according to rumor, for a large kickback. Only the military disbursing agent's refusal to pay the traders ultimately led to the exposure of the fraud. One eyewitness to this episode subsequently claimed that it was worse than the

Crédit Mobilier scandal. An English visitor to Wisconsin several years after the incident reported that the acknowledgement of traders' claims during annuity payments was still a "potwallopping affair" in which the Indians left as empty-handed as when they had arrived. Both the Tyler and Polk administrations, in response to complaints from some congressmen, honest Indian agents, and concerned frontier residents, denounced the practice of acknowledging traders' debts in treaties. But the tremendous political influence of the traders, together with the War Department's emphasis on the speedy removal of Indians from areas desired by whites, led the government to follow the path of expediency. Traders continued to receive payments for their claims throughout the Jacksonian era.

If the techniques already mentioned failed to entice the Indians to emigrate, there was always brute force. The state of Indiana probably had one of the worst records in this respect. The Potawatomis ceded their last holdings in Indiana in 1836, but the treaty provisions allowed them two years to emigrate. Whites quickly began moving onto their land in order to establish preemption rights. As tension between the Indians and the whites grew, the Indiana militia rounded up the Po-tawatomis in 1838. When Chief Menominee, who had refused to sign the removal treaty, objected to the proceedings, the soldiers lassoed him, bound him hand and foot, and threw him into a wagon. The militia then hastily set into motion the Potawatomi exodus to the West—the "Trail of Death" along which about one hundred and fifty men, women, and children died as a result of exposure and the physical hardships of the journey. Several years later the Indiana militia also rounded up the Miami Indians in similar fashion to expedite their removal to the West.

By the end of Jackson's second term, the United States had ratified nearly seventy treaties under the provisions of the Removal Act and had acquired about one hundred million acres of Indian land for ap-proximately sixty-eight million dollars and thirty-two million acres of land in the trans-Mississippi West. While the government had relocated forty-six thousand Indians by 1837, a little more than that number were still in the East under obligation to remove. According to the Office of Indian Affairs, only about nine thousand Indians, mostly in the Old Northwest and New York, were without treaty stipulations requiring their relocation, but there is evidence to indicate that the number of such Indians east of the Mississippi River at this time was much larger than the Indian Office reported. Indeed, there were probably more than nine thousand in Wisconsin Territory alone! The dearth of reliable population statistics for Indians during the Jacksonian era is a perplexing problem. By 1842, however, the United States had acquired the last area of any significant size still owned by the Indians in the Old Northwest. Only scattered remnants of the great tribes that had once controlled the region remained behind on reservations or individual holdings, chiefly in Michigan and Wisconsin.

The removal treaties of the Jacksonian era contained liberal provisions for emigrants and those remaining behind on reserves. They offered emigrants rations and transportation, protection en route to their new homes, medicine and physicians, reimbursement for abandoned property, funds for the erection of new buildings, mills, schools, teachers, farmers and mechanics, and maintenance for poor and orphaned children. The treaties read as if they were enlightened agreements. Yet there were several inherent defects in the treaty-making process. One of these was the assumption that the Indian leaders dealing with the government commissioners represented the entire tribe. Another was the assumption that the Indians clearly understood the provisions of the agreements. Still another was the fact that the Senate often amended or deleted treaty provisions without prior consultation with tribal leaders. Although treaty stipulations were provisional until ratified by the Senate, settlers rarely waited for formal action before they inundated Indian land. While Alexis de Tocqueville noted that "the most chaste affection for legal formalities" characterized American treaty making with the Indians, he also argued that "it is impossible to destroy men with more respect to the laws of humanity."

In spite of the favorable terms promised in removal treaties, most emigrants faced numerous hardships on their journeys to their new homes. A major reason for their misery was the system of providing them food and transportation by accepting the lowest bid from contractors. Many unscrupulous expectant capitalists furnished the Indians with scanty or cheap rations in order to make a sizeable profit from their contracts. The contractors were businessmen out to make money, and they were quite successful. Thomas Dowling, who received a contract in 1844 to remove six hundred Miami Indians from Indiana for nearly sixty thousand dollars, boasted to his brother that he would make enough profit to "rear the superstructure of an independence for myself, family, and relations."

In addition to the evils of the contract system, Indian emigrants also suffered from the government's perpetual concern for retrenchment. Although removal treaties provided for the medical care of emigrants, the War Department prohibited agents from purchasing medicine or surgical instruments until "actually required" during the economic hard times after 1837. Such instructions greatly hampered the effectiveness of the physicians accompanying migrating parties. To make matters worse, emigrants from the Old Northwest, many of them weakened by their constant battle with the elements of nature en route to the trans-Mississippi West, found themselves plagued with serious afflictions. Efforts to economize in removal expenditures by speeding up the movement of emigrants also led to much suffering. The War Department ordered in 1837 that only the sick or very young could travel west on horseback or by wagon at government expense. Even before this ruling, efforts to speed up the movement of migrating parties under orders from Washington officials proved detrimental to the Indians. An agent in charge of the removal of the Senecas from Ohio earlier in the 1830s, for example, wrote his superior that "I charge myself with cruelty in forcing these unfortunate people on at a time when a few days' delay might have prevented some deaths, and rendered the sickness of others more light, and have to regret this part of my duty."

Now let us examine the success of the removal policy in terms of the so-called benefits that government officials had argued it would bring to the Indians after their relocation. The first benefit was fixed and permanent boundaries outside the jurisdiction of American states and territories. Even before the Black Hawk War, the French travelers Alexis de Tocqueville and Gustave de Beaumont had voiced concern over the government's failure to establish a permanent Indian country for the northern Indians comparable to the one it was setting off west of Arkansas for the southern tribes. Sam Houston, a good Jacksonian Democrat, assured the travelers that Indian-white relations in the Old Northwest were not as critical as in the South. He pointed out that permanent boundaries were unnecessary for the northern tribes since they would eventually be "pushed back" by the tide of white settlement. Following the Black Hawk War, Houston's contention proved correct.

The history of the relocation of the Winnebago Indians from Wisconsin illustrates the government's failure to systematically plan fixed boundaries for emigrants from the Old Northwest. When the War Department pressured the Winnebagos into signing a removal treaty at the cessation of the Black Hawk War, it left them with two alternative locations. One was the so-called "neutral ground" in Iowa between the Sac and Fox Indians and their Sioux enemies to the north. This location proved too precarious for the Winnebagos, who quickly made their way back to the second designated area that was within the territorial limits of Wisconsin, north of the Wisconsin River. When the Winnebagos moved into this area, they found themselves too tightly crowded together to live according to their old life styles. As a result, they frequently returned to the sites of their old villages south of the Wisconsin River.

In returning to their old homesites, the Winnebagos encountered other Indians as well as white settlers. While the War Department had induced the Winnebagos to leave southern Wisconsin in order to free them from white contact in that area, it had relocated tribes from New York there in order to free them from white contact in New York. Both the Winnebagos and the New York Indians relocated in Wisconsin soon became the victims of the great land boom that swept the territory in the 1830s as whites eagerly sought Indian land for settlement and timber.

By 1838 the Winnebagos had ceded all of their land in Wisconsin and had promised to move to the neutral ground in Iowa, but the "final" removal of the last band of these Indians in 1840 required the use of troops. For several years after their relocation, the Indian Office attempted to transfer them from Iowa to the Indian country west of Missouri. In 1840 the Tyler administration planned to have them join other northern tribes in a new Indian territory north of the present Iowa-Minnesota border and south of, roughly, the 46th parallel. This new location would appease residents of Iowa who were clamoring for the removal of the Winnebagos and settlers in Wisconsin who were anxious to expel the Winnebago stragglers and the New York Indians who had settled there. Such a northern location would also placate the citizens of Arkansas and Missouri who opposed any additional influx of Indians on their western borders. The War Department favored this plan because it would provide a safe corridor for white expansion to the pacific through Iowa and would place the Indians of the Old Northwest far south of the Canadian border thus luring them away from British-Canadian influence.

In spite of the War Department's plans, large numbers of Winnebagos drifted back to Wisconsin during the 1840s. Efforts to relocate them in present-day Minnesota between the Sioux and their Chippewa enemies led again to Winnebago defiance. Despite the use of military force to compel them to go to their "proper homes," the Winnebagos were greatly dispersed in Wisconsin, Iowa, and Minnesota at the end of the decade, to the annoyance of white settlers in those areas. The condition of these Indians clearly indicates that the War Department was lax in undertaking long-range planning for a permanent home for the tribes of the Old Northwest. The government continually reshuffled these Indians in order to make room for northeastern tribes and the growing pressures of white settlement. Whenever the white population pattern warranted it, the War Department merely redesignated new locations for the Indians. Nor did the government pay much attention to the needs of emigrants. Menominee Chief Oshkosh, in complaining about Winnebago intrusions on Menominee land in Wisconsin in 1850, cited several reasons why the Winnebagos continually left their new locations and returned to Wisconsin; these included the poor soil in their new country, the scarcity of game there, and, most importantly, their dread of their fierce Sioux neighbors.

The agony of the Winnebagos was not unique. Many other tribes faced the prospect of removing to an allegedly permanent location more than once. Continued white hostility following the Black Hawk War led the United Nation of Chippewas, Ottawas, and Potawatomis, for example, to give up their claims to northern Illinois, southeastern Wisconsin and several scattered reserves in southern Michigan in 1833 for a tract of land bordering the Missouri River in southwestern Iowa and northwestern Missouri. The new Potawatomi lands included the Platte Country, the region in present-day northwest Missouri watered by the Little Platte and Nodaway rivers. This area was not included in the original boundaries of Missouri in 1820. The inclusion of the Platte Country in the land designated for the Potawatomis demonstrates once again the poor planning of the War Department. In 1832 Missouri Governor John Miller had called for the annexation of this region and Missouri Senators Lewis F. Linn and Thomas Hart Benton joined him in arguing that the area was necessary for the political and economic growth of their state. Although over one hundred Potawatomis had signed the original treaty, the War Department, in its effort to appease Missourians, secured an amended treaty, signed by only seven Indians, that substituted a similar amount of land in Iowa for the Platte Country.

While the government was seeking to modify the original treaty to placate Missouri, Potawatomis who had signed that document moved to the Platte Country. The number of tribesmen there grew as small bands from Indiana continued to travel West in accordance with the provisions of the original treaty. Many Potawatomis came to view the government's new proposed location for them in Iowa as being too close to the Sioux. The Jackson administration reluctantly permitted them to settle temporarily in the Platte Country until they could find suitable sites for new villages in southeastern Iowa. There were still approximately sixteen hundred Potawatomis in the Platte Country in March 1837 when President Martin Van Buren proclaimed the area part of the state of Missouri. The War Department soon ejected them from there and resettled them in southwestern Iowa and Kansas. Government officials consolidated the Potawatomis into one reservation in northcentral Kansas in 1846 and subsequently relocated them in Oklahoma during the 1860s.

The experiences of the Winnebago and Potawatomi Indians clearly indicate that the new boundaries for emigrants from the Old Northwest were far from permanent. Treaty commissioners merely reshuffled the tribes around as frontiersmen, speculators, and state officials pressured the War Department to open more Indian land to white settlement. Federal officials failed to undertake long-range planning for the establishment of permanent boundaries for the emigrant tribes from this region. The sole effort in this direction before 1848, the Tyler administration's attempt to create a northern Indian territory, failed because the War Department had neglected the needs and the desires of the Indians.

At the end of the Jacksonian era, Indian Commissioner William Medill reported that the Polk administration had begun to mark off a northern Indian "colony" on the headwaters of the Mississippi River for "the Chippewas of Lake Superior and the upper Mississippi, the Winnebagoes, the Menomonies, such of the Sioux, if any, as may choose to remain in that region, and all other northern Indians east of the Mississippi (except those in the State of New York), who have yet to be removed west of that river." Together with the removal of Indians from the "very desired" land north of the Kansas River to a southern "colony" west of Arkansas and Missouri, Medill hoped that the concentration of the northern Indians on the headwaters of the Mississippi River would provide "a wide and safe passage" for American emigrants to the Far West. Medill's report of November 30, 1848, was a tacit admission of the government's failure to provide Indian emigrants from the Old Northwest with fixed and permanent boundaries as guaranteed by the Removal Act of 1830. Throughout this period, the exigencies of the moment determined the boundaries that American officials provided for the Indians.

The second alleged benefit of removal was isolation from corrupt white elements such as gamblers, prostitutes, whiskey peddlers, and the like. The government's lack of planning for the permanent relocation of the tribes of the Old Northwest meant that these Indians were continually in the path of the westward tide of white settlement. Although Congress passed a Trade and Intercourse Act in 1834 to protect the Indians from land hungry whites, as well as whiskey peddlers and similar groups, nothing, including Indian treaty rights, stopped the advance of white settlement. Liquor was readily available to most tribes. In 1844 Thomas McKenney, an expert on Indian affairs, reported that the Menominees in Wisconsin, who had undergone several relocations, were "utterly abandoned to the vice of intoxication." Efforts to strengthen the Trade and Intercourse Laws in 1847 failed once again to halt the liquor traffic. Frontier citizens, especially the traders and their powerful political allies, blantantly refused to cooperate in enforcing the laws.

Tribal self-government unfettered by state or territorial laws was the third benefit that removal was supposed to bring the Indians. Yet the Trade and Intercourse Acts of 1834 and 1847 placed the Indians at the mercy of the white man's conception of justice. The legislation clearly provided that American laws would take precedence over Indian laws and customs in all cases involving both groups. Since the local judicial officers in the white communities adjoining Indian settlements reflected the dominant attitudes of their respective communities and often had ties with local businessmen and traders, they were not always effective administrators of the federal laws designed to protect the Indians from whiskey peddlers or other avaricious whites. The presence

of federal Indian agents and military detachments near Indian settlements, moreover, meant that the Indians were not completely sovereign.
Indian agents and the commanding officers of frontier posts often
played "Indian politics." They found it much easier to deal with a
central tribal authority rather than a series of chiefs or headmen and
encouraged the recognition of one individual as the principal tribal
leader. One vehicle used to accomplish this purpose was the allocation
of Indian annuities. By determining who would receive the annuities,
the War Department manipulated tribal politics. The result of such
efforts was the emasculation of tribal self-government.

The fourth alleged benefit of removal was "civilization." American
officials involved in the formulation and execution of Indian policy
argued that the Indians lacked the essentials of civilized society—Christianity, private property, and knowledge of agriculture and the mechanical arts. Indian removal, they maintained, would provide ample
opportunities for the uplifting of the Indians. Yet the removal policy
did not bring great benefits, in terms of the white man's "civilization,"
to a significant number of Indians.

The constant reshuffling of tribes to new "permanent" locations
failed to promote Indian interest in the white man's "civilization." How
could the Winnebagos who had suffered tremendous social and psychological strains as a result of their continuous uprooting and relocation be expected to have interest in, or make significant advances in,
the adoption of Christianity or any of the other so-called prerequisites
of "civilized" society? Other Indians had similar reactions.

The events surrounding the acquisition of Chippewa and Ottawa
lands in Michigan demonstrate some of the reasons for the failure of
government efforts to promote its "civilization" program among the
Indians of the Old Northwest. In 1836 the Chippewas and Ottawas
had ceded their lands with the understanding that the government
would allot them permanent reservations in northern Michigan and
provide blacksmiths, farmers, and teachers to help them learn white
trades and farming techniques. The land cession treaty provided federal
funds to accomplish the "civilization" of these Indians, but the entire
project was doomed before it began.

When the Senate considered the ratification of the treaty, it amended
the document so that the reserves in northern Michigan would only be
temporary residences. The Indians were understandably disturbed by

this unilateral alteration of the treaty, and they were reluctant to move to temporary reserves in order to clear the land and to take up farming. Commissioner of Indian Affairs Carey Allen Harris, moreover, urged that government funds for these Indians be kept to a minimum until they settled at a permanent location.

Because their "permanent" boundaries always seemed to be temporary ones, the Indians of the Old Northwest found it more convenient to live off their annuities than to labor in their fields. As Chippewa Indian George Copway lamented, "no sooner have the Indians gone on and made improvements, and our children began to like to go to the school houses which have been erected, than we hear the cry of the United States government, 'We want your lands'; and, in going from one place to another, the Indian looses [sic]all that he had previously learned." As a result of this situation, the Indians paid more attention to the fur traders than to the school teachers. The tribes in this region relied heavily on the traders for food and goods. Government officials tended to see this dependence on the traders as a sign of idleness or weakness of character. Their ethnocentricism blinded them to the fact that farming had long been women's work among these tribes. The fur trade, wild grain, and fish were traditionally much more important to the livelihood of these Indians than American agricultural products.

Other problems inherent in the "civilization program" included the personnel employed to "civilize" the Indians. Such appointments offered patronage-hungry politicians a means of rewarding their supporters. Consequently, the teachers hired to work with the Indians did not always bring altruistic motives to their jobs. Some of them were even "indolent and shif[t]less." The employment of missionaries as civilizing agents caused special problems. Interdenominational rivalries greatly impeded their work. Some Indians demonstrated open hostility to missionaries because they associated them with efforts to remove their people from their ancient homes. Presbyterian minister Peter Dougherty found that his preaching of the Gospel to the Chippewa Indians in Michigan was greatly impeded by the belief of "heathen" Chippewas that the acceptance of Christianity would lead to their removal. For several reasons, therefore, the "civilization" program actually suffered because of the removal policy.

Regardless of the intentions of federal officials, the Indian removal policy in the Jacksonian era did not bring the tribesmen the benefits that they had predicted. Scholars such as Prucha, Schultz, and Viola have argued that the architects of the removal policy had thought that it was in the best interests of the Indians. If the formulators and executors of the policy actually believed this, their assumption proved erroneous for the Indians of the Old Northwest. While there was no policy of racial extermination or genocide perpetrated against the Indians of this region, there can be no doubt that the removal policy led to tribal demoralization. Whether noble intentions or nefarious ones lay behind the removal policy, the results were disastrous for the Indians. As one scholar recently asserted, "it is sometimes difficult to tell whether the Indian has suffered more at the hands of his 'friends' or at the hands of his 'enemies.' "

Frances Trollope, an English visitor to the United States, wrote in 1832 that Indian removal epitomized everything despicable in American character, especially the "contradictions in their principles and practice." "You will see them one hour lecturing their mob on the indefeasible rights of man," she wrote, "and the next driving from their homes the children of the soil, whom they have bound themselves to protect by the most solemn treaties." American Indian policy in the Old Northwest during the Jacksonian era serves as a grim reminder of what can happen to a politically powerless minority in a democratic society. It also demonstrates that scholars must be careful not to confuse the rhetoric of government policies with the realities involved in executing these policies.

13

Women, Work, and Protest
in the Early Lowell Mills

THOMAS DUBLIN

● *The United States underwent a profound industrial trans-formation in the years between 1820 and 1860. At the earlier date, agriculture and foreign trade dominated the economy, and more than three-fourths of the labor force worked on farms. Such manufacturing as there was typically took place in houses or in very small establishments serving a local mar-ket. By the outbreak of the Civil War, the proportion of the work force employed outside agriculture had jumped to 41 percent, and the cotton textile and boot and shoe industries were well developed.*

No section of the nation was more affected by the impact of early industrialization than the Northeast. In 1790, Samuel Slater set up the first permanent spinning mill in Pawtucket, Rhode Island; in 1793, Alexander Hamilton established the Society for Useful Manufacturers in Paterson, New Jersey; and in 1813, the first fully integrated textile factory began operating in Waltham, Massachusetts. Soon thereafter, the factory system began to dominate the economies of the grow-ing urban centers throughout the region.

As Thomas Dublin indicates in the following essay, women had an important place in this emerging industrial economy. The new mills tempted farmers' daughters to leave their rural homes—at least temporarily—to accumulate savings for mar-riage. By 1860, more than 60,000 women were employed in the cotton textile industry in New England alone. The pattern for such work was set in Massachusetts at the junction of the Merrimack and Concord rivers just below the Pawtucket Falls.

Reprinted by permission from Thomas Dublin, "Women, Work, and Protest in the Early Lowell Mills," *Labor History*, 16 (Winter 1975), 99–116. Copyright © 1975 by *Labor History*.

In 1821, a group of Boston businessmen began to buy land secretly in the area, and the following year they began to build the Merrimack Manufacturing Company. The town which grew up there was incorporated as Lowell in 1826, and by 1850 it was the leading textile center in the United States. More importantly, it was seen as an experiment, as a vindi-cation of American methods that would prove superior to those of the Old World. As Dublin indicates, however, the experiment was not as idyllic as its proponents wanted to believe, and the dream of a new United States industrial order soon gave way to the grim realities of debilitating factory work and labor strife.

In the years before 1850 the textile mills of Lowell, Massachusetts, were a celebrated economic and cultural attraction. Foreign visitors invariably included them on their American tours. Interest was prompted by the massive scale of these mills, the astonishing produc-tivity of the power-driven machinery, and the fact that women com-prised most of the workforce. Visitors were struck by the newness of both mills and city as well as by the culture of the female operatives. The scene stood in sharp contrast to the gloomy mill towns of the English industrial revolution.

Lowell was, in fact, an impressive accomplishment. In 1820, there had been no city at all—only a dozen family farms along the Merrimack River in East Chelmsford. In 1821, however, a group of Boston cap-italists purchased land and water rights along the river and a nearby canal, and began to build a major textile manufacturing center. Open-ing two years later, the first factory employed Yankee women recruited from the nearby countryside. Additional mills were constructed until, by 1840, ten textile corporations with thirty-two mills valued at more than ten million dollars lined the banks of the river and nearby canals. Adjacent to the mills were rows of company boarding houses and tenements which accommodated most of the eight thousand factory operatives.

As Lowell expanded, and became the nation's largest textile man-ufacturing center, the experiences of women operatives changed as well. The increasing number of firms in Lowell and in the other mill towns brought the pressure of competition. Overproduction became a problem and the prices of finished cloth decreased. The high profits of the early years declined and so, too, did conditions for the mill operatives. Wages were reduced and the pace of work within the mills was stepped up. Women operatives did not accept these changes without protest. In 1834 and 1836 they went on strike to protest wage cuts, and between 1843 and 1848 they mounted petition campaigns aimed at reducing the hours of labor in the mills.

These labor protests in early Lowell contribute to our understanding of the response of workers to the growth of industrial capitalism in the first half of the nineteenth century. They indicate the importance of values and attitudes dating back to an earlier period and also the transformation of these values in a new setting.

The major factor in the rise of a new consciousness among operatives in Lowell was the development of a close-knit community among women working in the mills. The structure of work and the nature of housing contributed to the growth of this community. The existence of community among women, in turn, was an important element in the repeated labor protests of the period.

The organization of this paper derives from the logic of the above argument. It will examine the basis of community in the experiences of women operatives and then the contribution that the community of women made to the labor protests in these years as well as the nature of the new consciousness expressed by these protests.

The pre-conditions for the labor unrest in Lowell before 1850 may be found in the study of the daily worklife of its operatives. In their everyday, relatively conflict-free lives, mill women created the mutual bonds which made possible united action in times of crisis. The existence of a tight-knit community among them was the most important element in determining the collective, as opposed to individual, nature of this response.

Before examining the basis of community among women operatives in early Lowell, it may be helpful to indicate in what sense "community" is being used. The women are considered a "community" because of the development of bonds of mutual dependence among them. In this period they came to depend upon one another and upon the larger group of operatives in very important ways. Their experiences were not simply similar or parallel to one another, but were inextricably intertwined. Furthermore, they were conscious of the existence of community, expressing it very clearly in their writings and in labor protests. "Community" for them had objective and subjective dimensions and both were important in their experience of women in the mills.

The mutual dependence among women in early Lowell was rooted in the structure of mill work itself. Newcomers to the mills were particularly dependent on their fellow operatives, but even experienced hands relied on one another for considerable support.

New operatives generally found their first experiences difficult, even harrowing, though they may have already done considerable hand-spinning and weaving in their own homes. The initiation of one of them is described in fiction in the *Lowell Offering*:

> The next morning she went into the Mill; and at first the sight of so many bands, and wheels, and springs in constant motion, was very frightful. She felt afraid to touch the loom, and she was almost sure she could never learn to weave...the shuttle flew out, and made a new bump on her head; and the first time she tried to spring the lathe, she broke out a quarter of the treads.

While other accounts present a somewhat less difficult picture, most indicate that women only became proficient and felt satisfaction in their work after several months in the mills.

The textile corporations made provisions to ease the adjustment of new operatives. Newcomers were not immediately expected to fit into the mill's regular work routine. They were at first assigned work as sparehands and were paid a daily wage independent of the quantity of work they turned out. As a sparehand, the newcomer worked with an experienced hand who instructed her in the intricacies of the job. The sparehand spelled her partner for short stretches of time, and occasionally took the place of an absentee. One woman described the learning process in a letter reprinted in the *Offering*:

> Well, I went into the mill, and was put to learn with a very patient girl.... You cannot think how odd everything seems.... They set me to threading shuttles, and tying weaver's knots, and such things, and now I have improved so that I can take care of one loom. I could take care of two if only I had eyes in the back part of my head.

After the passage of some weeks or months, when she could handle the normal complement of machinery—two looms for weavers during the 1830s—and when a regular operative departed, leaving an opening, the sparehand moved into a regular job.

Through this system of job training, the textile corporations contributed to the development of community among female operatives. During the most difficult period in an operative's career, the first months in the mill, she relied upon other women workers for training and support. And for every sparehand whose adjustment to mill work was aided in this process, there was an experienced operative whose work was also affected. Women were relating to one another during the work process and not simply tending their machinery. Given the high rate of turnover in the mill workforce, a large proportion of women operatives worked in pairs. At the Hamilton Company in July 1836, for example, more than a fifth of all females on the Company payroll were sparehands. Consequently, over forty percent of the females employed there in this month worked with one another. Nor was this interaction surreptitious, carried out only when the overseer looked elsewhere; rather it was formally organized and sanctioned by the textile corporations themselves.

In addition to the integration of sparehands, informal sharing of work often went on among regular operatives. A woman would occasionally take off a half or full day from work either to enjoy a brief vacation or to recover from illness, and fellow operatives would each take an extra loom or side of spindles so that she might continue to earn wages during her absence. Women were generally paid on a piece rate basis, their wages being determined by the total output of the machinery they tended during the payroll period. With friends helping out during her absence, making sure that her looms kept running, an operative could earn almost a full wage even though she was not physically present. Such informal work-sharing was another way in which mutual dependence developed among women operatives during their working hours.

Living conditions also contributed to the development of community among female operatives. Most women working in the Lowell mills of these years were housed in company boarding houses. In July 1836, for example, more than 73 percent of females employed by the Hamilton Company resided in company housing adjacent to the mills. Almost three-fourths of them, therefore, lived and worked with each other. Furthermore, the work schedule was such that women had little opportunity to interact with those not living in company dwellings. They worked, in these years, an average of 73 hours a week. Their work day ended at 7:00 or 7:30 P.M., and in the hours between supper and the 10:00 curfew imposed by management on residents of company boarding houses there was little time to spend with friends living "off the corporation."

Women in the boarding houses lived in close quarters, a factor that also played a role in the growth of community. A typical boarding house accommodated twenty-five young women, generally crowded four to eight in a bedroom. There was little possibility of privacy within the dwelling, and pressure to conform to group standards was very strong (as will be discussed below). The community of operatives which developed in the mills it follows, carried over into life at home as well.

The boarding house became a central institution in the lives of Lowell's female operatives in these years, but it was particularly important in the initial integration of newcomers into urban industrial life. Upon first leaving her rural home for work in Lowell, a woman entered a setting very different from anything she had previously known. One operative, writing in the *Offering*, described the feelings of a fictional character: "The first entrance into a factory boarding house seemed something dreadful. The room looked strange and comfortless, and the women cold and heartless; and when she sat down to the supper table, where among more than twenty girls, all but one were strangers, she could not eat a mouthful."

In the boarding house, the newcomer took the first steps in the process which transformed her from an "outsider" into an accepted member of the community of women operatives.

Recruitment of newcomers into the mills and their initial hiring was mediated through the boarding house system. Women generally did not travel to Lowell for the first time entirely on their own. They usually came because they knew someone—an older sister, cousin, or friend— who had already worked in Lowell. The scene described above was a lonely one—but the newcomer did know at least one boarder among the twenty seated around the supper table. The Hamilton Company Register Books indicate that numerous pairs of operatives, having the same surname and coming from the same town in northern New England, lived in the same boarding houses. If the newcomer was not accompanied by a friend or relative, she was usually directed to "Number 20, Hamilton Company," or to a similar address of one of the other corporations where her acquaintance lived. Her first contact with fellow operatives generally came in the boarding houses and not in the mills. Given the personal nature of recruitment in this period, therefore, newcomers usually had the company and support of a friend or relative in their first adjustment to Lowell.

Like recruitment, the initial hiring was a personal process. Once settled in the boarding house a newcomer had to find a job. She would generally go to the mills with her friend or with the boarding house keeper who would introduce her to an overseer in one of the rooms. If he had an opening, she might start work immediately. More likely, the overseer would know of an opening elsewhere in the mill, or would suggest that something would probably develop within a few days. In one story in the *Offering*, a newcomer worked on some quilts for her house keeper, thereby earning her board while she waited for a job opening.

Upon entering the boarding house, the newcomer came under pressure to conform with the standards of the community of operatives. Stories in the *Offering* indicate that newcomers at first stood out from the group in terms of their speech and dress. Over time, they dropped the peculiar "twang" in their speech which so amused experienced hands. Similarly, they purchased clothing more in keeping with urban than rural styles. It was an unusual and strongwilled individual who could work and live among her fellow operatives and not conform, at least outwardly, to the customs and values of this larger community.

The boarding houses were the centers of social life for women operatives after their long days in the mills. There they ate their meals, rested, talked, sewed, wrote letters, read books and magazines. From among fellow workers and boarders they found friends who accompanied them to shops, to Lyceum lectures, to church and church-sponsored events. On Sundays or holidays, they often took walks along the canals or out into the nearby countryside. The community of women operatives, in sum, developed in a setting where women worked and lived together, twenty-four hours a day.

Given the all-pervasiveness of this community, one would expect it to exert strong pressures on those who did not conform to group standards. Such appears to have been the case. The community influenced newcomers to adopt its patterns of speech and dress as described above. In addition, it enforced an unwritten code of moral conduct. Henry Miles, a minister in Lowell, described the way in which the community pressured those who deviated from accepted moral conduct:

> A girl, suspected of immoralities, or serious improprieties, at once loses caste. Her fellow boarders will at once leave the house, if the keeper does not dismiss the offender. In self-protection, therefore, the patron is obliged to put the offender away. Nor will her former companions walk with her, or work with her; till at length, finding herself everywhere talked about, and pointed at, and shunned, she is obliged to relieve her fellow-operatives of a presence which they feel brings disgrace.

The power of the peer group described by Miles may seem extreme, but there is evidence in the writing of women operatives to corroborate his account. Such group pressure is illustrated by a story (in the *Offering*)—in which operatives in a company boarding house begin to harbor suspicions about a fellow boarder, Hannah, who received repeated evening visits from a man whom she does not introduce to the other residents. Two boarders declare that they will leave if she is allowed to remain in the household. The house keeper finally informed Hannah that she must either depart or not see the man again. She does not accept the ultimatum, but is promptly discharged after the overseer is informed, by one of the boarders, about her conduct. And, only one of Hannah's former friends continues to remain on cordial terms.

One should not conclude, however, that women always enforced a moral code agreeable to Lowell's clergy, or to the mill agents and overseers for that matter. After all, the kind of peer pressure imposed on Hannah could be brought to bear on women in 1834 and 1836 who on their own would not have protested wage cuts. It was much harder to go to work when one's roommates were marching about town, attending rallies, circulating strike petitions. Similarly, the ten-hour petitions of the 1840s were certainly aided by the fact of a tight-knit community of operatives living in a dense neighborhood of boarding houses. To the extent that women could not have completely private lives in the boarding houses, they probably had to conform to group norms, whether these involved speech, clothing, relations with men, or attitudes toward the ten-hour day. Group pressure to conform, so important to the community of women in early Lowell, played a significant role in the collective response of women to changing conditions in the mills.

In addition to the structure of work and housing in Lowell, a third factor, the homogeneity of the mill workforce, contributed to the development of community among female operatives. In this period the mill workforce was homogeneous in terms of sex, nativity, and age. Payroll and other records of the Hamilton Company reveal that more than 85 percent of those employed in July 1836 were women and that over 96 percent were native-born. Furthermore, over 80 percent of the female workforce was between the ages of 15 and 30 years old; and only ten percent was under 15 or over 40.

Workforce homogeneity takes on particular significance in the context of work structure and the nature of worker housing. These three factors combined meant that women operatives had little interaction with men during their daily lives. Men and women did not perform the same work in the mills, and generally did not even labor in the same rooms. Men worked in the picking and initial carding processes, in the repair shop and on the watchforce, and filled all supervisory positions in the mills. Women held all sparehand and regular operative jobs in drawing, speeding, spinning, weaving and dressing. A typical room in the mill employed eighty women tending machinery, with two men overseeing the work and two boys assisting them. Women had little contact with men other than their supervisors in the course of the working day. After work, women returned to their boarding houses, where once again there were few men. Women, then, worked and lived in a predominantly female setting.

Ethnically the workforce was also homogeneous. Immigrants formed only 3.4 percent of those employed at Hamilton in July 1836. In addition, they comprised only 3 percent of residents in Hamilton company housing. The community of women operatives was composed of women of New England stock drawn from the hill-country farms surrounding Lowell. Consequently, when experienced hands made fun of the speech and dress of newcomers, it was understood that they, too, had been "rusty" or "rustic" upon first coming to Lowell. This common background was another element shared by women workers in early Lowell.

The work structure, the workers' housing, and workforce homogeneity were the major elements which contributed to the growth of community among Lowell's women operatives. To best understand the larger implications of community it is necessary to examine the labor protests of this period. For in these struggles, the new values and attitudes which developed in the community of women operatives are most visible.

II

In February 1834, 800 of Lowell's women operatives "turned-out"— went on strike—to protest a proposed reduction in their wages. They marched to numerous mills in an effort to induce others to join them; and, at an outdoor rally, they petitioned others to "discontinue their labors until terms of reconciliation are made." Their petition concluded:

> Resolved, That we will not go back into the mills to work unless our wages are continued . . . as they have been.
> Resolved, That none of us will go back, unless they receive us all as one.
> Resolved, That if any have not money enough to carry them home, they shall be supplied.

The strike proved to be brief and failed to reverse the proposed wage reductions. Turning-out on a Friday, the striking women were paid their back wages on Saturday, and by the middle of the next week had returned to work or left town. Within a week of the turn-out, the mills were running near capacity.

This first strike in Lowell is important not because it failed or succeeded, but simply because it took place. In an era in which women had to overcome opposition simply to work in the mills, it is remarkable that they would further overstep the accepted middle-class bounds of female propriety by participating in a public protest. The agents of the textile mills certainly considered the turn-out unfeminine. William Austin, agent of the Lawrence Company, described the operatives' procession as an "amizonian [*sic*]display." He wrote further, in a letter to his company treasurer in Boston: "This afternoon we have paid off several of these Amazons & presume that they will leave town on Monday." The turn-out was particularly offensive to the agents because of the relationship they thought they had with their operatives. William Austin probably expressed the feelings of other agents when he wrote: "Notwithstanding the friendly and disinterested advice which has been on all proper occasions [sic]communicated to the girls of the Lawrence mills a spirit of evil omen . . . has prevailed, and overcome the judgment and discretion of too many, and this morning a general turn-out from most of the rooms has been the consequence."

Mill agents assumed an attitude of benevolent paternalism toward their female operatives, and found it particularly disturbing that the women paid such little heed to their advice. The strikers were not merely unfeminine, they were ungrateful as well.

Such attitudes notwithstanding, women chose to turn-out. They did so for two principal reasons. First, the wage cuts undermined the sense of dignity and social equality which was an important element in their Yankee heritage. Second, these wage cuts were seen as an attack on their economic independence.

Certainly a prime move for the strike was outrage at the social implications of the wage cuts. In a statement of principles accompanying the petition which was circulated among operatives, women expressed well the sense of themselves which prompted their protest of these wage cuts:

UNION IS POWER

Our present object is to have union and exertion, and we remain in possession of our unquestionable rights. We circulate this paper wishing to obtain the names of all who imbibe the spirit of our Patriotic Ancestors, who preferred privation to bondage, and parted with all that renders life desirable—and even life itself—to procure independence for their children. The oppressing hand of avarice would enslave us, and to gain their object, they gravely tell us of the pressure of the time, this we are already sensible of, and deplore it. If any are in want of assistance, the Ladies will be compassionate and assist them; but we prefer to have the disposing of our charities in our own hands; and as we are free, we would remain in possession of what kind Providence has bestowed upon us; and remain daughters of freemen still.

At several points in the proclamation the women drew on their Yankee heritage. Connecting their turn-out with the efforts of their "Patriotic Ancestors" to secure independence from England, they interpreted the wage cuts as an effort to "enslave" them—to deprive them of their independent status as "daughters of freemen."

Though very general and rhetorical, the statement of these women does suggest their sense of self, of their own worth and dignity. Elsewhere, they expressed the conviction that they were the social equals of the overseers, indeed of the mill owners themselves. The wage cuts, however, struck at this assertion of social equality. These reductions made it clear that the operatives were subordinate to their employers, rather than equal partners in a contract binding on both parties. By turning-out the women emphatically denied that they were subordinates; but by returning to work the next week, they demonstrated that in economic terms they were no match for their corporate superiors.

In point of fact, these Yankee operatives were subordinate in early Lowell's social and economic order, but they never consciously accepted this status. Their refusal to do so became evident whenever the mill owners attempted to exercise the power they possessed. This fundamental contradiction between the objective status of operatives and their consciousness of it was at the root of the 1834 turn-out and of subsequent labor protests in Lowell before 1850. The corporations could build mills, create thousands of jobs, and recruit women to fill them. Nevertheless, they bought only the workers' labor power, and then only for as long as these workers chose to stay. Women could always return to their rural homes, and they had a sense of their own worth and dignity, factors limiting the actions of management.

Women operatives viewed the wage cuts as a threat to their economic independence. This independence had two related dimensions. First, the women were self-supporting while they worked in the mills and, consequently, were independent of their families back home. Second, they were able to save out of their monthly earnings and could then leave the mills for the old homestead whenever they so desired. In effect, they were not totally dependent upon mill work. Their independence was based largely on the high level of wages in the mills. They could support themselves and still save enough to return home periodically. The wage cuts threatened to deny them this outlet, substituting instead the prospect of total dependence on mill work. Small wonder, then, there was alarm that "the oppressing hand of avarice would enslave us." To be forced, out of economic necessity, to lifelong labor in the mills would have indeed seemed like slavery. The Yankee operatives spoke directly to the fear of dependency based on impoverishment when offering to assist any women workers who "have not money enough to carry them home." Wage reductions, however, offered only the *prospect* of a future dependence on mill employment. By striking, the women asserted their actual economic independence of the mills and their determination to remain "daughters of freemen still."

While the women's traditional conception of themselves as independent daughters of freemen played a major role in the turn-out, this factor acting alone would not necessarily have triggered the 1834 strike. It would have led women as individuals to quit work and return to their rural homes. But the turn-out was a collective protest. When it was announced that wage reductions were being considered, women began to hold meetings in the mills during meal breaks in order to assess tactical possibilities. Their turn-out began at one mill when the agent discharged a woman who had presided at such a meeting. Their procession through the streets passed by other mills, expressing a conscious effort to enlist as much support as possible for their cause. At a mass meeting, the women drew up a resolution which insisted that none be discharged for their participation in the turn-out. This strike, then, was a collective response to the proposed wage cuts—made possible because women had come to form a "community" of operatives in the mill, rather than simply a group of individual workers. The existence of such a tight-knit community turned individual opposition of the wage cuts into a collective protest.

In October 1836, women again went on strike. This second turn-out was similar to the first in several respects. Its immediate cause was also a wage reduction; marches and a large outdoor rally were organized; again, like the earlier protest, the basic goal was not achieved; the corporations refused to restore wages; and operatives either left Lowell or returned to work at the new rates.

Despite these surface similarities between the turn-outs, there were some real differences. One involved scale: over 1,500 operatives turned out in 1836, compared to only 800 earlier. Moreover, the second strike lasted much longer than the first. In 1834 operatives stayed out for only a few days; in 1836, the mills ran far below capacity for several months. Two weeks after the second turn-out began, a mill agent reported that only a fifth of the strikers had returned to work: "The rest manifest good '*spunk*' as they call it." Several days later he described the impact of the continuing strike on operations in his mills: "We must be feeble for months to come as probably not less than 250 of our former scanty supply of help have left town." These lines read in sharp contrast to the optimistic reports of agents following the turn-out in February 1834.

Differences between the two turn-outs were not limited to the increased scale and duration of the later one. Women displayed a much higher degree of organization in 1836 than earlier. To co-ordinate strike activities, they formed a Factory Girls' Association. According to one historian, membership in the short-lived association reached 2,500 at its height. The larger organization among women was reflected in the tactics employed. Strikers, according to one mill agent, were able to halt production to a greater extent than numbers alone could explain; and, he complained, although some operatives were willing to work, "it has been impossible to give employment to many who remained." He attributed this difficulty to the strikers' tactics: "This was in many instances no doubt the result of calculation and contrivance. After the original turn-out they [the operatives]would assail a particular room— as for instance, all the warpers, or all the warp spinners, or all the speeder and stretcher girls, and this would close the mill as effectually as if all the girls in the mill had left."

Now giving more thought than they had in 1834 to the specific tactics of the turn-out, the women made a deliberate effort to shut down the mills in order to win their demands. They attempted to persuade less committed operatives, concentrating on those in crucial departments within the mill. Such tactics anticipated those of skilled mulespinners and loomfixers who went out on strike in the 1880s and 1890s.

In their organization of a Factory Girls' Association and in their efforts to shut down the mills, the female operatives revealed that they had been changed by their industrial experience. Increasingly, they acted not simply as "daughters of freemen" offended by the impositions of the textile corporations, but also as industrial workers intent on improving their position within the mills.

There was a decline in protest among women in the Lowell mills following these early strike defeats. During the 1837–1843 depression, textile corporations twice reduced wages without evoking a collective response from operatives. Because of the frequency of production cutbacks and lay-offs in these years, workers probably accepted the mill agents' contention that they had to reduce wages or close entirely. But with the return of prosperity and the expansion of production in the mid–1840s, there were renewed labor protests among women. Their actions paralleled those of working men and reflected fluctuations in the business cycle. Prosperity itself did not prompt turn-outs, but it evidently facilitated collective actions by women operatives.

In contrast to the protests of the previous decade, the struggles now were primarily political. Women did not turn-out in the 1840s; rather, they mounted annual petition campaigns calling on the State legislature to limit the hours of labor within the mills. These campaigns reached their height in 1845 and 1846, when 2,000 and 5,000 operatives respectively signed petitions. Unable to curb the wage cuts, or the speedup and stretch-out imposed by mill owners, operatives sought to mitigate the consequences of these changes by reducing the length of the working day. Having been defeated earlier in economic struggles, they now sought to achieve their new goal through political action. The Ten Hour Movement, seen in these terms, was a logical outgrowth of the unsuccessful turn-outs of the previous decade. Like the earlier struggles, the Ten Hour Movement was an assertion of the dignity of operatives and an attempt to maintain that dignity under the changing conditions of industrial capitalism.

The growth of relatively permanent labor organizations and institutions among women was a distinguishing feature of the Ten Hour Movement of the 1840s. The Lowell Female Labor Reform Association was organized in 1845 by women operatives. It became Lowell's leading organization over the next three years, organizing the city's female operatives and helping to set up branches in other mill towns. The Association was affiliated with the New England Workingmen's Association and sent delegates to its meetings. It acted in concert with similar male groups, and yet maintained its own autonomy. Women elected their own officers, held their own meetings, testified before a State legislative committee, and published a series of "Factory Tracts" which exposed conditions within the mills and argued for the ten-hour day.

An important educational and organizing tool of the Lowell Female Labor Reform Association was the *Voice of Industry*, a labor weekly published in Lowell between 1845 and 1848 by the New England Workingmen's Association. Female operatives were involved in every aspect of its publication and used the *Voice* to further the Ten Hour Movement among women. Their Association owned the press on which the *Voice* was printed. Sarah Bagley, the Association president, was a member of the three-person publishing committee of the *Voice* and for a time served as editor. Other women were employed by the paper as travelling editors. They wrote articles about the Ten Hour Movement in other mill towns, in an effort to give ten-hour supporters a sense of the large cause of which they were a part. Furthermore, they raised money for the *Voice* and increased its circulation by selling subscriptions to the paper in their travels about New England. Finally, women used the *Voice* to appeal directly to their fellow operatives. They edited a separate "Female Department," which published letters and articles by and about women in the mills.

Another aspect of the Ten Hour Movement which distinguished it from the earlier labor struggles in Lowell was that it involved both men and women. At the same time that women in Lowell formed the Female Labor Reform Association, a male mechanics' and laborers' association was also organized. Both groups worked to secure the passage of legislation setting ten hours as the length of the working day. Both groups circulated petitions to this end and when the legislative committee came to Lowell to hear testimony, both men and women testified in favor of the ten-hour day.

The two groups, then, worked together, and each made an important contribution to the movement in Lowell. Women had the numbers, comprising as they did over eighty percent of the mill workforce. Men, on the other hand, had the votes, and since the Ten Hour Movement was a political struggle, they played a crucial part. After the State committee reported unfavorably on the ten-hour petitions, the Female Labor Reform Association denounced the committee chairman, a State representative from Lowell, as a corporation "tool." Working for his defeat at the polls, they did so successfully and then passed the following post-election resolution: "*Resolved,* That the members of this Association tender their grateful acknowledgements to the voters of Lowell, for consigning William Schouler to the obscurity he so justly deserves." Women took a more prominent part in the Ten Hour Movement in Lowell than did men, but they obviously remained dependent on male voters and legislators for the ultimate success of their movement.

Although co-ordinating their efforts with those of working men, women operatives organized independently within the Ten Hour Movement. For instance, in 1845 two important petitions were sent from Lowell to the State legislature. Almost ninety percent of the signers of one petition were females, and more than two-thirds of the signers of the second were males. Clearly the separation of men and women in their daily lives was reflected in the Ten Hour petitions of these years.

The way in which the Ten Hour Movement was carried from Lowell to other mill towns also illustrated the independent organizing of women within the larger movement. For example, at a spirited meeting in Manchester, New Hampshire, in December 1845—one presided over by Lowell operatives—more than a thousand workers, two-thirds of them women, passed resolutions calling for the ten-hour day. Later, those in attendance divided along male-female lines, each meeting separately to set up parallel organizations. Sixty women joined the Manchester Female Labor Reform Association that evening, and by the following summer it claimed over three hundred members. Female operatives met in company boarding houses to involve new women in the movement. In their first year of organizing, Manchester workers obtained more than 4,000 signatures on ten-hour petitions. While men and women were both active in the movement, they worked through separate institutional structures from the outset.

The division of men and women within the Ten Hour Movement also reflected their separate daily lives in Lowell and in other mill towns. To repeat, they held different jobs in the mills and had little contact apart from the formal, structured overseer-operative relation. Outside the mill, we have noted, women tended to live in female boarding houses provided by the corporations and were isolated from men. Consequently, the experiences of women in "these early" mill towns were different from those of men, and in the course of their daily lives they came to form a close-knit community. It was logical that women's participation in the Ten Hour Movement mirrored this basic fact.

The women's Ten Hour Movement, like the earlier turnouts, was based in part on the participants' sense of their own worth and dignity as daughters of freemen. At the same time, however, it also indicated the growth of a new consciousness. It reflected a mounting feeling of community among women operatives and a realization that their interests and those of their employers were not identical, that they had to rely on themselves and not on corporate benevolence to achieve a reduction in the hours of labor. One woman, in an open letter to a State legislator, expressed this rejection of middle-class paternalism: "Bad as is the condition of so many women, it would be much worse if they had nothing but your boasted protection to rely upon; but they have at last learnt the lesson which a bitter experience teaches, that not to those who style themselves their 'natural protectors' are they to look for the needful help, but to the strong and resolute of their own sex." Such an attitude, underlying the self-organizing of women in the ten-hour petition campaigns, was clearly the product of the industrial experience in Lowell.

Both the early turn-outs and the Ten Hour Movement were, as noted above, in large measure dependent upon the existence of a close-knit community of women operatives. Such a community was based on the work structure, the nature of worker housing, and workforce homogeneity. Women were drawn together by the initial job training of newcomers; by the informal work sharing among experienced hands; by living in company boarding houses; by sharing religious, educational, and social activities in their leisure hours. Working and living in a new and alien setting, they came to rely upon one another for friendship and support. Understandably, a community feeling developed among them.

This evolving community as well as the common cultural traditions which Yankee women carried into Lowell were major elements that governed their response to changing mill conditions. The pre-industrial tradition of independence and self-respect made them particularly sensitive to management labor policies. The sense of community enabled them to transform their individual opposition to wage cuts and to the increasing pace of work into public protest. In these labor struggles women operatives expressed a new consciousness of their rights both as workers and as women. Such a consciousness, like the community of women itself, was one product of Lowell's industrial revolution.

The experiences of Lowell women before 1850 present a fascinating picture of the contradictory impact of industrial capitalism. Repeated labor protests reveal that female operatives felt the demands of mill employment to be oppressive. At the same time, however, the mills provided women with work outside of the home and family, thereby offering them an unprecedented [opportunity]. That they came to challenge employer paternalism was a direct consequence of the increasing opportunities offered them in these years. The Lowell mills both exploited and liberated women in ways unknown to the preindustrial political economy.

14

Fifty-four Forty or Fight! Oregon Territory Becomes American at Last

ROBERT MADDOX

● *American foreign policy has traditionally been rooted in two cardinal beliefs: the Monroe Doctrine and Manifest Destiny. Indicating that the United States would consider it a threat to itself if any European nation attempted to gain a foothold in the Western Hemisphere, President James Monroe's message to Congress in 1823 has been sanctioned by most Americans as having the effect of an international law. Manifest Destiny is a more indeterminate concept, but it might generally be defined as the belief that God has chosen us to do His will on earth. Whether Americans moved westward, booted the Indians off their ancestral lands, freed the Cubans from Spanish tyranny in 1898, took over the Philippines, entered World War I to make the world safe for democracy, or acted as leader of the free world to thwart Communist expansion, federal policymakers have usually justified their actions in moral terms. Thus, the United States seized almost half of Mexico (including most of what is now California, New Mexico, Arizona, Utah, and Nevada) during the 1840s while insisting that it was acting on behalf of democracy and justice. In actuality, the colossus of the North was stronger, richer, more populous, and more technologically advanced than its neighbor and hence able to enforce its will.*

The dispute over the proper boundary of the Oregon territory, which included all or part of what would later become five separate states, was another matter entirely. In this instance, the competitor was not a weak and backward Latin neighbor but Great Britain, then the most powerful nation on earth. Indeed, the British Empire stretched around the

Reproduced through the courtesy of Cowles Magazine, publisher of *American History Illustrated*.

*globe, and its mighty Royal Navy had no serious competitor
on any ocean. The nature of the "fifty-four forty" dispute and
the peaceful way it was finally resolved not only reveals how
the United States came to have its present boundary, but it
also points out that powerful nations can settle strong disagreements in a permanent fashion without resorting to armed
conflict.*

The United States government granted territorial status to Oregon on
August 14, 1848. The area then included what would become the states
of Oregon and Washington, as well as portions of Idaho, Wyoming,
and Montana. At one time or another most of the major European
powers had laid claim to the region, and on several occasions came
close to war. Indeed, in the mid–1840s there was talk of conflict between the United States and Great Britain over the Oregon question.
How important was the region? South Carolina Senator McDuffie had
said he would not give "a pinch of snuff for the whole territory" and
thanked God "for his mercy" in placing the Rocky Mountains between
it and the interior. Others thought differently. As one newspaper, the
Washington *Madisonian*, put it, "*Oregon is ours*, and we will keep it,
at the price, if need be, of every drop of the nation's blood." Fortunately, most Americans stood between these extremes and acquired the
area—most of it, anyway—without shedding a drop of blood.

The first whites to reach the coast of the Pacific Northwest most
likely were Spanish explorers during the middle of the sixteenth century.
They were searching for the Strait of Aniàn, a mythical passageway
which was supposed to connect the Atlantic and Pacific Oceans. Sir
Francis Drake, during one of his raids against Spanish shipping a few
decades later, may also have sailed as far north as Oregon, though the
evidence is inconclusive. In any event, almost two hundred years passed
before renewed explorations again created interest in the region—this
time with implications for Americans.

In 1774, the year when the First Continental Congress met in Philadelphia, Spain sent an expedition to the coast of Oregon which, among
other things, discovered Nootka Sound on the western side of what
later became known as Vancouver Island. Several more Spanish probes
followed, and in 1776 the great British explorer Captain James Cook
set sail to explore the northwestern coast. Aside from particular find-

ings, important in themselves, the most significant aspect of Cook's expedition was that its journals later were published and were widely read. What caused a sensation was the report that furs secured from the local Indians for a small amount later fetched as much as fifty to seventy dollars per skin when sold in China. "The rage with which our seamen were possessed to return," recorded one officer, "...to make their fortunes, at one time, was not far short of mutiny." The result of this news, according to one historian of Oregon, "was to send the first of a multinational flotilla to the Northwest coast," and to set in motion a train of events with far-reaching consequences.

Although Spain claimed sovereignty over the Pacific Northwest by virtue of a papal bull of 1494 and by her own explorations, her British rivals showed no inclination to back off. The matter came to a head during the summer of 1789 when Spanish authorities seized several British ships that had dropped anchor in Nootka Sound. The affair immediately took on international implications, especially for the new American government under George Washington, which had taken office only a few months earlier. If, as for a time seemed likely, war broke out between the two European rivals, Washington and his advisors assumed the British in Canada would strike at Spanish possessions in Louisiana and Florida. They could only do so by crossing American territory.

Washington was placed in a quandary. Agreeing to the anticipated British request to cross American soil might mean war with Spain; refusal might mean war with Great Britain. As became his habit, Washington placed the matter before his cabinet only to find it badly divided. Alexander Hamilton, the pro-British secretary of the treasury, favored granting the right of access. Secretary of State Thomas Jefferson suggested ignoring any such request. Fortunately, Washington did not have to decide. Spain was unable to stand alone against Great Britain, but when she turned to her ally, France, the latter nation was convulsed in revolution and unable to help. Spain had no choice but to capitulate and, in what became known as the Nootka Convention of 1790, recognized the right of British subjects to trade and settle along the coast of the Pacific Northwest. This greatly strengthened future British claims on the region and signaled "the beginning of the end of the Spanish Empire in America."

The Oregon country faded as a source of political friction among the powers for the next several decadse, but explorations of its coastline and harbors continued as did the trade in furs. Americans played an active role in both activities. In 1792 Captain Robert Gray located the mouth of the Columbia River, and by the mid–1790s Yankee traders dominated the sea otter trade. During this period the first expedition from the interior to reach the Pacific through Oregon was made by the Canadian explorer Alexander Mackenzie.

Finally, a few years after the turn of the century, President Thomas Jefferson authorized the historic expedition of Meriwether Lewis and William Clark, the last great overland survey of the Oregon country. Jefferson was motivated by several considerations in mounting this project, not the least of which was to strengthen American claims on Oregon for the future.

Oregon surfaced as a diplomatic issue several times during the decade following the War of 1812—and the United States profited in every instance. Most important was the Convention of 1818, negotiated with the British by Albert Gallatin and Richard Rush. This agreement settled a number of issues which had been hanging fire since the end of the war, including the establishment of the Canadian-American border at the forty-ninth parallel between the Lake of the Woods and the Rocky Mountains. Both parties claimed land west of the Rockies—Oregon— and no boundary could be agreed upon. In a spirit of compromise, however, the negotiators decided to leave the territory "free and open" to both Americans and Britons. Commonly referred to as"joint occupation," this arrangement had the effect of bolstering subsequent claims by the latecoming Americans.

Negotiations with Spain during this period also bore fruit with regard to Oregon. Although the most pressing issue had to do with acquiring Spanish possessions in Florida, President Monroe's secretary of state, John Quincy Adams, also sought to pressure Spain into relinquishing her claims on all territories lying north of the forty-second parallel, the northern border of California. Spain, weak militarily and beset with internal problems, had no wish either to knuckle under or to fight. Instead she simply dragged the negotiations out for as long as she could.

The Spanish thought their delaying tactics might pay off when, in April 1818, General Andrew Jackson conducted a punitive raid in Spanish Florida in "hot pursuit" of Indians and renegades who had been plundering American settlements. In the process Jackson's forces captured two British subjects and quickly executed them on the ground that they had incited the Indians. Spain hoped to play upon the resultant British indignation to secure an ally against the United States. When cooler heads prevailed—British officials had no desire to risk hostilities over two such obvious blunders—Spain realized she had to capitulate to Adams. The Adams-Onis Treaty of 1819, among other things, turned over Spanish claims to the Oregon territory to the United States.

Yet another European nation bowed out of the picture a few years later. During the late eighteenth and early nineteenth centuries Russian traders had moved south of Alaska—or Russian America, as it was then known—to establish outposts almost as far as San Francisco. In 1821 the tsar issued a proclamation, prohibiting the ships of other nations from coming within a hundred miles of the coast north of the fifty-first parallel. The proclamation was unenforceable, but seemed to Americans to indicate a potential threat to the Oregon country.

Secretary Adams responded to this move in terms very similar to those later found in the Monroe Doctrine. The United States, he warned, considered this hemisphere closed to "any new European colonial establishments." Adams did not frighten the Russians very much, but they were diplomatically isolated in Europe at the time and had grave domestic ills as well. In any event, Adams negotiated a treaty with them in 1824, the terms of which provided that Russia lay no claims to territory south of 54° 40'.

By the mid–1820s, therefore, only Great Britain and the United States were left to contest the territory between 42° and 54°40'. Britain's case for ownership rested upon the Nootka Convention of 1790, various explorations such as Captain Cook's, and the establishment of numerous fur trading posts then controlled by the mighty Hudson's Bay Company. The United States pointed to her own explorations, such as Gray's and the Lewis and Clark expedition, the acquisition of Spanish rights via the Adams-Onis Treaty, and the fact that Oregon was contiguous to American soil. Neither government thought the matter was important enough to squabble over during these years, and in 1827 the 1818 "joint occupation" agreement was extended indefinitely with the proviso that either party could terminate it by giving a year's notice.

This happy state of affairs lasted a decade and then began to disintegrate into an ominous situation.

The Oregon question became prominent during the early 1840s because of three developments, one of them potentially explosive. First, business interests became increasingly enamored with the idea of obtaining ports on the Pacific Ocean. Trade with the Far East had always figured in American thinking, but now visionaries dreamed of making the United States the center of world commerce by linking the Atlantic and Pacific oceans by means of transcontinental railroads. Second, more and more Americans began crossing the Rockies to settle in the Oregon territory. In 1841 there were about 500 Americans scattered throughout the region; by 1845 there were more than 5,000. And more were on the way, as what the Independence, Missouri *Expositor* called "Oregon fever" spread in the middle west.

Finally, a mood of militant expansionism was growing in the nation, a mood characterized by the term "Manifest Destiny." Though in the minority, more and more people began talking about America's right to *all* of Oregon and bandied about slogans such as "fifty-four forty or fight."

Over the years there had been several tentative efforts made to resolve the Oregon question diplomatically. Basically, the Americans wished merely to extend the 49° boundary west to the Pacific. In offering such a solution the United States implicitly recognized British claims to the area north of that line. The British, seeking to protect the interests of the Hudson's Bay Company, wanted the boundary drawn at the Columbia river, which meandered through Oregon to the sea several hundred miles south of the forty-ninth parallel.

Such a position, of course, implicitly recognized American claims south of the river. The crux of the issue, therefore, had been that triangle of land between the Columbia River and 49°. American settlers posed no obstacle to peaceful adjustment since they located almost exclusively in the lush Willamette Valley, which lay to the south of the Columbia. The desire for port facilities raised a thornier question, for these lay north of the river. Still, the British were inclined to be flexible, provided a decent regard was paid to the interests of the Hudson's Bay Company, whose operations in any event were becoming less profitable as the years went by. But the demand for *all* of Oregon, aside from being completely without foundation, was an intolerable affront to the British and unacceptable whatever the costs. In 1844, unfortunately, the entire question became enmeshed in "the noisy arena of Presidential politics."

The Oregon question by this time was irretrievably linked with the matter of admitting Texas to the union. This in turn involved sectional disputes and the slavery issue, among others. The Whig candidate, Henry Clay, sought to avoid dividing his party by equivocating on Mexico and Oregon. The lesser-known James K. Polk, whom the Democrats nominated, did the opposite by proclaiming his determination to acquire *both* areas, and the Democratic platform specifically referred to the "whole" of Oregon. Contrary to myth, the party never used the slogan "fifty-four forty or fight," but it amounted to the same thing.

Polk was a short, slender man with a shock of long hair and a perpetually mournful countenance. If he had a sense of humor he concealed it with great success. Stubborn and intense, he had no experience in diplomacy and was temperamentally unsuited for it. His guiding principle, if it can be called such, was that above all one should never trust the British. "The only way to treat John Bull," he confided to his diary, "was to look him straight in the eye." He appeared to be doing just that when he referred to Oregon in his inaugural address. America's claim to Oregon, Polk stated, was "clear and unquestionable," a phrase taken directly from the belligerent Democratic campaign platform. On the other hand he did not refer to "all" of Oregon, and later in the address said that "meantime every obligation imposed by treaty or conventional stipulation should be sacredly respected."

Actually Polk had no intention of risking war with Great Britain over unsupportable claims, particularly at a time when trouble with Mexico was brewing over the Texas issue. His real goal was modest and traditional—to extend the line of 49° west to the Pacific—and he was prepared to concede all of Vancouver Island to the British even though the southern portion of it lay below the parallel. His "clear and unquestionable" statement was a clumsy ploy designed in part to impress the British with his firmness, and in part to placate the hawks in his own party. It failed to do either. The more jingoistic elements in the British government and press howled in indignation and loosed their own broadsides against American treachery. And the hawks, or "ultras" as they were called, rushed to the attack over his failure to insist upon American rights to the entire territory.

Polk blundered again a few months later. When the furor over his inaugural address died down, the British instructed their minister in Washington, Richard Pakenham, to reopen the Oregon question. The British were willing to accept the forty-ninth parallel boundary, but wished to retain navigational rights on the Columbia River. After a delay of several weeks, on July 12 Polk formally replied through Secretary of State James Buchanan. He proposed extending the 49° boundary with all of Vancouver Island going to the British, but refused to offer use of the Columbia. Most important, Polk had written into the message a statement the gist of which was that the United States was making this proposal even though its claims to *all* of Oregon were valid.

It was insulting, to say the least. British acceptance of such terms would have amounted to an admission that *their* claims were invalid, and such territory as they received would represent a gift made by the generous Americans. Pakenham rejected the proposal without even referring it back to his government. Polk, angered by such ingratitude, broke off negotiations.

The Oregon question simmered along until December when Polk heated it up again in his first annual message to Congress. Referring to what had taken place thus far, the president placed the entire blame for failure on the British. The United States, he said, had acted in "a spirit of liberal concession" and "will be relieved of all responsibility which may follow the failure to settle the controversy." He asked Congress to provide armed escorts for wagon trains heading there, and said it would be desirable to serve Britain the required one-year's notice that the joint occupation agreement would be terminated.

Polk then specifically referred to the Monroe Doctrine, and there was no question as for whom his warning was meant. Looking John Bull "in the eye" again, Polk hoped to pressure the British into reopening negotiations on his own terms.

If the president hoped to obtain a show of national unity over Oregon, he was sadly mistaken. Instead his speech touched off a debate in and outside of Congress which lasted for months. The issue centered around terminating the joint occupation agreement. Moderates fought against serving any notice at all, while the more belligerent Democrats wished to accompany the notice with a defiant claim to all the Oregon territory. Finally a coalition of Whigs and administration Democrats secured for Polk a neutrally worded statement advising him to give notice of termination.

The belligerent language of Polk's annual message caused an uproar in Great Britain. British Foreign Secretary Aberdeen, a longtime proponent of compromise, told the American minister in London that "the possibility of a rupture with the United States" had to be considered. Fortunately, talk of war quickly faded as Great Britain at the time was wracked with internal disputes. Probably most Britishers wished to settle the issue provided it could be done with grace.

Finally, Aberdeen and the other moderates received a fortuitous break. Opponents of the 49° boundary had argued that the Columbia River was indispensable, not only for the Hudson's Bay Company, but for the western provinces of Canada. Now, however, news arrived in London that the Hudson's Bay Company had moved its main depot from the Columbia River to Vancouver Island. The company's voluntary withdrawal undercut the idea that the Columbia triangle was significant and permitted Aberdeen to begin negotiations on the basis of extending the 49° boundary.

Polk's stubbornness once again threatened a successful settlement. The British proposal provided that the treaty would guarantee the Hudson's Bay Company—and those doing business with it—free navigation of the Columbia. The president balked at this, and it required the strong arguments of a majority of the cabinet to convince him to go along. The fact that the nation was now in the midst of war with Mexico no doubt helped. His cabinet members also persuaded Polk to take an unusual step with the proposed treaty.

The normal procedure is for a president to sign a treaty and then send it to the Senate for passage. To have done so in this case would have exposed the administration to charges by the "fifty-four forty or fight" elements of signing away American rights. Instead, a reluctant Polk submitted the treaty to the Senate for its *previous* advice, thereby dropping a very hot potato into other people's laps. On June 12, 1846, by a vote of 38 to 12, the Senate advised the president to accept the proposal as it stood. He signed the treaty on June 15, and three days later the Senate passed it.

Oregon, at least that portion of it up to the forty-ninth parallel, was American at last! Rarely in human history has so much effort been expended to make a settlement over which the two parties were so close in goals all along. Both nations repeatedly had offered terms almost identical with those finally embodied in the treaty, and both repeatedly had been spurned.

Polk's willfulness had almost caused a rupture with Great Britain over the inconsequential matter of navigation rights to the Columbia. History credits his administration with acquiring Oregon, but it is fair to say that he succeeded in spite of himself. And to some of his contemporaries he had not even succeeded. "Oh," cried Senator Thomas Hart Benton, "mountain that was delivered of a mouse, thy name shall henceforth be fifty-four forty."

15

Florida's Slave Codes, 1821–1861

JOSEPH CONAN THOMPSON

● *Every human society, however small or primitive, of necessity develops rules of conduct that are enforced by threat of punishment if they are violated. In essence, such rules are denoted as law. Ordinarily, we like to think that the American legal system represents an honest attempt to produce a framework that will enforce our society's best ethical and moral mandates.*

What happens, however, when the law is placed at the service of an institution which is inherently evil? Slavery was a detestable practice that should have had no place in a society that presumed to be based upon the proposition that all men are created equal. Yet lawmakers and politicians in the South tried to make human bondage somehow compatible with ethical notions of fair play and justice. They developed slave codes that attempted to balance the contradictory desire of the white community to curtail the ability of slaves to act independently while at the same time extending to slaves certain guarantees against maltreatment. The attempt was doomed from the start, but, as Joseph Conan Thompson indicates in the following essay about Florida before the Civil War, it illustrates one of the many ways that this "peculiar institution" distorted American government.

As personal property capable of independent action, slaves posed a unique dilemma to antebellum Florida's ruling society. Statute law, which defined criminal behavior and affixed punishment for white criminals, could not be applied easily to the slaves lest whites compromise the hegemonic function of the law. A clear line of distinction between the two races was needed in order to maintain black subordination and race control. Had the ruling class consented to a body of laws that

Reprinted with permission of the editor from *Florida Historical Quarterly*, January, 1993.

would have applied equally to both master and slave, that line might have been disconcertingly ambiguous. Any hint of equality under the law would have raised questions as to the viability of a slave-labor-based economy and the validity of the doctrine of white supremacy, the very institutions upon which southern society rested. In addition, these laws protected the delicate balance, the uneasy peace, if you will, struck between the races. In this regard, slave codes, as they came to be known, were seen as precautionary measures designed to forestall the likelihood of slave insurrection, petty thievery, miscegenation, escapes, and countless other infractions associated with the frustrations of an oppressed people. This essay examines the legal apparatus that white Floridians used to preserve their social, political, economic, and psychological hegemony. Clearly evident in both territorial and state statutes as well as the rulings of Florida's highest court was an effort to maintain a balance in the law, to curtail the slaves' ability to act independently while at the same time extending to the slave certain guarantees against maltreatment. Indeed, Florida's slave code was designed to control both slaves and masters. Behind this dual function of the law lay the belief that the institution of slavery remained most secure when the bondsman was neither tempted with excessive liberties nor taunted by inhumane cruelties.

Florida's lawmakers drew upon models set by their fellow southern legislators when drafting their state's slave code. As a rule these enactments were harsher than the laws that governed white behavior. For example, Florida's slave code listed more felonies than did the regular statutes. Furthermore, the punishment meted out against offending slaves was generally more severe and often involved whipping or mutilation. By creating this code, Florida's lawmakers hoped to restrict the slaves' freedom of movement and limit their ability to communicate with one another. For instance, pass laws mandated that slaves receive some form of written permission before venturing off their master's property. Strict laws against instructing slaves to read, write, set type, or possess any sort of reading material were formidable legal barriers intended to prevent potentially seditious literature from reaching the bondsmen. Slaves could not legally carry or possess weapons of any sort, nor could they congregate in groups of eight or more without a white chaperon in attendance.

Between 1821 and 1861 most of Florida's slaves could be found working the cotton-rich plantations situated between the Suwannee and Apalachicola rivers, along the St. Johns River near St. Augustine, or harvesting sugar near the Manatee River south of Tampa. While slaves could be found as far south as Dade and Monroe counties, most of the whites in that area owned few if any bondsmen. In Florida, as in most southern states, masters enjoyed a great deal of latitude when disciplining their chattel. In practice most justice was carried out on the plantation, a fact that underscores the pre-bourgeois or manorial character of plantation life and the master's near-absolute control over his or her property. Florida's laws sanctioned branding, mutilation, and even death for certain crimes. However, most masters preferred to punish their slaves with whips specifically designed to inflict pain without leaving permanent scars, primarily because a scarred slave would be readily identified as "troublesome," thus depreciating his or her value. The pecuniary interests of the master further dictated that slaves not be imprisoned, for to do so would be to punish owners by temporarily denying them a productive asset. As the Civil War approached, the Draconian codes of the eighteenth century were gradually humanized. The revised code listed fewer capital crimes, and Florida's courts demonstrated a remarkable propensity for procedural fairness and justice when trying slaves. By 1845, the year Florida was granted statehood, the institution of slavery had been firmly established, so much so that legislators believed it to be secure enough to enact laws that protected slaves from arbitrary or excessive punishment.

Slaves codes served a variety of functions, the most pressing of which was to protect the white community from slave insurrections. The fear of rebellion, a fear exacerbated by the emergence of northern abolitionism, periodically spurred Florida's lawmakers into action. News of a recent uprising, regardless of its location or magnitude, was quite often followed by further revisions to the state's slave code. The reaction to Nat Turner's revolt in 1831 provides an example of this post-rebellion legislation. Soon after the failed mutiny, Florida's territorial legislature passed an act that empowered slave patrols to seize and punish (up to thirty-nine lashes on the bare back) any slave found violating local pass laws. Additional legislation made the act of inciting slaves to revolt a capital offense and defined the murder of a slave in the act of rebellion as justifiable homicide. The former act reflected an increasingly alarmist body of Florida lawmakers who imagined that rabble-rousing abolitionists lurked behind almost every tree and under every stone.

Floridians also enacted laws designed to punish slaveholders whose carelessness was deemed a threat to his or her neighbors. Fines of up to $100 were levied against any master whose runaway slave was captured by patrollers. Defined in the Florida code as any slave who was absent from his or her quarters and whose whereabouts were unknown, runaways represented an expensive burden to the master. Once captured, the runaway was to be housed in the local jail at the owner's expense. In addition, a nominal sum was to be paid, again by the owner, to the individual or group responsible for apprehending the fugitive. Legislators believed that these laws would encourage masters to keep a watchful eye on their more spirited chattel. While some codes specifically protected slaves from maltreatment, the vast majority were intended to "clarify beyond all question, to rationalize, to simplify, and to make more logical and symmetrical the slave's status in society."

Spanish Florida was home to so few slaves that its governors never saw the need to regulate the institution. Under British rule, however, the slave population experienced a substantial increase, necessitating the formulation of Florida's first slave code. The act was signed into law in May 1782, a year before Great Britain ceded Florida back to Spain. There exists no evidence to suggest that this particular code had a lasting impact on Florida's political culture. Nevertheless, there are certain basic similarities between the British and American codes, enough to warrant a brief look at the former code.

The British code projected the same desire to regulate the system and subjugate the slave, as evidenced in codes adopted in others parts of North America. British officials imposed stringent limitations on the bondsmen's movements and their ability to associate with other slaves. Likewise, masters were penalized for any number of infractions, including granting their slaves liberties beyond those proscribed by the law and, of a related nature, carelessly affording their bondsmen the opportunity to run away or transgress in any manner. Clearly, the uniform standards of slave codes are made manifest by the British model. But one can only speculate as to the correlation between the act of 1782 and Florida's later statutes.

Florida became a United States territory in 1821, but circumstances did not warrant the adoption of a body of criminal statutes governing its black inhabitants until 1828. At that time the territorial council enacted a law that came to form the basis for all subsequent slave-related legislation right up to emancipation. Even the so-called St. Joseph Constitution, drafted in 1839 and put into force in 1845 when Florida achieved statehood, did not substantively alter the 1828 code. Entitled "An Act relating to Crimes and Misdemeanors committed by Slaves, free Negroes, and Mulattoes," the 1828 code consisted of sixty-three sections defining a variety of criminal offenses and the appropriate penalties. It also included the legal definition of a slave and the circumstances under which one could be manumitted. With the passage of time, Floridians altered these codes in order to suit the demands of a changing social, political, and economic order. As sectional hostilities intensified, the white ruling class tightened its grip on the peculiar institution, a fact reflected in the law. The significance of this legislation mandates an in-depth examination of its pronouncements as well as any subsequent legislation adopted to revise it.

The first six sections of the Act of 1828 address the problem of determining who shall be deemed a slave. In Florida, as in the rest of the South, a child inherited the status of its mother. This inhibited the growth of a class of free mulattoes. These bastard children, the issue of illegal liaisons (miscegenation was prohibited by law), were social outcasts, pariahs whose presence served as reminders of the inherent contradictions between the moral pronouncements of the ruling race and its actual behavior. The law required free blacks to pay an annual head tax of $10, register with local magistrates, and select a white guardian to function as their representative in all legal matters. In 1829 manumission was outlawed, and a provision in the St. Joseph Constitution of 1839 gave the General Assembly power to prohibit the inmigration of free blacks and mulattoes. These aggressively prohibitive statutes prompted some free blacks to enter bondage on their own volition, a practice facilitated by legislative action in 1858. In short, successive legislative acts underscored a willingness on the part of the ruling race to segregate society into two clearly defined categories: free whites and enslaved blacks.

The first six sections of the 1828 code also governed the sale and importation of slaves. No slave convicted of a crime was permitted to enter Florida. Owners guilty of violating this article could be fined as much as $250 and ordered to remove the slave from the territory. In

1839 the St. Joseph Constitution specifically denied the General Assembly the power to emancipate slaves. Indeed, a reading of the slave code unmasks what antebellum white Floridians perceived to be the ideal black: he was obsequious, industrious, docile, loyal, and most importantly, enslaved.

Florida's lawmakers took care to see to it that slaves remained shut out of the marketplace. Seven of the sixty-three sections denied slaves the right to participate in the capitalist economy. The law forbade them from selling their labor, owning property (both real and personal), or trading without the written permission of their owners. Heavy penalties awaited both buyer and seller, regardless of race, if convicted of trading on the "black market." In practice whites could expect a more lenient form of correction. Selling intoxicating liquor to a slave was a particularly serious crime. Cognizant of the unruly behavior and violence associated with strong drink, the legislature ordered that any individual found guilty of this offense should pay a fine of $10 or be subjected to thirty-nine lashes across the back. Obviously this statute was intended to deny slaves access to alcohol by punishing potential suppliers. Section 45 of the 1828 code stated that slaves who bartered, bought, or sold anything of value were to receive a maximum of thirty-nine lashes. Part of the reasoning behind this penalty lay in the belief that much of what a slave had to sell had been illegally procured. Theoretically, if a slave could not own property then anything they sold could not have been their own. Unscrupulous whites often enticed slaves to pilfer from their masters by promising to buy all that the slave could steal. Lawmakers recognized this and adopted legislation designed to end it. Certain sections of the 1828 code enumerated those items that a slave could not trade. These included agricultural products, particularly staple crops. White masters feared their slaves' larceny would have a pernicious effect on their yield and, in turn, upon their margin of profit. Despite legislative diligence, Florida's "black market" flourished.

Slaves were also barred from owning property. The idea of a slave owning anything seemed ludicrous to the ruling race. This simple exercise in logic—the understanding that one cannot own property if one is property—was not lost on planters. Their law books affirmed this concept, and the courts concurred. Private ownership among the slaves, one Florida judge declared, tended "to make other slaves dissatisfied

... and thereby excite ... a spirit of insubordination." Sometimes masters allowed slaves to keep a horse, a few pigs, or even a boat, but only at the owner's discretion. Slaves could never be the genuine owner of anything. Any slave who claimed ownership of material goods could, by law, be forced to surrender said property to the court. In turn the court would sell the goods—the proceeds of the transaction to be divided between the prosecutor and the state treasury. The slave received nothing.

Despite laws denying slaves the right to hire out their labor for wages during their off hours, the practice proved fairly common throughout the South, particularly among those black artisans whose skills were in high demand. Free-born artisans objected to the lax enforcement of these laws, claiming that slaves worked at artificially depressed wages in order to attract business. These protests had some merit, for slaves usually had no overhead, and it was possible for them to cut prices without affecting their profit margins. One Florida legislator agreed, warning that hiring out caused a "relaxation of discipline and ... the forgetfulness of duty, gives them possession of money and affords them a means of debauchery and cannot but lead to the ultimate ruin of the slave, if not more disastrous consequences to the community." It was their fear for the safety of the white community, not their concern for the well-being of the slave, that moved lawmakers to action in 1855. In that year the city of St. Augustine repealed a city ordinance that sanctioned the practice of "hiring out." The next year the state followed suit by imposing heavier fines on owners convicted of violating the old statute. At the heart of these measures lay the pervasive desire to restrict the mobility of slaves. Regulating competition in the marketplace was a secondary concern.

Runaway slaves represented a severe financial strain on their masters. Based upon 1860 averages, the flight of a prime field hand could cost an owner as much as $1,500. Perhaps more disturbing, at least to most white Floridians, were the ubiquitous fugitives—both real and imagined—who might commit acts of petty thievery or encourage other slaves to join them. To combat this subversion to the state's economy and racial order, the slave code was amended to encourage whites to keep a tighter rein on their slaves. Florida law demanded that a master pay as much as $500 in order to recover a captured runaway. In addition, the unsuccessful runaway received the maximum number of "stripes" (100 lashes) allowed by law. Slave patrols had the authority to pursue runaways onto private property if necessary. They were also sanctioned to administer punishment, disperse illegal gatherings, and seize contraband. Relative to these statutes were those that prescribed the most severe forms of punishment for slave stealing. Whether the offender had acted as a noble-hearted abolitionist or as an ordinary thief, white Floridians regarded slave stealing as a despicable practice. Whites convicted of this offense either paid a fine of $1,000 or received thirty-nine lashes. In either case the guilty party was branded with the letters "ss." If the offender were black, however, he or she could receive the death sentence. As with all other slaves ordinances, Florida's laws against stealing slaves became more rigid with the passage of time.

The variety of violent crimes and crimes against property enumerated in Florida's slave codes reflected the standard Judeo-Christian ethic common to western legal traditions. The principal differences between the laws pertaining to whites and slaves were in the types and severity of punishment. In an age of enlightened penology, white criminals could expect to be fined or sentenced to a penitentiary to be reformed. Slaves, on the other hand, were too valuable to place behind bars. Their punishment was swift, painful, and inflicted with little thought given to the moral reformation of the offender. Capital crimes included murder, conspiracy to rebel or to commit murder, assault with intent to kill, poisoning with intent to kill, and attempted murder. In each case the law was resolute; the guilty slave was to be put to death. The courts could exercise discretion in other instances where death was listed as an option. Maiming, manslaughter, arson, robbery, burglary, and attempted rape fell within this category. Trespassing, possession of firearms, sedition, unlawful assemblage, rioting, verbal assault, larceny, perjury, and consulting or advising to murder came under the heading of crimes in which corporal punishment remained the sole recourse of judge and jury. Amendments to the codes support the contention that slave laws evolved to safeguard against insurrection by placing greater restrictions on the slaves. An example of this strategy can be found in Section 9 of the 1828 code and the subsequent repeal of that section in 1831. The original law permitted slaves to carry firearms provided that they had acquired the necessary permit from the local justice of the peace. The wisdom of allowing slaves to arm themselves came into question around the time of Nat Turner's rebellion. Apprehensive legislators struck down the provision, declaring that henceforth slaves could carry neither arms nor ammunition unless in the company of their masters.

The penalties prescribed by Florida law were, by present-day standards, cruel and unusual; by any standard they were painful. The whip remained the preferred instrument of punishment. Each infraction of the law stipulated the exact number of stripes or lashes to be applied to the guilty party's bare back. Ordinarily that number was thirty-nine, a recognized allusion to the Roman custom mentioned in the Bible. Other forms of punishment proved less humane. A slave convicted of perjury, for instance, in addition to being whipped could have one of his or her ears nailed to a post. The slave would remain standing beside the post for one hour, at which time the mutilated ear would be severed from the head. Such graphic displays, commonly known as cropping, were intended to remind potential malefactors that retribution was often swift and brutal. Other forms of non-lethal punishment dictated by Florida law included branding and nose splitting. Capital punishment was an extreme measure that most owners preferred to forego. In the event that a slave was executed by the state, however, the master was entitled to fair compensation because Floridians recognized the execution of a slave as something akin to the seizure or condemnation of property.

One should not confuse the letter of the slave code with the reality of its enforcement. Slavery was an institution based upon widely held assumptions regarding the relationship between whites and blacks, labor and capital, plain folk and gentry, and the individual and the state. All of these attitudes were ingrained in the characters of most white Floridians. The law simply mirrored their customs. While most laws merely reiterated local mores, others were nuisances, only to be enforced during times of social unrest or economic hardship. For example, slave owners generally consented to their slaves' weekly religious service unless cautioned by rumors of an insurrection plot. Then laws banning large gatherings were strictly enforced. Slave marriages, while prohibited by Florida law, were allowed by owners so long as his or her economic circumstances permitted the union. Otherwise the owner could disavow the marriage and separate the couple through sale. Some slaves kept rifles or livestock while others hired out their own time or traded with whites, often with their masters' knowledge and consent and always in violation of state ordinances. Noting these routine transgressions, a Florida Grand Jury in 1844 condemned "the great looseness or laxity that too generally prevails in the management of our slave population."

Owners were bound by a sense of moral accountability—an obligation often called "paternalism"—to treat their slaves in a humane fashion. Community pressure further dictated that masters behave in a socially responsible manner, exercising discretion when chastising disobedient slaves. Owners were also bound by the law. The St. Joseph Constitution required them to provide their servants with a healthy diet, adequate clothing, medical care, and shelter. Custom further dictated that they care for the elderly and infirm. In Florida, masters could be charged with murder if their abuse caused the death of a slave. However, most masters appear to have been guided by common economic pragmatism when it came to handling their bondsmen. Slaves represented capital assets; therefore, their misuse or neglect made little economic sense. Florida's slave code only codified the majority's mores; the master class functioned in its own best interests, and no law could dictate otherwise.

The patterns of legal change expressed in Florida's slave codes followed two divergent paths: the first led toward more restrictive legislation designed to limit the possibility of insurrection, while the second reflected a desire to protect the slaves. The former was largely the result of legislative action, the latter the work of the courts.

An accused slave rarely saw the inside of a courthouse. Instead, the plantation proved the more familiar venue. Masters preferred this alternative for it reaffirmed their authority and protected them from the caprice of outside interference. However, laws and social customs constrained owners by placing limitations on the severity of punishment that one could administer to a recalcitrant bondsman. For example, particularly serious offenses such as murder, theft, and attempted rape automatically came within the jurisdiction of the state. Crimes committed by slaves in any place other than their master's property necessitated the intervention of a disinterested or impartial third party. Again, the state filled this role. Civil suits also fell within the realm of the state's authority.

Slaves who knew of the court's reputation for fairness welcomed the intercession of the law, for it was in the courtroom that the slave stood the best chance for an impartial hearing. On the plantation justice was unchecked and arbitrary. Similarly, local justices of the peace offered little in the way of justice to the accused slave. Usually ignorant of legal subtleties or personally acquainted with the owner, slaves knew of their reputation for inconsistency and venality. Florida's Superior Court judges and Supreme Court justices, on the other hand, conformed to higher standards of practice. These men tended to be better educated and more responsive to public pressure than local justices. As a result, slaves could expect more justice from the state's higher courts.

The courts accorded the slaves a remarkable degree of judicial courtesy, closely adhering to the standards of procedure and decorum used for whites. The explanation for this curious departure from day-to-day race relations, aside from the two aforementioned, illustrate the oxymoronic quality of the definition "human property." In order to hold slaves accountable for their crimes, the court had to recognize that they were capable of exercising free will. To acknowledge this was to acknowledge their humanity. Slaves, therefore, had to be granted the same rights and privileges enjoyed by any other defendant who stood before the bench. To do otherwise would have opened the court up to charges of hypocrisy. The courts obliged this masquerade, granting the slaves rights in order that they may be legally punished. But in the process slaves came to enjoy the benefits of jury trials, the right to counsel, and the protection of the Constitution.

Unfortunately the courtroom was not entirely immune from the dictates of social custom. A black man's word alone was never sufficient to convict a white man of foul play. The white community would not countenance such a challenge in their daily lives, and they would not condone it in their courts. Consequently, no state, including Florida, allowed blacks to testify against whites. On occasion judges did allow a slave to enter a plea of "self-defense" for the murder of a white, but such was the exception rather than the rule. The possibility of an accused rapist receiving a fair hearing was even more remote; however, it did happen. In *State* v. *Charles (a slave)* the judge upheld a lower court ruling that dismissed an indictment for assault with an attempt to commit rape on the grounds that it did not specify the race of the alleged victim. Section 39 of the 1828 code, the pertinent statute, clearly stipulated race when describing both the victim and her alleged assailant. In another case of alleged rape, *Cato (a slave)* v. *State,* the

Florida Supreme Court granted a retrial to a convicted rapist because of the questionable veracity and character of the state's witnesses. Writing for the majority, Judge Charles H. DuPont proclaimed that "It is the crowning glory of our 'peculiar institution,' that whenever life is involved, the slave stands upon as safe ground as the master." These two cases illustrate an attempt to provide justice for those slaves accused of even the most serious crimes.

The perseverance of Cato's attorney demonstrates that some lawyers maintained their commitment to justice despite adverse public sentiment. Studies indicate that slaves generally received able representation. Indeed, the Florida Supreme Court, in the case of *Joe (a person of color)* v. *State*, granted a motion for a new trial because, among other things, the accused "lacked adequate council." Because slaves could not serve on juries, the likelihood of being tried by a true "jury of one's peers" was nil. In fact, slaves were adjudged by representatives of a superior caste. So, despite efforts at impartiality during voir dire, they remained at the mercy of prejudicial juries.

Courts made efforts to compensate for the slaves' legal vulnerability by making the appropriate allowances. Court-appointed attorneys were one such concession. Another was its willingness to challenge the admissibility of coerced confessions. Overzealous interrogators often employed torture and intimidation in order to compel suspect slaves to admit complicity in a crime. In *Simon (a slave)* v. *State* the Florida Supreme Court reversed a lower court's conviction because the latter had based its ruling upon a confession obtained through coercion. The presiding justice wrote that he could find "few cases ... where stronger influences were brought to bear ... to extract a confession."

The courts tended to construe the slave code quite literally, and sometimes this strict construction worked to the advantage of the slave. Paraphrasing Justice Albert G. Semmes in *Bryan* v. *Dennis*, the term "slave" had to appear in the wording of a law in order for that law to be applicable to slaves. In this particular case the ruling ordered that a family of slaves claiming freedom was, according to the law, still slaves. Although this particular ruling proved unfavorable to the litigants, it set a precedent for literalism that became a protective blanket for slaves against arbitrary legal action. In *Luke (a slave)* v. *State* Justice Leslie Thompson ruled that slaves could be punished only in the manner prescribed in the slave code. Thompson argued that "in order to punish a slave for a 'common law' offense, the court must examine the pertinent slave code," thereby insulating the slave against indiscriminate punishment. In *Francis (a slave)* v. *State* the Florida Supreme Court upheld the constitutionality of the slave code. In each of these cases, decided in the early 1850s, the justices ruled the slave code was the only law applicable to the enslaved. Clearly, Florida slaves benefited from the high court's predilection for constitutional and statutory literalism.

A Florida Supreme Court ruling in 1860 declared that a slave could only be charged with those crimes enumerated in the Florida slave code. The case in question involved a slave named Clem Murray who had been convicted of running an illegal gaming house. His attorney appealed the decision on the grounds that the relevant offense was not listed in the state's slave code and therefore could not be "extended to them [slaves] unless specifically named." Writing for the majority in the case of *Clem Murray (a slave)* v. *State,* Justice William A. Forward concurred, arguing that slaves were not "covered by the word 'person' in the penal statute [white code] except by necessary implication." The court, in deciding for Murray, sought to protect the slave from unrestrained persecution. By 1860 the courts had become the guardians of the slaves' legal rights.

Florida's slave code served to regulate and stabilize the "peculiar institution." It functioned as well as any body of law that enjoys the overwhelming support of its populace. The primacy of popular consensus in determining the scope and direction of the law is evident in the history of Florida's slave code. As demonstrated here, the exigencies of the era forced lawmakers to reexamine their priorities. An increasingly vocal anti-slavery movement in the North coupled with an almost obsessive fear of slave rebellion distorted the perceptions of many of Florida's lawmakers who determined that their slave code was too lax and therefore unable to prevent unrest and rebellion. In an effort to rectify this weakness, strict limitations were placed upon the slave's ability to act independent of his or her owner. But enlightened legislators and court officials paternalistically clothed their chattel in laws and court decisions that were designed to protect the slave's humanity. Referring to the treatment of slaves, the Florida Supreme Court declared in 1859 that a person who leased slaves should "bestow that degree of care and attention which a humane master would bestow on his servant." The statement served both as a warning to those who might abuse the slaves of another and as a mirror reflecting an image the courts held of how the slave should be treated.

16

Race, Class, and Gender in the Slave South

NELL IRVIN PAINTER

● *Among the many ways that slavery represented the exploitation of one human being by another, the most private and the least discussed was sexual. Officially, the southern leadership dwelt on the virtues of motherhood, chastity, and temperance and emphasized clean living and high moral standards. In particular, interracial sexual intercourse was regarded as an unspeakable abomination, and intimate relations between white women and black men were punishable by death to the offending male.*

Unofficially, everyone knew that interracial sex in the South was common, if only because white slaveowners had access to black women. As Professor Nell Irvin Painter of Princeton University indicates in the following essay, that fact disgusted white women, black women, and black men. Only white men seemed to benefit from the arrangement. Lifting the veil of secrecy that once covered the physical intimacy of owners and slaves, Professor Painter argues that sexuality and its repression belonged not to one race, or one class, or one gender, but resided squarely in the history of the region as a whole.

In my work on sexuality in the nineteenth- and twentieth-century South, my mind returns often to what the late Herbert Gutman used to say about Karl Marx, but with application to Sigmund Freud: "He raises some very good questions." While I have plenty of feminist company in my turn toward psychoanalysis, the Freud I am using here is not quite the Freud who has been making recent appearances. As a historian of the nineteenth- and early twentieth-century American South who remains tethered to a history project grounded in the archives, I find Freud is valuable mainly as an acute observer of nineteenth-century bourgeois society, as an analyst (no pun intended) who recognized the

From the *Georgia Historical Quarterly*, 76 (Summer, 1992).

relationship between sexuality and identity. His writing permits unu-
sually clear views into the ways in which social, economic, and ethnic
hierarchies affected households and families, for he was accustomed
to dealing with people in households that encompassed more than one
economic class. Such vision enriches southern studies, which is still
impoverished by exceptionalism and a tendency to see race as an opaque
obstacle that blocks feminist investigation.

My subject is the family relations that affected the richest and the
poorest of antebellum southern daughters. The tragically tiny number
of black daughters, who would have been actually or nominally free,
and the large cohort of white daughters, who would have lived beyond
the reach of the aristocracy, belonged to families who were able to
shelter them from predatory wealthy men and were more likely to
escape the fate of the daughters under discussion here. But whether
black or white, if young women lived in households where men had
access to the poorest and most vulnerable, these daughters ran gendered
risks related to sexuality that did not respect barriers of class and race.

It has been no secret, then or now, that in the plantation South,
owners and slaves lived on terms of physical closeness and often engaged in sexual intimacy. Yet historians have followed the lead of
privileged nineteenth-century southerners who, though well aware that
sex figured among the services masters demanded of slaves, briskly
pushed the matter aside. Even psychoanalysts like Abram Kardiner and
L. Ovesey pass quickly over the repercussions of interracial sexuality
in southern white families and hence on southern society generally.
Virtually by default, the conclusion in southern history was that master-
slave sex was a problem for the slaves, not the master; thus as a social
phenomenon, interracial, interclass sexuality has been relegated to African-Americans alone. This is not the position I hold. Because intimate
relations affected white as well as black families, I argue that such
sexuality and its repercussions belong not to one race or the other, but
must reside squarely in southern history.

One needs only to read the works of class- and gender-conscious
historians of Great Britain and Europe to recognize the parallels between nineteenth-century European bourgeois societies and that of the
antebellum South. Such usefulness is not limited to historians' insights.
Though very much in vogue with literary critics, Freudian psychoanalysis also offers thought-provoking assistance to historians, partic-

ularly on the formation of individual identity. Specifically, Sigmund
Freud's "Dora" case history raises fundamental questions about the
dynamics of elite families in a hierarchical society where the employment of servants (and here I concentrate on female servants) is routine.
This essay addresses the pertinence of three pieces of Freud's writing
to southern society, as reflected in two mid-nineteenth-century southern
characters known as "Lily" and "Linda Brent."

Lily is the title character of an 1855 novel by Sue Petigru King
(Bowen) (1824–1875). King was a daughter of the very respectable
Charlestonian Thomas Petigru. Having been educated in Charleston
and New York, she had returned to South Carolina to pursue her career
as a writer. Her Lily is the quintessential young plantation mistress:
hyper-white, wealthy, and beautiful. Much better known today, thanks
largely to the work of Jean Fagan Yellin and others, is "Linda Brent,"
who in contrast to Lily, was a slave. Brent is both the central character
and the pseudonym under which the Edenton, North Carolina fugitive
slave, Harriet Jacobs (1813–1897), used in her autobiography, *Incidents in the Life of a Slave Girl*, originally published with the help of
Boston abolitionists in 1861.

If rich, white, and free Lily represents the top of the antebellum
South's economic and racial hierarchies, then poor, yellow, and enslaved Linda Brent represents the near bottom. Linda, after all, has
some free relations, and her grandmother, nominally enslaved, lives in
her own house in town. Things could have been much worse for Linda
Brent. Both Linda's and Lily's stories are about very young women and
sex, and taken together with Freud's "Dora" they tell us a great deal
about southern family dynamics in slaveholding households. As both
texts are about sex and race, a word about the phenomenon of master-
slave sex, as I discovered it in Gertrude Thomas' journal, precedes the
discussion of Lily, Linda Brent, and "Dora."

Although historians have not begun to quantify its incidence, it is clear
that sexual relations between male slavemasters and female slaves were
exceedingly common in the antebellum South—as in any other slave
society, as Orlando Patterson points out. Nineteenth-century fugitive
slave narratives, such as those of Frederick Douglass and Moses Roper,
and the Fisk and WPA ex-slave narratives from the 1930s, are full of
evidence that masters did not hesitate to sleep with their women slaves,

despite the marital status of either. Although I have not had an opportunity to pursue this hunch, I suspect that about 10 percent of masters also slept or wanted to sleep with their enslaved men and boys; some mistresses possibly also regarded their female slaves as objects of desire. On the other side of the class and racial continuums from the Frederick Douglass and Moses Ropers, white women—southerners and observers—penned and sometimes published criticisms of the institution of slavery based on what they perceived as the demoralization of white men who engaged in adultery and/or polygyny.

I began to draw my own conclusions as I concentrated on the journal of Ella Gertrude Clanton Thomas (1834–1907), published in 1990 as *The Secret Eye*. Thomas, wealthy, educated, and white, lived in and around Augusta, Georgia, for most of her life. She began keeping a journal in 1848, when she was fourteen years old, and stopped writing definitively in 1889, when she was fifty-five. Although she was born into an immensely wealthy, slave-owning family, Thomas married a man who was a poor manager. Her husband, Jefferson Thomas, succeeded financially as a planter before the Civil War, thanks to unpaid labor and continual financial help from Gertrude's father. But her father died in 1864 and their slaves were emancipated in 1865. After the war the Thomases entered a long cycle of debt that sent Gertrude into the paid labor force as a teacher. Her earnings kept the family afloat economically, but poverty imposed great strains on the family. This journal, therefore, chronicles a life of privilege before the Civil War, the trauma of supporting the losing side, the loss of the labor and prestige that slavery had assured her, and the chagrin of downward mobility. Thomas joined the Woman's Christian Temperance Union in the 1880s and became a suffragist in the 1890s. She died in Atlanta.

Initially I appreciated this journal for its value as a primary source for the study of the social history of the South, for which Thomas was an excellent witness. Extraordinary as her record is, however, it works on yet another level, which psychoanalysis is well equipped to explore. The journal contains a veiled text, characterized by the keeping of secrets, lack of candor, and self-deception. Whereas the surface of this text presents a southerner of a certain class at given historical junctures, a less straightforward message also emerges, though it is not so easy to glimpse. The veiled text, less bounded chronologically, is about families and gender, and it contains and reveals a great secret that is relatively timeless: adultery. I know from the "deception clues" and leakage in the journal that most certainly by the 1860s, probably by the 1850s, Thomas was painfully aware but unable to admit that her father had had children by at least one of his slaves. By the 1870s, possibly as early as the 1850s, Thomas also knew that her husband had fathered at least one child by a woman who was not white.

This should come as no surprise. Harriet Martineau in the 1830s spoke of the plantation mistress as "the chief slave of the harem." Fredrika Bremer in the 1850s coined a famous phrase that Thomas quotes in her journal, "these white children of slavery." And Mary Chestnut wrote of the mulatto children in every slaveholding household. Gertrude Thomas was far from alone.

Some of the most interesting evidence comes from fiction, which, considering the subject, should not be surprising. Most respectable nineteenth-century people retreated—or attempted to retreat—behind the veil of privacy, rather than reveal their actual patterns of sexuality. The very ability to conceal the rawer aspects of the human condition, an ability that we sum up in the term privacy, served as a crucial symbol of respectability when the poor had no good place to hide. Nonetheless the topic of interracial sexuality was of enough fascination to reappear in fiction under various disguises. Taking my cue from Gertrude Thomas, who was hypersensitive about sexual competition between women, I began to pursue sexuality through the theme of competition. Tracked in that guise, southern fiction reveals some interesting manifestations.

Sue Petigru King sounded themes that occur in the works of several white southern women writers, such as Caroline Lentz, Grace King, and Willa Cather. For example, Cather's final novel, *Sapphira and the Slave Girl* (1940), is precisely and openly about a white woman's perception of sexual competition between herself and a Negro woman. In its racial candor, *Sapphira* is exceptional. More often the competition between women is not about individuals with different racial identities, but about two white characters who are color-coded in black and white. While I realize that European writers such as Sir Walter Scott and Honoré de Balzac used light (blonde) and dark (*la belle juive*) female characters symbolically, Anne Goodwyn Jones, Mary Kelley, and Jane Pease, scholars familiar with southern writing, corroborate my view that nineteenth- and early twentieth-century white southern women writers were singularly fascinated by competition between light and dark women. While most publications by these women followed the usual theme of a young woman's quest for autonomy and her eventual marriage to a good man, they also very much echoed Gertrude Thomas' fixation on female rivalry.

Sue Petigru King is no longer very well known, but she loomed large in Gertrude Thomas' literary world and was known in Great Britain. William Thackeray, one of Britain's most celebrated authors, visited her on a trip to the United States. In the mid-nineteenth century King published several novels which repeatedly stressed themes of jealousy and competition between women, the best known of which is *Lily*.

Very briefly, *Lily* is the story of Elizabeth Vere, whom her father calls "Lily" because she is "as white as any lily that ever grew." Over the course of the novel's plot, Lily goes from age seven to seventeen. King described her heroine with words like "white," "pure," "innocent," "simple," and "lovely." The character with whom King paired Lily is her cousin, Angelica Purvis. Angelica is also a rich white woman, but King focused on the blackness of her dresses and the intense blackness of her hair. At one point, King contrasted Lily, who "seemed made up of light and purity," with Angelica, who "was dark, designing, distracting." Angelica is exotic; King described her as an "Eastern princess" and called her looks "Andalusian." Whereas Lily is pure, Angelica is passionate, evil, voluptuous. Angelica says of her attractiveness to men: "I am original sin. . . . " At the age of seventeen, Lily is engaged to her first great love, Clarence Tracy, a childhood friend who is a graduate of Princeton University. Despite all her goodness, however, Lily is not rewarded with love for Clarence is crazy in love with Angelica, who is married.

On the face of it, the most obvious theme in *Lily* is competition between two white women, which the less virtuous is winning. But race hovers in the very near background. First, these ostensibly white competitors are color-coded in black and white. Then, as though to make the point unambiguously, King abruptly introduces a new character, Lorenza, at the very end of the novel. Lorenza is Clarence's Negro mistress. On the night before Lily's wedding, Lorenza murders Lily out of jealousy over her impending marriage.

King left nothing to guesswork in this novel, and to hammer home her message she also addressed her readers directly. Her point was the same made by Mary Chesnut in her Civil War diary: that southern planter husbands repaid their wives' faithful virtue with base infidelity. Wealthy southern men married young, pure, rich, white girls like Lily, then left them for mistresses tinged by blackness, whether of descent or intimation. King summed up Mary Chestnut's conviction and Gertrude Thomas' fears: "It is not the woman most worthy to be loved who is the most loved." This conclusion is also echoed in the writing of Sigmund Freud.

In 1912, Freud discussed exactly that phenomenon in his second contribution to the Psychology of Love: "On the Universal Tendency to Debasement in the Sphere of Love." Freud appraised the practical results of "civilized morality" and the sexual double standard from the standpoint of middle- and upper-class men who were susceptible to psychosomatic impotence with women of their own class. Freud said, making King's point: "Where such men love they have no desire and where they desire they cannot love."

In *Lily,* the pure, young, rich, white daughter is the most dramatic loser in the southern sexual sweepstakes. In this interpretation of southern sexuality, the motif is competition between women and the victims are wealthy white women. Writers from the other side painted a disturbingly similar, yet differently shaded portrait.

While many ex-slave narratives discuss master-slave sexuality, the most extended commentary comes from Harriet Jacobs, who, writing under the pseudonym Linda Brent, told of being harassed by her master for sex from the time she was thirteen. Her character, Linda, becomes the most literal embodiment of the slave as sexual prey in the literature of slave narratives.

Harriet Jacobs depicted puberty as a "sad epoch in the life of a slave girl." As she became nubile, Linda Brent's master began to whisper "foul words in my ear," which is the kind of act whose consequences Freud understood. Jacobs generalized from Linda's predicament that "whether the slave girl be black as ebony or as fair as her mistress"— she, the slave girl, is sexually vulnerable. This vulnerability robbed her of her innocence and purity. Hearing "foul words" from her master and angry and jealous outbreaks from her mistress, the slave girl, in Jacobs' phrase, became "prematurely knowing in evil things." The more beautiful she is, the more speedy her despoliation. Beauty, for Linda Brent and young women like her, was no blessing: "If God has bestowed beauty upon her, it will prove her greatest curse."

Incidents is of great interest in this discussion because Jacobs confronted the sexual component of servitude so straightforwardly. She recognized, too, that slaves and owners interpreted the situation very differently. Jacobs dedicated an entire chapter of *Incidents in the Life of a Slave Girl* to "The Jealous Mistress." Here and elsewhere, Jacobs maintained that mistresses whose husbands betrayed them felt no solidarity whatever with their slaves. Like other ex-slave narrators, Jacobs could ascertain the view of slave-owning women but emphatically did not share their conclusions. Writing as Linda Brent, Jacobs supplied the key word, "victim," and recognized that it was a matter of contention between slave and mistress.

White women, black women, and black men all resented deeply white men's access to black women. But the comments from the two sides of the color line are contradictory: where white women saw sexual competition—with connotations of equality—black men and women saw rank exploitation that stemmed from grossly disparate levels of power. Moses Roper, his master's child, relates the story of his near-murder, shortly after his birth, by his father's jealous wife. Frederick Douglass also noted that slave-owning women were distressed by the bodily proof of their husband's adulteries.

For Jacobs, as for other ex-slave narrators, the prime victim was the slave woman, not the slave-owning woman, no matter how the latter perceived the situation. Slave owners' sexual relations with their women slaves constituted one of several varieties of victimization by men whose power over them was absolute. Slaves of both sexes were oppressed by class and by race, but women suffered a third, additional form of oppression stemming from their gender. Extorted sex was part of a larger pattern of oppression embedded in the institution of slavery.

Harriet Jacobs and Gertrude Thomas provide examples of the family dynamics of cross-class adultery. Located in very different places within the complicated families of slavery, each explicates the deleterious effects of adultery within their households. Like Jacobs and Thomas, Sigmund Freud, in his analysis of "Dora," recognized the damage that a father's adultery caused a daughter.

"Dora" was eighteen-year-old Ida Bauer, whose father took her to see Freud in October 1900 after she threatened suicide. Phillip Bauer hoped that Freud would cure his daughter's mental and physical ailments and stem her wild accusations of sexual harassment. Ida had claimed that a close family friend, "Herr K" (Hans Zellenka), had made several sexual advances toward her and she told Freud that in one instance, "Herr K" had approached her with the same phrases he had used to proposition a servant woman. The entanglements ran deeper, for it was revealed that Herr K's young wife "Frau K" was Phillip Bauer's lover. In this adulterous game between her father and the Ks, Ida felt as though she were a helpless pawn, attached emotionally to Frau K and the female servant, as well as to her estranged mother and father. Freud diagnosed the distraught young woman as hysterical and used her case to put certain theories to the test.

Freud had been thinking about hysteria for several years and had worked out his notions in letters to his close friend and regular correspondent, Wilhelm Fliess. These comments are exceedingly helpful to me, particularly in observations that Freud enclosed with a letter dated May 2, 1897. Here Freud noted that children, even very young babies, hear things that later become the raw material for fantasies and neuroses. Accompanying this letter was "Draft L," which includes a paragraph on "The Part Played by Servant Girls."

In Draft L, Freud echoed his society's assumption that the poor young women who worked in bourgeois households were "people of low morals" because they were likely to become sexually involved with the men and boys of the household. Here Freud was echoing the most common of assumptions about black people in the South. But whereas Freud identified morals with class, white southerners saw low morals as a racial characteristic of African-Americans. For my purposes, however, this is not the crucial insight that Freud took from his failed analysis of Ida Bauer. For me Freud's most useful observation relates to the critical importance of servants in the psychological and, hence, social dynamics of the families in which they work. Although Freud thought mainly of the ramifications of the situation on the family of the employers, as we saw in the case of Linda Brent, servants, too, felt the effects of adulterous—should I add incestuous?—family dynamics.

Freud wrote Fliess that in households in which servant women are sexually intimate with their employers, the children (here I believe he means female children) develop an array of hysterical fantasies: fear of being on the street alone, fear of becoming a prostitute, fear of a man hidden under the bed. In sum, said Freud, "There is tragic justice in the circumstance that the family head's stooping to a maidservant is atoned for by his daughter's self-abasement.

Freud underscored the degree to which women in a household are emotionally intertwined. "Dora" identified with the servant that her would-be lover had tried to seduce. Observing situations in which race was not a factor, Freud understood that the very structure containing class and gender power dynamics is virtually Foucauldian in its leakiness. No class of women remained exempt from a degradation that aimed at the least of them. Just as Gertrude Thomas saw that her adulterous father and husband treated rich and poor and black and white women as interchangeable sexually, Freud saw there was a "part played by servant girls" and an object connection between "Dora" and her father's mistress. A recent Freud scholar, Hannah Decker, put her finger on the phenomenon that poisoned young women's lives in Freud's Vienna and that also characterized the nineteenth-century South: the careless sexual abuse of *das süsse Madel*—the sweet young thing.

Freud's letters to Fliess, "On the Universal Tendency to Debasement in the Sphere of Love," and especially the "Dora" case analysis, show that "Dora's" predicament is reflected in both *Lily* and *Incidents of the Life of a Slave Girl,* but in somewhat different ways. Linda Brent is more directly comparable with "Dora," for she was the object of unwanted sexual advances, as was young Ida Bauer. The case of Lily Vere is less obvious, for she is the daughter of "Draft L," of "The Part Played by Servant Girls." Lily is the daughter whose affective value is lowered by the existence of the sexually vulnerable servant class and the allure of enticing dark/Negro women like Angelica and Lorenza. While Linda Brent is a clear victim of her society's hierarchies of race and gender, Lily, unloved by her fiancé, and murdered by his servant lover, is victimized as well. Her fiancé, Clarence, is the very figure of the Freud patient suffering from psychically induced impotence.

Examining these southern women's stories and taking Freud to heart leads to two conclusions: First, that historians of the United States South, sheltered too long in southern exceptionalism, have let an intellectual color bar obstruct their view of the complexity of gender roles within households that were economically heterogeneous. Lily and Linda Brent, two examples of a spoliation of young women that was no respecter of race or class, underscore both the sexual vulnerabilities and the psychological interrelatedness of southern daughters. Second, Freud contributed to our understanding that families and societies cannot designate and thereby set apart one category of women as victims. The victimization spread, in different ways and in different degrees. But where historians have been prone to construe southern family relations within watertight racial categories, the stories of these three daughters pose complicated new questions whose answers do not stop at the color line.

Historians have wanted to reach a single conclusion that would characterize the relationship between slave-owning and slave women in the antebellum South: *either* slave women were at the bottom of a hierarchical society, as the ex-slave narrators testify, *or* all southern women were, finally, at the mercy of rich white men. The relationship between black and white women through white men deserves to be named, for slavery often made women of different races and classes into co-mothers and co-wives as well as owners and suppliers of labor. The question is whether there should be one name or, reflecting the number of races involved, more than one.

So far no historian of southern women has given more than a chapter or its equivalent to interracial sexuality and the gender relations that flowed from it, but the work is coming along. Yet the older, full-length studies of race and gender in the antebellum South by Deborah Gray White, Catherine Clinton, and Elizabeth Fox-Genovese and the newer work that builds upon them all tend toward the use of one concept to characterize relations within extended southern households: oppression. Deborah Gray White, in *Ar'n't I a Woman* stresses the "helplessness" and "powerlessness" of slave women vis-à-vis slave owners and in American society in general. Conceding that white women and black men may have envied black women, White nonetheless views black women at the bottom of a malevolent system that disempowered all women, even those who were rich and white. She places slave women at the negative end of a continuum of power, on which white women also occupied positions of relative powerlessness and exploitation.

Viewing matters from the other side of the class/race divide, Catherine Clinton, in *The Plantation Mistress,* also acknowledges a "parallel oppression of women, both white and black." But where Deborah

White cites instances of aggression on the part of white women against black, Clinton stresses plantation mistresses' roles as nurturers, mediators, and nurses. Clinton speaks of a patriarchy in which rich white men possessed slaves of both sexes as they possessed their own wives. In *The Plantation Mistress,* slave-owning women do not appear in hierarchical relationships with slave women. Rather than portray slave-owning women as rulers of their workers, Clinton sees white male masters as the font of all power and all evil.

In *Within the Plantation Household,* Elizabeth Fox-Genovese departs from the view of black and white women's parallel exploitation that White and Clinton evoke. Stressing the spacial and emotional intimacy in which many slave and slaveholding women lived in plantation households, Fox-Genovese softens the domination of the master. She prefers the term "paternalism" to Clinton's "patriarchy," because paternalism carries an air of "legitimate domination," which was how slaveholding men viewed their role. (Let us not quibble about whether slave owners should be allowed to choose the words we historians use to characterize them a century and a half later.)

But Fox-Genovese stiffens the authority of slave-owning women over their female slaves, providing theoretical and empirical arguments for a somewhat ambiguous but clearly hierarchical relationship between women of different races and classes. Rather than see masters as the proximate wielders of power, Fox-Genovese shows that slaveholding women and slave women were cognizant of who held the power between them and who could inflict the greatest violence with impunity. To make her point, Fox-Genovese enumerates instances of violence and minimizes slaveholding women's abolitionist leanings. For her, slaveholding women who saw themselves as victims of the kind of adultery that the slave system allowed were simply misguided.

Clinton's more recent essays reveal the pathologies of planter families in which rape and adultery distort descent and parental attachment. While "Caught in the Web of the Big House" glimpses the ways in which owner-slave rape affected mistresses, the emphasis still falls mainly on the tragedy of the direct victim of assault: the slave woman. "Southern Dishonor," Clinton's spiked critique of both southern historiography and slavery's brutal system of reproduction, announces themes and works-in-progress in the study of sexuality and slavery. Martha Hodes' 1991 dissertation and Mary Frances Berry's 1991 presidential address to the Organization of American Historians further enrich the historical literature by revealing the complexities of southern sexuality.

So far this work, though intriguing, stops short of completing the investigation of the relationship between southern families, society, and history. If feminist history has taught us anything in the last two decades, it is that important private matters become important historical matters. The example of the South Carolina fire-eater, James Henry Hammond—whose emotional turmoil following his wife's desertion when he took a second slave wife so incapacitated him psychologically that he missed an important secessionist meeting that would have bolstered his sagging political career—makes the point. Hammond's wife serves as a reminder that Gertrude Thomas' preoccupation—competition—needs to reenter the equation, or historians risk missing much of the psychodrama of southern history. Focusing on one part of the picture, even if more compatible with present-day understandings of power relations, flattens out the inherent complexity of southern history. If historians do not acknowledge that wealthy white women saw themselves in competition with women who were black and poor and powerless, they miss a vital dimension of southern history that helps explain the thorniness of women's contacts across the color line well into the twentieth century. We must acknowledge the existence of two ways of seeing, even while we keep our eyes on fundamental differentials of power.

What my approach means for southern history is a renunciation of a "the South" way of thinking. For me there is seldom a "the South," for simple characterizations eliminate the reality of sharp conflicts over just about everything in southern culture, slavery most of all. Saying that "the South" was pro-slavery (or, later, pro-segregation) equates the region with its ruling race and annihilates the position of at least one-third of its inhabitants. As a labor historian with a keen sense of the historical importance of all groups of people within a society (not simply the prestigious, published, and politically powerful), I insist on going beyond lazy characterizations in the singular. Recognizing the complex and contradictory nature of southern society, I can rephrase my conclusions about the study of southern history succinctly: Southern history demands the recognition of complexity and contradiction, starting with family life, and therefore requires the use of plurals; and though southern history must take race very seriously, southern history must not stop with race.

17

Slavery, the "More Perfect Union," and the Prairie State

PAUL FINKELMAN

● *The Civil War is the central event in the history of the United States. Measured in terms of loss of life, property damage, and enduring bitterness, it has been the costliest of American wars. The surrender at Appomattox of Robert E. Lee's Army of Northern Virginia effectively ended the armed rebellion. But it represented more than battlefield accomplishment; it signaled the ascendancy of industrialism over agriculture, of the city over the farm, and of centralized authority over states' rights. Charles A. Beard called it the "Second American Revolution."*

Most of the men who died in the struggle probably had no clear commitment either to abolition or to slavery; General Robert E. Lee himself refused to defend either slavery or secession. Why then did the war come? Was it the moral question posed by involuntary servitude, or was it a constitutional question relating to the powers reserved for the federal government? Or was it the inevitable result of irresistible economic forces? The question has puzzled scholars for more than a century.

Illinois was a major battleground in this ante-bellum ideological and political contest. Led by booming Chicago on Lake Michigan, a city which rose from nothing in 1833 to become the Midwest's railroad hub by 1861, the prairie state exemplified in microcosm the problems that were agitating Americans everywhere. Among those people who articulated the choices and the issues before the Civil War were Abraham Lincoln and Stephen A. Douglas, both citizens of Illinois and

Paul Finkelman, "Slavery, the 'More Perfect Union,' and the Prairie State," *Illinois Historical Journal*, 80 (Winter, 1987), 248–69. Reprinted with permission of the Illinois Historic Preservation Agency, Springfield, Illinois, and the author.

> *both among the finest orators and statesmen the United States*
> *has yet produced. As Paul Finkelman reveals in the following*
> *essay, they demonstrated that Illinois itself was a house*
> *divided.*

In accepting the Republican nomination for United States senator in
1858, Abraham Lincoln told his supporters that "a house divided
against itself cannot stand." He asserted that the American "government cannot endure, permanently half *slave* and half *free*." Lincoln
predicted that the nation would "become *all* one thing, or *all* the other."
He warned his audience that the decision was in the balance; that the
outcome was uncertain; and that freedom might lose out. "We shall
lie down pleasantly dreaming that the people of *Missouri* are on the
verge of making their State *free*; and we shall *awake* to the *reality*,
instead, that the *Supreme* Court has made *Illinois* a *slave* State."

Lincoln spoke in the wake of the Supreme Court decision in *Dred
Scott v. Sandford*. That case is best known for two specific holdings
of the Court: that the Missouri Compromise was unconstitutional, and
that free blacks could never be citizens of the United States, and thus
they had no standing to sue in federal court. But, in upholding Scott's
status as a slave, the Court also ruled on the meaning of the Illinois
Constitution. Besides living north of Missouri, in what eventually became Minnesota Territory, Scott had lived in Illinois. Part of his claim
to freedom, which the Court brushed aside, rested on his Illinois re-
sidency. Thus, when Lincoln warned of awakening to discover "that
the *Supreme* Court has made *Illinois* a *slave* State," he was making
more than simply a rhetorical point. He was certainly fearful of "another Supreme Court decision, declaring that the Constitution of the
United States does not permit a *state* to exclude slavery from its limits."
A case that might have led to such a decision was in fact then making
its way through the New York courts.

Lincoln's speech was also informed by his experiences as an attorney
in Illinois, a state where tensions between slavery and freedom were
often apparent. Indeed, few states better illustrate the problems of
trying to maintain "a more perfect Union" of slave and free states.

From its early settlement until at least the Civil War, Illinois was in
many ways as much a southern state as a northern one. Almost half
of the state was geographically south of the Mason-Dixon line. Much

of Illinois bordered on two slave states. The area's first European settlers
were French, many of whom owned slaves. Most of the state's earliest
Anglo settlers came from the South. A few masters, such as Edward
Coles, came to Illinois to free their slaves. But most who came north
to Illinois brought with them their pro-Southern, proslavery biases.
Some hoped to create a slave state on the northern banks of the Ohio.
Despite the prohibition on slavery in the Northwest Ordinance, slavery
remained prevalent throughout the Illinois Territory. The Illinois Constitution of 1818 protected existing slavery in the state and allowed
the limited introduction of new slaves for short periods of time. In
1823 a proslavery majority in the Illinois legislature passed a resolution
calling for a state constitutional convention for the purpose of legalizing
slavery throughout the state. An influx of northern settlers, vigorous
campaigning by anticonventionists, and the fortuitous failure of a pro-
convention newspaper prevented the convention from being called. The
failure of the convention movement did not end proslavery sympathies
in the state, however. Nor did it change the status of slaves already in
Illinois. Thus, as late as 1848 slaves were legally held in the state.

The voters' decision to reject a constitutional convention—and thus
keep Illinois a free state—did not end the state's dilemma as a free
jurisdiction in a house divided. On the contrary, by remaining a free
state with slave-state neighbors, Illinois was inevitably drawn into the
crisis of the Union that developed between 1820 and 1860. In that
period Illinois' leaders were forced to make hard choices over their
obligations to the United States Constitution, comity and good faith
to their slave-state neighbors, and fidelity to their own constitution and
free-state status. Judicial and political leaders of the state faced three
slavery-related constitutional issues: interstate transit of slaves across
Illinois, prevention of the kidnapping of free blacks living in Illinois,
and return of fugitive slaves.

Illinois officials often went out of their way to develop smooth and
harmonious relations with their slave-state neighbors. More than any
other Northern state (except Indiana), Illinois cooperated with its slaveholding neighbors. Part of the tradition of cooperation developed from
the state's heritage of slaveholding and its large number of citizens of
southern ancestry. Also affecting Illinois' response to slavery was a
profound Negrophobia, especially in the southern and central parts of
the state. Illinois' support of Southern demands was not complete,

however. All three branches of Illinois government, but especially the judiciary, were sometimes more sensitive to the claims of free blacks, fugitive slaves, and abolitionists.

In order to understand the role Illinois played in the crisis of the Union, it is first necessary to examine briefly how Illinois responded to the presence of slaves and free blacks. Here the position of Illinois was unique among all the free states.

SLAVERY IN EARLY ILLINOIS

Slavery was prohibited in the Illinois Territory by the Northwest Ordinance. Despite the Ordinance, slavery and other forms of involuntary servitude flourished. Territorial governors, starting with Arthur St. Clair in 1790, interpreted the Ordinance to be prospective, and to free only those slaves brought into the territory after July 13, 1787. Thus, the "French settlers" were allowed to retain their slaves throughout the territorial period and well after statehood.

Settlers of the Illinois country persistently, although futilely, petitioned Congress to amend or repeal the Ordinance to allow them to bring new slaves into the territory. The failure of those petitions led to elaborate statutes designed to evade the slavery prohibition of the Ordinance. The first was adopted by the Indiana territorial government in 1803. Reenacted in later years and supplemented by other acts designed to protect the property rights of those who held indentured "servants," the statutes allowed for the indenture of former slaves for virtually unlimited periods of time. Under those laws hundreds of slaves were brought into the territory as "indentured servants." With indentures running up to ninety-nine years, such blacks were, for all practical purposes, slaves. They could be beaten and punished by their owners, jailed for running away, and their indentures (and thus their persons) could be sold, traded away, or bequeathed.

Most of the pressure for allowing slavery in the Indiana Territory had come from settlers in present-day Illinois. With the division of the two territories in 1809, Illinois residents were able to move closer to creating a slave jurisdiction in the Old Northwest. In 1809 the new territorial government adopted all of the older Indiana territorial laws, including those creating a pseudo-slavery through indentures. In 1813 the legislature set a new standard for treating free blacks by prohibiting them from coming into the territory. The following year, "An act concerning negroes and Mulattoes" explicitly allowed the hiring of slaves in Illinois. The legislature guaranteed the owners of such hired slaves that the law would "not operate in any way whatever to injure the right of property in the master, in and to the service of such slave or slaves."

Under the law, slaves could be brought into the territory as laborers for up to twelve months, but there was no limit on the number of twelve-month periods that a slave could work. It would have been perfectly legal to bring slaves in for twelve months, remove them from the territory for a day, and then bring them back for another twelve months. Since the law did not contain any sanction against keeping the slave longer than twelve months, the subterfuge may have been unnecessary. Continuous twelve-month contracts, without any removal from the territory, might have been legal. Since the majority of the political and legal figures in the territory were proslavery—and many, like Governor Ninian Edwards, were slaveowners themselves—it is not surprising that there is no known instance of any slave being freed during the territorial period through the intervention of any political official or judge.

Illinois entered the Union in 1818, ostensibly as a free state. Unlike every other free state, however, Illinois allowed some forms of slavery to remain within its jurisdiction and provided no mechanism for ending slavery. Between 1780 and 1804 Pennsylvania, Connecticut, Rhode Island, New York, and New Jersey had all passed gradual emancipation statutes that guaranteed an eventual end to slavery in those places. Massachusetts, New Hampshire, and the new free states of Vermont, Ohio, and Indiana had ended slavery by their constitutions. Illinois took none of those steps.

The Illinois Constitutional Convention of 1818 would probably have made Illinois a slave state, except that doing so would have delayed statehood. By that time, however, the leaders in Illinois were adept at maintaining slavery while appearing to have a free jurisdiction. The Illinois Constitution of 1818 contained a clause declaring, "Neither slavery nor involuntary servitude shall hereafter be introduced into this state otherwise than for the punishment of crimes whereof the party shall have been duly convicted." By prohibiting slavery that might "*hereafter* be introduced" (emphasis added), the clause implied that slaves already in the state would not be freed.

The Constitution, written in August, 1818, also preserved indentures made prior to December, 1818. In that four-month period Illinois residents were free to bring in more indentured blacks, which some Illinois whites apparently did. Finally, the 1818 Constitution allowed the limited hiring of slaves in the state until 1825. Illinois came as close to permitting slavery as possible while still being considered a free state. In 1823–1824 Illinois came within a few hundred votes of calling another constitutional convention that would have explicitly allowed slavery in the state.

FREE BLACKS IN THE STATE OF ILLINOIS

Given the proslavery implications of the 1818 Constitution and the biases of many of the state's early political leaders, it is perhaps to be expected that free blacks were unwelcome in Illinois. Free blacks were the antithesis of slaves. Moreover, the presence of free blacks undermined slavery and involuntary servitude. Like the slave states of the South, Illinois restricted the immigration of free blacks and severely limited their rights in the state.

In 1819 Illinois adopted "An Act respecting Free Negroes, Mulattoes, Servants, and Slaves" designed to preserve slavery and involuntary servitude and to regulate free blacks. The act provided for the registration of slaves and servants already in the state. The law prohibited persons from bringing slaves into the state for the purpose of emancipating them. If a slave was emancipated in the state, however, the former owner was required to give a bond "in the penalty of one thousand dollars" against the ex-slave's ever seeking public assistance. It further provided that no black could settle in the state without producing a certificate of freedom.

This law was supplemented by a new statute of the same title passed in 1829. It required that blacks entering the state find sureties to give bond to insure they would not become a burden to the county. Anyone hiring or harboring a black who had not fulfilled those requirements could be fined $500. Any black entering the state without a certificate of freedom from another state would, under this law, be considered a runaway slave. Such a black could be held in jail for up to a year, while the sheriff advertised for the owner. Finally, slaves who entered the state seeking employment could not sue for their freedom. The law was amended in 1831 to provide for fining free blacks who failed to comply with its provisions.

Illinois passed a number of other statutes designed to regulate blacks and limit their access to the state. The government of Illinois made its policies quite clear. Existing slavery was to be preserved and the growth of a free black population was to be discouraged. Such policies would affect how Illinois dealt with slaves and slaveowners in other states during the thirty years leading to the Civil War.

INTERSTATE TRANSIT

The interstate movement of slaves raised important legal and constitutional questions for free states. Put simply, the interstate transit of slaves forced free states to choose between enforcing their own constitutions, which prohibited slavery, and granting comity—or legal force—to the laws of states that allowed slavery. How a free state dealt with visiting slaves said much about its commitment to its own ideals of freedom and its commitment to the Union. The actions of a free state also reflected attitudes toward free blacks. By the eve of the Civil War most Northern states resolved the questions in favor of freedom and against interstate harmony. A few Northern states, including Illinois, came down on the other side of the question.

The legal problems raised by the interstate transit of slaves were complicated and technical. Slavery was traditionally viewed as a local institution. By the time of the American Revolution the status of *slave* was considered an anamoly in Anglo-American law that could be supported only by the force of positive law. Thus, in *Somerset v. Stewart* (1772), William Murray, Lord Mansfield freed a slave voluntarily brought to England by his master on the theory that "The state of slavery is of such a nature, that it is incapable of being introduced on any reasons, moral or political; but only by positive law, which preserves its force long after the reasons, occasion, and time itself from whence it was created, is erased from memory: it's so odious, that nothing can be suffered to support it, but positive law."

Before 1836 Northern states accepted the force of the *Somerset* precedent but did not implement it because they felt an obligation to grant comity to visiting slaveowners from other states. That comity was simply one of the many compromises necessary to maintain a union of free and slave states.

In the nation's first six decades, few cases involving the *Somerset* precedent were brought before Northern courts. Thus, while *Somerset* had not been adopted by Northern courts, neither had it been rejected by them. Then, starting with *Commonwealth v. Aves*, an 1836 Massachusetts case in which a slave in transit was freed, antislavery lawyers successfully brought into most Northern courts cases that placed *Somerset* squarely before Northern judges. Responding to shrewd antislavery activism, most Northern courts quickly adopted the *Aves* precedent. Antislavery activists were also successful in generating legislative support for statutes that declared slaves free the moment their masters brought them into free states. These laws were similar to judicial adoptions of *Somerset*. Both the laws and the court decisions simply reaffirmed what Northerners had always believed: that slavery was incompatible with a free-state constitution, and unless restricted by the United States Constitution, a state had the power to free any person within its jurisdiction. Thus, slaveowners who brought their human property into Massachusetts, New York, Pennsylvania, and other free states did so at their own peril.

The situation in Illinois was different. Before the 1840s no cases involving slave transit reached courts in Illinois. Slaveowners heading for Missouri or Kentucky often traveled in Illinois, or even lived there before reaching their final destination in a slave state. Kentucky and Missouri masters also used their slaves in Illinois if they owned property in both states. Some slaves were also rented out in Illinois. Such uses of slave labor were accomplished with no apparent interference from the Illinois courts. Indeed, court action may have been precluded by two statutes—one passed in 1827 and the other in 1829.

The 1827 Illinois Criminal Code provided for a $500 fine or six months in jail for anyone who harbored a slave or servant "owing service or labor to any other person or persons, whether they be residents of this state[,]of any other state, territory, or district within the limits and under the jurisdiction of the United States." The same penalties applied to those who might "hinder or prevent" an owner "from retaking or possessing" his slaves in a "lawful manner." The law apparently applied to slaves in transit as well as fugitives. The law does not appear to have prevented slaves in transit from claiming their freedom, but it would seem to allow for the prosecution of any whites aiding those slaves.

An 1829 statute prohibited suits for freedom by slaves who came into Illinois and hired themselves out. Whether a court would have applied the statute to slaves "brought" into Illinois by their masters is unknown. The thrust of the statute, however, was clearly both to prevent the growth of a black population in Illinois and to protect the slave property of masters from other states.

The 1829 law did not lead to any reported litigation. In 1843, however, two cases arose under the 1827 act. In Bureau County, abolitionist Owen Lovejoy was convicted of harboring a slave brought into the state by her owner. Lovejoy appealed to the circuit court, and Judge John D. Caton ruled that the moment a master voluntarily brought a slave into Illinois the slave became free under the state's constitution. The decision had little precedential value because it was an unreported circuit court case, but it did indicate that one of the most prestigious judges on the Illinois bench wished to adopt the *Somerset-Aves* line of cases.

A majority of the Illinois bench was not prepared to join Caton in bringing the jurisprudence of the Prairie State in line with the rest of the North. That same year, in *Willard v. The People*, the Illinois Supreme Court upheld the conviction of Julius Willard for harboring a slave who escaped after she had been brought into the state by her master.

The *Willard* case reveals the support given by Illinois to comity and harmony within the Union. The slave in question, Julia, had been voluntarily brought to Illinois by Sarah Liles, her owner, who was passing through Illinois on her way to Louisiana. Willard hid Julia, and for that he was convicted under the 1827 law for harboring a slave owing service or labor to someone in another state. From the arguments of counsel it appears that Willard was initially charged with aiding a fugitive slave. The Illinois Supreme Court recognized this as a transit case, however, and ultimately dealt with it in that way.

There were two reasonable grounds for overturning Willard's conviction. The court might have treated it as a case involving a fugitive slave, as the initial prosecution had done. As such, the court could have declared that the 1827 law was unconstitutional because it usurped the exclusive power of Congress to regulate the rendition of fugitive slaves. Such a ruling would have been based on the United States Supreme Court's 1842 decision in *Prigg v. Pennsylvania*, which contained language implying that Congress had exclusive jurisdiction over the return of fugitive slaves. That position was strenuously argued by Willard's counsel. While some Northern jurists used the *Prigg* decision to avoid hearing cases involving fugitive slaves, the Illinois court, in 1843, declined to take that route. While recognizing the connections between the *Willard* case and the case of a fugitive slave, the Illinois Supreme Court correctly refused to classify it as a fugitive slave case because Julia had not actually escaped into Illinois. The Illinois court might also have held that Julia became free the moment her owner voluntarily brought her into Illinois. That position would have been a simple application of the *Somerset-Aves* precedents to the facts of the case and would have followed the analysis made by Judge Caton in Lovejoy's case.

Although Caton sat on the Illinois Supreme Court, he was unable to persuade his brethren to follow his Lovejoy opinion. In rejecting a *Somerset-Aves* approach to slave transit, the majority went out of its way to support interstate harmony at the expense of Julia's freedom, reflecting the sympathies of the legislature. Both the legislature and the court placed a higher value on interstate comity and harmony than on freedom for a slave. In his opinion of the court, Judge Walter B. Scates stressed the need for interstate harmony, including accommodating the needs of citizens of slave states who visited free states. Thus, Scates asserted that Illinois "does most distinctly recognize the existence of the institution of slavery" in the United States, leading him to conclude that "the slave does not become free by the Constitution of Illinois by coming into the State for the mere purpose of passage through it."

Scates believed that to rule otherwise "would be productive of great and irremediable evils, of discord, of heart burnings, and alienation of kind and fraternal feeling, which should characterize the American brotherhood, and tend greatly to weaken, if not destroy the common bond of union amongst us, and our nationality and character, interest, and feeling." Scates continued: "Thousands from Kentucky, Virginia, Maryland, Tennessee, and the Carolinas . . . have sought and found free and safe passage with their slaves" across Illinois. Unlike virtually every other Northern judge, Scates interpreted the Privileges and Immunities Clause of the United States Constitution to protect the right of transit with slaves for American citizens from other states.

The *Willard* decision clearly reflected the intent of the Illinois legislature and was consistent with other proslavery decisions by the state's highest court. Nevertheless, not everyone in the state approved of the decision. The *Alton Telegraph* noted that the decision was "in direct conflict" with decisions in Massachusetts, Pennsylvania, and other Northern states. The *Telegraph* clearly tried to shame the state's court by pointing out that Illinois was out of step "with what is regarded *now* as the settled law of the land."

In 1847 the Illinois court began to move in step with the rest of the North on the adoption of the *Somerset* principle. In that year Chief Justice William Wilson freed Jane Bryant and her four children, slaves owned by General Robert Matson of Kentucky. Matson also owned land in Illinois, where he had kept Jane for two years. Chief Justice Wilson ruled that "by bringing Jane" to Illinois "and domiciling" her there, Matson lost all claim to her. The case was heard while Wilson was riding circuit, and was not appealed. Nevertheless, it signaled a change in the decision-making of the Illinois court.

The change was confirmed in *Hone v. Ammons* in 1852, when the full supreme court affirmed that in Illinois "the presumption of the law" was that all blacks were free. The only exception was fugitive slaves. Slaves in transit were not fugitives and thus were free if found in Illinois. Judge Lyman Trumbull, although ill and about to leave the court for the United States Senate, wrote a long concurring opinion attacking slavery. He cited cases from New York, England, and Massachusetts, as well as the recently adopted Illinois Constitution of 1848, in arguing that slavery could not exist in Illinois. Illinois had finally entered the mainstream of Northern legal thought.

The *Willard* and *Hone* decisions violated two long-standing aspects of public policy in Illinois. First, they led to an increase of the state's black population by freeing slaves in transit, with the likely result that former slaves would remain in the state. Second, the decisions undermined the interstate harmony that Illinois, the quintessential border state, wished to preserve. The legislature reaffirmed those policies in 1853 with a statute that prohibited any free black from moving into the state and also declared that masters in transit had a right to pass through the state with their slaves.

The right to transit was incorporated into a comprehensive statue enacted to prevent all blacks—slaves, fugitive slaves, and free blacks—from entering the state. For the Illinois legislature a commitment to interstate harmony happily coincided with Negrophobia and racism. Antiblack attitudes made it far easier for the Illinois legislature to support comity.

Political support for a proslavery position is illustrated by Jane Bryant's suit for freedom. Her master, General Robert Matson, in seeking to retain his property right in Jane and her children, hired the best lawyer he could find. In Illinois, in 1847, that meant hiring Abraham Lincoln. Lincoln, of course, was more than just a lawyer. He was also an extremely ambitious politician at the height of his pre-presidential success. Lincoln's role in the case suggests his own ambivalence about slavery and race. His action contrasts with his future cabinet members, Salmon P. Chase and William H. Seward, who had consistently defended fugitive slaves, free blacks, and abolitionists, but would have never thought of taking the case of a slaveowner. Lincoln's willingness to represent a slaveowner is also indicative of antiblack, antiabolitionist, pro-Southern sentiments in Illinois, and the weakness of the Illinois antislavery movement in 1847. Lincoln could take the case and not worry that it would destroy his chances for future elective office. One cannot imagine a similar case being taken by a politician—particularly a Whig—in most of Ohio, Pennsylvania, New York, or New England.

On the eve of the Civil War, Illinois was one of three Northern states that granted visiting masters a right of transit with their slaves. In the crisis of the Union, at least on that issue, Illinois clearly stood for compromise. Indeed, during the Oregon debates of 1848 Senator Sidney Breese of Illinois admitted that courts in his state "uniformly decided against . . . freedom," although in similar cases the slave states of Kentucky and Missouri would have granted freedom based on residence or transit in Illinois. Breese, described by an antislavery congressman from Ohio as a "cold-hearted, dough-faced scoundrel," clearly reflected the racist views of many of his constituents. Yet the position of Illinois was not one of complete capitulation to every Southern demand. Even after the legislature specifically protected slave transit, the Illinois bench continued to maintain its recently adopted position that there was a presumption of freedom for all people in Illinois.

PERSONAL LIBERTY AND FREE BLACKS

While the Illinois court accepted a presumption of freedom on the eve of the Civil War, the state nevertheless remained generally hostile to free blacks. That hostility, as has already been noted, began in the territorial period. After statehood Illinois adopted a complex series of laws designed to make the migration of free blacks difficult and complicated. In 1848 Illinois attempted to stop black immigration entirely through a provision in the state's new constitution that required the general assembly to "pass such laws as will effectually prohibit free persons of color from immigrating to and settling in this state, and to effectually prevent the owners of slaves from bringing them into this state, and to effectually prevent the owners of slaves from bringing them into this state, for the purpose of setting them free." The laws were to be passed at the first session of the assembly after the adoption of the constitution. Not until 1853, however, did the state legislature finally pass such a law.

The Black Laws seem to have had little effect on the actual migration of blacks into Illinois, although many individuals suffered anxiety from registration procedures and fear of prosecution. Between 1820 and 1860 the state's total black population increased by more than 500 percent, from 1,374 to 7,628. In 1850 half the blacks recorded by the census were born outside the state. In the decade from 1850 to 1860 the Illinois black population increased by over two thousand—a 40 percent jump. Two factors make the increase particularly notable. First, the Fugitive Slave Law of 1850 had made life difficult for runaways in the North. This was especially true in Illinois because of its close proximity to the South. Many fugitive slaves and free blacks along the Ohio River fled north to the upper Midwest, northern New York, or New England. Other blacks, fugitive and free, abandoned the United States altogether and emigrated to Canada. Second, while pressure from the 1850 federal law should have reduced the black population in Illinois, black migration was absolutely prohibited by state legislation after 1853. Nevertheless, the state's black population increased dramatically.

Clearly, anti-immigration statutes did not discourage blacks from moving to the state.

The ever-growing free black population created an enormous dilemma for Illinois lawmakers, judges, and politicians. On one hand, the state was firmly on record as opposing any black migration. On the other hand, the question for legislators was what to do with those blacks, and how much protection to give them. Because free blacks were often claimed as fugitive slaves, the protection of free blacks was inextricably tied to the rendition of fugitive slaves.

Most Northern states passed personal liberty laws designed to prevent the kidnapping of free blacks. Those laws also complicated the rendition of fugitive slaves. Some of the laws were in fact good-faith efforts to balance the need for free blacks to be protected from kidnappers with the rights of slaveowners to recover their runaway slaves. That was the purpose of Pennsylvania's 1826 act "to Give Effect to the Provisions of the Constitution of the United States Relative to Fugitives From Labour, For the Protection of Free People of Colour, and To Prevent Kidnapping."

In the 1840s and 1850s a number of Northern states passed new and stronger personal liberty laws that were in fact designed to thwart the return of fugitive slaves, under the guise of preventing kidnapping. New York's 1840 act "to extend the right of trial by jury" was aimed at protecting fugitive slaves in that state. So too was Ohio's 1857 law, which prohibited the use of state facilities for the incarceration of alleged fugitive slaves. The laws were a result of the growing abolitionist movement in the North, the increasing Northern hostility towards slavery expansion, and the return of fugitive slaves.

The personal liberty laws stemmed from two distinct, although interrelated, philosophies. The anti-kidnapping laws reflected a Northern commitment to due process that has been underestimated by most scholars of the period. Despite the racism of the antebellum North, most Northern states in fact did protect the liberty and basic human rights of their black neighbors. The personal liberty laws were a key component of that protection.

The personal liberty laws also reflected a wide range of abolitionist, antislavery, and Christian sentiment against the rendition of fugitive slaves. Whites and blacks throughout the North opposed the enforcement of the federal fugitive slave laws through a variety of violent and non-violent, legal, extralegal, and illegal methods. Slaves were rescued from the hands of federal marshals, slaveowners, and professional slave catchers in Massachusetts, Pennsylvania, New York, Ohio, and Wisconsin. Blacks organized vigilance committees, often with white allies, to prevent the return of fugitives. Thousands of Northerners aided fugitive slaves. A few—like James G. Birney and John Van Zandt in Ohio and John Hossack and Julius Willard in Illinois—ended up caught in the meshes of the law. Many others, however, working on the "underground railroad" or operating openly above ground, helped runaway slaves without ever facing legal action.

Countless citizens petitioned against the fugitive slave laws and voted against those who supported them. Many Northerners no doubt sympathized with the fictional Mary Bird of *Uncle Tom's Cabin*. When her husband, Senator Bird, asserted that there were no legal, constitutional, or political reasons for returning runaway slaves, Mary Bird responded: "Now, John, I don't know anything about politics; but I can read my Bible; and there I see that I must feed the hungry, clothe the naked, and comfort the desolate; and that Bible I mean to follow." Such religiously based sympathy for fugitive slaves helped motivate political abolitionists, who in turn worked for the passage of personal liberty laws.

The history of personal liberty legislation in Illinois differs from that of most of the North. Throughout the antebellum period the Illinois legislature went out of its way to prevent free blacks from settling in the state. The legislature was far more concerned with helping masters recover fugitive slaves than with preventing the kidnapping of free blacks.

In 1825 the state passed "An Act to more effectively prevent Kidnapping," which was directed at persons taking "any negro, mulatto, or person of color" out of the state against their will in order to enslave them. Despite its title, the law was not very effective. The penalties for violation included fines, but not imprisonment. There is no record that anyone was ever prosecuted under that section of the law.

Any prosecutions under the law would have been severely handicapped by an 1827 act that prohibited the testimony of any "negro, mulatto, or Indian" against a white person. Such laws were of course not uncommon. Illinois, however, remained unusual because it kept that prohibition right through the end of the Civil War. By 1860 only four Northern states—Indiana, Illinois, Oregon, and California—prohibited black testimony. The two Pacific Coast states repealed their restrictions in 1862 and 1863.

The 1825 anti-kidnapping law also prohibited the removal to other states of blacks indentured for a term of years. The only penalty for such a removal was the loss of services of the indentured black, however. The penalty obviously was not a deterrent, since—once out of the state—an indentured black might be treated as a slave or sold as one.

In 1855 the legislature authorized the governor to appoint agents to secure the liberty of Illinois residents kidnapped and sold as slaves in other states. The act appears to have been a bona fide attempt to help rescue free blacks taken out of the state against their will.

The 1855 act was apparently a response to two controversies between Illinois and Missouri over the alleged kidnapping of free blacks living in the Prairie State. In 1849 Governor Augustus C. French sought the extradition of three men accused of kidnapping a black named Wade. Missouri Governor Austin King asserted that Wade was in fact a fugitive slave, and thus the alleged kidnappers could not be extradited to Illinois. In a heated exchange of letters, French defended the right of Illinois to define kidnapping and to punish those who violated the law. In the end, however, the alleged kidnappers remained in Missouri.

In 1852 Governor French again sought the extradition of three alleged kidnappers. The victim was Charles Bartelle, a black descendant of slaves owned by French settlers. Bartelle had been born after the adoption of the Northwest Ordinance. French argued that Bartelle was never the slave of anyone, and therefore those who took him to Missouri were kidnappers. The Governor of Missouri, asserting that Bartelle was in fact a fugitive slave, refused to comply with the extradition requisition.

The actions of Governor French suggest the limits of Illinois' interstate cooperation. Illinois would willingly capture fugitive slaves, incarcerate them, and advertise for their owners. Similarly, Illinois would punish its own citizens who helped slaves escape. But, at least in the 1840s and 1850s, Illinois would not tolerate the kidnapping of its free black residents. French's actions and the 1855 law may have stemmed in part from a sense of humanitarian obligation, but the main thrust of the issue was sovereignty. Illinois demanded

the right to define for itself what constituted a crime within its jurisdiction. It was not inconsistent, therefore, for Illinois to punish people who helped slaves escape in Illinois and also to seek to punish
people who kidnapped free blacks from Illinois. There is no indication that the 1855 law was in fact ever used to secure the liberty of
any kidnapped blacks.

FUGITIVE SLAVES AND THE OBLIGATIONS OF THE UNION

Despite the 1855 statute and Governor French's correspondence with
his Missouri counterparts, Illinois' personal liberty laws were weak and
relatively impotent against kidnappers. The weakness of Illinois' personal liberty legislation contrasts sharply with other states, which closed
their facilities to slave catchers in the 1840s and 1850s and in other
ways attempted to deter the removal of blacks from their jurisdictions.
The state legislation also contrasts with actions by the city of Chicago.
In 1850 the Chicago Common Council strongly urged citizens of that
city, including police officers whose salaries were appropriated by the
council, to refuse to participate in the enforcement of the new Fugitive
Slave Law. The council condemned the law as "revolting to our moral
sense and an outrage upon our feelings of justice and humanity."

Few antebellum issues were as explosive as the rendition of fugitive
slaves. The stakes were high for all concerned. The cases were also
complicated. For the runaway a rendition meant not only an end to
freedom but return to almost certain punishment. The fugitive Anthony
Burns was partially crippled by the treatment he received after he was
returned to Virginia. Even more than the physical pain was the mental
and emotional anguish. A return to slavery signaled, for most fugitive
slaves, an end to a hope and a dream. Few slaves were as desperate as
Margaret Garner, who took the lives of her own children in order to
prevent their return to servitude. Similarly, the fugitive Jerry begged a
crowd to kill him, rather than allow his return to slavery. He was more
fortunate than most and was rescued that same night by a mob in
Syracuse, New York. At Christiana, Pennsylvania, fugitive slaves risked
their lives in a gun battle with a posse led by their master and a federal
deputy marshal.

For a master the return of a fugitive slave was a matter of dollars—
lots of them. Slaves, worth between $500 and $1,200, were extremely

valuable possessions; but also at stake was an issue of constitutional right. Masters often spent more than a slave was worth to assert their rights as slaveowners under the Constitution. For masters the return of their slaves was a moral issue from which they could not back away. Burns's owner, for example, refused an offer for more than his slave was worth if he would free him. The offer was refused, at least in part, to vindicate his rights. At Christiana, Edward Gorsuch declared he would get his slaves back or "go to Hell trying." Where he ended up in the afterlife is unclear, but when the gunfire stopped, his slaves were on their way to Canada, and he was on his way to an early grave.

For Northern whites the rendition of a fugitive could also be a painful experience. Abolitionists could not bear the thought of a rendition happening in their communities. Ann Phillips, wife of abolitionist Wendell Phillips, urged her cousins to agitate against the return of Burns because "if this man is allowed to go back *there is no* antislavery in Massts.—We may as well disband at once if our meetings and papers are all talk." After his conviction for violating the Fugitive Slave Law of 1850, John Hossack told the federal court in Illinois that he acted because he was "opposed to carrying out wicked and ungodly laws" and because he loved the "freedom" of his state and country. To preserve that freedom, Hossack rescued a fugitive slave, for which he paid a fine and spent a short time in jail. Preventing the rendition of a fugitive slave was as much a matter of honor for abolitionists as returning the slave was a matter of honor for the slaveowner. Similarly, for politicians seeking Southern support, a successful rendition was equally one of honor.

All of those competing interests and sentiments were felt by Northern legislators and judges. For the judge hearing the case of a fugitive slave, the issue was often one between natural law and positive law. It was equally one of justice to the slave, who deserved to be free, and justice to the master, who had a constitutional right to his property. It was an issue that few judges willingly faced. Legislators faced similar dilemmas, although perhaps not as sharply. Neither the master demanding his property nor the slave pleading for his liberty ever argued their case in the state assemblies. Yet the conscientious legislator could not avoid knowing that a vote for a personal liberty law would cut one more strand of the bonds of Union, while a vote against personal liberty law might bring sleepless nights and electoral defeats. In most states personal liberty won out over the Northern cries of disunion coming from the South. Illinois, however, was not with the majority of the North on this question.

In its willingness to aid in the rendition of fugitive slaves, Illinois went further than other Northern states to support the Constitution and the Union. Legislation supporting the return of fugitive slaves contrasts sharply with the paltry protections Illinois offered its own free blacks. Not until 1825 did Illinois adopt legislation to protect free blacks from kidnapping. The 1825 anti-kidnapping law provided no jail sentences for kidnappers.

The Prairie State's concern with fugitive slaves began before the passage of the anti-kidnapping law and continued through the secession crisis. The 1819 act "respecting free Negroes, Mulattoes, Servants and Slaves" provided penalties for slaves and servants leaving their master's premises without a pass. The law, however, did not directly affect those who might aid a runaway slave. That "defect" was partially remedied by the 1827 criminal code, which provided a jail term and fines for anyone convicted of harboring a slave or servant owing service or labor under the laws of any American jurisdiction.

The 1829 "Act Respecting Free Negroes and Mulattoes, Servants and Slaves" dealt at greater length with the problem of fugitive slaves. Section One provided a $500 fine for anyone harboring a black who had entered the state without a certificate of freedom. Of that amount, half would be paid to the informant. The clause obviously made helping a fugitive slave a risky act and at the same time may have induced some Illinois citizens to act as slave catchers. Section Two of the law dealt directly with fugitive slaves by asserting that any black who could not prove his or her freedom "shall be deemed a runaway slave or servant." Such a legal provision was quite common in slave states, but virtually unknown in free states. In essence, Illinois adopted the Southern presumption that all blacks were slaves, unless they could prove otherwise—a rejection of the law of freedom that distinguished the North from the South. Blacks without free papers could be jailed for six weeks and then hired out "month to month, for the space of one year" while the sheriff advertised the existence of the "runaway." If no owner claimed the "runaway," the next circuit court would grant freedom papers. Finally, the law provided that any slaves coming into the state and claiming to be free would be arrested and returned to their owners.

The laws of the 1820s were reenacted in later years, and were incorporated into the official revised statutes of Illinois published in 1858.

The contrast between the meager protections for free blacks and assistance to slaveowners went beyond legislation. While there were no known prosecutions under the 1825 law designed to prevent kidnapping, there were a number of arrests and jailings both of blacks believed to be fugitive slaves and those accused of helping them. In 1847, for example, in the famous Matson case, a court ordered that the blacks claiming their freedom be held in jail on the ground that they were "in Illinois without certificates of freedom." Only after the court held Jane and her children to be free were they released. Had the court held that Jane was still a slave, then the whites who helped her would have been subject to prosecution. A similar situation had occurred in Bureau County in 1841, when Jonathan Holbrook was indicted for harboring an alleged fugitive slave named John Dolan (alias Black Jack). The grand jury admitted it did not know who Dolan's owner was but nevertheless approved the prosecution of Holbrook. Similarly, abolitionists Julius Willard, Owen Lovejoy, and Richard Eells were prosecuted for aiding blacks alleged to be fugitives. Both Lovejoy and Willard aided slaves brought into the state by their owners. Lovejoy's conviction was reversed by Judge Caton, while riding circuit. Willard, however, was fined $20 and court costs by Judge Samuel D. Lockwood, who was also riding circuit at the time. Willard appealed to the full Illinois Supreme Court, which affirmed the conviction.

The case of Richard Eells was more correctly one involving a fugitive slave. Eells gave employment and lodging to a fugitive slave owned by a Missouri resident. For that he was indicted under the 1827 law, as Willard and Lovejoy had been. Eells appealed his conviction on two separate grounds. The Illinois court's rejection of those arguments further illustrates the position of the state with regard to interstate harmony.

Eells first argued that the indictment did not charge that he knew he was harboring a fugitive slave. This defect in the indictment led to the argument that Eells in fact had no "notice" that the person he hired was a fugitive slave. Eells could legitimately state that he did not *know* that the person in his house was a slave. That argument could have provided an easy, noncontroversial, and constitutionally legitimate way for the Illinois court to overturn Eells's conviction. In a similar case in

1837 the Ohio Supreme Court had accepted such arguments, made by
Salmon P. Chase, in overturning a conviction of the abolitionist James
G. Birney. Unlike its Ohio counterpart, however, the Illinois court was
not looking for an easy way to avoid upholding Eells's conviction.
Thus, Justice James Shields dismissed the argument with the rather odd
conclusion that "[t]he essence of the offence consists in the attempt to
defraud the owner of his property," and not in harboring the slave.
Justice Shields, of course, failed to explain how Eells could have attempted to defraud the owner of a slave when he did not know that
the person in his house was a slave. However illogical Shields's point,
he nevertheless made it clear that the Illinois court was intent on upholding the conviction and the interstate harmony it implied.

The second objection went to a complicated constitutional question.
In 1793 Congress had passed a fugitive slave law that set out methods
for returning fugitive slaves and punishing those who aided them. In
1842, in *Prigg* v. *Pennsylvania,* the United States Supreme Court had
not only upheld the validity of the 1793 law but also struck down a
Pennsylvania personal liberty law that had added requirements to the
rendition process. In his opinion of the court, Justice Joseph Story had
implied that states might be precluded from legislating on fugitive slave
rendition because that was exclusively the jurisdiction of Congress.

Attorneys for Eells argued that under *Prigg* only the federal government could prosecute people for helping fugitive slaves; therefore, the
Illinois law was unconstitutional, and Eells had to go free. Shields
responded that *Prigg* only prevented states from passing laws "which
may interfere with the right of the master to the service of his fugitive
slave." Illinois had no such laws, and so both the statute and the
conviction were sustained. Three justices—Lockwood, Thomas C.
Browne, and Chief Justice William Wilson—dissented.

In *Eells* the Illinois court showed its willingness to convict citizens
of the state for helping fugitive slaves. That position contrasted with
virtually all other free state courts, which by that time consciously
avoided aiding slaveowners and slave catchers. The *Eells* opinion demonstrated that Illinois, unlike most other Northern states, placed interstate harmony and fidelity to the national Constitution far above
any concepts of natural law or the pro-freedom implications of the
state's own constitution.

The Eells affair indicated the distance that Illinois would go in supporting the needs of its slave-state neighbors while also illustrating the

limits of that policy. While Eells was under indictment in Illinois, Governor Thomas Reynolds of Missouri sought his extradition as a fugitive from justice for harboring a fugitive slave from Missouri. Reynolds claimed that Eells had stolen the slave from Missouri, and thus he should be tried in that state. Illinois Governor Thomas Ford initially agreed to extradite Eells, but then changed his mind when he discovered that Eells had not been in Missouri for the previous two years, and therefore could not have "fled" from that state. Ford noted that Eells was a physician in Quincy and was "all the time publicly about in the city" when he allegedly committed the crime of slave stealing in Missouri. Ford told Governor Reynolds that he had been "furnished with a great mass of written testimony, too voluminous to be set forth," that convinced him that Eells was innocent of the charges against him in Missouri.

Ford's refusal to extradite Eells has been ascribed to protest meetings by antislavery activists in northern Illinois. Such meetings may have affected Ford—as they might any politician—but, since Ford was totally unsympathetic to abolitionists, the meetings may not have been crucial. Ford assured Reynolds that "the fanatical and misguided Sect called Abolitionists" had "no countenance or encouragement from the people" of Illinois. Nevertheless, the "arrest, imprisonment and transportation of an innocent man" could not be allowed, even "under pretence of suppressing or punishing the excesses of a Sect."

More important, no doubt, than Ford's sense of justice toward an innocent man—especially an innocent abolitionist—was his sense of state sovereignty. He asserted that "the first and highest duty of a Governor, is to the people of his own State." He argued that "State Governments were erected upon this principle." Ford would not extradite Eells, because to do so would violate the sovereignty of his state. Illinois would willingly prosecute Eells for crimes committed in Illinois against the slaveowners of Missouri, but Missouri could not try a citizen of Illinois for a crime committed in Illinois. That would violate the sovereignty of Illinois.

FUGITIVE SLAVES AND THE CRISIS OF THE UNION

Throughout the 1820s, 1830s, and into the 1840s, the three branches of Illinois government generally granted comity to visitors and travelers passing through the state with slaves. The governors were willing to allow the extradition of abolitionists if they had actually gone to slave states and helped slaves escape. The policies developed out of a general concensus on two issues: that blacks should be kept out of the state, and that interstate harmony was a major political goal.

The concensus began to break down in the 1840s. The Illinois judiciary initiated that change. In 1841, in *Kinney v. Cook,* the Illinois court asserted that in cases involving the status of blacks living in that state "the presumption is in favor of liberty." The burden of proof in claiming a black's labor rested with the alleged owner. The court, however, did not deny that with proper proof a claim to a black's labor as an indentured servant or slave might be sustained. Four years later, in *Jarrot v. Jarrot,* the Illinois high court declared that all blacks born in Illinois after the adoption of the 1818 Constitution were free, regardless of the status of their parents. In his opinion of the court, Justice Walter B. Scates also asserted that any black born in Illinois since the adoption of the Northwest Ordinance of 1787 was also free. A majority of Scates's colleagues, however, did not endorse his second conclusion.

The *Kinney* and *Jarrot* decisions ran counter to legislative actions dating from 1819. They clearly undermined the concensus on the status of blacks in Illinois. The decisions reflected, at least in part, the development of a sophisticated antislavery bar. The prevailing attorney in both cases was Lyman Trumbull, who would ultimately serve on the Illinois Supreme Court. The change in attitude—and the limits of that change—were apparent in the convention that wrote the 1848 Illinois Constitution. That document finally ended all slavery and indentured servitude in the state. Yet it also prohibited free blacks from immigrating to the state.

In 1852, in *Hone* v. *Ammons,* the Illinois court expanded its "presumption of freedom" to include all blacks found in the state. Two years earlier, in *Thornton's Case,* the court had struck down an 1829 law that required sheriffs to arrest and incarcerate alleged fugitive slaves. The court ruled, as it had refused to do in the cases of Willard and Eells, that Congress had exclusive jurisdiction over fugitive slaves. In *Thornton's Case,* Chief Justice Samuel Treat, citing Justice Story's decision in *Prigg* v. *Pennsylvania,* declared the Illinois statute void "because it assumes to legislate upon a subject matter over which congress has exclusive jurisdiction." Taken together, the two cases put the Illinois court on the cutting edge of the legal attack on slavery. The court had asserted that it would assume all blacks in the state to be free and that it would not allow state officials to help in the capture and return of fugitive slaves.

The results were unacceptable to the Illinois General Assembly. In 1853 the legislature effectively overruled the implications of *Home* by declaring that slaves in transit were not entitled to claim their freedom. In 1857 the court reasserted that Illinois would have no part in the rendition of fugitive slaves. In *Rodney* v. *Illinois Central Railroad,* the court refused to allow a Missouri slaveowner to recover the value of a slave who had escaped by boarding an Illinois Central train at Cairo. Until 1850 the state, through its courts and legislature, had readily aided masters seeking fugitive slaves and had willingly prosecuted those who helped fugitive slaves. But *Thornton* and *Rodney* signaled that the Illinois court, like most of its Northern counterparts, would not play the role of slave catcher.

The Illinois legislature was unwilling to follow the court's leadership on this issue, just as it had rejected the court's decisions on slaves in transit. Although the court emphatically declared unconstitutional Illinois' fugitive slave law, the legislature nevertheless included it as part of the 1858 revised statutes. Thus, a statute declared unconstitutional in 1850 remained on the books after an official revision of the laws in 1858. On paper, at least, the state of Illinois supported harmony within the Union at the expense of liberty for all.

ILLINOIS: A HOUSE DIVIDED

By the eve of the Civil War, Illinois was truly a house divided against itself on the question of fugitive slave rendition. In southern Illinois fugitive slaves were easily captured and returned while those who helped them faced prosecution under state laws. After 1850 federal officials and slave catchers operated with little direct interference from local citizens. All fugitives captured south of Champaign were either returned to their owners by a federal court or taken back to slavery without any court hearing at all.

In northern Illinois the situation was quite different. Slave catchers entered Chicago at their own risk. Citizens in that city openly aided fugitive slaves without fear of capture. In 1846, for example, Dr. Charles V. Dyer, a prominent physician, employed a fugitive slave from

Kentucky in his house. When his master seized him, Dyer rescued the fugitive and beat off the Kentuckians with his cane. Dyer faced no prosecution even though he had harbored a fugitive slave in violation of Illinois law. Nor did the alleged master seek to prosecute Dyer for the battery or sue him for the value of the slave. Two years later Dyer stalled a courtroom proceeding until a crowd gathered and rescued a captured fugitive.

The passage of the new fugitive slave law in 1850 led to more organized opposition. Within weeks after the passage of the 1850 law, Chicago blacks had formed the "Liberty Association," whose members were assigned to "patrol the city, each night and keep an eye out for interlopers." When slave hunters appeared in the city, they were warned that their safety could not be guaranteed. Meanwhile, as already noted, the city council went on record as opposing enforcement of the law. In the first fugitive slave case under the federal law the judge determined that the person was not a fugitive slave. In 1860 a Chicago judge had a sheriff's deputy remove a slave from federal custody on an alleged violation of a city law. The slave was then released and escaped. In nearby Ottawa, mobs rescued slaves in 1851 and 1859. While some slaves were returned from the northern part of the state, the successful returns were accomplished without legal action. In other words, slaveowners could bring slaves out of the northern part of the state only if they did so quietly and without being discovered.

Illinois lawmakers were also divided on how to deal with the return of fugitive slaves. The courts chose fidelity to fundamental justice, the Constitution of Illinois, the legal trends in other free states, and a narrow and strict reading of the United States Constitution. The legislature chose fidelity to a broad reading of the United States Constitution and to a spirit of comity and interstate harmony.

Those questions, like so many other critical legal issues, ultimately became political issues. They emerged, quite appropriately, in the Lincoln-Douglas debates of 1858. Geographically, the two men seemed to be on the wrong side of the question. Douglas, a native of New England and since 1847 a resident of northern Illinois, represented a proslavery position. Lincoln, originally from Kentucky and a resident of southern Illinois, took the opposite position. Although neither man expressed it in these terms, the two debaters also reflected the division between the Illinois legislature and the Illinois Supreme Court. Oddly enough, Douglas, a former member of the state supreme court and a defender of the United States Supreme Court, took the side of the legislature. Lincoln, a former state legislator, came down on the side of the Illinois Supreme Court.

Put another way, Douglas favored the state's long-standing hostility to free blacks and sympathy for slaveowners. Lincoln took the opposite position. Douglas, Lincoln correctly told his audience in Chicago, "cares not if slavery is voted up or down." Lincoln, of course, did care. Similarly, Douglas would relegate all blacks to servitude because he feared there would otherwise be interracial marriage and the destruction of white society. Lincoln was less fearful and protested "against that counterfeit logic which presumes that because I do not want a negro woman for a slave, I do necessarily want her for a wife." Lincoln understood he "need not have her for either."

Lincoln was also not ready to argue for total racial equality. To do so would have been political suicide. It also would have run counter to his own thoughts. The Lincoln of 1858 was clearly ambivalent about race although certainly in favor of white supremacy. In that regard he was fully in tune with his constituents, including the entire Illinois Supreme Court. But, like the court, he was unwilling to relegate blacks to the status of permanent servitude. Douglas, like the legislature, looked to the past as a model for the place of blacks in Illinois and America. At the most basic level Lincoln anticipated the future, arguing:

> There is no reason in the world why the negro is not entitled to all the rights enumerated in the Declaration of Independence— the right of life, liberty and the pursuit of happiness. I hold that he is as much entitled to these as the white man. I agree with Judge Douglas that he is not my equal in many respects, certainly not in color—perhaps not in intellectual and moral endowments; but in the right to eat the bread without leave of anybody else which his own hand earns, he is my equal and the equal of Judge Douglas, and the equal of every other man.

Had the 1858 senatorial election been decided by a popular vote, Lincoln might have won. But, win or lose, the closeness of the outcome suggests the vast changes in Illinois from the 1830s to the 1850s. The debates, like the conflicting court decisions and statutes of Illinois, underscore the dilemmas of a state on the border between slavery and freedom. These problems illustrate the nature of a constitution in a house divided.

18

What Took the North So Long?

WILLIAMSON MURRAY

• *The Civil War is the central event in the history of the United States. On April 12, 1861, Confederate artillery began the attack on Fort Sumter in Charleston harbor. President Abraham Lincoln then called for volunteers to defend the American flag and all that it represented. Four years later, almost to the day, General Robert E. Lee surrendered his broken and almost starving Army of Northern Virginia to the victorious Union commander Ulysses Simpson Grant. Along the way, more than 620,000 Americans lost their lives—or about as many as in all the other wars in which the United States has thus far fought. The conflict killed one-quarter of the Confederacy's white men of military age, and it destroyed half of its industries and railroads and about two-fifths of its livestock.*

Why did the Civil War last so long? Why was the human cost so terrible? There is no easy answer to these questions, but Professor Williamson Murray of Ohio State University reminds us of the enormous distances involved and compares the scale of the conflict with the Napoleonic invasion of Russia. Moreover, he points out that the struggle between the North and the South was in many respects the first modern war, the first total war, the first occasion in history in which technology and industry were harnessed to the killing fields. Initially, Professor Murray argues, the Union lacked a unified, comprehensive strategy. Once General Grant took command, however, the North had its visionary leader, and the Confederacy was doomed.

The Civil War devastated the South and savaged the armies of both sides, exacting a casualty toll that made it one of the costliest wars in modern times and the worst in American history. At the heart of the

"What Took The North So Long?" by William Murray, © 1989 by *MHQ: The Quarterly Journal of Military History.*

bloody struggle lay the grand strategy of the North. As so often had happened in history, Northern strategy emerged only gradually. The path to victory was not clear on either side in 1861. Nor was the outcome of the war preordained. Political and military leaders on both sides enjoyed few of the prerequisites in education, inclination, and background to wage a war of this magnitude and intensity.

The North was eventually victorious because its leadership learned from its mistakes and adapted to the "real" conditions of war. In particular, Abraham Lincoln, a backwoods Illinois lawyer with only ninety days of militia experience in the Black Hawk War of 1832, and Ulysses S. Grant, perhaps the clearest-thinking general in American history, solidified Northern strategy and grasped victory from the wreckage of the early days.

The North, of course, relied on its great superiority in population, industrial resources, financial reserves, and agricultural production. Why, then, did it take so long for the federal government to achieve victory? We might begin by examining several popular explanations for the length of the war. The most persistent is that Southern soldiers, largely drawn from a yeoman class of farmers, had spent their lives shooting game and inuring themselves to hardship in a healthy outdoor environment. The Northern population, on the other hand, condemned to work in dark, dank factories, supposedly had developed few of the attributes that an army requires. Such a view, however, flies in the face of social evidence and the testimony of those who fought. One Southern officer, writing to a Northern friend immediately after the war, put the case differently. "Our officers were good," he commented, "but considering that our rank and file were just white trash and they had to fight regiments of New England Yankee volunteers, with all their best blood in the ranks, and Western sharpshooters together, it is only wonderful that we weren't whipped sooner." The fact is that nearly 80 percent of the Northern population lived in rural areas, like their Southern counterparts, and it is hard to see much difference in the social composition of the armies.

A corollary argument holds that the crucial factor in the war's length lay in the natural superiority of Southern officers and generals, an aristocratic group of West Point cavaliers who had been raised in the antebellum South to appreciate warrior values. The legends surrounding Robert E. Lee, Stonewall Jackson, and Jeb Stuart lend a certain plausibility to the argument, and the dismal record of the Union Army of the Potomac in the eastern theater of operations supports it. With two victories (Gettysburg and Five Forks), twelve defeats, and one draw (Antietam), the Army of the Potomac had a record of unambiguous failure matched by no other unit of equivalent size in the history of the United States Army. But historians have for too long overemphasized the war on the eastern front.

In fact, in the West, the reverse was true: There, Confederate forces fared just as badly as their counterparts in the Army of the Potomac and as a result of the same kind of wooden-headed leadership. Floyd, Pemberton, Bragg, and Hood on the Confederate side in the West fully matched the incompetence of McDowell, McClellan, Hooker, and Burnside in the Army of the Potomac. In his memoirs, Ulysses S. Grant recounts one anecdote from the pre-war army that captures the nature of Bragg's leadership:

> On one occasion, when stationed at a post of several companies commanded by a field officer, [Bragg] was himself commanding one of the companies and at the same time acting as post quartermaster and commissary. He was first lieutenant at the time, but his captain was detached on other duty. As a commander of the company he made a requisition upon the quartermaster—himself—for something he wanted. As quartermaster he declined to fill the requisition, and endorsed on the back of it his reasons for doing so. As company commander he responded to this, urging that his requisition called for nothing but what he was entitled to, and that it was the duty of the quartermaster to fill it. As quartermaster he still persisted that he was right. In this condition of affairs Bragg referred the whole matter to the commanding officer of the post. The latter, when he saw the nature of the matter referred, exclaimed, "My God, Mr. Bragg, you have quarrelled with every officer in the army, and now you are quarrelling with yourself."

One of the soldiers in the Army of Tennessee reflected a perfect understanding of Bragg's leadership when asked whether he was in the general's army. "Bragg's army? Bragg's got no army. He shot half of them himself up in Kentucky, and the other half got killed at Murfreesboro!" The superior command skills of the Confederate generals in the East were more than counterbalanced by the quality of Union leadership in the West.

As for the romantic image that clings to eastern Confederate generals, one might well remember Jackson's and Lee's ruthless brand of leadership. The former's marches up and down northern Virginia were frequently punctuated by summary executions of deserters; under his cold-eyed Presbyterian command, there was nothing cavalier about serving in his army. As for Lee, he was as ferocious a combat leader as the American army has produced. At Malvern Hill he brashly threw his men against a Union artillery concentration deadlier than any in the war. He won the day, but only at tremendous cost. War is a nasty business, and the Confederate generals in the East were extremely good at it.

The length of the war has far more to do with the immensity of the geographic arena and the complexities of modern war than with the supposed superiority of Southern manhood and the competence of Southern generals. Geography offers a major clue as to why the North found it so difficult to project its industrial and military power into the Southern states and end the rebellion. Taken together, Mississippi and Alabama are slightly larger than present-day West Germany. The distance from central Georgia to northern Virginia is approximately the distance from East Prussia to Moscow. The distance from Baton Rouge to Richmond exceeds the distance from the Franco-German border to the current Soviet-Polish frontier. Considering that it took Napoleon from 1799 to 1807 to reach the frontiers of czarist Russia, one should not be surprised that it took the North so long to conquer the South. Exacerbating the challenge was the fact that primeval wilderness covered substantial portions of the South, particularly in the western theater of operations. While the eastern theater was relatively close to the centers of Northern industrial power, the starting point for the western armies—Cairo, Illinois—was nearly a thousand miles from the North's industrial center. Without railroads and steamships, the North would not have been able to bring its power to bear and probably would have lost the war.

The first formidable problem confronting the North in the Civil War lay in mobilizing its industrial strength and population and then deploying that power into the Confederacy. The problems of mobilization were daunting. The regular army was little more than a constabulary designed to overawe Indians on the frontier; it was certainly not prepared for large-scale military operations. Nowhere was there a body

FIGURE 1 The North's strategy for defeating the Confederacy had three features: blockading the coast, securing the Mississippi, and capturing the capital at Richmond. But tactical setbacks—most notably in the East, where Union commanders engaged in little more than stop-gap maneuvers—forced a new operational feature: Sherman's March to the Sea. It was so successful that the taking of Richmond proved unnecessary.

of experience from which to draw in solving the issues that now arose; the armies and their support structure had to come from nothing. The politicians knew nothing about war. The military leaders may have read a little of Baron de Jomini's works on the Napoleonic Wars, but the knowledge they derived was probably more harmful than helpful. Certainly no one had read Clausewitz; and though by 1864 Lincoln and Grant were to evolve an approach resembling Clausewitz's, their success resulted more from trial and error and common sense than from military history or theory.

The South did possess one significant advantage at the beginning of the war. Since it had no regular army, officers who resigned their commissions in the federal army to return home and serve the Confederacy found themselves spread throughout the newly formed state regiments, where their experience could at least provide an example to others.

But in the North, since regular units continued to exist, the experience of those within the professional officer corps was not used to best advantage in creating the Northern volunteer armies. Grant records the value of just one experienced officer—himself—in training the Twenty-first Illinois. "I found it very hard work for a few days to bring all the men into anything like subordination; but the great majority favored discipline and by the application of a little regular army punishment all were reduced to as good discipline as one could want." The Twentieth Maine, trained by another lone regular officer, Adelbert Ames, also suggests the importance of experience in the training process. Not only did Ames turn out one of the best regiments in the Army of the Potomac, but Joshua Chamberlain, second-in-command of the regiment and up to July 1862 a professor of Greek at Bowdoin College, arguably became the best combat commander in the Army of the Potomac by the end of the war. All too often Union regiments did not have that one officer and therefore had to learn on the battlefield—which was an expensive process.

The armies themselves, whichever side one describes, retained a fundamentally civilian character. Photographs of even the units of the Army of the Potomac, supposedly the most spit-and-polish of all the Civil War armies, suggest a casualness that perhaps only the Israelis have exemplified in the twentieth century. When properly led, however, these troops were capable of sacrifices that few units in American military history have equaled. The performance of the First Minnesota at Gettysburg is only one case among hundreds. Although it sustained 80 percent casualties on the second day, it was back in the line receiving Pickett's charge on the third.

The whole first year of the war largely revolved around the complex task of raising, equipping, training, and deploying the forces that the strategic and political requirements of the war demanded. These problems presented themselves concurrently, not sequentially. Nor could Civil War military leaders depend on former certainties of war. The rifled musket had drastically altered combat. With killing ranges extended by 300 to 400 yards, Napoleonic set-piece tactics were no longer valid. Through a process of learning on the battlefield, Civil War armies substantially changed the manner in which they deployed and defended themselves as the war proceeded. How to wage offensive warfare against modern long-range firepower, however, remained an unsolved problem. Ultimately it would require the four long years of the First World War before answers to this question began to appear.

The initial strategic moves of the war turned out entirely in favor of the federal government. Above all, Lincoln's political acuity brought the all-important border states over to the Union camp. Ruthless action secured Maryland and Missouri, while cautious maneuvering led the South to mistakes that tipped Kentucky to the North. Gaining Maryland secured Washington; Missouri represented the first step down the Mississippi; and the securing of Kentucky would in early 1862 allow an obscure Union brigadier general to move against Forts Donelson and Henry. The latter success may have been among the most decisive in the war; the Tennessee and Cumberland rivers were now open to federal naval power as far as they were navigable. In effect Grant not only captured an entire Southern army but also made Tennessee indefensible by the South, while affording the Union the opportunity to cut the only east-west railroad that the Confederacy possessed.

However, the North's grand strategy took considerable time to emerge, at least in its fullest, winning form. The federal government's senior commander at the start of the war, General Winfield Scott, had a three-point strategic framework, the famous Anaconda Plan: (1) to blockade the South, (2) to capture its capital, and (3) to open up the Mississippi. It was a start, but only a start; the North would have to add a number of elements to achieve victory. The Battle of Shiloh in April 1862, which underlined how drastically the tactical game had changed, should have warned how difficult this war would prove to be. The federal government was going to have to break the will of a population—a population, moreover, inflamed by nationalism and possessing both a huge territory on which to draw and a Confederate government willing to take drastic measures to keep shirkers in line. Little of that was clear in April 1862; thus Grant was widely criticized in the North when Shiloh's casualties became known. But Grant at least sensed the depth of Southern hostility and its implications after the slaughter of Shiloh:

> Up to the battle of Shiloh, I, as well as thousands of other citizens, believed that the rebellion against the Government would collapse suddenly and soon, if a decisive victory could be gained over any of its armies. Donelson and Henry were such victories. An army of more than 21,000 men was captured or destroyed. Bowling Green, Columbus, and Hickman, Kentucky, fell in consequence, and Clarksville and Nashville, Tennessee, the last two with an immense amount of stores, also fell into our hands. The Tennessee and Cumberland rivers, from their mouths to the head of navigation, were secured. But when Confederate armies were collected which not only attempted to hold a line farther South, from Memphis to Chattanooga, Knoxville and on to the Atlantic, but assumed the offensive and made such a gallant effort to regain what had been lost, then, indeed, I gave up all idea of saving the Union except by complete conquest.

Grant's emergence in 1862 was seemingly one of the great surprises of the war; certainly the vicious back-biting that characterized Major General Henry Halleck's reports on the future Northern commander did little to speed the process. Nevertheless, one should not assume that Grant was entirely an unknown quantity. Confederate General Richard S. Ewell wrote in spring 1861: "There is one West Pointer, I think in Missouri, little known, and whom I hope the Northern people will not find out. I mean Sam Grant. I knew him in the Academy and in Mexico. I should fear him more than any of their officers I have yet heard of...."

Grant, of course, exercised little influence over Union grand strategy at the beginning; that was left to supposed prodigies such as George McClellan, whose sense of personal importance came close to losing the war in the East. Grant's conquest of the Mississippi in 1862 and 1863 opened up the great inland waterway, split the Confederacy, and cemented the alliance of the eastern and western states that would ultimately crush the Confederacy. His opening move at Forts Donelson and Henry exposed the one crucial geographic weakness of the Confederacy: the fact that its rivers in the West allowed Northern armies to penetrate into the very heartland of the Confederate nation. Tennessee, northern Alabama, and northern Georgia were all now within reach of invading Union troops. But under the constraints of Halleck's insipid leadership and Brigadier General William Rosecrans's tardy drive, the Union push took a considerable length of time to develop. There were some in the Confederacy who recognized how dangerous this threat might become, but Jefferson Davis continued to emphasize the eastern theater at the expense of the West and to support the inflexible and incompetent leadership of Braxton Bragg.

Unfortunately, Grant's second great victory—and his second battle of annihilation—at Vicksburg never realized its full potential. Once the Mississippi had been opened, his victorious army dispersed and the Union high command wasted Grant during the summer of 1863. The humiliating September defeat at Chickamauga, however, forced the high command to reorganize the western theater under Grant's control, sending him considerable reinforcements from the East. Lincoln and Secretary of War Edwin Stanton redeployed two corps from the Army of the Potomac, moving 25,000 men, along with their artillery and horses, over 1,200 miles in less than two weeks. This awesome logistic accomplishment underlines how far the North had advanced in its ability to mobilize and utilize its resources. Grant more than repaid the trust of the Lincoln administration with his smashing victory at Chattanooga in late November. His devastating defeat of Bragg's army solidified the Northern hold over Tennessee and established a solid base from which the Union's western armies could break the South apart at its very heart: Georgia. None of this had been imaginable at the onset of war. By now the North could logistically deploy, maintain, and put into battle an army of 100,000 men in the very center of the Confederacy.

Chattanooga set the stage for the Lincoln-Grant partnership—and the full evolution of Northern grand strategy—that saw the war through to its victorious conclusion in spring 1865. By the beginning of 1864, the Anaconda Plan had for the most part been realized: The Mississippi was open; the blockade was largely effective; and only Richmond remained untaken. Northern strategy moved in new directions. Lincoln had seen early in the war that a concerted, concurrent

Union effort in all theaters would be required to break the outer ring of Confederate resistance. But George McClellan had babbled about the foolishness of such an approach and had contemptuously dismissed Lincoln's proposal. McClellan, as a disciple of Jomini, could think only in terms of capturing the enemy's capital or seizing some central position that would lead to a decisive battle. Lincoln thought in far broader terms. He would learn, while McClellan, like the Bourbons who briefly regained power between Napoleon's two reigns, learned nothing.

Both Lincoln and Grant looked beyond the eastern theater. Grant's grand strategy for 1864, after he was made commander of all the U.S. armies, aimed to crush the Confederacy with thrusts from a number of different directions. His instructions to General William Sherman (similar orders were given to General George Meade) made his intentions clear.

> It is my design, if the enemy keep quiet and allow me to take the initiative in the spring campaign, to work all parts of the army together and somewhat toward a common center. For your information I now write you my programme as at present determined upon.
>
> I have sent orders to [Major General Nathaniel P.] Banks by private messenger to finish up his present expedition against Shreveport with all despatch.... With [his] force he is to commence operations against Mobile as soon as he can. It will be impossible for him to commence too early.
>
> [Major General Quincy] Gillmore joins [Major General Benjamin F.] Butler with 10,000 men, and the two operate against Richmond from the South side of the James River.... I will stay with the Army of the Potomac, increased by [Major General Ambrose E.] Burnside's corps of not less than 25,000 effective men, and operate directly against Lee's army wherever it may be found.
>
> [Major General Franz] Sigel collects all his available force in two columns...to move against the Virginia and Tennessee....
>
> You I propose to move against [Joseph E.] Johnston's army, to break it up and to get into the interior of the enemy's country as far as you can, inflicting all the damage you can against their war resources.
>
> I do not propose to lay down for you a plan of campaign, but simply to lay down the work it is desirable to have done, and leave you free to execute in your own way.

Grant concluded by telling Sherman that Sigel probably had the smallest chance of achieving his objective, but, as Lincoln had suggested during the strategy briefing, "if Sigel can't skin himself, he can hold a leg whilst someone else skins." There is no clearer, more concise strategic conception in American military history. It spelled the end of the Confederacy by 1865.

Why it did not spell defeat for the Confederacy in 1864 is worth examining. Failure to achieve victory before 1865 reflected the extraordinary difficulty in planning, coordinating, and executing military operations, as well as the inevitable impact of political reality on the world of military operations. Unfortunately, two key elements in Grant's strategy—Banks's move against Mobile, and Butler's move from Bermuda Hundred to cut the Petersburg–Richmond railroad—failed to materialize. Banks remained tied to the disastrously inept Red River campaign; consequently his move against Mobile, which would have tied one corps of the Army of Tennessee to Alabama, did not occur and that unit reinforced Johnston's defense of Atlanta. Butler's attack from Bermuda Hundred collapsed in a welter of incompetence rarely seen this late in the Civil War. As Grant noted in his memoirs, Butler "corked" himself and his army into a position where he could exercise no influence on the unfolding campaign. Had he succeeded, Lee would have been forced to divide his forces against two foes. As it was, Butler's army was simply subsumed into the Army of the Potomac. The results of these failures prevented victory in 1864. Sherman faced far more effective resistance in his offensive against Atlanta, while the Army of the Potomac confronted an Army of Northern Virginia that was able to devote full attention to the defense of northern Virginia.

Significantly, Grant did not complain in his memoirs that the great spring offensive failed because of the incompetent leadership of "political" generals. He was well aware that Lincoln needed the support of "war Democrats" in the upcoming presidential campaign and that keeping Butler and Banks in positions of high responsibility was therefore essential for political reasons; both were "war Democrats." Good strategy, as with all things in war, is a fine balance of choices. As the British commander James Wolfe commented before Quebec in 1757: "War is an option of difficulties." The delicate coalition that Lincoln was holding together in the North was essential to the successful settlement of a war that had opened wounds not only between the North and the South but also within the North itself. To risk damaging that coalition by removing Banks and Butler was to risk losing the presidential election, and defeat in November might well have eviscerated whatever battlefield successes the Union army would achieve in 1864.

In assuming his position as commander of all Union forces, Grant was initially inclined to remain in the West. But his justified trust in Sherman's competence led him to change his mind: He would accompany the Army of the Potomac. Meade's competent but hardly driving brand of leadership in the last half of 1863 suggests that the Army of the Potomac's commander required the support of a more senior officer upon whom he could rely in moments of crisis. Grant would provide that support. He understood, however, that as an outsider he was not in a position to replace that army's senior leadership. He therefore was compelled to fight the coming battles of spring 1864 with a fundamentally flawed instrument—a military organization whose cohesion, willingness to sacrifice, and dogged determination were second to none in American military history, but whose repeated failures to seize the initiative, incapacity to take risks, and sheer bad luck resulted in a long record of defeat and reversal.

Thus, the Army of the Potomac fought the spring and summer battles in Virginia at appalling cost to itself and the nation. As a brigadier in the Army of the Potomac wrote his wife after Spotsylvania Court House: "For thirty days it has been one funeral procession past me and it has been too much." However, while Grant pinned Lee and the Army of Northern Virginia to Richmond, Sherman battled General Johnston back in Atlanta. The pressure on Lee prevented the Confederate government from reinforcing Johnston. Jefferson Davis then made the fatal mistake of replacing Johnston with General John B. Hood. Hood's slashing attacks from Atlanta wrecked his army, lost Atlanta, and opened the way for Sherman's March to the Sea. The march again allowed Union forces to bisect the Confederacy and further fragment the span of Southern control, while opening up the last undamaged areas of the South to attack.

It also opened the way for the final chapter in the evolution of the war's strategy: a straight-out Union policy aimed at breaking the will of the Southern population by destroying the property, homes, and sustenance on which the survival of the South rested. In May 1864

Sherman had already confided to his wife his perplexity that the Southern population had not yet given up: "No amount of poverty or adversity seems to shake their faith.... [N]iggers gone, wealth and luxury gone, money worthless, starvation in view, yet I see no sign of let up—some few deserters, plenty tired of war, but the masses determined to fight it out." Sherman's frustration in front of Atlanta had led to bombardment of the city irrespective of the danger to civilians or to its military usefulness. The March to the Sea had taken place soon afterward, and while Sherman's progress through Georgia was not aimed directly at civilian lives, its "collateral" effects—the ruthless destruction of homes and foodstuffs and the starvation and disease that followed in its wake—indicated how far the North was willing to go in this war. As Sherman warned in a letter to the citizens of northern Alabama in 1864:

> The government of the United States has in North Alabama any and all rights which they choose to enforce in war, to take their lives, their houses, their land, their everything, because they can not deny that war exists there, and war is simply power unconstrained by constitution or compact. If they want eternal warfare, well and good. We will accept the issue and dispossess them and put our friends in possession. To those who submit to the rightful law and authority all gentleness and forbearance, but to the petulant and persistent secessionists, why, death is mercy and the quicker he or she is disposed of the better. Satan and the rebellious saint[s] of heaven were allowed a continuance of existence in hell merely to swell their just punishment.

Sherman then noted that the American Civil War, unlike traditional European warfare, was "between peoples," and the invading army was entitled to all it could get from the people. He cited as a like instance the dispossession of the people of North Ireland during the reign of William and Mary.

General Philip Sheridan's conduct of the Shenandoah campaign suggests that Sherman's treatment of Georgia, Alabama, and South Carolina was not a matter of idiosyncratic choice but rather represented a larger strategic and policy design of the authorities in Washington and the Union high command. Clearly indicating this were Grant's instructions to Sheridan to turn the Shenandoah into "a barren waste ... so that crows flying over it for the balance of this season will have to carry their provender with them." Sheridan followed his orders. His remark to the Prussians during the Franco-Prussian War of 1870–71 that they were "too humanitarian" in their treatment of the French population suggests how far the Union's strategy had descended into a relentless crushing of popular resistance. As he added to his European listeners, "Nothing should be left to the people but eyes, to lament the war!" Admittedly, neither Sherman nor Sheridan reached the level of Bomber Command's "dehousing" campaign of World War II. But Northern military forces were on the ground; they could spare the inhabitants their wretched lives while destroying the economic infrastructure, homes, foodstuffs, and farm animals far more effectively than "Bomber" Harris's force could ever dream of in World War II.

The Civil War was the first modern war, one in which military power, built on popular support and industrialization, and projected by the railroad and steamships over hundreds of miles, approached the boundary of Clausewitz's "absolute" war. Neither the strategic vision nor the military capacity to win the war existed at the onset. The mere creation of armies and their requisite support structure created problems that were neither readily apparent nor easily solved. The Union leadership did evolve a strategy that at last brought victory, but the cost was appalling: somewhere around 625,000 dead on both sides, equaling the total losses of all our other conflicts up to the Vietnam War. A comparable death toll in World War I would have been about 2.1 million American lives. Given what we now know of the cost of war in the modern world, we should not be surprised at the cost of this terrible conflict. We should, rather, wonder how the leaders of the Union—unversed in strategy at the beginning of the war, masters by its end—were able to see it through to its successful conclusion.

19

Reconstruction: A Reinterpretation

ERIC FONER

● *The phrase "radical reconstruction" once appeared in almost every textbook in American history. The general theory was that after the Civil War, a misguided nation imposed black rule on the subjugated South. The result was that ignorant "freedmen" bankrupted state treasuries by unleashing a torrent of ill-conceived legislative initiatives upon the politically disenfranchised citizenry of the old Confederacy. Fortunately, northerners soon learned the error of their ways, and cooler and wiser heads prevailed. Blacks were returned to the menial positions to which they were supposedly best suited, and educated white southerners once again took their rightful places as the political and business leaders of the region.*

Since World War II, however, this interpretation of Reconstruction has come under devastating scholarly criticism. We now know that almost no permanent changes of a radical nature resulted from Reconstruction policies. The Civil War itself led to the thirteenth amendment, which abolished slavery, and to the fourteenth amendment, which granted citizenship to anyone born or naturalized in the United States and which required states to proceed with "due process of law" (however ambiguous that may be) before depriving any citizen of life, liberty, or property. These momentous changes passed through Congress and became part of the Constitution before Reconstruction in the South even began.

After 1867, blue-uniformed military forces occupied the southern states to enforce the authority of the United States government. But in crucial areas such as social mobility, education, and occupational opportunities, little was done to help the former slaves. No major political or military figures of the Confederacy suffered anything more than temporary

*imprisonment and suspension of political rights for a few
years. The structure of southern society remained relatively
intact, and the descendants of the pre-Civil War leaders
emerged as the key personages in the post-Reconstruction
South.*

*Professor Eric Foner of Columbia University has been the
most prominent of the many scholars who have recently redefined the Reconstruction era. Although admitting that it
failed in its original purposes, Foner here argues that Reconstruction nevertheless transformed southern blacks and mo-
bilized the black community. Reconstruction, he suggests,
may be thought of as America's "unfinished revolution."*

In the past generation, no period of American history has been the
subject of a more thoroughgoing reevaluation than Reconstruction, the
violent, dramatic and still controversial era that followed the Civil War.
Race relations, politics, social life, and economic change during Reconstruction have all been reinterpreted in the light of new attitudes
toward the place of blacks within American society. The traditional
interpretation that dominated historical writing for much of this century has finally been laid to rest.

According to the interpretation that dominated historical writing
before 1960, Reconstruction was an era of unrelieved sordidness in
American political and social life. When the Civil War ended, according
to this view, the white South genuinely accepted the reality of military
defeat, stood ready to do justice to the emancipated slaves, and desired
above all a quick reintegration into the fabric of national life. Before
his death, the martyred Lincoln had embarked on a course of sectional
reconciliation. President Andrew Johnson, his successor, attempted to
carry out Lincoln's policies, but was foiled by the Radical Republicans
(also known as "Vindictives" or "Jacobins"). Motivated by an irrational
hatred of "rebels" or by ties with northern capitalists out to plunder
the South, the Radicals swept aside Johnson's lenient program and
fastened black supremacy upon the defeated Confederacy. An orgy of
corruption followed, presided over by unscrupulous carpetbaggers
(Northerners who ventured south to reap the spoils of office), traitorous
scalawags (Southern whites who cooperated with the new governments
for personal gain) and the ignorant and childlike freedmen, who were

incapable of properly exercising the political power that had been thrust upon them. After much needless suffering, the white community of the South banded together to overthrow these "black" governments and restore Home Rule (their euphemism for white supremacy). All told, Reconstruction was the darkest page in the American saga.

Originating in anti-Reconstruction propaganda of Southern Democrats during the 1870s, this traditional interpretation achieved scholarly legitimacy around the turn of the century through the work of William Dunning and his students at Columbia University. It reached the larger public through films like *Birth of a Nation* and *Gone With the Wind*, and that best-selling work of myth-making masquerading as history, *The Tragic Era*, by Claude G. Bowers, which told how Southern whites "literally were put to the torture" by "emissaries of hate" who manipulated the "simple-minded" freedmen, "inflaming the negroes' egotism" and even inspiring "lustful assaults" by blacks upon white womanhood.

The long reign of the old interpretation is not difficult to explain. It presented a set of easily identifiable heroes and villains. It enjoyed the imprimateur of the nation's leading scholars. And it accorded with the political and social realities of the first half of this century. This image of Reconstruction helped freeze the mind of the white South in unalterable opposition to any movement for breaching the ascendancy of the Democratic party, eliminating segregation, or readmitting disenfranchised blacks to the vote.

Nevertheless, the demise of the traditional interpretation was inevitable. For it ignored the testimony of the central participant in the drama of Reconstruction—the black freedman. Furthermore, it was grounded in the conviction that blacks were unfit to share in political power. As Dunning's colleague John W. Burgess put it, "a black skin means membership in a race of men which has never of itself succeeded in subjecting passion to reason, has never, therefore, created any civilization of any kind." Once objective scholarship and modern experience rendered that assumption untenable, the entire edifice was bound to crumble.

The work of "revising" the history of Reconstruction began with the writings of a handful of survivors of the era, such as former slave John R. Lynch, who had served as a Congressman from Mississippi after the Civil War. In the 1930s, white scholars like Francis Simkins and Robert Woody carried the task forward. Then in 1935, the black historian and activist W. E. B. Dubois produced *Black Reconstruction in America*, a monumental reevaluation that closed with an irrefutable indictment of a historical profession that had sacrificed scholarly objectivity on the altar of racial bias. "One fact and one alone," he wrote, "explains the attitude of most recent writers toward Reconstruction: they cannot conceive of Negroes as men." In many ways, *Black Reconstruction* anticipated the findings of modern scholarship. At the time, however, it was largely ignored.

It was not until the 1960s that the full force of the revisionist wave broke over the field. Then, in rapid succession, virtually every assumption of the traditional viewpoint was systematically dismantled, and a drastically different portrait emerged to take its place. President Lincoln did not have a coherent "plan" for Reconstruction but, at the time of his assassination, had been cautiously contemplating black suffrage. Andrew Johnson was a stubborn, racist politician, who lacked the ability to compromise. By isolating himself from the broad currents of public opinion that had nurtured Lincoln's career, Johnson created an impasse with Congress that Lincoln would certainly have avoided, thus throwing away his political power and destroying his own plans for reconstructing the South.

The Radicals in Congress were acquitted of both vindictive motives and the charge of serving as the stalking-horses of northern capitalism. They emerged instead as idealists in the best nineteenth-century reform tradition. Radical leaders like Charles Sumner and Thaddeus Stevens had worked for the rights of blacks long before any conceivable political advantage flowed from such a commitment. Stevens refused to sign the Pennsylvania Constitution of 1838 because it disenfranchised the state's black citizens; Sumner led a fight in the 1850s to integrate Boston's public schools. Their Reconstruction policies were based on principle, not petty political advantage, for the central issue dividing Johnson and these Radical Republicans was the civil rights of the freedmen. Studies of Congressional policy-making also revealed that Reconstruction legislation, ranging from the Civil Rights Act of 1866 to the Fourteenth and Fifteenth Amendments, enjoyed broad support from moderate and conservative Republicans. It was not simply the work of a narrow radical faction.

Even more startling was the revised portrait of Reconstruction in the

South. Imbued with the spirit of the civil rights movement and rejecting the racial assumptions that had underpinned the traditional interpretation, these historians portrayed Reconstruction as a time of extraordinary political, social, and economic progress for blacks. The establishment of public school systems, the granting of equal citizenship to former slaves, the effort to restore the devastated Southern economy, the attempt to construct an interracial political democracy from the ashes of slavery, all these were commendable achievements, not the elements of Bowers's "tragic era."

Unlike earlier writers, the revisionists stressed the active role of the freedmen in shaping Reconstruction. Black initiative established as many schools as did northern religious societies and the Freedmen's Bureau. The right to vote was not simply thrust upon them by meddling outsiders, since blacks began agitating for the suffrage as soon as they were freed. In 1865, black conventions throughout the South issued eloquent, though unheeded appeals for equal civil and political rights.

With the advent of "Radical Reconstruction" in 1867, the freedmen did enjoy a real measure of political power. But "black supremacy" never existed. In most states, blacks held only a small fraction of political offices, and even in South Carolina, where they comprised a majority of the state legislature, effective power remained in white hands. As for corruption, moral standards both in government and private enterprise were at low ebb throughout the nation in the postwar years—the era of Boss Tweed, the Credit Mobilier scandal and the Whiskey Ring. Southern corruption could hardly be blamed on the former slaves.

Other actors in the Reconstruction drama also came in for reevaluation. Most carpetbaggers were former Union soldiers seeking economic opportunity in the postwar South, not unscrupulous adventurers. Their motives, a typically American amalgam of humanitarianism and the pursuit of profit, were no more insidious than those of pioneers in the West. Scalawags, previously seen as traitors to the the white race, now emerged as "Old Line" Whig Unionists who had opposed secession in the first place, or poor whites who had long resented planters' domination of southern life, and who saw in Reconstruction a chance to recast Southern society along more democratic lines. Strongholds of Southern white Republicanism like East Tennessee and western North Carolina had been the scene of resistance to Confederate rule throughout the Civil War; now, as one scalawag newspaper put it, the choice was "between salvation at the hand of the Negro or destruction at the hand of the rebels."

At the same time, the Ku Klux Klan and kindred groups, whose campaign of violence against black and white Republicans had been minimized or excused in older writings, were portrayed as they really were. Earlier scholars had conveyed the impression that the Klan intimidated blacks mainly by dressing as ghosts and playing on the freedmen's superstitions. In fact, black fears were all too real: the Klan was a terrorist organization that beat and killed its political opponents to deprive blacks of their newly won rights. The complicity of the Democratic party and the silence of prominent whites in the face of such outrages stood as an indictment of the moral code the South had inherited from the days of slavery.

By the end of the 1960s, the old interpretation had been completely reversed. Southern freedmen were the heroes, the "Redeemers" who overthrew Reconstruction the villains, and if the era was "tragic," it was because change did not go far enough. Reconstruction had been a time of real progress and its failure a lost opportunity for the South and the nation. But the legacy of Reconstruction—the Fourteenth and Fifteenth Amendments—endured to inspire future efforts for civil and political equality.

The reevaluation of the first Reconstruction was inspired in large measure by the impact of the second—the modern civil rights movement. And with the waning of that movement, writing on Reconstruction underwent still another transformation. Instead of seeing the Civil War and its aftermath as a second American Revolution (as Charles and Mary Beard had), a regression into barbarism (as Bowers argued), or a golden opportunity squandered (as the revisionists saw it), many writers of the 1970s and 1980s argued that "Radical Reconstruction" was not really very radical. Since land was not distributed to the former slaves, they remained economically dependent on their former owners. The planter class survived the war and Reconstruction with its property (apart from slaves) and social prestige more or less intact.

Many historians also found little to praise in federal policy toward the emancipated blacks. A new sensitivity to the strength of prejudice and laissez-faire ideas in the nineteenth-century North led some to doubt whether the Republican party ever made a genuine commitment to racial justice in the South. The granting of black suffrage was an alternative to a long-term federal responsibility for protecting the rights of the former slaves. Once enfranchised, blacks could be left to fend for themselves. With the exception of a few Radicals like Thaddeus Stevens, nearly all northern policy-makers and educators were criticized for assuming that, so long as the unfettered operations of the market-place afforded blacks the opportunity to advance through diligent labor, federal efforts to assist them in acquiring land were unnecessary.

The revisionist historians of the 1960s effectively established a series of negative points: the Reconstruction governments were not as bad as had been portrayed, "black supremacy" was a myth, the Radicals were not cynical manipulators of the freedmen. Their successors rightly pointed to elements of continuity that spanned the nineteenth-century Southern experience, especially the survival, in modified form, of the plantation system. But by denying the real changes that did occur, they failed to provide a convincing portrait of an era characterized above all by drama, turmoil, and social change. Indeed, in current writing, the term "revolution" has reappeared as a way of describing the Civil War and Reconstruction.

Building on the findings of the past twenty years of scholarship, today's historians view Reconstruction not so much as a specific time period, bounded by the years 1865 and 1877, but as an episode in a prolonged historical process—American society's adjustment to the consequences of the Civil War and emancipation. The Civil War, of course, raised the decisive questions of America's national existence: the relations between local and national authority, the definition of citizenship, the balance between force and consent in generating obedience to authority. The war and Reconstruction, as Allan Nevins observed over fifty years ago, witnessed the "emergence of modern America." This was the era of the completion of the national railroad network, the creation of the modern steel industry, the conquest of the West and final subduing of the Indians, and the expansion of the mining frontier. Lincoln's America—the world of the small farm and artisan shop—gave way to a rapidly industrializing economy. The issues that galvanized postwar Northern politics—from the question of the greenback currency to the mode of paying holders of the national debt—arose from the economic changes unleashed by the Civil War.

Above all, the war irrevocably abolished slavery. Since 1619, when "twenty negars" disembarked from a Dutch ship in Virginia, racial injustice had haunted American life, mocking its professed ideals even as tobacco and cotton, the products of slave labor, helped finance the nation's economic development. Now, the implications of the black presence could no longer be ignored. The Civil War resolved the problem of slavery but, as the Philadelphia diarist Sidney George Fisher observed in June 1865, it opened an even more intractable question: "What shall we do with the Negro?" Indeed, he went on, this was a problem "*incapable* of any solution that will satisfy both North and South."

As Fisher realized, the focal point of Reconstruction was the social revolution known as emancipation. Plantation slavery was simultaneously a system of labor, a form of racial domination, and the foundation upon which arose a distinctive ruling class within the South. Its demise threw open the most fundamental questions of economy, society, and politics.

The transition from slavery to freedom was a complex process that involved bitter conflict. Under slavery, most blacks had lived in nuclear family units, although they faced the constant threat of separation from loved ones by sale. Reconstruction provided the opportunity for blacks to solidify their preexisting family ties. Conflicts over whether black women should work in the cotton fields (planters said yes, many black families said no), and over white attempts to "apprentice" black children revealed that the autonomy of family life was a major preoccupation of the freedmen. Indeed, whether manifested in their withdrawal from churches controlled by whites, the blossoming of black fraternal, benevolent, and self-improvement organizations, or the demise of the "slave quarters" and their replacement by small tenant farms occupied by individual families, the quest for independence from white authority and control over their own day to day lives shaped the black response to emancipation.

In the post-Civil War South, the surest guarantee of economic autonomy, blacks believed, was land. To the freedmen, the justice of a claim to land based on their years of unrequited labor appeared self-evident. As an Alabama black convention put it, "the property which they [the planters]hold was nearly all earned by the sweat of *our* brows." Many freedmen in 1865 and 1866 refused to sign labor contracts, expecting the federal government to give them land. In some localities, as one Alabama overseer reported, they "set up claims to the plantation and all on it." In the end, of course, most blacks remained propertyless and poor. Planters succeeded in stabilizing the plantation system, but only by blocking the growth of alternative enterprises, like factories, that might draw off black laborers, thus locking the region into a pattern of economic backwardness.

The United States was not the only nation to experience emancipation in the nineteenth century. Neither plantation slavery nor abolition were unique to the United States. And as in every society that abolished slavery, emancipation was followed by a comprehensive struggle over the shaping of a new labor system to replace it. The conflict between former masters aiming to recreate a disciplined labor force and blacks seeking to carve out the greatest degree of economic autonomy, profoundly affected economics, politics, and race relations in the Reconstruction South. Planters were convinced that their own survival and the region's prosperity depended on their ability to resume production using disciplined gang labor, as under slavery. To this end, the governments established by President Johnson in 1865, in which blacks had no voice, established a comprehensive system of vagrancy laws, criminal penalties for breach of contract, and other measures known collectively as the "Black Codes" and designed to force the freedmen back to work on the plantations. Blacks strongly resisted the implementation of these measures, and the evident inability of the leaders of the white South to accept the implications of emancipation fatally undermined Northern support for Johnson's policies.

Out of the conflict on the plantations, new systems of labor emerged in different regions of the South. Sharecropping—a compromise between blacks' desire for land and planters' for labor discipline, in which each black family worked its own plot of land, dividing the crop with the landlord at the end of the year—came to dominate the cotton South. In the rice kingdom, the great plantations fell to pieces, and blacks were able to acquire small plots of land and take up self-sufficient farming. And in the sugar region, gang labor survived the end of slavery. In all these cases, blacks' economic opportunities were limited by whites' control of credit and by the vagaries of a world market in which the price of agricultural goods suffered a prolonged decline. But the degree to which planters could control the day-to-day lives of their labor force was radically altered by the end of slavery.

The sweeping social changes that followed the Civil War were also reflected in the experience of the white yeomanry. Wartime devastation set in motion a train of events that permanently altered their self-sufficient way of life. Plunged into poverty by the war, they saw their plight exacerbated by successive crop failures in early Reconstruction. In the face of this economic disaster, yeomen clung tenaciously to their farms. But, needing to borrow money for the seed, implements, and livestock required to resume farming, many became mired in debt and were forced to take up the growing of cotton. A region in which a majority of white farmers had once owned their land was increasingly trapped in a cycle of tenancy and cotton overproduction, and unable to feed itself.

The South's postwar transformation proundly affected the course of Reconstruction politics. As the Black Codes illustrated, state governments could play a vital role in defining the property rights and re-stricting the bargaining power of planters and laborers. Not surprisingly, when Republicans came to power, largely on the basis of the black vote, they swept away measures designed to bolster plantation discipline. They also launched an ambitious program of aid to railroads, hoping to transform the region into a diversified, modernizing society with enhanced opportunities for black and white alike. But raiload aid not only failed to achieve its economic goals, but generated most of the corruption that plagued Reconstruction government in several states.

To blacks, however, Reconstruction represented the first time they had ever been given a voice in public affairs, and the first time Southern governments even attempted to serve their interests. Former slaves, less than two years removed from bondage, now debated the fundamental questions of the polity—what is a republican form of government; should the state provide equal education for all; how reconcile political equality with a society in which property was so unequally distributed? There was something inspiring in the way such men met the challenge of Reconstruction. "I knew nothing more than to obey my master," James K. Greene, an Alabama black politician later recalled. "But the tocsin of freedom sounded and knocked at the door and we walked out like free men and we met the exigencies as they grew up, and shouldered the responsibilities."

"You never saw a people more excited on the subject of politics than are the negroes of the south," one planter observed in 1867. And there were more than a few Southern whites as well who in these years shook off the prejudices of the past to embrace the vision of a new South dedicated to the principles of equal citizenship and social justice. One South Carolinian expressed the new sense of possibility in 1868, to the state's Republican governor: "I am sorry that I cannot write an elegant stiled letter to your excellency. But I rejoice to think that God almighty has given to the poor of S. C. A Gov. to hear to feel to protect the humble poor without distinction to race or color.... I am a native borned S. C. a poor man never owned a Negro in my life nor my father before me.... Remember the true and loyal are the poor of the whites and blacks, outside of these you can find none loyal."

Few modern scholars believe the Reconstruction governments established in the South in 1867 and 1868 fulfilled the aspirations of their humble constituents. While their achievements in such realms as education, civil rights, and the economic rebuilding of the South are now widely appreciated, historians today believe Reconstruction failed to affect either the economic plight of the emancipated slave, or the ongoing transformation of independent white farmers into cotton tenants. Yet their opponents did perceive the Reconstruction governments as representatives of a revolution that had put the bottom rail, both racial and economic, on top. This perception helps explain the ferocity of the attacks levelled against them, and the pervasiveness of violence in the post-emancipation South.

The spectacle of black men voting and holding office was anathema to large numbers of southern whites. Even more disturbing, at least in the view of those who still controlled the South's wealth, was the emergence of local officials, black and white, who sympathized with the plight of the black laborer. Alabama's vagrancy law, was "a dead letter" in 1870, "because those who are charged with its enforcement are indebted to the vagrant vote for their offices and emoluments." Political debates over the level and incidence of taxation, the control of crops, the resolution of contract disputes, revealed that a primary issue of Reconstruction was the role of government in a plantation society. During Presidential Reconstruction, and after "Redemption," with planters and their allies in control of politics, the law emerged as a means of stabilizing and promoting the plantation system. If Radical Reconstruction failed to redistribute the land of the South, the ouster of the planter class from control of politics at least ensured that the sanctions of the criminal law would not be employed to discipline the black labor force.

An understanding of this fundamental conflict over the relation between government and society helps explain the pervasive complaints concerning corruption and "extravagance" during Radical Reconstruction. Corruption there was aplenty; tax rates did rise sharply. More significant than the rate of taxation, however, was the change in its incidence. For the first time, planters and white farmers had to pay a significant portion of their income to the government, while propertyless blacks often escaped scotfree. Several states, moreover, enacted heavy taxes on uncultivated land, to discourage land speculation and force land onto the market, benefitting, it was hoped, the freedmen.

As time passed, complaints about the "extravagance" and corruption of southern governments found a sympathetic audience among influential Northerners. The Democratic charge that universal suffrage in the South was responsible for high taxes and governmental extravagance coincided with a rising conviction among the urban middle classes of the North that city government had to be taken out of the hands of the immigrant poor and returned to the "best men"—the educated, professional, financially independent citizens unable to exert much political influence at a time of mass parties and machine politics. Increasingly, the "respectable" middle classes began to retreat from the very notion of universal suffrage. The poor were no longer perceived as honest producers, the backbone of the social order; now they became the "dangerous classes," the "mob." As the historian Francis Parkman put it as Reconstruction drew to a close, too much power rested with "masses of imported ignorance and hereditary ineptitude." To Parkman, the Irish of the Northern cities and the blacks of the South were equally incapable of utilizing the ballot: "Witness the municipal corruptions of New York, and the monstrosities of negro rule in South Carolina." Such attitudes helped to justify Northern inaction as, one by one, the South's Reconstruction regimes were overthrown by political violence.

In the end, neither the abolition of slavery nor the advent of Reconstruction succeeded in resolving the debate over the meaning of freedom in American life. In the United States, as in nearly every plantation society that experienced the end of slavery, a rigid social and political dichotomy between former master and former slave, an ideology of racism, and a dependent labor force with limited economic opportunities all survived abolition. Unless one means by freedom the simple fact of not being a slave, emancipation thrust blacks into a kind of no-man's land, a partial freedom that made a mockery of the American ideal of equal citizenship.

Yet however brief its sway, Reconstruction allowed scope for a remarkable political and social mobilization of the black community. It opened doors of opportunity that could never be completely closed. Reconstruction transformed the lives of southern blacks in ways unmeasurable by statistics and unreachable by law. It raised their expectations and aspirations, redefined their status in relation to the larger society, and allowed space for the creation of institutions that enabled them to survive the repression that followed. And it established constitutional principles of civil and political equality that, while flagrantly violated after Redemption, planted the seeds of future struggle.

Certainly, in terms of the sense of possibility with which it opened, Reconstruction failed. But, as W. E. B. DuBois observed, it was a "splendid failure." For its animating vision—a society in which social advancement would be open to all on the basis of individual merit, not inherited caste distinctions—is as old as America itself, and remains relevant to a nation still grappling with the unresolved legacy of emancipation.